ELEMENTS OF COMPUTER SCIENCE

JAMES W. ESTES
University of Connecticut

B. ROBERT ELLIS
University of New Hampshire

CANFIELD PRESS/SAN FRANCISCO

A Department of Harper & Row, Publishers, Inc.

New York, Evanston, London

to

Carlie, Evie,
Scott, Peggy, Gena, and David

PREFACE

Each year courses in computer science attract more college students, increasing the demand for texts that are pedagogically sound and structurally flexible for use in introductory courses. Such courses often service the entire college or university community in the basic principles of computer science, without regard to the background of the students. Additionally, students may be expected to learn programming in a particular language, along with the basic principles underlying problem solution and basic computer systems principles. This situation usually requires the combined use of some programming text and an available introductory computer science text. However, the difference in philosophy among authors, combined with a redundancy of information, necessarily results in poor correlation. Certain topics must be omitted, and the order of at least one of the texts must be altered. The attempt to cover both areas in one text generally proves inadequate making two separate texts necessary. To insure complete compatibility, these texts should be authored by the same person or persons.

Designed to serve as a core text, *Elements of Computer Science* presents a complete introduction to basic principles of computing and computer science, with an algorithmic approach to problem-solving. Three language texts by the same authors, FORTRAN IV with WATFOR/WATFIV, PL/I, and BASIC, allow students to implement the principles found in the core text. While each text can be used alone, the design of the core text and any particular programming language text is arranged so that the development of the programming languages parallel and complement the development of the principles in the core text. The user can either utilize the core text together with one of the language texts, utilize the core text without the language text (or with the user's own language text), or utilize one of the language texts without the core text (suitable solution for a course dealing exclusively with programming). The texts therefore provide maximum flexibility of approach, dependent upon the user's unique requirements.

Elements of Computer Science emphasizes fundamental problem-solving techniques, starting with the initial design of algorithms and covering such concepts as looping, searching and sorting, data structures and subalgorithms. The text does not concentrate on one discipline, but instead introduces concepts of problem-solving common to all types of problems which extend to cover more complex techniques.

A unique feature of this text enables a student to progress from problem-solving in general to a more detailed knowledge of how a computer realizes a problem solution by including such topics as internal representation and computer organization (using a hypothetical computer). Details of computer operations appear throughout the text at key locations where the student can best benefit from them. For example, certain concepts are introduced via the hypothetical computer whose operation is then compared to that of two popular existing machines—the PDP-8/E and the IBM System/360. Thus, with the aid of a programming language text, a student can immediately develop computer solutions while gradually mastering the details of computer data representations and operations—a technique successfully employed by the authors in their one-semester introductory computer science courses.

Elements of Computer Science takes into account the existence of varying levels of introductory courses. A strong chapter on data structures is included since it is a topic essential to all types of problem-solving. For a course with a lesser degree of rigor, the more advanced topics in this chapter can easily be eliminated. The survey of programming languages, intended for comparative purposes only, makes its use in any particular course flexible. The history has been placed at the end of the text because the authors feel that at that point students gain a better perspective of where we are now, how we got here, and where we are going from here. But the material in that chapter could be used at any point in a course, again dependent on the user's objectives. Finally, the detailed discussion of magnetic storage devices found in the Appendix can be used according to the demands of a course.

Exercises appear at the end of each chapter, affording practical applications of the concepts covered. Students should be encouraged to solve as many of these as possible. A bibliography and list of references accompany each chapter to help students further expand their knowledge of topics in computer science. The extensive use of flowcharts, tables, and examples highlights and illustrates the concepts presented in the text.

The authors gratefully acknowledge the invaluable assistance given to us in the preparation of this text by William L. French, Edward G. Fisher, Karin W. Frobig, Janice C. King, Susan W. MacKenzie, Richard C. Schofield, Jr. and Susan E. Whitcomb. In particular, the constructive comments and suggestions offered by Professors Peter Calingaert and William H. Cotterman have been extremely helpful. The resources offered by both the Department of Mathematics and the Computation Center at the University of New Hampshire aided us in the development of this material and its use in our classes. A very special recognition goes to our students, who directly and indirectly contributed to this text from its original conception to its final version. We also wish to thank our typist Jean Caldwell for a job well done under pressure of time, along with Jean Gahan and Gail Perrault for their secretarial assistance. Most of all, however, we thank our families for their long-suffering endurance and understanding throughout this entire endeavor.

January 1973   JAMES W. ESTES
                                              B. ROBERT ELLIS

CONTENTS

Introduction

Modern technology has provided us with many tools for use in problem-solving. Among them is the general purpose, automatic electronic digital computer—known to most people simply as the computer. A wide variety of today's problems have been solved with the aid of computers. Manned space flights, national defense networks, and satellite communication networks all utilize computers in an impressive way, and almost everyone is aware of and at least indirectly affected by such spectacular achievements. But the increased use of telephone lines for data transmission is rapidly causing the impact of computers to become more personalized. Most individuals can now see firsthand evidence of a computerized society in their immediate surroundings—even, in some cases, in their own homes. This expanding role of the computer can best be illustrated by a hypothetical case study.

John Stoke is a student attending Continental University. As a member of this year's freshman class (1900 students), he is acutely aware of the influence of computers on his life. His personal encounters with our computerized society began in high school, where he took a part-time job at the local printing plant to help finance his future college expenses. This printing company uses a computerized typesetting system. Copy to be set is entered on a typewriter that is connected to a magnetic tape unit. As the operator types copy, the characters are recorded on tape. The tape is then used as input to the computer, and a new tape containing the completely edited text (with justified margins) is produced. This final tape is used to operate either a phototypesetter or a Linotype machine, ultimately producing the required printing plate. The use of tape increases the versatility of this printing company, since the firm can now satisfy the demand for repeated printings of annual indexes (completely updated), produce abridged versions of larger works, and quickly revise editions to be reprinted. Storage is no longer a problem, since the tapes require less space than trays of set type. A daily newspaper is also published by this company. Daily, abbreviated stock reports as well as the complete weekly report are transmitted with the aid of a computerized system originating in New York and are automatically typeset as they are received by the printing company's computer. Even the subscription labels for the newspaper are prepared in coded form by using punched cards, magnetic tape, and an optical scanner.

John kept his earnings in a savings account and also maintained a small checking account at the local bank. Before long, he became aware of the role of the computer in banking. His deposits to and withdrawals from his checking account, the transfer of funds directly from his checking account to his savings account, the computation of interest on his savings, the calculation of service charges on his checking account, and the preparation of his monthly statement are all processed by the bank's computer. Rapid clearance of checks from central banks to his bank are made possible with the aid of computers. Many of the firms in town make use of the bank's computer to prepare their payrolls and perform auditing tasks.

As an employee, John became an active taxpayer. The Internal Revenue Service keeps a record of his Federal tax payments through a computer system that includes a National Computer Center in West Virginia and seven regional centers across the country. This system becomes extremely active during tax time. Each return that is filed is checked for accuracy; then the information is submitted to a regional computer. A tape is prepared and sent to the national center, where a master file is retained. Conditions such as failure to pay the proper tax, failure to file a return, or qualification for a refund are checked. Selected information is then returned by tape to regional centers for further action. In the future, banks and employers may supply information directly to the computers via magnetic tapes and data communication lines. John also made the usual contributions to the Social Security System, the administration of which depends heavily on computers to continuously update the records of millions of citizens and supervise benefit payments to qualified claimants. The state income tax system, also highly computerized, operates very much like the Federal system; it records figures from filed returns, processes the information, issues refunds, and checks for possible circumventions of state tax laws.

According to the results of the recent census conducted by the Federal Bureau of the Census, the Stoke family is a typical, middle-class American family. The information they supplied on the comprehensive questionnaire was compiled along with all the information gathered across the country. The files constructed from this data are stored on tapes, divided into categories, and analyzed by computers to generate useful statistics and to examine a wide variety of patterns. Certain basic information is also made available on tape for use by state and local agencies in planning for future development. For example, John's father works at a nearby steel mill, where a computer is used to control the automated production line that processes the steel. The computer supervises all aspects of the operation in such detail that the slightest deviation sends a signal to the operator, who then takes action. He may personally intervene and correct the difficulty, or he may direct the computer to analyze the situation and then alter the production process through selective changes that it is pro-grammed to initiate. Such instantaneous identification of potential problem areas, accompanied with rapid correction, has protected the company from loss in both time and production. Quality control has increased to maximum efficiency, and the quantity of output has increased proportionately. Similarly, John's mother works as a part-time, check-out clerk in a local branch of a major discount store. At the end of her shift, she is required to report to the manager's office with two items: the cash drawer from her register and the drawer containing the top portions of sales tickets that she has removed from each customer's merchandise. The tickets contain either punch-hole patterns or coded symbols. They are sent to the central business office, where they are read by machines capable of producing punch cards or punched tapes containing such information as item code numbers, unit prices, and department code numbers. This information is then processed by a computer and used to prepare inventory reports, sales reports, and other statistics useful in the operation of the discount store.

While John was a junior in high school, his town was one of several communities selected for the first experiment in a "cashless society." Plastic ID cards were issued to the town's financially responsible citizens. All business establishments were supplied with special Touch-Tone telephones capable of communicating directly with a central computer. When any customer makes a transaction in a store, the clerk inserts the ID card into a slot in the telephone, and the pertinent data regarding the sale are transmitted directly to the computer. The verification of the customer's identity, the validation of his transaction, the updating of both his account and the store account, and the arrangement of any necessary credit are all processed in a matter of moments by the computer system. No cash is exchanged! The participants in the experiment even pay their utility bills, rents, and other home expenses with their ID cards. The residents involved in this experiment are already familiar with the credit-card system in general, since most of them previously used two or more of the major, nationwide charge-account plans and oil-company credit cards. Many of these systems are tied into a single computer network to assist in checking customer credit ratings and the illegal use of stolen or invalid credit cards. Yet billing cycles differ; service charges vary; and credit conditions are not consistent. The cashless experiment is designed to eliminate these discrepancies by processing *all* financial transactions at one central location, while concurrently eliminating the fraudulent use of credit systems.

During the same year, John's high school made an arrangement with the state university whereby three terminals were installed at the high school and connected to the university computer by a special telephone line. The school thus became part of a time-sharing system that included ten high schools throughout the state as well as the entire university campus. The terminals permitted teachers to use stored programs previously prepared at the university as instructional aids in their classes. Concepts of chemistry, physics, math, and foreign languages are both taught and tested, allowing each student to learn at the rate most comfortable for him. The high school also has a contract with the university under which grade reports for all students are prepared by computer, courses are scheduled, and student records are maintained.

John Stoke traveled to college on one of the five, nonstop weekend flights originating from the airport near his home town. The airline's computerized registration system provided instant confirmation of John's choice of available flights along with the arrival and departure times. Arrangements for rental cars at the point of destination, special dietary restrictions for meals on long flights, constantly updated information on cancellations, and information concerning entertainment available on certain flights are also possible with this system. Using a special electronic console or a typewriter terminal tied into a large computer network, a clerk at the reservation desk or at a travel agency requests information from a central system, which may be many miles distant. The system operates in real-time, since it responds to the constantly changing aspects of the airline environment and simultaneously produces the most current information for many users.

The first week at college was both confusing and informative for John Stoke. He found himself registering for courses under a system that was computerized and discovered that his personal records were processed by the same computer. The university library utilizes a special information-retrieval system in which anyone can query files containing records such as book titles, graduate theses, cross-reference indexes, and catalog listings. The university medical center had already received a complete medical record for John Stoke and had added this information to the computerized medical files maintained for all in- and out-patients. Shock and intensive care units in the hospital utilize computerized monitoring devices that constantly survey the progress of critical cases, detecting even the slightest variations and notifying the nurse in charge. Training sessions are initiated for hospital staff during which human physical conditions are simulated in a plastic-skinned mannequin, including the lifelike functioning of such major organs as the heart, kidneys, and lungs. Driven by a small computer, the mannequin can be made to react exactly like a human being, thus affording a realistic yet safe means for studying the best steps to take in response to a variety of medical problems.

John is presently taking courses in the College of Technology, where his interest in engineering has led him to investigate several possible areas in which to major. Departments within the College are currently involved in many projects, three of which have attracted his attention. The first project involves the use of computers to design other computers. Optical display screens picture design structures that can be altered by using a light pen. The result of such changes are immediately indicated on the screen. The entire picture can be rotated as if it were a real, three-dimensional object, thus enabling the design to be viewed from all angles. After all investigation and research are complete, the actual physical counterpart will be constructed. The second project, partially funded by a Federal grant, was initiated in response to the need for simulation devices in the aircraft industry. The project goal is to improve existing systems and produce new methods for training commercial pilots through the use of flight simulators. All possible combinations of actual flight conditions in normal and emergency situations are generated by a computer, which also processes the responses of the trainee. The computer produces information concerning aircraft performance, control readings, radar reports, warning signals, weather conditions, and a simultated picture of the pilot's field of vision. The project is also designed to develop a computer system for training air-traffic controllers in which a realistic control-tower environment, including a computer-operated radar scope, is simulated. Simulation is also the key element of the third project, which is in its second year of research and development. A computer system is being designed to control traffic in a major city. Hundreds of intersections must be monitored and controlled to produce the maximum efficiency in the flow of traffic. Capable of recognizing the most complex traffic patterns, the system will continuously modify its control program in response to such changes. Electrified road signs as well as traffic lights will be operated by the system to direct drivers through traffic or reroute them if necessary. Conditions such as accidents, fires, or utility repairs, which cause traffic delays that are not detected directly by the computer, will be reported to the computer center and made available immediately to the system by the operator.

John Stoke has accepted the fact that computers will continue to affect all our lives; yet his personal experiences have given him a balanced perspective. He knows that computers may fail to perform the tasks required or, at times, may produce results that are unexpected. He knows that computer systems depend on humans and therefore possess only the capabilities that human intelligence can create and control. He is also aware that all the wonders of the "computer age" are a direct result of a very basic premise: *machines can assist in the solution of problems only if the problem-solving process itself is clearly defined.*

In any given problem, information is "fed into" a computer, and a short time later, results will be relayed back from the machine. Yet a complete understanding of this process requires full knowledge of the concepts and techniques of problem-solving, as well as a thorough study of the internal workings of a computer and its use as a problem-solving tool. A brief introduction to both these aspects will illustrate their close relationship.

Once a particular situation has been identified as a problem requiring a solution, there is a basic pattern to follow to achieve that solution.

1. *Formulate a precise statement of the problem.* This may be the most difficult part of problem-solving, especially if the original statement of the problem is vague and sketchy. It is therefore necessary to establish first what essential facts have been given and then state the desired goal.

2. *Develop a representative structure of the problem.* Any problem has associated with it certain variables used to represent actual events. These have to be identified and related to each other or to the desired solution. Mathematical structures will most often be selected for this purpose, due to the precise manner in which such relationships can be expressed.

3. *Analyze relationships existing in the structure.* Observations regarding cause and effect occur at this

stage. Only those relationships pertinent to the solution of the problem will be assimilated. The structure must be refined to the level at which an answer can be obtained; at the same time, the influence of the variables on that answer must be clarified.

4. *Generate a solution.*   Eventually, we reach the point where the variables will be assigned real values in key relationships, and calculations will be carried out that will result in specific answers.

Throughout this process, assumptions will be made and tested—some of these will require a new approach and thus the design of a new representative structure. Results may often generate new problems requiring new solutions. Many times, the problem will become illustrative of a whole class of problems, thus extending the solution.

A computer is a machine designed to assist in the process of problem-solving. The instructions, commands, and operations utilized by a computer must be precise and unambiguous. Computers make use of such primitive arithmetic and logical operations as adding one quantity to another or comparing two quantities to see if they are equal. These instructions and operations are expressed internally in a numerical machine language. Within this context, any task performed by a computer must be done in a logical, step-by-step sequence. To make use of the computer as a problem-solving tool, it is therefore necessary

1. *to reduce the problem-solving process already described to a specific and finite sequence of unambiguous intructions leading to a solution,* and
2. *to establish a basis of communication with the machine by expressing these instructions in a language that the machine can understand.*

Our goals in this text will be to develop a precise, algorithmic approach to problem-solving, to examine in detail the internal operations of the computer, and to introduce some basic methods of communicating with the computer. The ultimate objective is to answer clearly the question: "How can we utilize the computer as a tool in the field of problem-solving?"

SELECTED REFERENCES

Baer, Robert M., *The Digital Villain*, Reading, Mass.: Addison-Wesley, 1972.
Joslin, Edward O. (editor), *An Introduction to Computer Systems*, Washington, D.C.: College Readings, 1969.

Martin, James, and Adrian R.D. Norman, *The Computerized Society*, Englewood Cliffs, N.J.: Prentice-Hall, 1970.

Rothman, Stanley, and Charles Mosmann, *Computers and Society*, Chicago: Science Research Associates, 1972.

Taviss, Irene (editor), *The Computer Impact*, Englewood Cliffs, N.J.: Prentice-Hall, 1970.

Weiss, Eric A. (editor), *Computer Usage: Applications*, New York: McGraw-Hill, 1969.

Weiss, Eric A. (editor), *Computer Usage: Fundamentals*, New York: McGraw-Hill, 1969.

White, Peter T., "Behold the Computer Revolution," The National Geographic Magazine, Vol. 138, No. 5 (November 1970), pp. 593-633.

Withington, Frederic G., *The Real Computer: Its Influences, Uses, and Effects*, Reading, Mass.: Addison-Wesley, 1969.

Algorithms and Flowcharts—
An Introduction

Most basic algebra courses devote a certain amount of time to the study of *word problems*. These often become a pitfall for students who are otherwise quite skilled in algebra. Throughout their lives, many individuals continue to profess a total inability to solve problems. On the other hand, we often encounter problems whose solutions have become so automatic that the step-by-step solution process has been obscured. The frustration of problem-solving leads to questions that must be answered.

What constitutes a problem? How do you solve a problem? Is the answer to a problem really the solution of the problem? Or is "solving the problem" actually the problem?

PROBLEM-SOLVING AND ALGORITHMS

A *problem* exists when a specific set of related data requires some change from its present form to an equivalent form, thus providing a basis for action that will produce useful information. Scheduling students for courses, developing a payroll for employees, and solving a quadratic equation are all problems. They all contain unique information describing the events in an environment in which each problem exists. The *solution* of a problem consists of the development of meaningful actions taken to analyze the problem and to generate a set of instructions that will convert or process the original data and yield a new set of useful data. This output data constitutes the *answer* to the problem. In the payroll

9

case, for example, data exist relating to hourly pay scales, salary deductions, number of employees, classification of workers, etc. All this must be processed by a predetermined set of instructions designed to yield one paycheck per employee.

The solution of a problem and the answer to a problem are quite distinct. A solution consists of the steps taken to analyze given information and to structure a means for doing something with that information. An answer is the information that is output as a result of those steps. The following problem and its solution will better illustrate these definitions.

Example: Big City Airlines needs to develop a reservation system. The company has flights that originate in Boston and fly daily to New York, Philadelphia, Chicago, Pittsburgh, Houston, Los Angeles, San Francisco, Seattle, Miami, and Phoenix.

This forms the basic environment of the problem. Establishing a reservation on any flight involves analysis of such data as available flights, class accommodations, numbers of seats, prices, and time schedules. It is possible to devise a coding system for all this pertinent data and thus transform it into an equivalent form that would be very precise and easily manipulated. For example, the cities could be replaced by numbers from 1–11 or by letter codes such as BSTN for Boston. Accommodations could be designated by 0 for economy class and 1 for first class. For the present, however, we will ignore this aspect of problem-solving and illustrate the solution to this problem as a set of instructions given in a series of numbered steps to be followed in sequence (see p. 11). Useful output from this solution would consist of a ticket satisfactory to the person requesting a reservation; such output therefore becomes the answer to the problem.

This set of instructions constitutes an *algorithm,* a complete and unambiguous sequence of instructions that will lead to the solution of a problem in a finite number of steps. The word algorithm is derived from the name Al-Khowarizmi, a ninth-century Arabian mathematician whose works were instrumental in introducing current methods of counting to the Western world. A close examination of the solution for the airline reservation problem will illustrate the key factors involved in the construction of algorithms.

An algorithm must consist of complete and unambiguous rules.   Some individuals would probably consider the solution to the airline problem to be incomplete. Indeed, certain things have been taken for granted. There is no mention of conditions that

1. Accept person's request for flight to a particular city.
2. Does airline fly to that city?   *Yes*: go directly to step 5.
   No: proceed to step 3.

3. Direct person to different airline.
4. Go directly to step 17.
5. Clerk shows person flight schedule.
6. Are there any satisfactory   *Yes*: go directly to step 7.
   flight times?   *No*: return directly to step 3.
7. Does the person require first-   *Yes*: go directly to step 15.
   class accommodations?   *No*: proceed to step 8.
8. Are there enough vacant econ-   *Yes*: go directly to step 16.
   omy seats on the requested   *No*: proceed to step 9.
   flight?
9. Will the person change to a dif-   *Yes*: proceed to step 10.
   ferent flight time?   *No*: go directly to step 11.
10. Have all possible flights on   *Yes*: proceed to step 11.
    requested day been checked?   *No*: return directly to step 8.
11. Have other accommodation   *Yes*: return directly to step 3.
    classes been checked?   *No*: proceed to step 12.
12. Is the original request for   *Yes*: go directly to step 14.
    economy?   *No*: proceed to step 13.
13. Will the person change to   *Yes*: return directly to step 8.
    economy class?   *No*: return directly to step 3.
14. Will the person change to first   *Yes*: proceed to step 15.
    class?   *No*: return directly to step 3.
15. Are there enough first-class   *Yes*: proceed to step 16.
    seats on the requested flight?   *No*: return directly to step 9.
16. Issue appropriate tickets.
17. Is it closing time?   *Yes*: proceed to step 18.
    No: return directly to step 1.

18. Terminate procedure.

would cancel flights or of alternative action to be taken in such cases. What about such factors as the type of plane available for certain flights or the extras offered on some flights?

An algorithm should be a solution of any member of a class of problems. In this case, the algorithm for the airline problem should be designed to cover all aspects of the successful operation of that particular reservation system. The given solution is obviously restricted to a particular airline company having only two types of accommodations, but the problem and solution do make use of the fact that, in general, certain things have to be checked to determine availability of reservations. Big City Airlines might very well make use of an available master reservation system designed in a form so general that it can easily be modified to meet the specific needs of any particular airline.

An algorithm should lead to a solution in a finite number of steps. The airline problem can certainly become a very detailed set of instructions, but the solution would still contain a definite, countable number of steps that must be followed in sequence.

The term algorithm can be applied to essentially any list of instructions. How complete and unambiguous the algorithm is depends on the interpreter. Sometimes, algorithms can be expressed sufficiently in a language such as English. A person reading the algorithm has the ability to interpret the idiosyncracies inherent in that language. A computer does not have this capacity; therefore, special languages, called *programming languages,* have been developed in which instructions are written for implementation on computers. These languages have been constructed using a small subset of the English language but with a much more restricted syntax (grammar) to reduce the possibility of misinterpretation.

FLOWCHARTING

Descriptions of algorithms using the English language or programming languages are necessarily linear in nature, since the instructions are stated line after line in numerical sequence. Such descriptions may be adequate for cases in which each instruction follows directly from the one numerically preceding it, but more complex algorithms do not fit this pattern. The solution to the airline problem, for example, contains many instructions that are followed not with respect to their strict numerical sequence but with respect to their logical sequence. Yet the linear structure of the solution makes the logic involved very difficult to follow and may even obscure it completely. Therefore a special, two-dimensional language called flowcharting has been developed to express algorithms.

A *flowchart* is a pictorical representation of the algorithm for a problem or class of problems in which several types of enclosures are connected by lines, called flowlines. Each enclosure represents a basic operation necessary for the solution of the problem. The flowlines determine the sequence of these operations, thereby providing a visual conception of the logic involved in the algorithm.

The types of enclosures used in this text are listed here.

Rectangle. It is used to indicate a particular *process* within the algorithm.

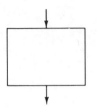

The processes within an algorithm result in a transformation of information (data) associated with the problem either through computation or through movement of information from one place to another. The following are three examples of the use of the process symbol.

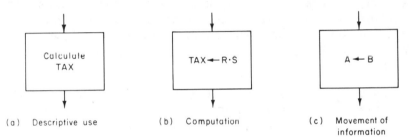

(a)   Descriptive use   (b)   Computation   (c)   Movement of information

The left-pointing arrow (←) is used to denote assignment. In (b) the result of the multiplication R × S is assigned to TAX. In general, any computation is allowed that makes use of a valid combination of symbols, numbers, and operators following the simple algebraic rules for such expressions. In (c) the value of B is assigned to A, and the value of B remains unchanged.

Parallelogram. It is used to indicate *input of information* (data) to the algorithm and *output of results* from the algorithm.

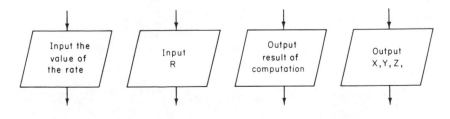

Starting and Stopping.   The *oval* is used to define the *starting point* of the flowchart and the *logical end* of the flowchart.

Flowlines. Enclosures are connected by flowlines that show *the paths the solution is to follow.* For clarity, flowlines should be only vertical or horizontal and should never cross. The standard paths of travel are top to bottom and left to right. These directions may be indicated by flowlines without arrowheads (−, |). Bottom to top and right to left should be indicated by lines with arrowheads (←, ↑). To avoid confusion, however, we shall use arrowheads to indicate all directions of flow. Any number of flowlines may enter an enclosure, but only one flowline may leave it. An exception is the decision diamond, which will be discussed next.

Decision Making. It is often necessary to test for certain conditions within an algorithm. Then, depending on whether the result of the test is true (*T*) or false (*F*), we must go to different sections of the algorithm. The *decision diamond* is used to represent *tests* in a flowchart.

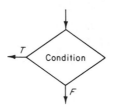

Some examples are

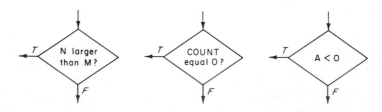

In general, a decision will take the form

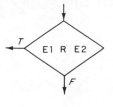

where E1 and E2 are variables or mathematical expressions and R is one of the relational operators $<$, $\leq$, $\geq$, $>$, $=$, $\neq$, representing less than, less than or equal, greater than or equal, greater than, equal, and not equal, respectively.

Whenever two variables or mathematical expressions are specifically compared, they are related to each other in only one of three possible ways: the first quantity can be less than the second quantity; it can be equal to the second quantity; or it can be greater than the second quantity. It is not possible for two of these relationships to exist simultaneously. A decision diamond may be used to indicate a separate course of action for each of these three relationships. For example,

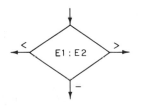

The order in which the relational operators are placed on the flowlines leaving the diamond is dependent only on the requirements of the particular algorithm.

The basic path that a solution follows in a flowchart is indicated by flowlines connecting enclosures, but the nature of some solutions is such that it becomes necessary to bypass certain enclosures. This is referred to as a *branch* (transfer of control). A *conditional* branch is the result of a test or comparison made in a decision diamond. Any other transfer of control is labelled *unconditional.*

Connectors. When it becomes necessary to *temporarily termi-nate a flowchart* and continue it from another position on the page because of space limitations, a *small circle with a symbol inside* is used, and another circle with the same symbol inside is placed where the flowchart continues.

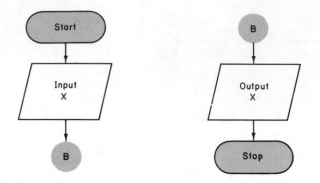

These connectors are also used to avoid crossing flowlines. If a flowchart is to be continued on another page, the following symbol is used.

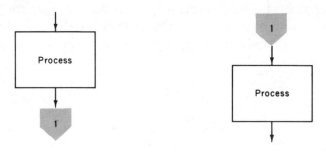

Annotation Symbol. A *rectangle with one open end* is used to write *additional explanatory information* within the flowchart. The dotted line indicates that the explanation is not part of the algorithm.

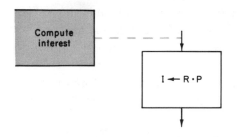

Using the tools of flowcharting, we can now write the algorithm for the airline reservation system in flowchart form. To "translate" the algorithm stated earlier into flowchart form, we must first identify each step as a *process*, an *input* or *output,* or a *decision.* The chart in Figure 2.1 should help illustrate this identification process.

The flowchart contains a "Start" symbol at the very beginning of the algorithm, just prior to step 1. The initial four steps of the

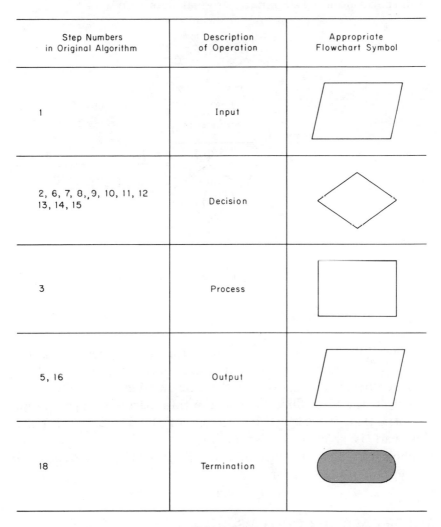

Step Numbers in Original Algorithm	Description of Operation	Appropriate Flowchart Symbol
1	Input	
2, 6, 7, 8,,9, 10, 11, 12 13, 14, 15	Decision	
3	Process	
5, 16	Output	
18	Termination	

FIGURE 2.1

algorithm therefore take the flowchart form in Figure 2.2. Since the original algorithm contained many statements such as "proceed to step 18," the flowchart contains flowlines directed to the appropriate flowchart symbols corresponding to those steps. Furthermore, to avoid crossing flowlines and due to limitations of space on the printed page, connectors containing capital letters are used. To facilitate the translation process, each flowchart symbol is accompanied by a number in parentheses to indicate reference to the corresponding step in the original algorithm.

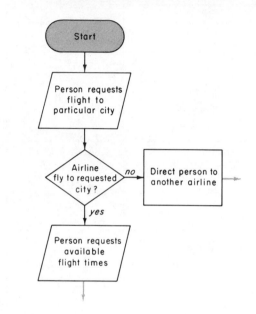

FIGURE 2.2

The fully constructed flowchart for the airline reservation system [see Figure 2.3] should be closely examined. The numbers in parentheses correspond to the line numbers in the English version of the algorithm. At first, the flowchart may appear more complex than the original description of the algorithm. Yet the flowchart is simpler to use because it combines a few basic symbols with definite lines of flow, thus creating a better visual conception of the solution.

THREE BASIC ALGORITHMS

The use of flowcharts to express algorithms can be illustrated by a simple mathematical problem (see p. 20).

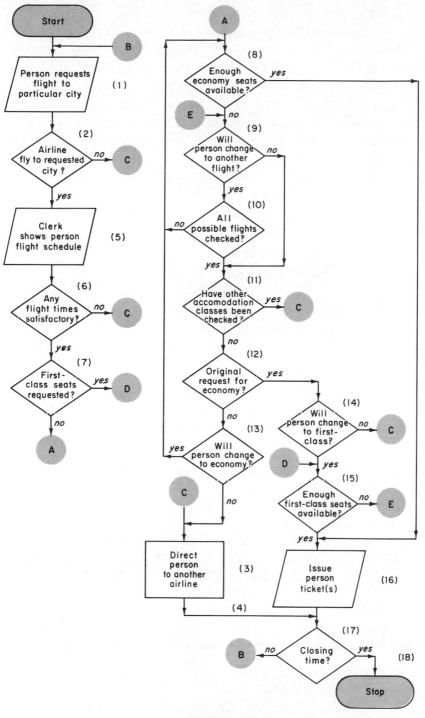

FIGURE 2.3

Example: Find the area of a triangle when given the measure of the base and the height (altitude). The formula is $k = (b \cdot h)/2$, where k, b, and h are variables representing the area, the base, and the altitude of the triangle, respectively.

Solution.   Before the solution of any problem can be expressed as an algorithm in flowchart form, key elements must be isolated from the initial statement of the problem. A process has to be developed whereby nonessential information is eliminated and focus is centered only on relevant facts. For many people, this may well be the most difficult aspect of problem-solving.

We start with a precise statement of the problem.

1.   We are to *find* the *area* of a triangle.
2.   The *measure of the base and the altitude* of the triangle are *given*.
3.   The area is *related to* the base and altitude by a *formula*: base X height/2.

These three statements contain italicized words or phrases that indicate the essential facts needed in the solution. Delineating this even further, we can now select variables to represent key elements.

1.   K will be used to represent *area*.
2.   B will represent the measure of the *base*.
3.   H will represent the measure of the *height*.
4.   The *formula* for the area becomes $K = (B \cdot H)/2$.

Finally, we need to identify the input and output associated with the solution. Having been "given," the values of the measures of B and H are identified as input. Note that the formula for the area clearly requires the values of those two variables. Output will consist of the value of the area—the thing we were asked to "find." At the same time, the values of B and H will also be output, since they are directly related to the value of the area and might be needed to check the final results of the algorithm. The chart in Figure 2.4 summarizes this discussion.

All that remains is the ordering of the steps so that the flowlines in the flowchart will indicate the proper sequence.

1.   Input B and H.
2.   Calculate K.
3.   Output B $\cdot$ H and K.
4.   Terminate procedure.

Key Elements from Original Problem Statement		Represented by	Operation	Flowchart Symbol
Given	Measure of base and height of triangle	B, H	Input	
Find	Area	K	Output	
Formula	$Area = \dfrac{base \times height}{2}$	$K = \dfrac{B \cdot H}{2}$	Process	

FIGURE 2.4

One very basic assumption is made in this algorithm, illustrated in Figure 2.5; namely, the measure of the base and the altitude is always valid. If either measure is less than or equal to zero,

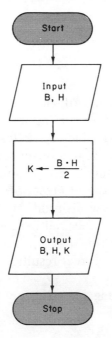

FIGURE 2.5

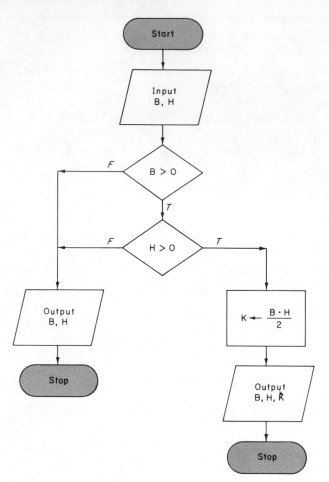

FIGURE 2.6

the algorithm will yield meaningless results. Since it may not be known in advance whether all input values are valid, we shall redesign the algorithm to include a test for validity. Incorrect input values will result in the output of these values with no further processing of data. The new solution is found in Figure 2.6. Note that it is necessary to test *both* the measure of the base, B, and the measure of the altitude, H, before proceeding to the computation of the area, since neither measure can be less than or equal to zero. Although this may appear to be time-consuming, it is necessary to guarantee correct results.

The concept of testing for valid input is further illustrated in the next problem.

Example: A government agency supplies milk to needy families by using a predetermined set of conditions: A family with no children will receive two quarts of milk per week. A family with at least one child but no more than three children will receive four quarts per week. If the family has more than three but fewer than six children, the weekly milk allotment is eight quarts. With six or more children, the family will receive each week a basic quota of three quarts of milk, plus one quart for every child.

Solution. A close examination of the problem reveals that the key elements necessary for a solution are the *number of children* in the family and the corresponding *number of quarts of milk* to be supplied per week. These two elements are *related*, as shown in the table in Figure 2.7. The variables to be used in the flowchart are defined as

NCHILD—number of children in family, and

MILK—number of quarts of milk per week supplied to family.

Number of Children in Family	Number of Quarts per Week
0	2
1 to 3	4
More than 3 but fewer than 6	8
6 or more	3 quarts + 1 quart per child

FIGURE 2.7

First, we must construct a series of tests to arrive at the proper relationship of NCHILD to MILK, based on our table. In fact, each line of the table requires a test for the number of children to be followed with an appropriate action—either issue the corresponding number of quarts of milk or go to the next line for the next test. The only case not handled by this process is the one in which the number of children given is negative, a condition that could not exist realistically within the context of the problem. Such a value will be eliminated from processing by the algorithm.

The value of NCHILD will be *input* to the algorithm. *Output* will consist of the value of MILK and the corresponding value of NCHILD. For the case where NCHILD is not valid, that value is output, and the process is terminated.

Working with this information, we can then identify the steps in the solution of the problem.

1. Input NCHILD.
2. Is NCHILD < 0?   If true, output NCHILD and terminate procedure.
   If false, go to step 3.
3. Is NCHILD = 0?   If true, MILK ← 2, go to step 7.
   If false, go to step 4.
4. Is NCHILD ≤ 3?   If true, MILK ← 4, go to step 7.
   If false, go to step 5.
5. Is NCHILD < 6?   If true, MILK ← 8, go to step 7.
   If false, go to step 6.
6. MILK ← 3 + NCHILD.
7. Output NCHILD and MILK.
8. Terminate procedure.

Finally, the algorithm is stated in flowchart form in Figure 2.8.

The algorithm just illustrated does test for invalid input values of NCHILD, and it will compute the proper results if the input is correct. Yet it is not a *generalized* solution. Suppose the government agency changes the criteria for receiving milk, or suppose the agency changes the number of quarts of milk to be given out? Certain sections of the algorithm would have to be rewritten to change specific constants. For example, it might be decided to give five quarts of milk to families having four or fewer children. This would require changing

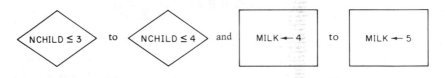

Thus a maximum of six alterations could be required. To overcome this difficulty, we could input the values of the limits on the number of children and the quarts of milk assigned. Consider the table in Figure 2.9. If we contrast this table with the previous

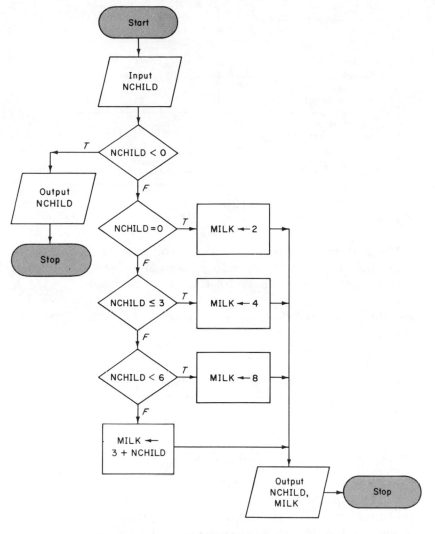

FIGURE 2.8

table, where the specific case was first examined, we see that MAX1 = 3, MAX2 = 6, M1 = 2, M2 = 4, M3 = 8, and MB = 3. A new set of criteria would result in new values being supplied to the variables.

The flowchart in Figure 2.10 illustrates the generalization of the algorithm for the needy family problem. Note that the need for validity tests has also increased.

Number of Children in Family	Number of Quarts per Week
0	M1
MAX1 or fewer but more than zero	M2
More than MAX1 but fewer than MAX2	M3
MAX2	MB + 1 quart per child

FIGURE 2.9

The first problem in this section produced an algorithm for finding the area of a triangle. Now, we will present an alternate method, using Hero's Formula for the area of a triangle.

Example: Given the three sides of triangle a, b, and c

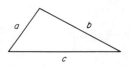

the area is determined by

$$k = \sqrt{s(s-a)(s-b)(s-c)}$$

where $s = (a + b + c)/2$, that is, the semi-perimeter.

This problem illustrates one method of structuring a formula or group of formulas into an algorithm. The process involves the development of a chain of relationships between variables and formulas, which in turn requires a search for values that are known or given. In this case, we have two formulas: one for the area and one for the semi-perimeter of a triangle. The first formula is dependent on the second in the sense that until s is calculated, k cannot be determined. Furthermore, the formula for s is itself dependent upon values of a, b, and c, since s cannot be determined without them. The basic information needed is the measure of each of the three sides of the triangle, which is given. A procedure for solving the problem must consequently start with identifying these three variables.

Solution.   A, B, C will represent the measures of the three sides of

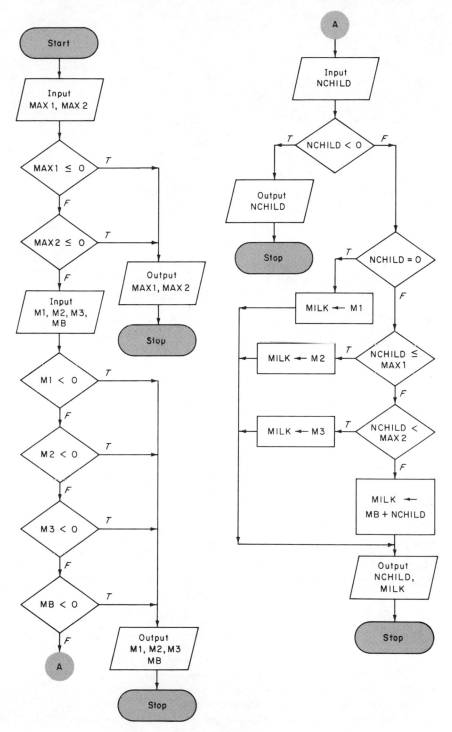

FIGURE 2.10

the triangle. Next, we represent the semi-perimeter by S and relate it to these three values.

$$S = (A + B + C)/2$$

Finally, using K to represent the area of the triangle, we can state the relationship of the area to A, B, C, and S as

$$K = \sqrt{S(S - A)(S - B)(S - C)}$$

Since the measures of all three sides of the triangle will serve as input, it must be determined if they truly form a triangle. This is done by making certain that the measures of any two sides have a sum greater than the measure of the remaining side. We must check *all* possible pairs.

An outline of the algorithm will identify the key steps in the procedure.

1. Input A, B, C.
2. Test for validity of input values.
3. Test for the sum of pairs of sides.
4. Calculate S.
5. Calculate K.
6. Output A, B, C and K.
7. Terminate procedure.

The algorithm is given in flowchart form in Figure 2.11. The calculation of K involves raising a quantity to the 1/2 power, which is equivalent to taking the square root of the quantity.

The problems presented thus far have been simple in order to introduce the basic concepts of algorithms and flowcharts. Regardless of the problem, however, the process has remained constant: the problem has been clearly stated, an algorithm has been developed, and that algorithm has been expressed in flowchart form. Now, it is time to examine more complex properties of algorithms and flowcharts.

EXERCISES

1. Define an algorithm in flowchart form that will convert U.S. dollars ($) to German marks (D.M.), or vice versa. The input to the algorithm consists of a pair of numbers. If the value of the first number in the pair is −1, convert the second number from dollars to marks. If the value of the first number is +1, convert the second number from marks to dollars. Use the conversion formula:

1 D.M. = $0.3171

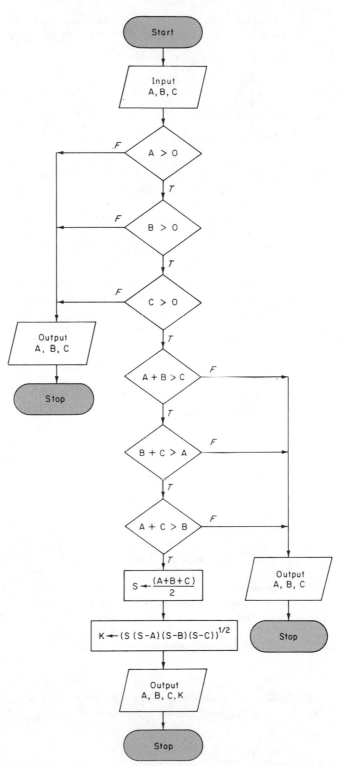

FIGURE 2.11

2. Define an algorithm in flowchart form that will compute the following for a value of x, which is determined by input.

$$y = \begin{cases} (x^3 + 2x^2 + x - 4)/(2x + 7) & \text{if } x > 0 \text{ and } x \leq 12 \\ 0 & \text{if } x = 0 \\ (x - 12)/x & \text{if } x < 0 \end{cases}$$

Note: $x > 12$ is invalid.

3. A bartender mixes gin and tonic in the following way: if the capacity of the glass is less than or equal to 8 oz, he uses 1 shot of gin; if the capacity of the glass is more than 8 oz but less than 13 oz, he uses 2 shots of gin; and if the capacity of the glass is 13 oz or more, he uses 3 shots of gin. Define an algorithm in flowchart form that accepts the capacity of the glass in ounces and determines the number of shots of gin to be used. Output both the capacity of the glass and the number of shots of gin.

4. In Exercise 1, the stated problem is limited in two ways: the exchange rate is not constant (it fluctuates daily), and the solution applies only to dollars and marks. Correct this situation by assigning the conversion factor between dollars and the desired currency through input.

5. Generalize the solution to the gin problem in Exercise 3 by assigning values to the upper and lower limits for each range and the number of shots of gin associated with each range through input. Include the capacities of the smallest and largest allowable glass sizes and test whether the given glass capacity falls within this range.

6. Define an algorithm in flowchart form that will accept three numbers as input and determine the largest value. Output the three original values and the largest value.

7. A local shoe store started the new year with an inventory of 350 pairs of men's suede-look tennis shoes, purchased for $9.50 a pair, and 170 pairs of hiking boots, purchased for $10.95 a pair. For the first five months of the year, the store sold 82 pairs of tennis shoes at $16.95 per pair and 20 pairs of hiking boots at $13.95 per pair. The store then reduced the price of the tennis shoes to $12.50 and increased the price of the hiking boots to $15.95. The total sales for the year consisted of 118 pairs of tennis shoes and 80 pairs of hiking boots. Define an algorithm that calculates and outputs the value of the initial inventory, the value of the total sales, and the profit for the year. The algorithm should be made general to yield the desired outputs for any values of initial inventory, prices, and numbers of sales.

8. Define an algorithm that will accept the real coefficients a, b, and c of a quadratic equation of the form $ax^2 + bx + c = 0$ and determine

the roots of the equation using the quadratic formula

$$x = \frac{-b \pm \sqrt{b^2 - 4ac}}{2a}$$

If the discriminant $(b^2 - 4ac)$ is positive, output the coefficients and the two roots. If the discriminant is zero, output the coefficients and the double root $x = -b/2a$. If the discriminant is negative, output the coefficients only.

9. Define an algorithm that will accept four numbers as input and rearrange the numbers into a smallest-to-largest order and output the results.

10. A system of linear equations of the form

$$ax + by = c$$

$$dx + ey = f$$

can be solved using the equations

$$x = (ce - bf)/(ae - bd) \quad \text{and} \quad y = (af - cd)/(ae - bd)$$

Define an algorithm that will accept the values of a, b, c, d, e, and f as input and determine the values of x and y. Be sure to test that $ae - bd$ is not equal to zero.

SELECTED REFERENCES

Bohl, Marilyn, *Flowcharting Techniques,* Chicago: Science Research Associates, 1971.

Farina, Mario V., *Flowcharting,* Englewood Cliffs, N.J.: Prentice-Hall, 1970.

Forsythe, A.I., T.A. Keenan, E.I. Organick, and W. Stenberg, *Computer Science: A First Course,* New York: John Wiley, 1969.

Gleim, George A., *Program Flowcharting,* New York: Holt, Rinehart and Winston, 1970.

Maisel, Herbert, *Introduction to Electronic Digital Computers,* New York: McGraw-Hill, 1969.

Moursund, David G., *How Computers Do It,* Belmont, Calif.: Wadsworth, 1969.

Schriber, T.J., *Fundamentals of Flowcharting,* New York: John Wiley, 1969.

Sterling, T.D., and S.V. Pollack, *Computing and Computer Science, A First Course With Fortran IV,* New York: Macmillan, 1970.

Walker, Terry M., *Introduction to Computer Science: An Interdisciplinary Approach,* Boston: Allyn and Bacon, 1972.

Walker, Terry M., and William W. Cotterman, *An Introduction to Computer Science and Algorithmic Processes,* Boston: Allyn and Bacon, 1970.

3

Algorithms and Flowcharts — Looping

Although the three basic algorithms presented in Chapter 2 provide a good introduction to the method of expressing algorithms in flowchart form, they all contain one severe limitation. Each algorithm is executed with only *one* set of input values and is then terminated. To repeat the algorithm for a new set of values, it must be started again. This means that each algorithm is a "once only" operation and therefore lacks the generalization necessary for continuous processing of many different sets of values. The concept of problem-solving must now be expanded to include such generalization.

CONCEPT OF LOOP STRUCTURE

Processing of input data can be made continuous only if algorithms contain a means of returning to the point of input. The structure that accomplishes this is called a *loop*. The flowchart in Figure 3.1 is a slightly altered form of the original algorithm given in Chapter 2 for finding the area of a triangle. The flowlines leaving the output enclosure and returning to the point in the flowchart just prior to the input enclosure form a loop. The input, test, process, and output enclosures are said to be contained in the loop. Input values of B and H are still tested for validity, but invalid values no longer cause termination of the algorithm. Such values are now output, followed by an unconditional branch to

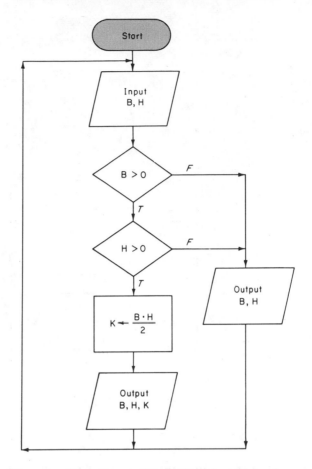

FIGURE 3.1

the input step. We can therefore utilize the algorithm for any number of sets of input values of B and H without having to restart it.

The use of loop structures is not limited to situations requiring many sets of input values. Some algorithms make use of an *iterative procedure* in which values that have already been generated within the solution are used to generate new values. Consider the following problem.

Example: A sum of money is invested in a savings account that pays interest at the rate of 5%, compounded annually.

Solution. The formula for calculating the interest is $I = 0.05(P)$, where P is the principal. Each year the interest is calculated and the amount is added to the principal, thus forming a new principal. The repetitive nature of the process is revealed as a loop in the flowchart in Figure 3.2. Note that the initial amount

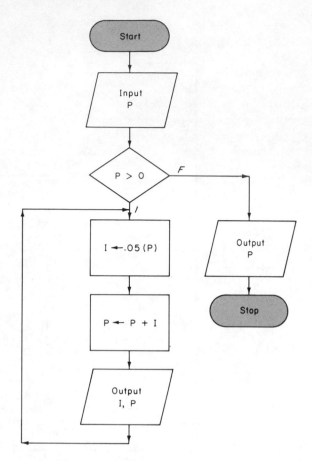

FIGURE 3.2

invested is the only input to the problem. A validity test is applied to P, and if the value is not greater than zero, P is output. The algorithm is then terminated without any execution of the loop. Otherwise, each execution of the loop yields output consisting of the amount of interest earned and the resulting new principal for each year.

The two algorithms just described—if left in their present form—contain a serious error commonly associated with the use of loop structures. The processing of values is indeed continouous, but it is also *endless* (nonterminating). There is no indication of a final value and therefore no way to stop the algorithm. Several methods are available for removing this obstacle.

METHODS OF TERMINATING LOOPS

The algorithm for the airline reservation system in Chapter 2 contains a loop that directs processing from Step 18 back to Step 1.

Yet the algorithm also contains a provision for termination. Both of these features are made available through the use of a test in Step 18, given in the form of a question: Is it closing time? If the answer is *yes*, the algorithm is terminated. If the answer is *no*, processing continues with new input. This illustrates a general procedure for terminating a loop. A test for a critical value supplies the condition for determining the next action to be taken by the algorithm.

The application of this method to the algorithm for finding the area of a triangle produces the flowchart in Figure 3.3. There are two conditions tested in the algorithm (due to the nature of the problem), both involving values less than or equal to zero. We can now use the algorithm to continuously process any number of pairs of values for B and H, provided one or both of an extra pair of values are not positive. Yet the condition for termination is not quite satisfactory, since it is not unique. *Any* negative or zero value for B or H, occurring *anywhere* prior to the last pair of input

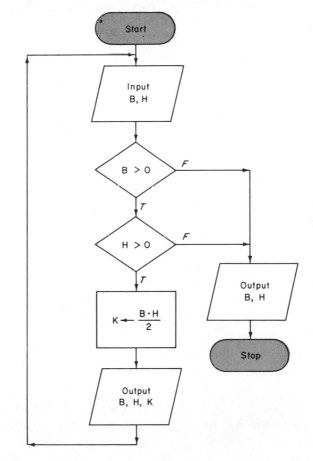

FIGURE 3.3

values, will terminate processing, even if such a value was a mistake. Taking this into consideration, the algorithm is redesigned in Figure 3.4 so that processing is stopped only if *both* B and H are equal to zero. Note that any other invalid input values are now output, followed by a return to the input enclosure. This provides a means by which values for B and H that are eliminated from processing can be indentified.

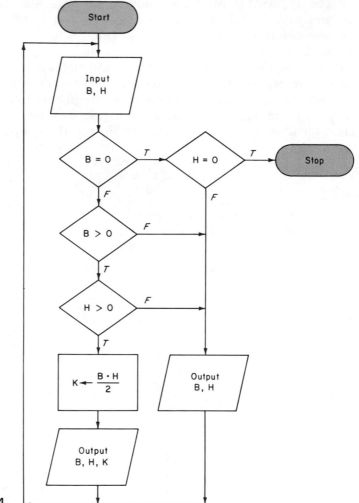

FIGURE 3.4

The next problem and its solution further illustrate the use of a unique input value for terminating a loop—in this case, a nonzero value.

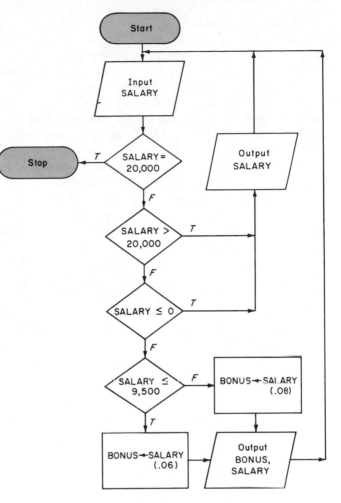

FIGURE 3.5

Example: A small company employs a number of salaried workers none of whom earns more than $20,000 a year. At the end of the year, the company pays each employee a bonus based on his salary. If the salary is $9,500 or less, the bonus is 6% of the salary. Otherwise, the bonus is 8% of the salary.

Solution. The algorithm given in flowchart form in Figure 3.5 solves the problem of calculating the bonuses for all salaried employees. The variable names SALARY and BONUS are used to identify, respectively, the value that is input and the value that is calculated. The given information that all salaries are less than $20,000 supplies the condition for terminating the loop. The algorithm makes additional use of this fact to eliminate from processing any values greater than $20,000 and, of course, to eliminate any values less than or equal to zero.

Since this solution to the salary problem depends on fixed values for the maximum salary, the cutoff point for the new bonus rate, and even the bonus rates themselves, it is not general enough to apply to circumstances requiring changes in these values. In a real situation, however, such changes can occur quite frequently.

The method of generalizing an algorithm to accommodate all possible cases has already been examined in the needy family problem in Chapter 2. Applying this procedure to the salary problem, the table in Figure 3.6 and the flowchart in Figure 3.7 produce the required generalization. Note that the variables RATEHI, RATELO, CUTOFF, and TOP do not have validity checks applied to them. It is possible to guarantee that the values of the first two variables be reasonable percentage rates, but in practice, the maximum allowable rate may change quite frequently. The condition that the values of the last two variables have to be positive can also be guaranteed, but these values may also change quite frequently. Since all the values are input at one time outside the loop, there is only one set of values, and their validity can be easily verified before they are input to the algorithm. In fact, validity tests can become ridiculous if we force every algorithm to perform the testing of *all* values. For those cases in which large amounts of data are processed, however, validity checks are necessary and useful.

Variable Name	Information Represented
TOP	Value greater than maximum salary
CUTOFF	Value of salary where bonus rate changes
RATELO	Percentage for calculating bonus on salary CUTOFF
RATEHI	Percentage for calculating bonus on salary CUTOFF

FIGURE 3.6

The question still remains whether such unique input values are sufficient for terminating loops. It is possible for such values to be input at the wrong time, that is, to be out of sequence in the set of data being supplied to the algorithm. In such cases, the processing of information would terminate before all the desired values were input. If the unique value is not found anywhere in the set of input values, we would encounter a situation in which

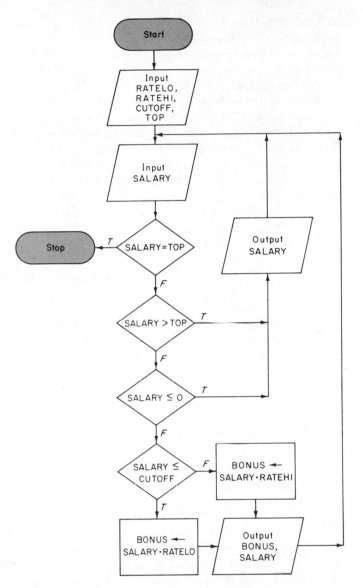

FIGURE 3.7

the algorithm is searching for data that is not there. We could circumvent these difficulties by checking all data before it is used as input to the algorithm, but in problems requiring enormous amounts of data, this method is somewhat slow and wasteful. Furthermore, all problems do not automatically have some unique value that can be used in this way without restricting the generality of the solution.

The difficulties inherent in the use of unique input values necessitate the development of an alternate method for terminating loops—one that is based on counting the number of input values and using the resulting total as a condition for termination. The full application of such a method to a particular problem, however, requires that we direct our attention to some basic, background principles.

First, a distinction has to be made between an *accumulator* and a *counter*. If the solution of a problem involves answering the general question "how many?" the algorithm needs a counter. For example, the algorithm for finding the area of a triangle [see Fig. 3.4] can be expanded to include a counter that would enable us to determine the total number of areas that are calculated by the algorithm. An accumulator is used to answer the question "how much?" The algorithm for the salary problem [see Fig. 3.5] can be altered to include an accumulator that would carry a total of all salaries paid. Secondly, the use of an accumulator or counter implies that a sum is to generated, thus requiring a variable whose value at any given time is the current sum. This variable has to be *initialized* (assigned a starting value), and it also has to be *incremented* (increased periodically by some predetermined amount). In the case of an accumulator, the increment is a varying quantity, whereas the increment for a counter is a fixed quantity. Both the initial value and the value of the increment depend on the nature of the total that is required by a specific problem.

At this point, we return to the area problem and present three examples of the application of these basic concepts.

Example: The first case [see Figure 3.8] makes use of a counter to find the total number of actual areas computed by the algorithm. The variable name NUMBER is the counter. It is assigned an initial value of zero, since no areas have yet been evaluated. Immediately after the area is calculated, the counter is incremented by one; the result is that the new value for NUMBER is the number of areas calculated up to that point. Note that the loop does *not* include the initialization enclosure, since this value is set only once at the start of the algorithm. Incorrect placement of such a step within an algorithm can cause invalid final results or, worse yet, no results at all. In this case, if the initialization step were included in the loop, transferring control back to the beginning of the loop would cause NUMBER to be assigned the value of zero for every execution of the loop. Nothing would be counted, because although a valid calculation of area would result in NUMBER increasing to one, this increment would be replaced by zero upon return to the start of the loop. The final output value of NUMBER would therefore be zero—no matter what the algorithm processed. To eliminate such a meaningless execution of the algorithm, the initialization enclosure is placed outside the

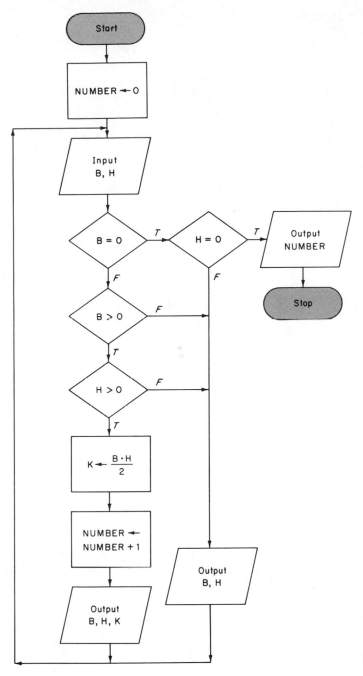

FIGURE 3.8

loop. At the end of the loop, control is transferred back to the
input enclosure so that new values can be input to the algorithm.
The process counts only valid area calculations, since the step in

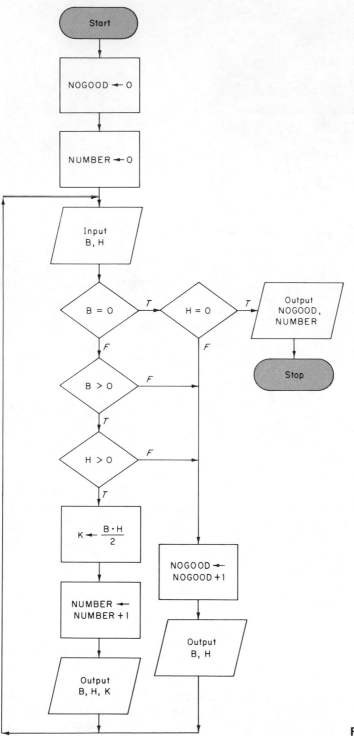

FIGURE 3.9

which NUMBER is incremented is bypassed in the case of invalid input values. The last step before terminating the algorithm outputs the current value of NUMBER, that is, the total number of areas that were calculated by the algorithm.

A further alteration in the area algorithm results in Figure 3.9, a case in which the number of pairs of invalid input values is also counted.

Example: This requires a new counter variable, identified as NOGOOD, with an initial value of 0. An enclosure is also needed in which NOGOOD is incremented by 1; it should be placed after the testing of the values of B and H and just prior to the output of such invalid data. The two branches are distinct; thus every set of input values will cause one and only one counter to be incremented for each execution of the loop. Final output consists of the current value of both NOGOOD and NUMBER. The initializations of NUMBER and NOGOOD are again placed outside the loop, thus making certain that accurate totals are obtained by the algorithm.

The last case, seen in Figure 3.10, makes use of a counter to find the total number of pairs of input values, regardless of their validity. In other words, the assumption is that there will always be at least one pair of values, which establishes a minimum requirement for any execution of the algorithm.

Example: NUMBER is again identified as the counter variable but is assigned an initial value of 1, since *every* pair of values will be counted, including the extra pair used to terminate the algorithm. It is important to note that now the incrementing of NUMBER is placed after *both* possible branches in the algorithm, since it is not necessary to distinguish between valid and invalid data. Even the pair of values used to terminate the loop is counted. In fact, this flowchart can be used to identify the numerical placement of each pair of values in the entire data set by allowing the current value of NUMBER to be output along with B and H each time such an output occurs. This utilization of a counter can help in tracing input values that are misplaced in a set of data and that consequently cause either errors in processing or premature termination.

Several facts are apparent from the three preceding cases. First, the location of the step in which a counter variable is initialized is critical. Placing such a step inside the range of a loop will simply cause the same initial value to be assigned repeatedly.

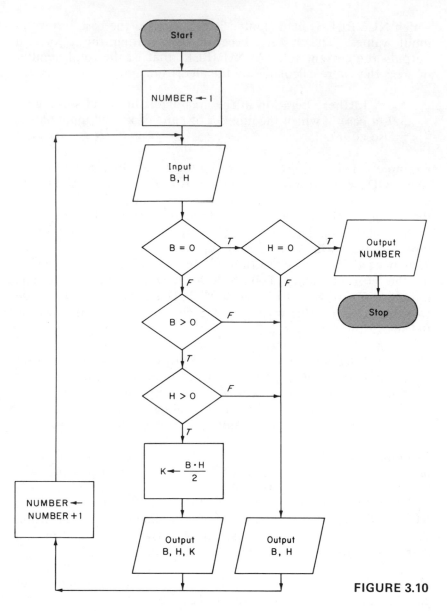

FIGURE 3.10

Secondly, the location of the step in which the counter is incremented is critical. Placing such a step necessitates full knowledge of the requirements for a solution of a particular problem. Finally, counters are not always initialized with the same value, nor do they need to be incremented by 1 each time. For example, it may be necessary to increase a counter by two, three, or some other fixed amount. To permit maximum utilization of such counters, the value of the increment is assigned to a variable at the time the counter is initialized. This variable is added to the counter at all points where the counter is to be incremented.

Although counters do accumulate totals, we have reserved the concept of accumulators for those cases in which sums are generated with no reference to the number of elements involved. For example, Figure 3.2 represented the flowchart form of an algorithm for computing compound interest. The variable P is considered an accumulator, since each execution of the loop causes an amount to be added to P—an amount determined by multiplying the current value of P by the interest rate. The concept of accumulators is further illustrated in Figure 3.11, where the original flowchart for the salary problem now includes a means for determining the total salaries paid to all empoyees. The variable TOTAL is initialized with a value of 0, but the increment associated with TOTAL is not a fixed amount. Since TOTAL will eventually contain the sum of all salaries paid, the value of each increment is variable and is equal to the value of each salary. At the same time, invalid input values are not accumulated in TOTAL, due to the position of the increment step.

Many variations of this flowchart can be designed, allowing for such features as calculating the total bonus money paid or separating the salary totals on the basis of the different bonus scales. For example, the problem could require that a solution contain output indicating the total number of salaries qualifying for the low bonus rate, along with the total number that qualified for the high rate and the total sum of salaries paid. Such a solution combines the use of counters and accumulators and is given in flowchart form in Figure 3.12.

Algorithms can now be designed containing loops that are terminated either by counting to some predefined maximum value or by accumulating a sum until a prescribed maximum value is reached. The use of such methods allows all input values to be either processed or eliminated, since the condition for terminating the algorithm is made dependent on the number of items or on a total amount rather than on the value of a particular input item.

Example: Consider again the problem of a sum of money invested in a savings account paying interest at the rate of 5% compounded annually. The given solution was incomplete, since it contained a nonterminating loop. A complete solution results by adding the condition that the algorithm must be designed to find the value of that investment at the end of 15 years. Note that this new condition translates into the need for a counter that must be

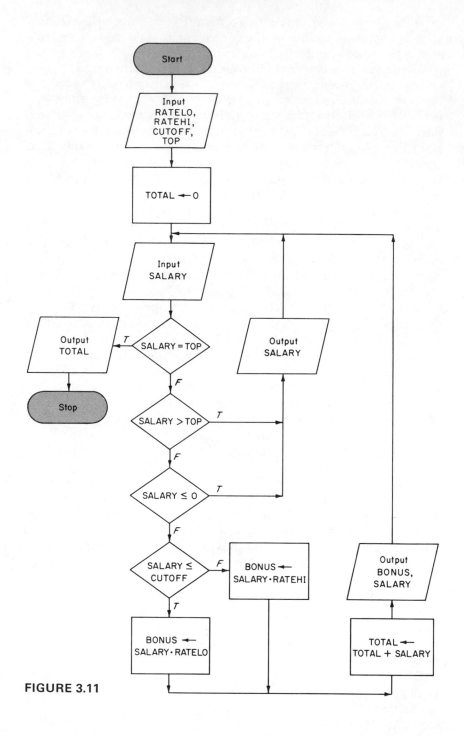

FIGURE 3.11

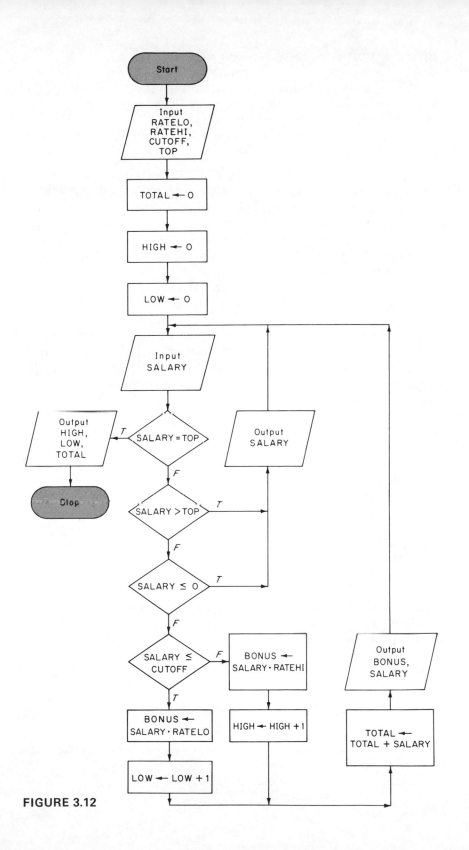

FIGURE 3.12

identified, initialized, and incremented to a maximum value of 15. The counter is tested each time the loop is executed. Upon exceeding the prescribed maximum, the loop is terminated, thus making the solution complete and also independent of any one value of P or I.

Solution. The flowchart in Figure 3.13 illustrates the complete solution. N is the variable name assigned to the maximum number of years (in this case, 15). The use of a variable for the maximum value makes the algorithm applicable to cases involving different upper limits, since only a change in the assignment step is necessary. YEAR is the variable name for the counter, which is initialized at 1 to indicate the first year calculation, incremented by one at the end of the loop to account for each successive annual calculation, and tested prior to each execution of the loop to ensure that the value is less than or equal to N.

A final note regarding this last problem concerns the placement of the increment step with respect to the test step. It is preferable to use the sequence indicated in the solution, especially if the maximum value is to be used to count the last execution of the loop. The interest problem required the fifteenth calculation to be carried out, since the interest is compounded annually for 15 years. Initializing YEAR at 1 indicates that the first year calculation is actually counted before it occurs, making it necessary for YEAR to equal 15 for the counting of the final execution of the loop. Placing the test between the calculation of the interest and the incrementing of YEAR—while preserving the original intent of the problem—would require the test to be changed to strictly less than 15, as illustrated in Figure 3.14. Although such a change does not alter the final results of the algorithm, it does cause the purpose of the test itself to be interpreted quite differently. Emphasis is shifted from determining whether the loop is to be executed again to determining whether the counter is to be incremented. This text will be consistent in applying the first emphasis, reserving the use of variations for those problems that contain special conditions making such an application awkward or impossible. The process is summarized as follows.

1. Initialize counter.
2. Test to determine if value of counter is less than or equal to predetermined maximum. If true, continue with step 3. Otherwise, cease execution of the loop.
3. Execute loop.
4. Increment counter and return to step 2.

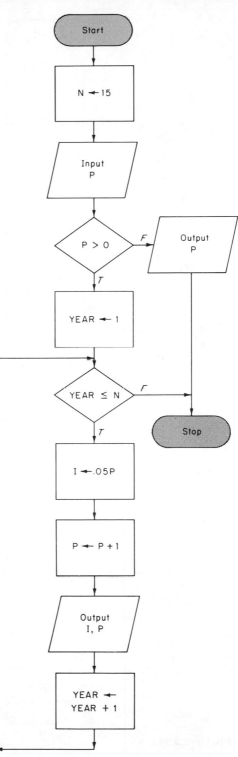

FIGURE 3.13

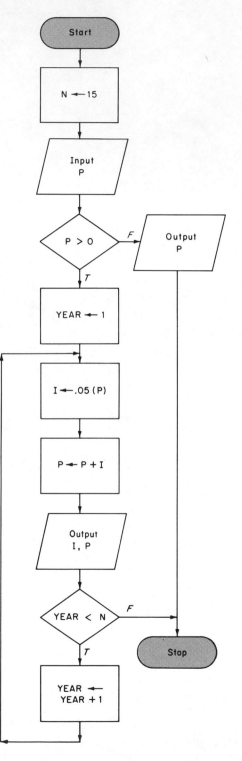

FIGURE 3.14

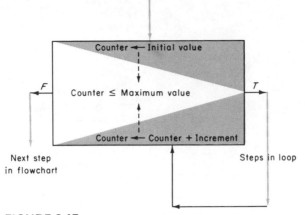

FIGURE 3.15

A new flowchart symbol is introduced (Figure 3.15) that expresses this concept visually and presents a concise statement of the steps in the process. Figure 3.16 illustrates the use of the symbol in the interest problem.

Maximum values can also be used with accumulators to indicate the point at which a loop is terminated. The interest problem, if reworded in the following manner, produces the solution given in flowchart form in Figure 3.17.

Example: A sum of money less than $1,000 is invested in a savings account paying interest at the rate of 5% compounded annually. Determine the number of years it takes that investment to exceed $5,500 in value, assuming the interest rate remains fixed. Output the number of the year, the amount of interest for that year, and the total principal at the end of that year.

Solution. This solution makes use of a counter identified by YEAR, but not for use in terminating the loop. YEAR is assigned an initial value of zero, thus allowing the first year calculation to be counted within the first execution of the loop. Consequently, the value of YEAR does not need to be tested, since it merely counts the number of years for which calculations are performed. The value of MAX, however, is initialized at 5500, and the accumulator P is then tested against this value prior to each execution of the loop. Placing the increment of YEAR after the test step simply guarantees that the year count will be accurate for output purposes. The choice of less than or equal for the test makes use of the condition in the problem requiring the value of the investment to exceed $5,500. Finally, the problem indicates that any solution will make use of original values of P less than

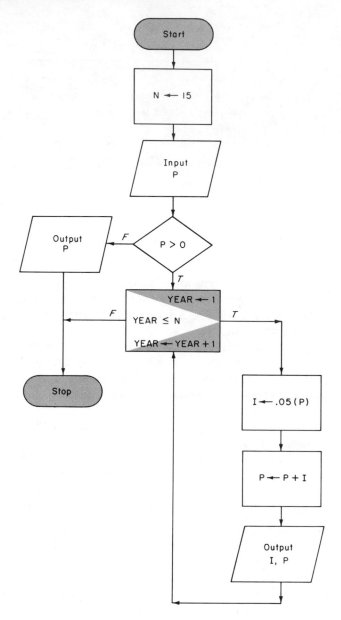

FIGURE 3.16

$1,000. A test for an invalid value of P is thus provided immediately after input.

A further examination of the flowchart in Figure 3.17 reveals the fact that accumulators can use the same process and be described with the same flowchart symbol designed for counters. The accumulator P is initialized by input. It is incremented by the

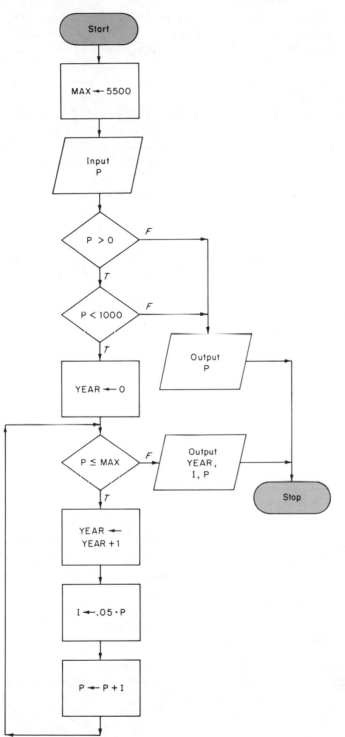

FIGURE 3.17

current value of I within each execution of the loop. The accumulator is also tested with respect to a maximum value. Therefore, the symbol designed for use with counters is definitely applicable in this case. Incorporating this symbol in the interest problem (Figure 3.18) does make one other minor change necessary. The input enclosure now identifies PRIN as the variable name associated with the initial principal. This allows P to assume the value of PRIN in the initialization section of the loop symbol and avoids the necessity of having P replaced by the value of P itself. It also preserves the initial input value, a feature that is useful in many types of problems. Thus the four-step loop process, as stated earlier for counters, and the accompanying flowchart symbol for loop counters can both be generalized by alternately supplying the word "accumulator" wherever the word "counter" appears.

Our use of counters has thus far been restricted to the concept of increasing to a prescribed maximum. But counters can also be *decremented* (decreased) from a given value to a prescribed *minimum* value. The following problem illustrates such a procedure.

Example: Determine the factorial of a given nonnegative integer N. Output the original integer and the value of its factorial. The factorial is represented symbolically by N!, and is defined as

$$N = N(N - 1) (N - 2) \ldots (3) (2) (1)$$

That is, the factorial of any given positive integer N is the product of all the integers less than or equal to N. For example,

$$8! = 8 \cdot 7 \cdot 6 \cdot 5 \cdot 4 \cdot 3 \cdot 2 \cdot 1 = 40320$$

A special case exists for zero, since 0! equals 1 by definition.

Solution. The statement of the problem indicates that we are given a nonnegative integer and a formula for determining factorials. The solution therefore requires

1. a variable name to represent the number, to be assigned a value by input, and
2. a method for counting down from the given number to 1, using each of the resulting numbers in a cumulative product.

The first condition is satisfied if the given number is represented by the variable name NUMBER. The second condition involves several factors.

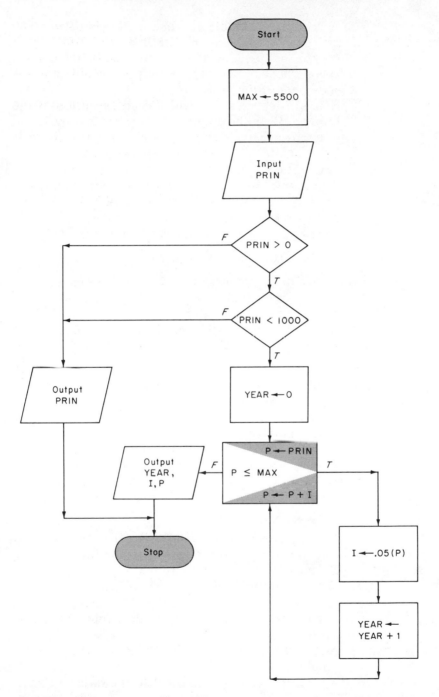

FIGURE 3.18

1. A counter variable is necessary, initialized by assigning it the value of NUMBER. [NUMBER itself cannot be used as the counter, since its original value is to be preserved for output, according to the statement of the problem.]
2. A loop is necessary in which each execution of the loop results in the counter being *decreased* by 1.
3. A test is necessary to control execution of the loop by guaranteeing that the decreasing counter value does not drop below 1.
4. A variable is necessary to carry the cumulative product, initialized with the value of NUMBER and multiplied by the next smaller value of the decreasing counter each time the loop is executed.

The required variables can now be identified as

NUMBER—the number for which the factorial is calculated,

N   —the loop counter,

FACT   —the cumulative product, which is equal to the required factorial value when the loop is terminated.

Finally, as indicated by the problem statement, 0! is a special case, thus requiring a test immediately following input. Of course, 1! is equal to the same value; therefore the test can cover both of these input values at the same time. A restriction has also been given that does not allow for input values less than 0, making a validity check necessary immediately after the input of NUMBER.

We have now collected sufficient information to generate the basic steps in the solution.

1. Input NUMBER.
2. Test to determine if NUMBER is less than zero. If true, output NUMBER and terminate the algorithm. Otherwise, continue with Step 3.
3. Test to determine if NUMBER is less than or equal to 1. If true, set FACT equal to 1, output NUMBER and FACT, and terminate the algorithm. Otherwise, continue with Step 4.
4. Assign the value of NUMBER to the counter variable N.
5. Assign the value of NUMBER to the variable FACT.
6. Start loop by decreasing N by 1.
7. Test value of N to make certain it is greater than 1. If true, continue with Step 8. Otherwise, output NUMBER and FACT and terminate the algorithm.

8. Replace the current value of FACT with the product of FACT $\cdot$ N.
9. Repeat the loop by returning to Step 6.

The complete solution is given in flowchart form in Figure 3.19. Note that the value of FACT is constantly changing, since at any given time the product just calculated becomes the new value for FACT, which is then used in the subsequent multiplication of FACT times the next smaller value of N. Also, the test for N greater than 1 eliminates the multiplication of FACT times 1, since no change in the product would result.

Throughout the discussion of counters and accumulators, the purpose has been to devise a method of terminating loops dependent on the number of items being processed rather than on the value of the input items. One final generalization needs to be examined before all the tools for such an application are available—namely, the process by which the maximum values for counter or accumulator variables are set. One method, used in the last solution of the interest problem, is to place a step at the beginning of the algorithm in which some variable is assigned a specific numerical value (e.g., MAX $\leftarrow$ 5500). This method is general only if the assignment step is changed to correspond to any change in the maximum, in which case the algorithm itself has to be physically changed. If the maximum value always remains constant, there is no need for wasting an assignment step, since the actual maximum value can be put directly into the test step. A preferable method is to assign such maximum values by input. The specific numerical values become data, and future alterations of such values do not require any physical changes in the algorithm. The solution is therefore completely generalized, and variations in application are dependent only on the data that are input to the algorithm. This second method will now be illustrated by applying it to both the area problem and the salary problem.

The problem of determining the area of a triangle, as originally stated, required a solution [see Fig. 3.4] that was dependent on the use of unique input values of B and H to terminate the loop. Based on the given information, there seemed to be no other way to determine when the last pair of values had been processed. The need for such dependency is eliminated, however, if the given information is expanded to include the *number* of pairs of input values that the algorithm is expected to process. Consider the following restatement of the problem.

Example: Given a number, n, of pairs of values – each pair representing the measures of the base and height (or altitude) of a triangle—find the area of each triangle.

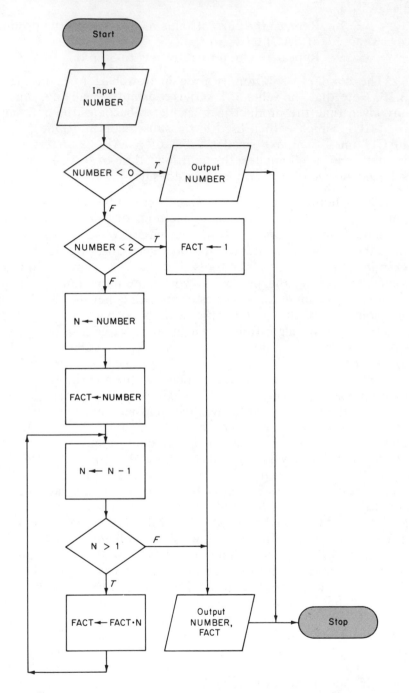

FIGURE 3.19

The actual number of triangles being considered is therefore determined, since all specific cases are covered if the number of pairs of values for B and H is represented by the variable N. When the set of data has as its *first* input value the specific number of pairs of values that follow and when N is assigned this value by input in the algorithm, the solution becomes generalized for all valid cases. Furthermore, the search for unique input values is eliminated, since using the number of pairs of values (n) as a maximum value and using a counter incremented to this maximum, a new condition is provided for terminating the loop.

Solution. The flowchart in Figure 3.20 illustrates the fully generalized solution to the area problem. Since N is critical to the proper execution of the loop, it is tested after input to ascertain its validity within the context of the problem. In this case, the number of pairs of values could not realistically be less than or equal to zero. The use of the loop flowchart symbol identifies NUMBER as the variable name for the counter, which is initialized at 1, incremented each time by 1, and tested to see whether or not it is less than or equal to N. For example, if 26 pairs of values made up the set of data, the first value to be input to the algorithm would be 26. In this specific case, N would therefore take on the value of 26. NUMBER would be incremented to this value, guaranteeing 26 executions of the loop. Consequently, with the loop controlling the input of values for B and H, no more than N inputs of these values can occur. Finally, it should be noted that the specific tests for B and H equal to zero have been removed. There is no longer a need for making a special case of such values. It is sufficient to ensure that both B and H are positive to guarantee valid calculations of areas.

Example: Earlier in this chapter, Figure 3.7 presented the flowchart form of a solution to the salary problem that made use of an upper salary limit as a means for terminating a loop. The generalization involved, among other things, the use of a variable TOP, which had the upper limit assigned to it by input. We can now eliminate the need for TOP as a termination value by using a variable N to represent the number of salaried employees. Each time the algorithm is executed, the specific value of N will be supplied as the first input value. Combining this with a counter incremented to that value used as a maximum completes the structure for the necessary loop.

Solution. The resulting solution, as given in flowchart form in Figure 3.21, requires a few comments. Since TOP is still

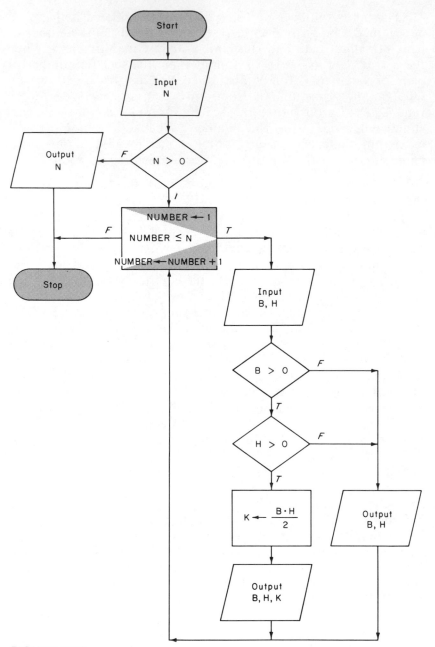

FIGURE 3.20

considered to be a maximum value that no salary can exceed, the test for validity remains. Testing the validity of the salary with respect to zero has also been retained to save unnecessary calculations. The use of various counters and accumulators, found

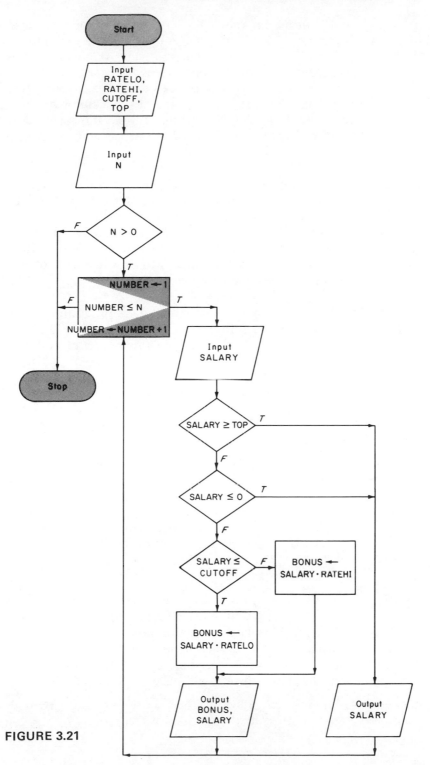

FIGURE 3.21

previously in Figures 3.11 and 3.12, has also been eliminated to focus attention on the use of the counter to terminate the loop.

All possibility for error is not automatically removed by this method of generalizing algorithms. Care must be taken to ensure that the specific input value for N does exactly equal the number of input items that follow. If N is too small, execution of the loop terminates too soon, thus leaving some input items unprocessed. If N is too large, the algorithm is expected to process more data than actually exists. Such errors are not difficult to correct, however, since it is the number of items that have to be checked—not the values themselves. This may not appear to make much difference when referring to single-item inputs or pairs of items, but if each input consisted of twenty items and if hundreds of such inputs are processed, finding the error becomes more difficult. In fact, checking the count of input items can be done by the algorithm itself simply by inserting a step that causes the value of the counter to be output when the loop is terminated.

Before examining some new techniques of looping, the following problem and its solution is presented to further illustrate those methods pertaining to the generalization of looping techniques.

Example: A set of test scores for a class of students must be analyzed to determine the total number of scores in each of the grade categories A, B, C, D, and F. The following general conditions exist.

> 1.   The class can contain any number of students.
> 2.   Each individual test score is recorded as a single item.
> 3.   Each score must lie between a highest possible score and a lowest possible score, but these bounds are flexible for any particular set of test scores.
> 4.   The upper and lower limits for each grade category are not always the same for every set of test scores.

Solution.   The first step in the solution is to identify the elements in the problem statement that must be represented by variables. The table in Figure 3.22 isolates this information.

Next, it is necessary to extract from the problem statement the relationships among these variables and to identify any new variables that such relationships might necessitate.

> 1.   Since each individual test score is a single item, N also represents the number of test scores.

Key Elements in Problem	Represented by
Number of students in class	N
Individual test score	SCORE
Highest possible test score	HIGH
Lowest possible test score	LOW
Lower limit for A category	A
Lower limit for B category	B
Lower limit for C category	C
Lower limit for D category	D
Total number of A grades	ASUM
Total number of B grades	BSUM
Total number of C grades	CSUM
Total number of D grades	DSUM
Total number of F grades	FSUM

FIGURE 3.22

2. The input of all these scores therefore requires a loop and a counter that uses N as its maximum value. The loop counter will be represented by the variable M.
3. Within the loop, each test score (when input) must be checked for validity and then checked for its proper letter-grade equivalent. [For example: Is SCORE less than the lower limit of B and greater than or equal to the lower limit of C?] Consequently, values for HIGH, LOW, A, B, C, and D will have to be assigned values (preferably by input) to satisfy the requirements of the general conditions stated in the problem.
4. The total number of test scores in each grade category requires the use of counters ASUM, BSUM, CSUM, DSUM, and FSUM, which must all be initialized at 0 to guarantee accurate totals. Each time a test score is identified as belonging to a letter-grade category, the corresponding counter will be increased by one.
5. Upon completion of the loop, the totals in ASUM, BSUM, CSUM, DSUM, and FSUM will be output.

As the final step of the solution, these relationships are translated into an algorithm, whose flowchart form is given in

Figure 3.23. These notes merely help to clarify a few steps in the flowchart.

1. The output of invalid values of SCORE immediately after the validity test is included to facilitate identification of such values.
2. Testing the value of SCORE to determine if it is strictly less than the lower limit of any particular letter grade does cause the proper branching to take place. For example, if SCORE is less than B but not less than C, then it must be greater than or equal to C, and CSUM is the proper counter to increment. Thus every value of SCORE can be associated with its appropriate letter-grade equivalent.
3. Once such a determination has been made, all other subsequent steps are bypassed, and control is transferred to the increment of the loop counter.

The grade problem algorithm does provide a general solution for any single class of students. One set of input data can be processed by any single execution of the algorithm. In fact, all the algorithms discussed in this chapter have exhibited the same property. But it is often necessary to process more than a single set of related data items at one time, and the restrictions requiring the restarting of the algorithm each time becomes inefficient. For example, the grade problem cannot be used to continuously process more than one class of students. The algorithm does not have the property of maximum utilization or generalization. A method must be developed so that any execution of the algorithm allows for continuous processing of any number of sets of related data.

NESTED LOOPS AND ALGORITHM GENERALIZATION

Initially, the need to continuously process a set of input items associated with a given problem was solved by developing a method for returning to the point of input, which made use of a loop structure. For some problems, the set consisted of only one input item, but the solution utilized a loop that processed this piece of information and generated the desired results. Extending algorithm generalization to include continuous processing of *many* such sets of input items also requires a loop—one that transfers control back to the starting point of the algorithm. If an algorithm makes use of both kinds of processing, then both loops are

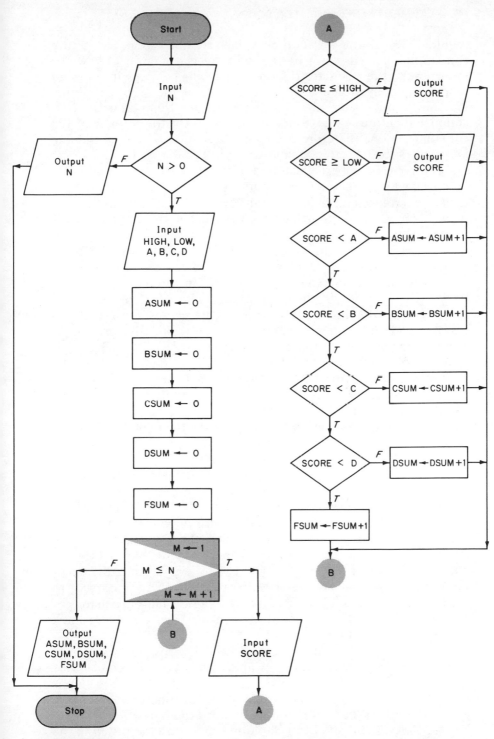

FIGURE 3.23

required. The result is a loop contained within a loop, a structure commonly referred to as a *nested loop.* Nests can consist of two or more levels; the main restriction is that all the steps in a nested loop completely reside within the bounds of the loop containing it. This implies that all counting done by the nested loop is completed before the next increment occurs for the counter of the containing loop; therefore each new execution of the containing loop causes the nested loop counter to be reinitialized.

The concept is best illustrated with reference to the odometer of a car, which is actually a set of nested counters. A number of dials are arranged in a horizontal row, each dial containing the digits from 0 to 9. Starting at the right of the row, the dials represent unit miles, tens of miles, hundreds of miles, etc. As each mile is traveled, the unit mile counter increments from 0 to 9, indicating 9 miles have been traveled. At the end of the tenth mile, the tens counter is incremented by 1, and the unit counter returns to 0. The process is then repeated, eventually involving the increment of the hundreds counter. This causes both the tens counter and the unit counter to start over, and the process of reinitializing and counting is thus repeated. In Figure 3.24 this nesting of loops is illustrated in a flowchart segment, where the flowlines clearly indicate the range of each loop. The variables MILE, TEN, and HNDRD identify the counters for units, tens, and hundreds of miles, respectively.

A complete flowchart would depend on the highest unit to be measured, and it would be *nonterminating* in the sense that odometers reach the maximum value and simply start counting all over again. It is also worth noting that if the tests applied to each counter had been made strictly less than 9, one more increment to 10 would have occured in each case—this factor apparently conflicts with the original discussion, since odometer dials do not contain the number 10 as such. In fact, the flowchart gives the impression that the tens counter is increased by one before the unit counter returns to zero. These two events actually occur simultaneously on a odometer; unfortunately there is no way to precisely represent such an occurrence in a flowchart. The steps of an algorithm must be executed in sequence, and one event must therefore precede the other.

The numbering of the levels of nested loops starts with the inner loop, the one that is repeatedly executed the most. For example, in Figure 3.24 the MILE loop is level 1; the TEN loop is level 2; and the HNDRD loop is level 3. Furthermore, the entry point into any nested loop always occurs at its initialization step, but transfer of control out of the loop can occur at any step in the loop. Of course, nested loops can also be identified in flowcharts by using the special loop enclosure, as illustrated in Figure 3.25,

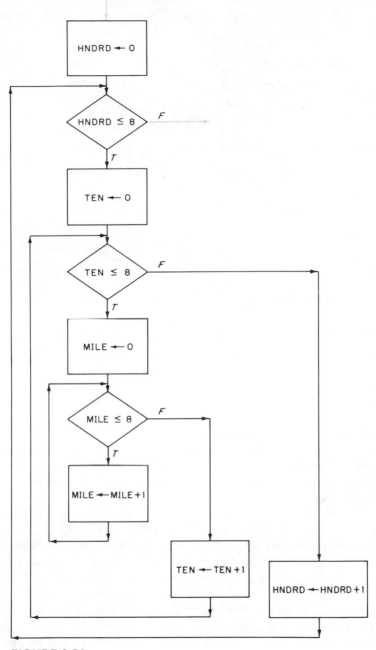

FIGURE 3.24

although at first the visual representation of the nesting is not quite as obvious.

All of this background material relating to the concept of nested loops is best understood through actual application. The

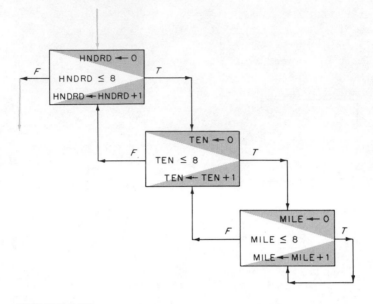

FIGURE 3.25

next three examples, all based on previously encountered problems, exhibit the further generalization that is gained by the use of
nested loops when a condition requiring continuous processing of
more than a single set of input items is added to the original
problem.

Example: A sum of money is invested in a savings account that
pays interest at *a given rate,* compounded annually. Find the value
of *any such investment at the end of any given number of years*,
assuming the given rate of interest remains the same for all
investments.

The problem is basically the same as the one for which a
solution was given in Figure 3.3. The difference in this restatement
of the problem can be found in the *italicized* phrases. First, the
previous solution used a rate of interest fixed at *5%*, whereas the
present problem is to be solved *for any given rate.* Second, where
the previous solution could evaluate *one* investment for *15* years,
this problem requires a solution that can handle *any number* of
investments for *any specified number* of years. Each set of input
values will now consist of two items: the number of years and the
amount of the the initial investment. Since the interest rate will
remain constant for all investments, there is no need to include its
value as one of the items in each set of input values. The rate will
be identified by a variable whose value is assigned only once by
input. In addition, the solution must be able to process more than

one set of input values, and the number of years must no longer be fixed. This requires both the number of sets of input items and the number of years to be identified by variables whose values are assigned by input. Consequently, two loops are necessary. One loop will count the number of yearly calculations associated with each input item, a process already illustrated in Figure 3.3. The other loop, which will contain the first one, will count the number of sets of input items to be processed.

Solution.   The solution, given in flowchart form in Figure 3.26, is most easily explained step by step.

1.   The first input item consists of the specific number of sets of input items to be processed. This number is identified by the variable name NSETS. [It is important to keep in mind that in this problem one set of input values consists of two items.] The value of NSETS will be a maximum for the variable used to count these input sets.

2.   Since any meaningful value of NSETS must be greater than zero, a validity test is supplied that results in termination of the algorithm upon encountering such a value. If the value of NSETS is valid, the given rate is input, identified by the variable name RATE.

3.   The preliminary discussion indicated the need for a loop to count the number of sets of input items being processed. This loop has a counter identified by the variable name M, which is initialized at 1, indicating the first set of values is to be input.

4.   Each input set consists of two items, the first of which is the number of years for which interest is to be calculated for a given initial investment. The variable N is assigned the value of this specific number by input. It is also the maximum value for the variable used to count the number of years.

5.   Only positive, nonzero values of N are meaningful; therefore a validity test is supplied. But invalid values of N do not cause termination of the loop. Instead, following the output of any such value, a transfer of control bypasses all calculations associated with this particular set of input values and proceeds directly to the increment and test associated with the loop that counts the number of input sets. This permits any remaining valid sets to be processed and also ensures that the count of the sets will be accurate.

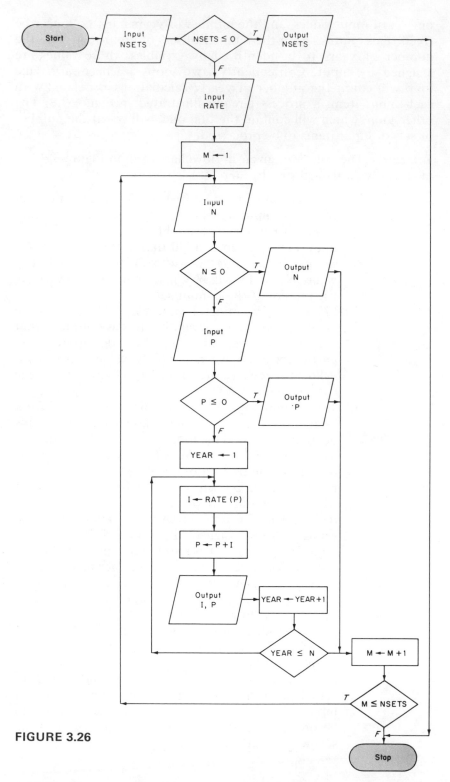

FIGURE 3.26

6. The second input item is the value of the initial investment or principal assigned to the variable name P.

7. A validity test is supplied for P, which accepts only nonnegative values. Invalid values are output, followed by the same transfer of control that was set up earlier for similar values of N.

8. The loop structure used to count the number of year calculations is identical to Figure 3.3 and requires no explanation. [It is worth noting that this becomes the inner loop, since it is the first level of the nest.]

9. Once YEAR has exceeded N in value, the variable M is incremented by 1 and tested to see whether it is still less than or equal to the value of NSETS. If it is, the outer loop is executed again. If not, there are no more sets of input items to be processed, and execution of the algorithm is terminated.

10. Any execution of the outer loop results in the input of new values for N and P. If these values are valid, YEAR is reinitialized at 1, and the inner loop is again carried to completion.

Example: Determine the factorial of *any nonnegative integer N belonging to a given set of such numbers.* Output the original integer along with the value of its factorial.

The *italicized* phrase indicates the major change from the original statement of the problem. In its original form, the problem made use of a solution [see Fig. 3.19] that was restricted to *one* input value for each execution of the algorithm. The problem now requires a solution for a set of *any number* of values. The original solution must therefore be expanded to include this new condition by the addition of another loop, as indicated in Figure 3.27. This means a variable must be supplied to identify the number of values in the set, with a specific value assigned to the variable by input.

Solution. The following points serve to highlight key features of the solution, taken in sequence.

1. The number of values in the set of data is identified by the variable name NSETS. The specific value for this variable is assigned by input; consequently the first input item of the data set must be the actual number of items in the set.

2. NSETS is checked for validity, since its value will be used as a maximum for the counter associated with the outer loop.

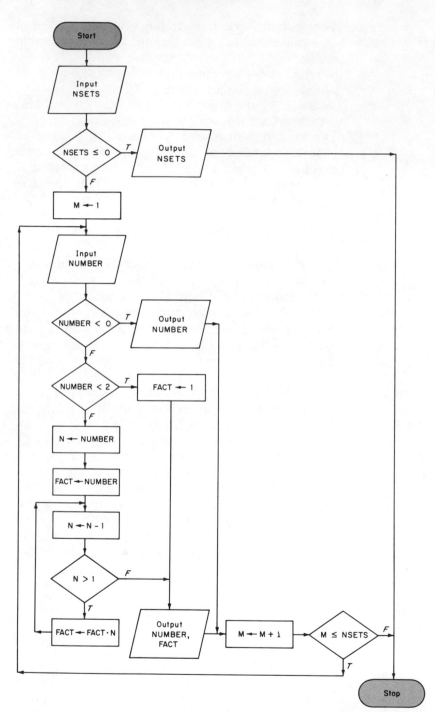

FIGURE 3.27

3. The loop that will count the number of input items has a counter identified by the variable name M. This counter is initialized at 1, indicating that the first number for which a factorial is to be calculated will be input and processed.

4. The steps for calculating the factorial are identical to those presented in Figure 3.19, with a *decreasing* counter controlling the execution of the inner loop.

5. Neither invalid values of NUMBER nor output of values of NUMBER and FACT cause termination of the algorithm. Such conditions now result in a transfer of control to the increment of the outer loop.

6. The inner loop counter M is incremented by 1 and tested against the value of NSETS. As long as M remains less than or equal to NSETS, the outer loop is again executed. Thus new values of NUMBER are input and processed. When the set of input values is finally depleted, the algorithm is terminated.

Example: A set of test scores for a class of students must be analyzed to determine the total number of scores in each of the grade categories A, B, C, D, and F. The following general conditions exist:

1. *Any number of classes can be processed at one time,* and each class can contain any number of students.

2. Each individual test score is recorded as a single item.

3. Each score must lie between a highest possible score and a lowest possible score, but these bounds are flexible for any particular set of test scores.

4. The upper and lower limits for each grade category are not always the same for every set of test scores.

Once again, the *italicized* phrase indicates the new condition that has been added to the original problem for which a solution was stated earlier [see flowchart in Fig. 3.23]. But the need to process any number of classes really translates into the need for continuous processing of more than one set of input values. In this case, one set of input values consists of several items:

1. the number of students in a given class,

2. the maximum and minimum numerical grades for the test that is administered to the class, along with the minimum values that serve as the lower limits for the letter grades A, B, C, and D, and

3. the test scores for each student in the class.

The new solution of the grading problem must therefore utilize a loop that properly inputs all of these items while keeping them grouped as a set of values. Such a solution is found in flowchart form in Figure 3.28.

Solution. The pattern is now familiar enough so that only a few comments are needed to emphasize the key features of this new solution.

1. NSETS is again the variable name used to identify the number of sets of input values.
2. The loop that controls the input of these sets is indicated by using the loop flowchart symbol. K is the variable name for the counter and is initialized at 1 and incremented in steps of 1 to the maximum value indicated by NSETS.
3. Each execution of this outer loop results in the input of the number of students in the class whose test scores are being processed, N, as well as the critical numerical values to be used in the calculation of the letter grades. Note that when any invalid value of N is encountered, it is output, and the algorithm is terminated. Since N identifies the number of students in each class, there is no way to determine how many input items must be bypassed before the next value of N is found and therefore no way to find the next set of student test scores. It is impossible to count to a maximum, if the maximum is unknown. Such input must be corrected before the algorithm can be properly executed.
4. The inner loop controls the input of the remaining values in each set, namely, the individual test scores. The calculations of the letter-grade totals are also done within this loop.
5. After the processing of a set of input values and the output of the appropriate results, the outer loop counter is increased and tested to determine whether more sets of input values remain to be processed. If so, the whole procedure is repeated. Otherwise, the algorithm is terminated.

The three examples just presented clearly indicate one specific use of nested loops to provide maximum generalization of algorithms. Multiple use of loops, however, is not restricted to the nested concept. In fact, many algorithms may require the use of a number of distinct or separate loops at the same level. In Figure 3.29 three variations of loop structures are outlined to illustrate

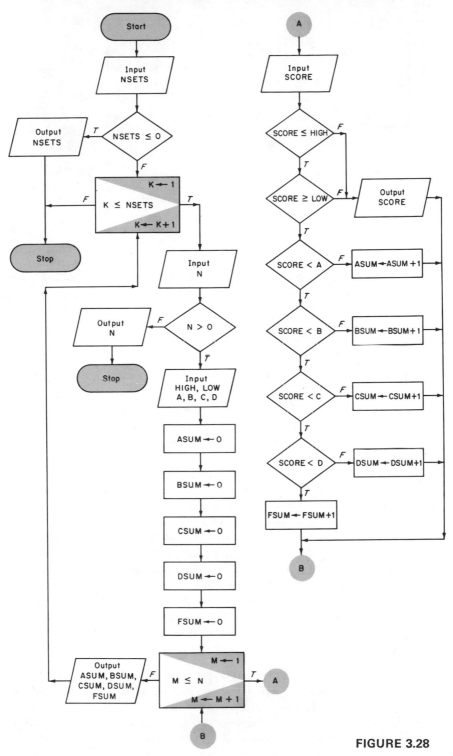

FIGURE 3.28

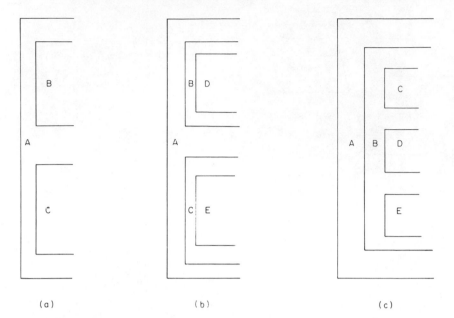

(a)   (b)   (c)

FIGURE 3.29

some of the possiblities in the multiple use of loops. In part (a) loops B and C are distinct, but both exist at the same level and are nested within loop A. Each execution of loop A causes complete execution of B and C, unless conditions within the latter two loops cause only partial execution. In part (b) loop A contains two sets of nested loops. The first set (B and D) are distinct from the second set (C and E). Each execution of A first causes complete execution of B. Each execution of B causes complete execution of D. Loops C and E are then executed similarly. Conditions within the loops may, of course, result in partial execution only. In part (c) loops C, D, and E are distinct loops, constituting the first level of the nest. They are completely executed in sequence for each execution of loop B, at the second level of the nest. Complete execution of B occurs with each execution of the third level loop A.

This chapter has stressed the structuring of loops and examined some ways in which loops can be terminated. The method used for terminating a loop is, in fact, closely associated with the function of the loop itself. Three basic relationships can be isolated.

1. A loop can be used to count a predefined number of things. Such a loop is terminated when a counter reaches that predefined value.
2. A loop can be used to accumulate a total. Such a loop is terminated when an accumulator reaches a

prescribed value. In this case, a counter might also be used simply to indicate the number of loop executions required before the total is reached.

3. A loop can be used to refine the value of a specific variable. Such a loop is terminated either when the value of the variable itself reaches a critical maximum or minimum, or when the value of the variable falls between a prescribed upper limit and a prescribed lower limit. This method is used most often for approximation purposes.

The first two cases have been adequately covered in the preceding material. The third case differs in the sense that the critical value is not a sum, nor is it the number of executions of a loop. The critical value is the *generated value* of some variable within the loop. Since the possbility exists that the critical value might not be generated, thus causing the loop to be executed endlessly, or that the value might require an unrealistically high number of iterations of the loop, it is not uncommon to combine this method with the use of a counter. The counter causes termination of the loop if the critical value is not generated after a certain number of executions. The following problem and its solution illustrate this particular aspect of the use of loops.

Example: Find an approximation of $\sqrt[N]{X}$ (the Nth root of X), satisfying a specified degree of accuracy, E, for any given number of sets of values of $N > 1$, $X > 0$, and $E < 1$. Use the following formula in an iterative process:

$$Y = \frac{1}{N} \cdot \left[(N-1) \cdot Q + \frac{X}{Q^{(N-1)}} \right]$$

Q is initially assigned the value of X/N, providing a convenient starting value for the iteration. After each value of Y is computed, Q is assigned this new value for the next iteration. The required accuracy for the approximation will be achieved when $-E \leq (Y - Q)/Y \leq E$, since this guarantees that Q/Y is as close to 1 as necessary.

Before stating a solution in flowchart form, let us examine the use of the formula for a specific case. Suppose we want to approximate the square root of 5 [$\sqrt{5}$, equivalent to $\sqrt[2]{5}$], correct to the nearest thousandth. E is therefore .001, and X is equal to 5. N is equal to 2, so $(N-1)$ is equal to 1. The first calculation of Y requires that Q initially equal $X/2$ (in this case, 2.5).

First calculation: Q = 2.5; so Y = $(1/2) \cdot (2.5 + 5/2.5) = (1/2) \cdot (4.5) = 2.25$. $(Y - Q)/Y$ is approximately $-.111$.

Second Calculation: $Q = 2.25$; so $Y = (1/2) \cdot (2.25 + 5/2.25) = (1/2) \cdot (4.47222) = 2.23611$. $(Y - Q)/Y$ is approximately $-.066$.

Third calculation: $Q = 2.23611$; so $Y = (1/2) \cdot (2.23611 + 5/2.23611) = (1/2) \cdot (4.4721359) = 2.23606795$. $(Y - Q)/Y$ is approximately $-.00002$.

With the third calculation, the ratio of $(Y - Q)$ to Y falls within the required limit; that value of Y is therefore the square root of 5 correct to the nearest thousandth. In this case, all the values of $Y - Q$ were negative, but that is not always true. The ratio is always compared to both the positive and negative limits, however, to make certain that Q/Y does not exceed 1 by the required amount *and*, at the same time, is not less than 1 by the required amount.

Solution.   The mathematical calculation just performed actually outlines the steps of a loop that will be required for the solution. The flowchart procedure would assume the following sequence.

1. Assign Q the value of X/N.
2. Calculate Y using the given formula.
3. Test the value of $(Y - Q)/Y$ to determine if it is greater than or equal to E. If it is not, assign Q the value of Y and return to Step 2. If it is, proceed to Step 4.
4. Test the value of $(Y - Q)/Y$ to determine if it is greater than or equal to $-E$. If it is not, assign Q the value of Y and return to Step 2. If it is, terminate the loop, since the approximation Y has reached the desired accuracy.

The formula used in the loop depends on values for N, X, and Q that must be determined prior to the first execution of the loop. Each test for the accuracy of the approximation depends on a specifed value of E. Since N, X, and E are given, they can be assigned values by input. The first value of Q is then determined by dividing X by N. After the first value of Y is calculated, the iteration can proceed indefinitely, since the formula actually generates each new value of Q. To satisfy the conditions stated in the problem, validity tests must be supplied for N, X, and E immediately after input. These checks will eliminate the values of N less than or equal to 1, the values of X less than or equal to 0, and the values of E greater than or equal to 1. Also, the problem required a solution capable of handling any number of these three values, so a loop is required that can count the number of sets of

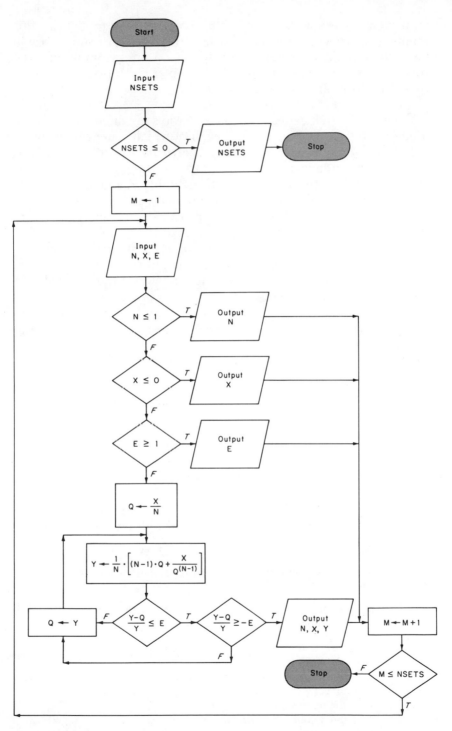

FIGURE 3.30

input items. The variable name NSETS will be used to identify this number, which will be assigned a value by input. A counter N will be initialized and incremented to this value, completing the structure of the outer loop. The complete solution is given in flowchart form in Figure 3.30 (see p. 79).

Obviously, there are a multitude of ways in which loops can be used in the design of algorithms, each of which is dependent upon the unique requirements of any particular problem. In this chapter, the applications have stressed the generalization of algorithms by using loops to count, accumulate, and approximate. All of these applications made use of data in whatever form it existed. Later, we shall see how loops can be utilized to structure the data itself into a form more suitable to the nature of any given problem. The general characteristics of loop structure, however, remain the same regardless of the specific applications. The concept of the loop is one of the most powerful tools available in the problem-solving process.

EXERCISES

Define generalized algorithms in flowchart form for each of the following problems.

1. In 1626 Peter Minuit bought Manhattan Island from the Indians for $24.00. If that money had been deposited in a savings account paying 4% compounded annually, what would be its value today? Output the value at the end of each ten year period, but after 1967, output the value for every year that is a multiple of 3.

2. The square of any positive integer, N, can be found by adding the first N consecutive odd integers, starting with 1. For example,

$$6^2 = 1 + 3 + 5 + 7 + 9 + 11 = 36$$

Input to the algorithm a list of positive integers and output a list of all the inputs and their squares.

3. From an unordered list of numbers in the range 0 to 1,000,000, determine the largest value in the list.

4. A class of students has taken an examination. From the resultant scores, determine
   (a) the number of students that passed the examination (60 or above),
   (b) the number that failed, and
   (c) the number that received 90 or above.

5. A circle is uniquely determined by an ordered pair (x,y), the coordinates of the center of the circle, and a radius, r. Given

these values for a circle and set of points of the form (u,v), determine how many of these points lie within the circle. Output the coordinates of the center of the circle followed by the coordinates of each point accompanied by an indication of whether the point was inside, outside, or on the circle. [*Note:* The distance between two points (x,y) and (u,v) is defined by the formula $d = \sqrt{(x-u)^2 + (y-v)^2}$.]

6. Given a set of grades arranged in a smallest-to-largest order and the number of elements in the list, determine the average grade and the median grade. The median is the middle grade if the length of the list is odd and is the average of the two middle grades if the length of the list is even. Output the list of scores, the average, and the median.

7. The Plastic Things Co. uses a method of forecasting sales for the coming month that is based on sales for the prior four-month period. But all prior months are not considered of equal importance. Therefore the following weighting scheme is used.
   (a) The oldest two months are summed.
   (b) The month-before-last is assigned a weight of 1.5 (i.e., is multiplied by 1.5).
   (c) Last month's sales and sales forecast are averaged, and this is assigned a weight of 3.
   (d) The sum of a, b, and c above is divided by 6.5, and this is used as the next month's forecast.

   The input to the forecasting algorithm consists of a set of values for each item in stock. Each set consists of an item identification number, last month's sales forecast, last month's actual sales, and sales for each of the second, third, and fourth months prior. In each case, output the original set of data along with the projected sales for the month.

8. The area under a curve between the x and y axes can be approximated by summing the areas of a number of rectangles that are inscribed under the curve.

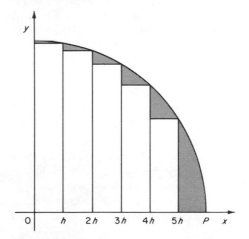

All rectangles will have width h, and the heights of the rectangles are found by evaluating the function (equation of the curve) at the points $h, 2h, 3h, \ldots, nh$, where n is the number of rectangles. [*Note:* h = (distance from 0 to P)/n.] Determine the area under the curve $y = \sqrt{4 - x^2}$, where $0 \leq x \leq 2$.

9. A better approximation of the area under a curve can be obtained by inscribing trapezoids, instead of rectangles, under the curve, and summing their areas. The area of a trapezoid is $h \cdot (a + b)/2$, where h is the width and a and b are the two heights.

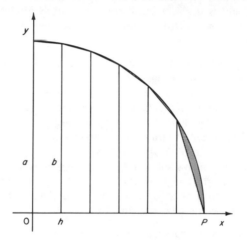

Determine the area under the curve $y = \sqrt{4 - x^2}$, where $0 \leq x \leq 2$, using this approximation method.

10. Three sailors, shipwrecked with a monkey on a desert island, gathered a pile of coconuts one day that are to be divided early the next day. Sometime during the night, one sailor arises, divides the pile into three equal parts, and finds one coconut left over, which he gives to the monkey. He then hides his share. Later during the same night, each of the other two saliors arises separately and repeats the performance of the first sailor. In the morning all three sailors arise, divide the pile into three equal shares, and find one left over, which they give to the. monkey. Given any number of sailors and a maximum possible number of coconuts, determine the number of coconuts in the original pile. [*Note:* The pattern indicated above may be satisfied for more than one solution within the given maximum.]

11. The students in a class have taken three examinations during the semester. The professor stated that the lowest exam score would not be counted in the final average. Given the number of students in the class and each student's exam scores,
    (a) compute each student's exam average by averaging his two highest exam grades,

    (b) compute the overall class average by averaging the individual student averages, and

    (c) determine the highest and lowest average in the class.

The output should consist of a list of the students' averages, the class average, and the highest and lowest averages. Test the validity of the input data (grades between 0 and 100) and make the solution general for any number of classes.

12. Given the amount of a purchase in a grocery store *in cents* and the amount of money given the cashier by the customer (in cents), compute the amount of change due. Next compute the number of dollar bills, quarters, dimes, nickels, and pennies necessary to make up the change. Assume you have an unlimited supply of each denomination. Output should consist of the original input, the amount of change, and the number of coins (bills) in each denomination.

13. The greatest common divisor of two integers, A and B, is the largest integer that will divide both A and B, evenly. If the greatest common divisor is 1, the numbers are said to be relatively prime. Given a set of pairs of numbers, determine the greatest common divisor of each pair. [*Hints*: Check that A is larger than B; if not, rearrange them and proceed as follows. Determine the remainder of A/B. If the remainder is zero, B is the greatest common divisor. If the remainder is one, the numbers are relatively prime. Otherwise, redefine A to have the value of B and B the value of the remainder; then continue the steps until the remainder is zero or one. Output each pair of integers and its greatest common divisor.]

14. Use the *interval-halving method* to find the roots of the polynomial

$$y = x^3 + 5x^2 + 3x - 4.$$

Interval Halving: Consider a function $f(x)$ such as $f(x) = x^3 + 5x^2 + 3x - 4$. The function has a root on the interval (a,b). That is, if the sign of $f(a)$ is the opposite of the sign of $f(b)$, then a value of x exists between $x = a$ and $x = b$ for which $f(x) = 0$. The root can be found as follows:

    (a) Evaluate $f(x)$ at the midpoint of the interval, where $x = c = (a + b)/2$.

    (b) If $f(c)$ is zero, the root is found.

    (c) If $f(c)$ is positive and $f(a) < 0$ then the root must lie on the interval (a,c); otherwise the root lies on the interval (c,b). If $f(c)$ is negative and $f(a) < 0$ then the root must lie on the interval (c,b); otherwise the root lies on the interval (a,c). In either case, the original interval has been cut in half.

    (d) The procedure is repeated for the next interval. If after 20 iterations, the midpoint of the final interval has not yet yielded an exact functional value of zero, it will be assumed to be the value of the root, since the size of the interval has become so small as to be negligible. Given a set of pairs of values, each indicating the intervals in which roots of

$y = x^3 + 5x^2 + 3x - 4$ are known to exist, determine the root for each interval. Output the given values along with each root.

15. A positive integer $N > 1$ is called *prime* if it is divisible only by itself and one. If an integer is even and greater than 2, it is automatically not prime, being divisible by 2. Given any two positive even integers, find all the prime numbers that lie between them. The output should consist of the two endpoints of the range and the list of primes. The algorithm should check that the endpoints of the range are positive even integers; if not, it should redefine them to be the next highest even number. [*Hint:* In testing whether an odd integer is prime, it suffices to divide it by only the odd integers from 3 up to the square root of the integer being tested.]

SELECTED REFERENCES

Forsythe, A.I., T.A. Keenan, E.I. Organick, and W. Stenberg. *Computer Science: A First Course,* New York: John Wiley, 1969.

Knuth, Donald E., *The Art of Computer Programming,* Vol. 1, "Fundamental Algorithms," Reading, Mass.: Addison-Wesley, 1968.

Knuth, Donald E., *Art of Computer Programming,* Vol. 2, "Seminumerical Algorithms," Reading, Mass.: Addison-Wesley, 1968.

Maisel, Herbert, *Introduction to Electronic Digital Computers,* New York: McGraw-Hill, 1969.

Moursund, David G., *How Computers Do It,* Belmont, Calif.: Wadsworth, 1969.

Rice, John K., and John R. Rice, *Introduction to Computer Science,* New York: Holt, Rinehart and Winston, 1969.

Sterling, T.D., and S.V. Pollack, *Computing and Computer Science, A First Course With Fortran IV,* New York: Macmillan, 1970.

Walker, Terry M., *Introduction to Computer Science: An Interdisciplinary Approach,* Boston: Allyn and Bacon, 1972.

Walker, Terry M., and William W. Cotterman, *An Introduction to Computer Science and Algorithmic Processes,* Boston: Allyn and Bacon, 1970.

4

Information Representation in Digital Computers

All the algorithms we have discussed so far can be realized by using a digital computer. To perform the necessary operations, however, the computer must first be able to represent the information (i.e., the numbers and letters) inherent in those algorithms. The *computer memory* is the physical medium of information representation.

CHARACTERISTICS OF COMPUTER MEMORY

The two binary digits 0 and 1, called *bits,* are the basis of information representation in digital computers. These bits are often represented in the computer memory by tiny ferrite cores. If a wire is threaded through a core and sufficient current is passed through the wire, a magnetic field is induced within the core. The direction of the magnetic field within the core is determined by the direction of the current in the wire, as shown in Figure 4.1 (p. 86). The ferrite core also has the property that the magnetic field within the core remains after the current is removed [Fig. 4.1(b)]. If sufficient current is passed through the wire from the opposite direction [Fig. 4.1(c)], the magnetic field within the core is flipped (reversed). To facilitate the setting of a core to the "0" or "1" state and to facilitate the determination of the state of a core, the cores are arranged in a plane (matrix). Each core is placed at the intersection of two perpendicular wires, which form one row

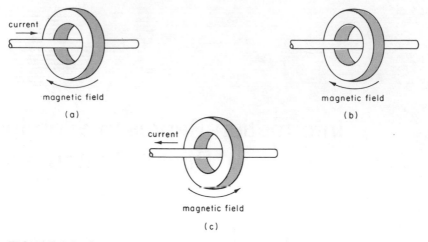

FIGURE 4.1   Operation of a Magnetic Core

and one column of the matrix, as shown in Figure 4.2. The amount of current necessary to magnetize a core in one of the two directions is divided into two parts. Half of the current is sent along a wire representing a *column* of the matrix, and the other half is sent along a wire representing a *row* of the matrix. Only the core at the intersection of the two wires selected receives enough current for magnetization. The other cores through which these selected wires pass are not affected; hence it is possible to change the direction of only one core in a plane at a given time. To read (determine) the state of a core in a plane, currents that will flip the core to the 0 state are sent through the proper row and column wires. If the core is in the 1 state, the reversal of direction of the magnetic field within the core causes a current to be induced in a third wire, called the *sense wire,* which passes through the core. If the core is in the 0 state, the magnetic field remains unchanged, and no current is induced in the sense wire. The sense wire passes through every core in the plane and is therefore used in the detection of the state of every core in the plane, one core at a time. After the state of a core is determined, the core now contains 0 and the previous state must be regenerated in case it is needed later. Currents that will flip the core to the 1 state are sent along the row and column wires. If the core was originally in the 0 state, a current is also sent through a fourth wire, called the *inhibit wire,* which passes through the core. The direction of this current is opposite to the current in the row wire and thus cancels it. The net result is that the core remains in the 0 state. If the core was originally in the 1 state, no current is passed through the inhibit wire, and the core is flipped from the 0 state back to the 1 state.

FIGURE 4.2

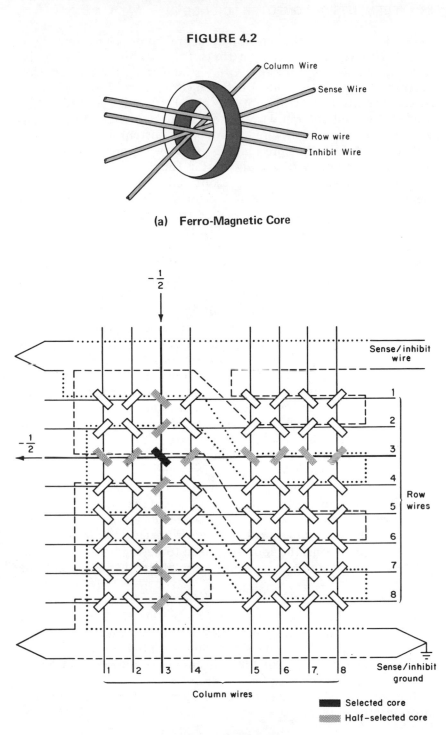

(a) **Ferro-Magnetic Core**

(b) **Magnetic Core Plane**

These actions give the illusion that readout from memory is nondestructive. The technique for setting a core to a particular state, called *writing into the core,* is similar to the regeneration portion of the core readout. First, the core is forced to the 0 state. Next, currents to flip the core to the 1 state are applied to the proper row and column wires. If a 0 state is desired, a current is sent through the inhibit wire to cancel the current in the row wire, and the 0 state in the core remains. Otherwise, no current is sent through the inhibit wire, and the core is flipped to the 1 state.

Since a single core can represent only two states, computer memories are designed to use groups of cores to represent information. These groups are formed from the same core position in several consecutive planes, since only one core in a plane can be accessed at a time, as shown in Figure 4.3. In most designs, the smallest group size is chosen to represent the computer's basic unit of information. This unit is commonly called one *storage location,* one *memory location,* one *byte,* or one *word* and is the smallest amount of information that can be referenced within the computer realization of an algorithm. Each group of core planes used to represent several storage locations is constructed so that the row and column wires are continuous from the first plane through the last plane of the group. Thus current applied to one row wire on the first plane reaches the same row of cores in each plane. Individual planes have different sense wires and inhibit wires; therefore to read the contents of a storage location, the proper row and column wires on the first plane are activated. The individual sense wires on each plane then yield the bit pattern of the storage location. The regeneration technique is then applied to each core plane. Writing into memory is accomplished by using the technique for the single core plane, except that it is applied to several planes simultaneously. Each storage location has associated with it a unique number, called its *address.* During memory read and write operations, the address is used to determine the group of core planes and the core within each plane that represent the storage location.

Different computer designs use different size storage locations, as shown in Figure 4.4 (p. 90). The bit pattern within one storage location is used for different purposes within the computer; thus its meaning at a given moment is dependent on the context in which it is used. Different uses of the contents of a storage location are discussed later in this chapter. First, however, we will examine the mathematical significance of using binary digits to represent information.

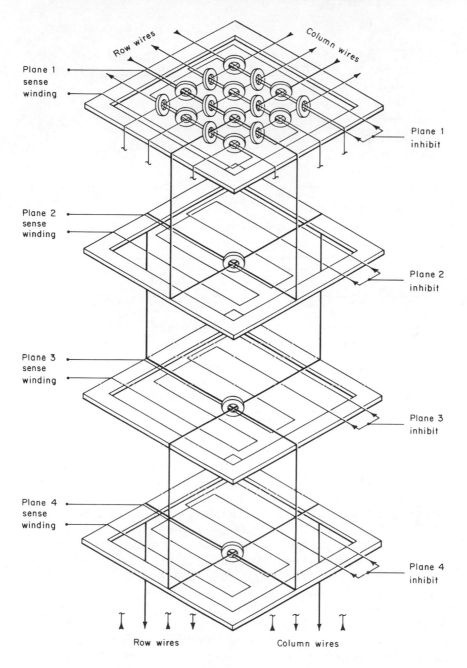

FIGURE 4.3

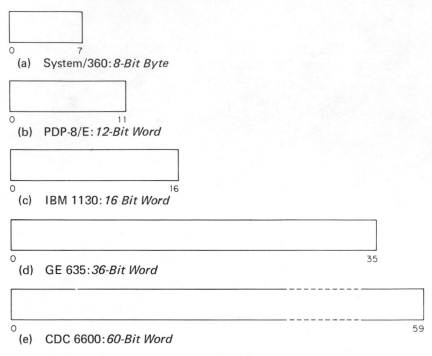

FIGURE 4.4   Examples of Computer Wordsizes

NUMBER REPRESENTATION SYSTEMS AND NUMBER CONVERSIONS

Numbers are concepts in the sense that they exist only in our minds. Symbols have been used to represent numbers since the time man first found it helpful to express these concepts in a physical form. Thus the number two can be represented by many symbols: "two," "II," "zwei," a raised dot pattern in Braille, or "2." Such symbols are referred to as *numerals*. A number has mathematical properites, but a numeral does not. The numeral "2" can be written down, while the number 2 cannot. Once the distinction is understood, numbers are commonly represented by their numerals (without the quotation marks).

Everyone is familiar with our method of counting using ten digits (zero through nine), which is called the *base ten* (decimal number representation) system. To understand how other methods of counting work, however, we must first examine the mathematical meaning of base ten numbers. For example, consider the number 1492. Mathematically we can write

$$1492 = 1000 + 400 + 90 + 2$$
$$= 1 \cdot 1000 + 4 \cdot 100 + 9 \cdot 10 + 2 \cdot 1$$
$$= 1 \cdot 10^3 + 4 \cdot 10^2 + 9 \cdot 10^1 + 2 \cdot 10^0$$

The final reduction yields 1492 expressed as a sum of products. Note that $10^0 = 1$. In fact, any positive number raised to the zeroth power is equal to one. Each product is one of the digits in the number times a power of ten. The power of ten used in each product is determined by the position of the digit in the number. The powers of ten start at zero with the least significant digit and increase in steps of one (moving from right to left) to the most significant digit in the number. This method of representation is called *positional representation*. The number 10 is called the *base* (*radix*) of the number system, and the digits 0, 1, 2, 3, 4, 5, 6, 7, 8, and 9 are the *coefficients* for the powers of the base. Hence any base ten number represented in its usual form,

$$d_{n-1} \ldots d_4 d_3 d_2 d_1 d_0$$

where d_i represents one of the digits 0 through 9 and the subscript denotes the position within the number representation, can be expressed as

$$d_{n-1} \cdot 10^{n-1} + \ldots + d_4 \cdot 10^4 + d_3 \cdot 10^3 + d_2 \cdot 10^2 + d_1 \cdot 10^1 + d_0 \cdot 10^0$$

Positional representation is also used to form numbers in bases other than base ten. For example, let B represent an arbitrary base and d_i represent one of the digits in the range 0 to $B - 1$. Then, if

$$d_{n-1} \ldots d_4 d_3 d_2 d_1 d_0$$

is a number representation in base B, it can be expressed as

$$d_{n-1} \cdot B^{n-1} + \ldots + d_4 \cdot B^4 + d_3 \cdot B^3 + d_2 \cdot B^2 + d_1 \cdot B^1 + d_0 \cdot B^0$$

Besides decimal, the bases 2(binary), 8(octal), and 16(hexadecimal) number representation systems are most important in computer usage. We shall therefore concentrate on their relationship to the base 10(decimal) number representation system.

A *binary number* is a number that is represented in base two. The binary number representation system has radix 2 and the digits 0 and 1 for coefficients. Hence all numbers in base 2 will be strings of zeros and ones. For example,

$$1011011_2 = 1 \cdot 2^6 + 0 \cdot 2^5 + 1 \cdot 2^4 + 1 \cdot 2^3 + 0 \cdot 2^2 + 1 \cdot 2^1 + 1 \cdot 2^0$$

Note: The subscript following the number is used to indicate the base (in decimal).

An *octal number* is a number that is represented in base eight. The octal number representation system has radix 8 and the digits

0 through 7 for coefficients. For example,

$$133_8 = 1 \cdot 8^2 + 3 \cdot 8^1 + 3 \cdot 8^0$$

A *hexadecimal number* is a number that is represented in base sixteen. The hexdecimal number representation system has radix 16, the digits 0 through 9, and the symbols A, B, C, D, E, and F for coefficients. For example,

$$5B_{16} = 5 \cdot 16^1 + 11 \cdot 16^0$$

Note: The graphic symbols A through F are used when writing hexadecimal numbers in standard form but are replaced by their numerical equivalent when the number is expanded in powers of 16.

When working in bases other than base ten, some confusion can be eliminated if we do not attach base ten names to numbers in other bases. For example, read 1001_2 as "one-zero-zero-one base two" instead of "one-thousand-one base two." The names we have for different sequences of digits are for base ten numbers only and should not be attached to numbers in other bases.

Since we are not accustomed to working with numbers in bases other than base ten, we will develop the skill of converting base ten numbers to other bases and numbers in other bases to base ten. Let us first examine the latter.

The examples just given actually demonstrate a method for converting numbers in other bases to base ten. To get the base ten equivalent in each case, we need only perform the arithmetic (in base ten) shown in each expansion. For example, consider the octal number

$$\begin{aligned}
133_8 &= 1 \cdot 8^2 + 3 \cdot 8^1 + 3 \cdot 8^0 \\
&= 1 \cdot 64 + 3 \cdot 8 + 3 \cdot 1 \\
&= 64 + 24 + 3 \\
&= 91_{10}
\end{aligned}$$

Hence $133_8 = 91_{10}$. The following is an algorithm for converting numbers in other bases to base ten.

1. Expand the number as a sum of products. Each product consists of a digit from the number times a power of the base from which you are converting. The power of the base is determined by the position of the digit in the number.
2. Perform all the arithmetic indicated (in base ten) to get the base ten number.

Here are two examples that illustrate the algorithm.

Example: $100101_2 = ?_{10}$

$$100101 = 1 \cdot 2^5 + 0 \cdot 2^4 + 0 \cdot 2^3 + 1 \cdot 2^2 + 0 \cdot 2^1$$
$$+ 1 \cdot 2^0$$
$$= 32 + 0 + 0 + 4 + 0 + 1$$
$$= 37_{10}$$

Example: $A13_{16} = ?_{10}$
$$A13 = 10 \cdot 16^2 + 1 \cdot 16^1 + 3 \cdot 16^0$$
$$= 2560 + 16 + 3$$
$$= 2579_{10}$$

In addition, the following algorithm eliminates raising the base to many powers.

1. Multiply the most significant (leftmost) digit of the number by the value of the base in which the number is represented and add the product to the next digit in the number.
2. Multiply the resultant sum by the value of the base and add the product to the next digit of the number.
3. Repeat Step 2, using the successive sums generated in that step until there are no digits left in the number.

This example points out the details of the algorithm.

Example: $110111_2 = ?_{10}$
$$1 \cdot 2 + 1 = 3$$
$$3 \cdot 2 + 0 = 6$$
$$6 \cdot 2 + 1 = 13$$
$$13 \cdot 2 + 1 = 27$$
$$27 \cdot 2 + 1 = 55$$

Now let us examine the conversion of base ten numbers into other bases.

The problem of converting a base ten number to its equivalent in another base is to find the sequence of coefficients from the new base that, when expanded as a sum of products and the arithmetic performed, yields the original base ten number. The algorithm for converting from base ten to another base is as follows.

1. Divide the base ten number by the value of the base to which you are converting and retain the remainder.
2. Divide the quotient of Step 1 by the value of the

base. Keep dividing subsequent quotients in a like manner, retaining the remainder at each step.
3. Stop the process when the quotient becomes zero.

The last remainder represents the most significant digit of the new number—the previous remainders become progressively less significant. The next two examples illustrate this algorithm, and the arithmetic on the right shows how the algorithm forms the new number in positional representation.

Example: $57_{10} = ?_2$

```
2 |57
2 |28   1    57 = 28 · 2 + 1
2 |14   0       = (14 · 2 + 0) · 2 + 1 = 14 · 2² + 0 · 2 + 1
2 | 7   0       = (7 · 2 + 0) · 2² + 0 · 2 + 1 = 7 · 2³ + 0 · 2²
                   + 0 · 2 + 1
2 | 3   1       = (3 · 2 + 1) · 2³ + 0.2² + 0 · 2¹ + 1 = 3 · 2⁴ + 1 · 2³
                   + 0 · 2² + 0 · 2¹ + 1
2 | 1   1       = (1 · 2 + 1) · 2⁴ + 1 · 2³ + 0 · 2² + 0 · 2¹ + 1
    0   1       = 1 · 2⁵ + 1 · 2⁴ + 1 · 2³ + 0 · 2² + 0 · 2¹ + 1 · 2⁰
                = 111001₂
```

$57 = 28 \cdot 2 + 1$
$= (14 \cdot 2 + 0) \cdot 2 + 1 = 14 \cdot 2^2 + 0 \cdot 2 + 1$
$= (7 \cdot 2 + 0) \cdot 2^2 + 0 \cdot 2 + 1 = 7 \cdot 2^3 + 0 \cdot 2^2 + 0 \cdot 2 + 1$
$= (3 \cdot 2 + 1) \cdot 2^3 + 0.2^2 + 0 \cdot 2^1 + 1 = 3 \cdot 2^4 + 1 \cdot 2^3 + 0 \cdot 2^2 + 0 \cdot 2^1 + 1$
$= (1 \cdot 2 + 1) \cdot 2^4 + 1 \cdot 2^3 + 0 \cdot 2^2 + 0 \cdot 2^1 + 1$
$= 1 \cdot 2^5 + 1 \cdot 2^4 + 1 \cdot 2^3 + 0 \cdot 2^2 + 0 \cdot 2^1 + 1 \cdot 2^0$
$= 111001_2$

Example: $5486_{10} = ?_8$

```
8 |5486
8 |685   6    5486 = 685 · 8 + 6
8 | 85   5         = (85 · 8 + 5) · 8 + 6 = 85 · 8² + 5 · 8 + 6
8 | 10   5         = (10 · 8 + 5) · 8² + 5 · 8 + 6 = 10 · 8³
                      + 5 · 8² + 5 · 8 + 6
8 |  1   2         = (1 · 8 + 2) · 8³ + 5 · 8² + 5 · 8 + 6
     0   1         = 1 · 8⁴ + 2 · 8³ + 5 · 8² + 5 · 8¹ + 6 · 8⁰
                   = 12556₈
```

$5486 = 685 \cdot 8 + 6$
$= (85 \cdot 8 + 5) \cdot 8 + 6 = 85 \cdot 8^2 + 5 \cdot 8 + 6$
$= (10 \cdot 8 + 5) \cdot 8^2 + 5 \cdot 8 + 6 = 10 \cdot 8^3 + 5 \cdot 8^2 + 5 \cdot 8 + 6$
$= (1 \cdot 8 + 2) \cdot 8^3 + 5 \cdot 8^2 + 5 \cdot 8 + 6$
$= 1 \cdot 8^4 + 2 \cdot 8^3 + 5 \cdot 8^2 + 5 \cdot 8^1 + 6 \cdot 8^0$
$= 12556_8$

Note: After dividing, the new number is read from bottom to top. The last example points out the correspondence between binary, octal, and hexadecimal representations of a number.

Example: $236_{10} = ?_2$ (binary) $236_{10} = ?_8$ (octal)

```
2 |236                          8 |236
2 |118   0                      8 | 29   4
2 | 59   0                      8 |  3   5
2 | 29   1                           0   3
2 | 14   1                      236₁₀ = 354₈
2 |  7   0
2 |  3   1                       236₁₀ = ?₁₆ (hexadecimal)
2 |  1   1                      16 |236
    0   1                       16 | 14   12 = C
                                     0   14 = E
                                236₁₀ = EC₁₆
```

$236_{10} = 354_8$

$236_{10} = ?_{16}$ (hexadecimal)

$236_{10} = EC_{16}$

If we write the binary number in groups of three bits, we can convert directly to the octal representation by replacing each group of three bits by this octal equivalent. Thus

$$\underbrace{11}_{3} \quad \underbrace{101}_{5} \quad \underbrace{100}_{4}$$

Similarly, we can convert from binary to hexadecimal by writing the binary number in groups of four bits and replacing each group of bits by its hexadecimal equivalent. Thus

$$\underbrace{1110}_{E} \quad \underbrace{1100}_{C}$$

Figure 4.5 is used as an aid in this type of conversion.

The preceding discussion dealt only with whole numbers, but it will also be necessary to convert fractional numbers to and from base ten. Consider the meaning of a fractional number in base ten:

$$
\begin{aligned}
.4375 &= .4 + .03 + .007 + .0005 \\
&= 4 \cdot (.1) + 3 \cdot (.01) + 7 \cdot (.001) + 5 \cdot (.0001) \\
&= 4 \cdot (1/10) + 3 \cdot (1/100) + 7 \cdot (1/1000) + 5 \cdot (1/10000) \\
&= 4 \cdot (1/10^1) + 3 \cdot (1/10^2) + 7 \cdot (1/10^3) + 5 \cdot (1/10^4) \\
&= 4 \cdot 10^{-1} + 3 \cdot 10^{-2} + 7 \cdot 10^{-3} + 5 \cdot 10^{-4}
\end{aligned}
$$

FIGURE 4.5   Equivalent Representations in Bases 2, 8, 10, and 16

Base 2 (binary)	Base 8 (octal)	Base 10 (decimal)	Base 16 (hexadecimal)
0	0	0	0
1	1	1	1
10	2	2	2
11	3	3	3
100	4	4	4
101	5	5	5
110	6	6	6
111	7	7	7
1000	10	8	8
1001	11	9	9
1010	12	10	A
1011	13	11	B
1100	14	12	C
1101	15	13	D
1110	16	14	E
1111	17	15	F

The expanded notation points out that positional notation is also used when writing fractional numbers in base ten. The powers of ten decrease toward the right, and the decimal point is not needed in the expansion. Fractional numbers in other bases are written as in base ten; the base point (called decimal point in base ten) is followed by a sequence of coefficients from the base. For example, if B is an arbitrary base, d_i represents coefficients between 0 and $B - 1$, and $.d_{-1}d_{-2}d_{-3}d_{-4}\ldots d_{-n}$ is a fractional number in base B, then

$$.d_{-1}d_{-2}d_{-3}d_{-4}\ldots d_{-n} = d_{-1} \cdot B^{-1} + d_{-2} \cdot B^{-2}$$
$$+ d_{-3} \cdot B^{-3} + d_{-4} \cdot B^{-4}$$
$$+ \ldots + d_{-n} \cdot B^{-n}$$

The first algorithm mentioned for converting whole numbers from other bases to base ten can be applied directly to fractional numbers.

Example: $.1011_2 = ?_{10}$
$$.1011 = 1 \cdot (1/2) + 0 \cdot (1/4) + 1 \cdot (1/8) + 1 \cdot (1/16)$$
$$= 1/2 + 1/8 + 1/16$$
$$= 11/16$$
$$= .6875_{10}$$

The same algorithm also applies to numbers that consist of both whole and fractional parts.

Example: $37.16_8 = ?_{10}$
$$37.16 = 3 \cdot 8 + 7 \cdot 1 + 1 \cdot (1/8) + 6 \cdot (1/64)$$
$$= 24 + 7 + 1/8 + 1/6$$
$$= 31\tfrac{7}{24}$$
$$\approx 31.29$$

Finally, an algorithm for converting fractional numbers to base ten that eliminates determining different powers of the base is as follows.

1. Multiply the *least* significant (rightmost) digit of the number by $1/B$, where B is the base of the number, and add the resultant product to the next digit to the left.
2. Multiply the resultant sum by $1/B$ and add the product to the next digit to the left.
3. Repeat Step 2, using the successive sums generated in that step until there are no digits left in the number.
4. Multiply the result of Step 3 by $1/B$.

Example: $.1011_2 = ?_{10}$

$1 \cdot (1/2) + 1 = 3/2$

$(3/2) \cdot (1/2) + 0 = 3/4$

$(3/4) \cdot (1/2) + 1 = 11/8$

$(11/8) \cdot (1/2) = 11/16 = .6875$

The algorithm for converting a base ten fraction to another base is similar to the algorithm for converting whole numbers.

1. Multiply the fraction by B (i.e., divide by $1/B$), the base to which you are converting, and retain the whole number part.
2. Multiply the new fractional part by B and retain the whole number part.
3. Repeat Step 2 until the fractional part becomes zero or the desired accuracy is reached.

The following example illustrates the algorithm and also shows the development of the positional representation of the new fraction.

Example: $.46_{10} = ?_2$

.46	
2	
0|.92	$.46 = (0 + .92) \cdot (1/2) = 0 \cdot (1/2) + .92 \cdot (1/2)$
2	
1|.84	$= (0 + (1/2) \cdot (1 + .84)) \cdot (1/2) = 0 \cdot (1/2)$
2	$+ (1 + .84) \cdot (1/4)$
1|.68	$= 0 \cdot (1/2) + [1 + (1 + .68) \cdot (1/2)] \cdot (1/4)$
2	$= 0 \cdot (1/2) + 1 \cdot (1/4) + (1 + .68) \cdot (1/8)$
1|.36	$= 0 \cdot (1/2) + 1 \cdot (1/4) + [1 + (1 + .36) \cdot (1/2)] \cdot (1/8)$
2	$= 0 \cdot (1/2) + 1 \cdot (1/4) + 1 \cdot (1/8) + (1 + .36) \cdot (1/16)$
0|.72	$= 0 \cdot (1/2) + 1 \cdot (1/4) + 1 \cdot (1/8) + [1$
	$+ (0 + .72) \cdot (1/2)] \cdot (1/16)$

$= 0 \cdot (1/2) + 1 \cdot (1/4) + 1 \cdot (1/8) + 1 \cdot (1/16)$
$+ 0 \cdot (1/32) + \text{remainder}$
$= 0 \cdot 2^{-1} + 1 \cdot 2^{-2} + 1 \cdot 2^{-3} + 1 \cdot 2^{-4} + 0 \cdot 2^{-5} + \ldots$
$\approx .01110_2$

The whole number parts that are retained are read from top to bottom to form the binary fraction. The binary representation was terminated after five digits had been determined. If this result ($.01110_2$) is converted to decimal, we get .4375! By adding another binary digit to the fraction ($.011101_2$), the conversion back to decimal yields $.453125_{10}$, a value much closer to the original number. The binary equivalent of $.46_{10}$ is a nonterminating expansion; hence, when the conversion is terminated, the result is only an approximation of $.46_{10}$. The use of binary numbers to represent decimal numbers can therefore introduce error. In fact, the use of any base which is a multiple of 2 to represent decimal fractions causes similar errors. When a nonterminating expansion in one base is approximated by a nonterminating expansion in another base, the errors are more serious.

Example: Approximate $(1/3)_{10}$ in binary.

$(1/3)_{10} \approx .3333_{10}$

$$
\begin{array}{r}
.3333 \\
\underline{2} \\
0|.6666 \\
\underline{2} \\
1|.3332 \\
\underline{2} \\
0|.6664 \\
\underline{2} \\
1|.3328 \\
\underline{2} \\
0|.6656 \\
\underline{2} \\
1|.3312
\end{array}
$$

Therefore, $.3333_{10} \approx .010101_2$

As in the previous example, reconverting the binary fraction to decimal will yield only an approximation of $.3333_{10}$, namely $.3281_{10}$. However, $.3333_{10}$ is already an approximation of $(1/3)_{10}$. The error inherent in the original representation is made worse by using a binary approximation. The effect of such errors in computer representations of fractions will be studied later in this chapter.

When converting a base ten number that consists of whole and fractional parts, convert the whole and fractional parts separately and combine the results to get the new number. Also, if a number to be converted is negative, the result in the new base will also be negative. Having studied number representation systems and number conversions, we shall now turn to their usage in computers.

CHARACTER REPRESENTATION

We have stated that the computer uses the binary digits 0 and 1 as a basis for information representation. But if we had to remember the meaning of different strings of zeros and ones, computer usage would be prohibitive. To utilize the computer efficiently and easily, therefore, we must develop a basis for communication between the external physical world and the computer's internal electronic world.

External Representation

The *punched card* (Hollerith card) is the most common medium for the external representation of numbers and characters. Most punched cards are $7\frac{3}{8}$ in. long by $3\frac{1}{4}$ in. high. There are eighty columns, numbered 1 to 80 from left to right, and twelve rows, numbered 12, 11, 0 to 9 from top to bottom on a punched card. Each alphabetic character, numerical digit, or special character that can be represented in the computer's memory has a unique representation in one column of a punched card. Punches in rows 12, 11, or 0 are called *zone punches,* and punches in rows 1 through 9 are called *numeric punches.* Cards are prepared on a keypunch machine, which operates from a keyboard similar to that of a typewriter. Figure 4.6 shows a punched card and the punches for a character set consisting of 64 symbols.

Card Readers

Electromechanical devices that interpret the patterns of holes punched in each column of a punched card are called *card readers.* The existence of a hole in a column is used to represent a one, and unpunched row positions within a column represent zeros, resulting in a 12-bit binary number. Each 12-bit pattern is translated to the internal character coding used by the computer. Commonly used character codings require six bits or eight bits of memory. Since the wordlength of most computers is greater than six or eight bits, the storage of only one character in a word would be a waste of memory space. Characters therefore are packed into

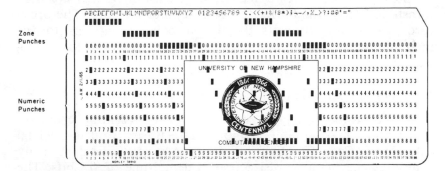

FIGURE 4.6   A Punched Card

words of memory to conserve storage. For example, a computer with a 36-bit word can pack six 6-bit characters into a single word of memory, and a computer with a 32-bit word can pack four 8-bit characters into a single word. The table in Figure 4.10 contains the card column punches for forty-eight different characters in two commonly used coding systems; the *binary coded decimal interchange code* (BCDIC) and the *extended binary coded decimal interchange code* (EBCDIC). These coding systems will be discussed in more detail in the next section. Card readers are available that read at rates of 300 − 1400 cards per minute.

In the photoelectric card reader (see Fig. 4.8), cards are placed in a hopper, and from there, they are fed to a preread station, as shown in Figure 4.7. Next, the cards pass columnwise under twelve photoelectric cells one cell for each row of the card. Holes in a column allow light through, thus indicating a 1. The resultant 12-bit pattern is converted to the internal binary code used by the computer for representing characters. After all columns on the card have been read, the card is passed on to the card stacker.

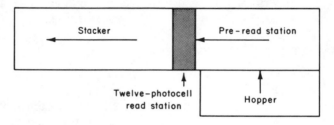

FIGURE 4.7

The brush-style card reader sends the cards from a hopper past two sets of read brushes rowwise. The holes in the card allow the brushes to make electrical contact with a drum on the opposite side of the card. The contents of an entire card are read to a memory area in the card reader, called a *buffer,* and are then transferred from the buffer to the computer memory. The brush card reader also converts the 12-bit column patterns to the internal binary code used by the computer for representing characters.

Internal Representation

There are three widely used codes for representing character information in computer memory. The Binary Coded Decimal Interchange Code (BCDIC) is a 6-bit code and is used by many computers having a wordsize that is a multiple of six bits. The Extended Binary Coded Decimal Interchange Code (EBCDIC) and

FIGURE 4.8 IBM 2501 Card Reader

the American Standards Code for Information Interchange (ASCII) are 8-bit codes and are used by computers having a wordsize that is a multiple of eight bits. For purposes of discussion, the amount of memory required to represent one character will be called one *byte*, and the number of bits in a byte will be determined from the context in which the term byte is used. For example, a 36-bit word can be used to represent six 6-bit characters and thus consists of six bytes with six bits per byte.

Each code divides a byte into two parts, as shown in Figure 4.9. In the EBCDIC and the ASCII, bits 0 through 3 are called *zone bits*, and bits 4 through 7 are called *numeric bits*. In the BCDIC, bits 0 and 1 are the zone bits, and bits 2 through 5 are the

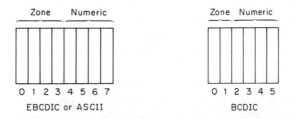

FIGURE 4.9 Zone and Numeric Bits in One Byte

**FIGURE 4.10   BCD and EBCDIC Codes and Card Punches and
Corresponding ASCII Codes**

	BCD	EBCDIC	BCD Code		EBCDIC Code		ASCII Code	
Character	cards	cards	binary	octal	binary	hex	binary	hex
A	12,1	12,1	010 001	21	1100 0001	C1	1010 0001	A1
B	12,2	12,2	010 010	22	1100 0010	C2	1010 0010	A2
C	12,3	12,3	010 011	23	1100 0011	C3	1010 0011	A3
D	12,4	12,4	010 100	24	1100 0100	C4	1010 0100	A4
E	12,5	12,5	010 101	25	1100 0101	C5	1010 0101	A5
F	12,6	12,6	010 110	26	1100 0110	C6	1010 0110	A6
G	12,7	12,7	010 111	27	1100 0111	C7	1010 0111	A7
H	12,8	12,8	011 000	30	1100 1000	C8	1010 1000	A8
I	12,9	12,9	011 001	31	1100 1001	C9	1010 1001	A9
J	11,1	11,1	100 001	41	1101 0001	D1	1010 1010	AA
K	11,2	11,2	100 010	42	1101 0010	D2	1010 1011	AB
L	11,3	11,3	100 011	43	1101 0011	D3	1010 1100	AC
M	11,4	11,4	100 100	44	1101 0100	D4	1010 1101	AD
N	11,5	11,5	100 101	45	1101 0101	D5	1010 1110	AE
O	11,6	11,6	100 110	46	1101 0110	D6	1010 1111	AF
P	11,7	11,7	100 111	47	1101 0111	D7	1011 0000	B0
Q	11,8	11,8	101 000	50	1101 1000	D8	1011 0001	B1
R	11,9	11,9	101 001	51	1101 1001	D9	1011 0010	B2
S	0,2	0,2	110 010	62	1110 0010	E2	1011 0011	B3
T	0,3	0,3	110 011	63	1110 0011	E3	1011 0100	B4
U	0,4	0,4	110 100	64	1110 0100	E4	1011 0101	B5
V	0,5	0,5	110 101	65	1110 0101	E5	1011 0110	B6
W	0 6	0,6	110 110	66	1110 0110	E6	1011 0111	B7
X	0,7	0,7	110 111	67	1110 0111	E7	1011 1000	B8
Y	0,8	0,8	111 000	70	1110 1000	E8	1011 1001	B9
Z	0,9	0,9	111 001	71	1110 1001	E9	1011 1010	BA

numeric bits. Each 8-bit byte of storage can be represented as two
hexadecimal digits, whereas 6-bit bytes are represented as two
octal digits. Figure 4.10 gives the internal codes for characters
common to BCDIC, EBCDIC, and ASCII.

We mentioned previously that characters are packed into
words to conserve storage. Figure 4.11 (p. 104) presents three
such examples. Several consecutive bytes of memory may be used
to represent groups of characters that are logically related (e.g.,
output labels or error messages). These groups are called *character
strings*. In byte-oriented computers, successive characters are
stored in successive bytes of memory, and in word-oriented
computers, groups of bytes are packed into successive words of
memory.

VENDREDI
AOÛT
31
AUGUST
FRIDAY

	EBCDIC Code		ASCII Code	
	binary	hex	binary	hex
0800				
0830				
0900				
0930	1111 0000	F0	0101 0000	50
1000 02	1111 0001	F1	0101 0001	51
	1111 0010	F2	0101 0010	52
1030	1111 0011	F3	0101 0011	53
	1111 0100	F4	0101 0100	54
1100	1111 0101	F5	0101 0101	55
1130	1111 0110	F6	0101 0110	56
	1111 0111	F7	0101 0111	57
1200	1111 1000	F8	0101 1000	58
1230	1111 1001	F9	0101 1001	59
1300				
1330	0100 0000	40	0100 0000	40
1400	0100 1011	4B	0100 1110	4E
1430	0100 1101	4D	0100 1000	48
	0100 1110	4E	0100 1011	4B
1500	0101 1011	5B	0100 0100	44
1530	0101 1100	5C	0100 1010	4A
	0101 1101	5D	0100 1001	49
1600	0110 0000	60	0100 1101	4D
1630	0110 0001	61	0100 1111	4F
	0110 1011	6B	0100 1100	4C
1700	0111 1101	7D	0100 0111	47
	0111 1110	7E	0101 1101	5D

9243

Printers and Card Punches

The most popular form of output from a digital computer is the printed page, produced by the line printer. The function of the printer is to translate the coded internal form of each character to be printed to a command that causes the equivalent external graphic symbol to be printed on the paper. Printers are available that print up to 144 characters per line. We shall discuss three different types of printers.

The *character printer* is simply a typewriter under computer control. This printer is capable of printing only $10 - 30$ characters/second. Typewriters can also be used as input devices. Their main usage is for direct operator intervention to the computer and for terminal stations in time-sharing systems.

FIGURE 4.11 Examples of Character Codes Packed into Words

C1 | C2 | C3 | C4

(a) EBCDIC *Coding (Hexadecimal) for ABCD in a 4-Byte Word*

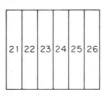

21 | 22 | 23 | 24 | 25 | 26

(b) BCDIC *Coding (Octal) for ABCDEF in a 6-Byte Word*

A1 | A2 | A3 | A4

(c) ASCII *Coding (Hexadecimal) for ABCD in a 4-Byte Word*

FIGURE 4.12 IBM 2741 Terminal

The *chain printer* has a continuously moving chain of type slugs with several replications of the character set on it, as shown in Figure 4.13. When the correct type slug passes the desired print position, a hammer hits the paper, pressing the paper against the ribbon and the type slug. The speed of the chain printer is related to the size of the character set used. A smaller character set can be duplicated more times on the chain; therefore the chain does not have to move as far to position each character. The range of speed for the chain printer is from 600 − 1100 lines/minute.

The *cylinder printer* uses a continuously rotating cylinder. Each character appears in all available print positions in one row across the face of the cylinder. A hammer hits the paper as it does in the chain printer, except all entries of a single character on one line are printed simultaneously.

A *card punch* performs the reverse operation of a card reader. The internal coding of each character to be punched is translated to its corresponding punch code in a single card column. Card

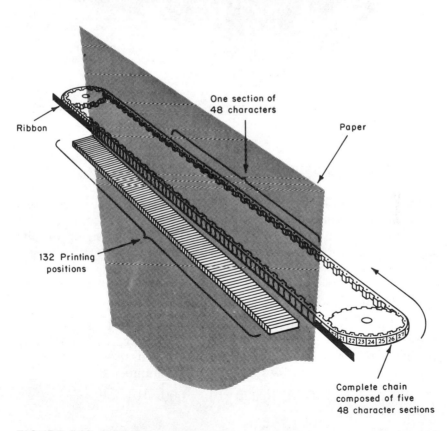

FIGURE 4.13 Chain Printer Mechanism

FIGURE 4.14 IBM 1403 Printer

punches are capable of operating in the range of 100 − 500 cards punched/minute.

INTERNAL NUMBER REPRESENTATION

The digits of an integer that are punched in consecutive columns of a card are read by a card reader and stored in consecutive bytes of memory in their internal coding. The resulting string of bits bears little relationship to the binary representation of the integer discussed in the preceding section.

Decimal Number Representation

If a computer codes characters in the BCD format, then each 6-bit byte represents each digit of a decimal number in binary. For example, if the number 235 is read from a card, the three bytes of memory that are necessary to represent the number are

$$000 \quad 010 \quad 000 \quad 011 \quad 000 \quad 101$$

or, in octal,

$$02 \quad 03 \quad 05$$

Since each decimal digit is coded in binary, the resulting representation is called *binary coded decimal* (BCD). Some computers are designed to perform arithmetic on data in this format. These computers do not have a fixed wordsize; instead they provide an address for each byte of memory. Bytes are grouped together to form *words* (fields) of varying length, and numbers are represented in BCD within these words. Since these numbers vary in length, a method is needed to determine the beginning and end of a number. The address of each word is specified as the address of the least significant digit, and an additional bit is set in the representation of the most significant digit. The sign of a number is represented by the zone bits of the least significant digit. With the exception of the first and last digits in each number, four bits are sufficient to represent each digit. The design of the System/360 series of computers eliminates these wasted bits.

The basic unit of memory in the System/360 is an 8-bit byte, which uses the EBCDIC for character representation. Each byte consists of four zone bits and four numeric bits and can be represented as two hexadecimal digits. For example, if we read the number 235, the three consecutive bytes of storage look like

$$1111 \quad 0010 \quad 1111 \quad 0011 \quad 1111 \quad 0101$$

zone   numeric

This is written in hexadecimal as

$$F2 \quad F3 \quad F5$$

Note that the original digits of the number are identifiable in the internal representation as the numeric part of each byte. This is true for all decimal integers, since the digits 0 through 9 can be represented using four binary digits. The sign of a number is represented by the zone bits associated with the least significant digit of the number. The combinations 1100 and 1111 represent a positive sign (+), and the combination 1101 represents a negative sign (−). If an integer is punched with a 12 punch in the same column containing the least significant digit, the zone bits 1100 are generated for that digit. If an 11 punch occurs in the same column with the least significant digit, the zone bits 1101 are generated. If no other punch occurs with the least significant digit, the zone bits 1111 are generated. The number 235 with a 12 punch in the column with the 5 yields F2 F3 C5 internally, while 235 with an 11 punch in the column with the 5 yields F2 F3 D5 internally. This type of integer representation is called *zoned decimal.*

The System/360, however, does not perform arithmetic on

numbers in the zoned decimal format. Since the zone bits require as many bits as a single decimal digit, the use of this format to represent decimal numbers requires twice as much storage as is necessary. The System/360 provides for conversion from the zoned decimal to a format that packs two digits in a byte. This form of representation is called *packed decimal*. Since the sign of the number is represented by the zone bits of the least signfiicant digit in the zoned format, they are retained in the packed format as the numeric bits of the rightmost byte of the representation. The following example shows two conversions from zoned decimal to packed decimal representation.

Example: 235 in its zoned form
F2   F3   F5

becomes   23 5F   in packed decimal,

and
−235 in its zoned form
F2   F3   D5

becomes   23 5D   in packed decimal.

The System/360 computers are designed to perform arithmetic on packed decimal data. Each packed decimal number is addressed by the address of its leftmost byte, and the length (in bytes) of the number is specified in the packed decimal instructions. The maximum size of numbers in this format is thirty-one digits and one sign digit, requiring sixteen bytes of memory.

Arithmetic performed on representations of decimal digits yields exact results. There is no accuracy lost in conversion from base ten to another base, since conversion is unnecessary. This form of data is used for such applications as payrolls and accounting, where exact results are necessary. Since the arithmetic is performed only on integral amounts, the user must keep track of the placement of the decimal point.

Binary Number Representation

Computers with a fixed wordsize represent integers in binary. If a computer word has N bits, numbered 0 through $N - 1$ from left to right, bit 0 represents the sign, and bits 1 through $N - 1$ represent the integer in binary, as shown in Figure 4.15. A sign bit of 0 is used to represent a positive number, and a sign bit of 1 is used to represent a negative number. Numbers are represented either in *sign/absolute* (S/A) form or in *two's-complement* form. In S/A

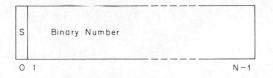

FIGURE 4.15   Binary Integer Representation in an N-bit Word

value representation, bit 0 represents the sign of the number, and bits 1 through $N - 1$ represent the number in pure binary. For example, assuming a 12-bit word, the number ten is represented by 000000001010, and negative ten is represented by 100000001010. These may be represented as 0012 and 4012 in octal or as 00A and 80A in hexadecimal. In two's-complement representation, discussed in the next section, a negative number is represented as its two's-complement with a sign bit of 1. The range of numbers that can be represented in S/A value in an N-bit word is $-2^{N-1} +1$ to $2^{N-1} -1$. In two's-complement representation, the range is -2^{N-1} to $2^{N-1} -1$. For example, if a computer uses a 12-bit word with S/A representation, the range of allowable number is $-2^{11} +1$ to $2^{11} -1$ or $-2{,}047$ to $2{,}047$. This range can also be represented by the octal and hexadecimal equivalents of the largest and smallest numbers, namely, 7777_8 to 3777_8 and FFF_{16} to $7FF_{16}$. The range of allowable numbers in a 16-bit word with two's-complement representation is -2^{15} to $2^{15} -1$, or $-32{,}768$ to $32{,}767$.

Since all integers are represented initially in a binary coded decimal (BCD) form, computers provide instructions for converting them from BCD to binary. Also, since the results of arithmetic operations performed in binary are binary, instructions are provided to convert from binary to BCD so that the results may by printed. The following examples illustrate the steps of conversion from BCD to binary.

Example: Assume the computer uses BCD coding and has a 36-bit word.

Solution.   The number 39 is converted from its BCD form

$$000011001001 \quad \text{or} \quad 0311 \text{ (octal)}$$

to its binary form

$$000000000000000000000000000100111 \quad \text{or}$$
$$000000000047 \text{ (octal)}$$

Example: Assume the computer uses EBCDIC coding and has a 32-bit word (e.g., System/360).

Solution. The number 39 is converted from its zoned-decimal form

    1111001111111001   or   F3F9 (hexadecimal)

to its packed form

    001110011111   or   39F (hexadecimal)

To its binary form

    00000000000000000000000000100111   or
                00000027 (hexadecimal)

Note: Although the System/360 provides an address for each byte of memory, 4 bytes are grouped together to form a fixed-length word for representing binary integers. Each word is addressed by the address of its leftmost byte.

Signed numbers are converted similarly with the conversion instruction(s) designed to test for the sign of the BCD numbers and to provide the proper sign bit in the resultant binary representation.

Two's-Complement Representation and Arithmetic

Before studying the two's-complement representation, we must study the basic rules for the addition and subtaction of binary numbers. The basic rules for addition are

$$0 + 0 = 0, \quad 0 + 1 = 1 + 0 = 1, \quad \text{and} \quad 1 + 1 = 10$$

The basic rules for subtraction are

$$0 - 0 = 0, \quad 1 - 0 = 1, \quad \text{and} \quad 10 - 1 = 1$$

When performing arithmetic on numbers in binary, "carries" and "borrowing" occur as they do in decimal arithmetic.

Example: Perform the addition
        1010
      + 1110
        11000

Discussion. Starting with the least significant bits, we have

        $0 + 0 = 0$;

        $1 + 1 = 0$ with a carry of 1;

        $0 + 1 + 1(\text{carry}) = 0$ with a carry of 1; and

        $1 + 1 + 1(\text{carry}) = 10 + 1(\text{carry}) = 11$.

Example: Perform the subtraction

$$10010$$
$$- 101$$
$$\overline{ 1101}$$

Discussion.   Starting with the least significant bits, we have

$0 - 1$, which requires a borrow giving $10 - 1 = 1$;

as a result of this borrow, we have $0 - 0 = 0$;

$0 - 1$ requires a borrow giving $10 - 1 = 1$; and

this borrow reduces the remaining 10 to 1, giving us $1 - 0 = 1$.

The two's-complement of a binary number is obtained by subtracting it from the next highest power of two greater than the number. The least power of two greater than a given binary number is easily found by placing zeros over each bit of the number and by then placing a one immediately to the left of the leftmost zero.

Example: Form the two's-complement of 1011.

Solution.   The next power of two greater than 1011 is 10000. Then perform the subtraction

$$10000$$
$$- 1011$$
$$\overline{ 0101}$$

0101 is the two's-complement of 1011.

Example: Form the two's-complement of 1101110.

Solution.   The next power of two greater than 1101110 is 10000000. Then perform the subtraction

$$10000000$$
$$- 1101110$$
$$\overline{ 0010010}$$

0010010 is the two's-complement of 1101110.

Note: This procedure can be carried out by writing the binary numbers as their hexadecimal equivalents and by performing the arithmetic in hexadecimal. The hexadecimal result is then called the *sixteen's-complement*.

Example: Form the two's complement of 1101110 using hexa-decimal arithmetic.

$$1101110_2 = 6E_{16} \quad \text{and} \quad 10000000_2 = 80_{16}$$

Solution. Then perform the subtraction

$$
\begin{array}{r}
80 \\
- 6E \\
\hline
12 = 0010010_2
\end{array}
$$

If we declare that all bits in a number are significant (including leading zeros) and set a limit for the number of bits permitted in a number, the two's-complement of a number in the resultant range can be used to represent negative numbers. For example, require that decimal numbers to be represented can have no more than five bits in their binary equivalent.

Example: Add 12 to the two's-complement of 12.

Solution. Form the two's-complement of $12_{10} = 01100$ in our 5-bit system. First perform the subtraction

$$
\begin{array}{r}
100000 \\
- 01100 \\
\hline
10100
\end{array}
$$

Now perform the addition

$$
\begin{array}{r}
01100 \\
+ 10100 \\
\hline
100000
\end{array}
$$

Recall that only five bits can be retained. The sixth bit in the sum is discarded, and the result is zero—just as if the number had been subtracted from itself. Suppose that we want to perform the subtraction $18 - 12$ in our restricted binary system.

Example: $18_{10} = 10010$

$-12_{10} = 10100$

and

$$
\begin{array}{r}
10010 \\
+ 10100 \\
\hline
1 \quad 00110
\end{array}
$$

Solution. The result $00110_2 = 6_{10}$ is the correct answer.

At this point, it seems that a negative number might be represented by the two's-complement of the number and that subtraction can be replaced by complementing and adding. To find the two's-complement of a number, however, we must perform a subtraction from a number that cannot be represented in the system! The two's-complement of a binary number in a fixed-length system is found as follows.

1. Change all 0's to 1's and all 1's to 0's to get the *one's complement*.
2. Add 1 to the result of Step 1.

Example: Find the two's-complement of 01100 in the 5-bit system.

Solution.   Form the one's-complement of 01100   10011
              Add 1   +   1
                                                      ———————
              To get   10100

The result is the same value that was computed by the subtraction in the example that added 18 to the two's-complement of 12.

We now have a means of eliminating subtraction from the system, but we still cannot distinguish between a negative number and a positive number. For example, does 11001 represent 25_{10} or -7_{10} ? To identify whether a number is positive or negative, an additional bit must be added to represent the sign. Each positive number is represented with a sign bit of 0, and negative numbers are represented as the two's-complement of their positive representation (including the sign bit). Negative numbers therefore have a sign bit equal to one, thus allowing us to distinguish between positive and negative numbers. Since computers with a fixed wordsize must necessarily limit the number of bits allowable in a binary representation, they can be designed to represent positive and negative numbers using the method just discussed. The remainder of our discussion of two's-complement representation is exemplified by using a computer with a 12-bit word. The largest positive integer that can be represented in twelve bits is $011111111111_2 = 3777_8 = 2^{11} - 1$, and the smallest negative integer is $100000000000 = 4000_8$. The magnitude of a negative integer is found by recomplementing. The two's complement of 100000000000 is $011111111111 + 1 = 100000000000 = 2^{11}$. Hence the smallest negative 12-bit integer is -2^{11}.

The use of two's-complement representation must also provide the correct sign after addition operations. This requirement is met by performing the arithmetic with all twelve bits of the representation. The following example illustrates that the correct sign results when two's-complement addition is used.

Example: (12-bit words):

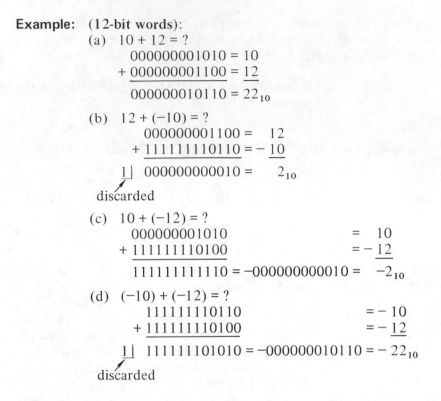

(a) $10 + 12 = ?$

$$000000001010 = 10$$
$$+ \ 000000001100 = \underline{12}$$
$$000000010110 = 22_{10}$$

(b) $12 + (-10) = ?$

$$000000001100 = \quad 12$$
$$+ \ 111111110110 = - \ \underline{10}$$
$$1| \ 000000000010 = \quad \ 2_{10}$$

discarded

(c) $10 + (-12) = ?$

$$000000001010 \qquad\qquad = \quad 10$$
$$+ \ 111111110100 \qquad\qquad = - \ \underline{12}$$
$$111111111110 = -000000000010 = \quad -2_{10}$$

(d) $(-10) + (-12) = ?$

$$111111110110 \qquad\qquad = - \ 10$$
$$+ \ 111111110100 \qquad\qquad = - \ \underline{12}$$
$$1| \ 111111101010 = -000000010110 = - \ 22_{10}$$

discarded

The reader is urged to work out the details of this example. All combinations of a positive integer and a negative integer have been summed, and the resultant sign has been correct in all cases. But the correct result occurs *only* if the final result can be represented in twelve bits, as the next example illustrates.

Example: The sum

$$011110101000$$
$$+ \ \underline{000111101111}$$
$$100110010111$$

cannot be represented in two's-complement form within a 12-bit word. The above addition of two positive numbers results in a carry into the sign-bit position. If the answer were left unde-tected, it would be interpreted as a negative number. This is called *overflow* and is caused by

1. a carry into the sign position and no carry out of the sign position, resulting from the sum of two large positive values, and
2. no carry into the sign position and carry out of the

sign position, resulting from the sum of two small negative numbers.

In general, an overflow occurs if the sum of two N-bit two's-complement numbers falls outside the range -2^{N-1} to $2^{N-1}-1$.

Besides determining the correct sign of results of arithmetic operations, two's-complement arithmetic is used to perform subtractions by complementing and adding. Thus the design of the computer is simplified and made less expensive by the elimination of circuitry that performs binary subtraction. Typically, computers can perform arithmetic on fixed-length binary integers faster than on BCD integers. It is therefore preferable to use the fixed-length data in applications that perform much integer arithmetic.

Although integers are used in scientific applications of computers, fractions must also be represented. Integer representations can be used, provided the user keeps track of the position of the radix point. Since only a limited number of values can be represented with this method, a number system representing a large range of values is needed.

Floating-Point Representation

Decimal numbers with fractional parts are often represented in *scientific notation*. For example, $-27.67 = -.2767 \cdot 10^2$ and $.00058 = .58 \cdot 10^{-3}$. The result in each case is a decimal fraction multiplied by a power of ten. This notation can be simplified by writing the exponent of the power of ten enclosed in parentheses immediately preceding the decimal point. Using this system, $-.2767 \cdot 10^2$ becomes $-(2).2767$ and $.58 \cdot 10^{-3}$ becomes $(-3).58$. As long as the base of the number system used to represent the fraction is known, the meaning of these representations is clear. Computers with a fixed wordsize represent fractions using floating-point notation that is similar to the coding just discussed.

Computers with a 36-bit word usually represent fractions using a 27-bit fraction, an 8-bit exponent field, and a 1-bit sign field, as shown in Figure 4.16. The fractions are *normalized*, meaning that the first digit to the right of the binary point is 1. The eight bits

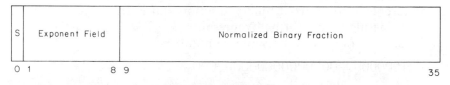

FIGURE 4.16   36-bit Floating Point Format

used to represent the exponent provide values in the range from 00000000_2 to $11111111_2 = 255_{10} = 377_8$. Since both negative and positive exponents are needed, the value $128_{10} = 10000000_2 = 200_8$ is used to represent an exponent of zero. The range of exponent values thus provided is -128 to $+127$. The following table shows the correspondence between the value of the exponent field and the exponent being represented.

Exponent	Exponent Field
−128	$00000000_2 = 0_{10} = -128 + 128$
−127	$00000001_2 = 1_{10} = -127 + 128$
.	.
.	.
.	∘
−1	$01111111_2 = 127_{10} = -1 + 128$
0	$10000000_2 = 128_{10} = 0 + 128$
1	$10000001_2 = 129_{10} = 1 + 128$
.	.
.	.
.	.
+126	$11111110_2 = 254_{10} = 126 + 128$
+127	$11111111_2 = 255_{10} = 127 + 128$

This exponent notation is called *excess−128* notation. Bit 0 is used as a sign bit with a zero representing a positive sign and a one a negative sign. The sign is interpreted as in the S/A representation for integers. Two's-complement arithmetic is not used. Thus, if F represents a normalized binary fraction and E the exponent field, this floating-point format represents $F \cdot 2^{(E\,-\,128)}{}_{10}$. In this format, the range of representable numbers is

$$.10000000000000000000000000000_2 \cdot 2^{0\,-\,128} = 2^{-1} \cdot 2^{-128}$$
$$= 2^{-129}$$
$$\approx 1.5 \cdot 10^{-39}$$

to

$$.11111111111111111111111111_2 \cdot 2^{255 \, - \, 128}$$
$$= (1 - 2^{-27}) \cdot 2^{127} \approx 1.7 \cdot 10^{38}$$

System/360 computers represent floating-point numbers as a normalized hexadecimal fraction multiplied by a power of sixteen. They are represented in either a 32-bit word (short form) or in a 64-bit double word (long form), as shown in Figure 4.17. In each form, bit 0 is the sign bit ($0 = +$, $1 = -$), and bits 1 through 7 represent an exponent. In the short form, the next twenty-four bits represent the fraction, and in the long form, the next fifty-six bits represent the fraction. The exponent represents the power of sixteen the fraction must be multiplied by to get the true value of the number. The value $1000000_2 = 40_{16}$ is used to represent an exponent of zero. Numbers greater than 40_{16} and less than or equal to $1111111_2 = 7F_{16}$ are used to represent positive exponents, and numbers less than 40_{16} and greater than or equal to zero are used to represent negative exponents. The true value of the exponent is found by subtracting $40_{16} = 64_{10}$. The method of exponent coding is called *excess-64* notation and allows for an exponent in the range -64_{10} to $+63_{10}$. In the short form, six hexadecimal digits are used to represent the fraction, and in the long form, fourteen hexadecimal digits are used to represent the fraction. The allowable range of values in the short form is $.1 \cdot 16^{-64} = 16^{-65}$ to $(1 - 16^{-6}) \cdot 16^{63}$. The allowable range of values in the long form is 16^{-65} to $(1 - 16^{-14}) \cdot 16^{63}$. In decimal, this range is approximately 10^{-78} to 10^{75} with seven digits of precision in the short form and sixteen digits of precision in the long form.

We shall conclude this section with two examples that illustrate conversion of fractions to and from System/360 floating-

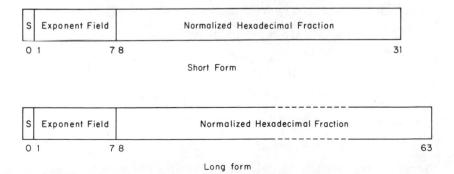

FIGURE 4.17 System/360 Floating Point Number Formats

point short form. Although floating-point numbers are stored initially in zoned-decimal format, the conversion to internal floating-point format from zoned-decimal format is too complicated to be discussed in this text.

Example: Code -29.36_{10} in floating-point short form.

Step 1.   Convert the whole number part to hexadecimal.

```
16  |29
16  |1   13
     0    1
```

The whole number part is $1D_{16}$.

Step 2.   Convert the fractional part to hexadecimal.

```
    .36
    16
  5|.76
    16
 12|.16
    16
  2|.56
    16
  8|.96
    16
 15|.36
```

The fractional part is $.5C29_{16}$. The conversion is terminated after five digits, and the result is rounded to four digits, since bits 8 through 31 can hold only six hexadecimal digits.

Step 3.   Normalize the hexadecimal number.

$$1D.5C29 = .1D5C29 \cdot 10_{16}^2$$

Step 4.   Determine the exponent.
An exponent of zero is

$$1000000_2 = 40_{16}$$

Our exponent is

$$40_{16} + 2 = 42_{16} = 1000010_2$$

Step 5.   Combine the sign bit with the exponent bits.

$$1\ 1\ 0\ 0\ 0\ 0\ 1\ 0 = C2_{16}$$
$$\text{sign}\quad\text{exponent}$$

Step 6. Combine the result of Step 5 with the hexadecimal fraction.

C21D5C29   is the internal floating-point
representation of -29.36_{10}

Example: Determine the decimal value of the internal floating-point number 3EC9D6FF.

Step 1. Express the first two hexadecimal digits in binary to get sign and exponent.

$$3E_{16} = 0\ 0\ 1\ 1\ 1\ 1\ 1\ 0$$
sign   exponent

Since bit 0 is zero, the number is positive, and the exponent is $3E_{16} - 40_{16} = -2$.

Step 2. Unnormalize the hexadecimal number.

$$.C9D6FF \cdot 10_{16}^{-2} = .00C9D6FF_{16}$$

Step 3. Convert the result of Step 2 to decimal.

$$\begin{aligned}
.00C9D6FF_{16} &= 0 \cdot (1/16) + 0 \cdot (1/16^2) + 12 \cdot (1/16^3) \\
&\quad + 9 \cdot (1/16^4) + 13 \cdot (1/16^5) + 6 \cdot (1/16^6) \\
&\quad + 15 \cdot (1/16^7) + 15 \cdot (1/16^8) \\
&= .0030914_{10} \text{ (approximate)}
\end{aligned}$$

Floating-Point Arithmetic and Roundoff Errors

System/360 short-form, floating-point numbers are used in this section to illustrate floating-point addition and subtraction and the errors that may result from these operations.

Example: Floating-point addition.
Perform the addition

425F6238
+ 40765294

Step 1. Align the fractional parts by shifting the fraction with the smaller exponent N hexadecimal digits to the right, where N is equal to the difference between the two exponents. In this case, $42 - 40 = 2$ and 765294 becomes 007652[9], where [9] is retained as a guard digit that participates in the addition. The guard digit of each number is initialized at zero.

Step 2. Add the fractions

5F6238 [0]
+ 007652 [9]

5FD88A[9]

Step 3. Attach the larger exponent field to the fraction to get 425FD88A and attach the correct sign.

Step 4. Normalize the fraction if necessary. [Not necessary in this example.]

Example: Floating-point subtraction.
Perform the subtraction

$$41AC5612$$
$$-41AB4837$$

Step 1. Align the fractions if necessary. [Not necessary in this example.]

Step 2. Subtract the fractions.

$$AC5612[0]$$
$$-AB4837[0]$$
$$010DDB[0]$$

Step 3. Attach the larger exponent and attach the correct sign.

$$41010DDB[0]$$

Step 4. Normalize the fraction and adjust the exponent to get

$$4010DDB0$$

Note that the guard digit has been shifted into the fraction.

Example. Floating-point addition with a carry out of the high order digit position.
Perform the addition

$$42A65F69$$
$$+42CA3811$$

Step 1. Align the fractions, if necessary.

Step 2. Add the fractions.

$$A65F69[0]$$
$$+CA3811[0]$$
$$\overset{\displaystyle 1}{} 70977A[0]$$

carry

Step 3. Attach the larger exponent and the correct sign to get

$$4270977A[0]$$

Since a carry occurred out of the high order digit position, shift the fraction one digit to the right, increase the exponent by one, and insert a one in the high-order digit position. The result is

$$43170977[A]$$

and the digit in the guard position is dropped.

Two exceptional conditions may occur during floating-point addition and subtraction operations. If the number generated is too large to be represented, it means that the exponent generated cannot be represented in the exponent bits. This is called *exponent overflow*. Similarly, *exponent underflow* occurs when an exponent results that is smaller than the smallest representable exponent.

The normalization step after each addition or subtraction often forces the guard digit back into the fraction, thus improving the accuracy of the result. Normalization, however, is not sufficient to guarantee completely accurate results. Most decimal fractions cannot be represented exactly by a finite hexadecimal fraction. Also, as was stated earlier, there is error in many decimal fractions and conversion to hexadecimal compounds the problem. Referring back to the first example in the preceding section, the conversion of the decimal number -29.36 was terminated when seven hexadecimal digits had been determined. Since only six hexadecimal digits can be retained, the sixth digit is rounded, depending on the value of the seventh digit. Restricting the fraction to six hexadecimal digits means that the distance between successive possible fractions is $.000001_{16}$ or 16^{-6}. Thus numbers whose true value lies between two possible representations must be approximated using one of these values. Rounding assures that the error in the representation will be no greater than one-half the distance between two successive representations. (i.e., $.00000075_{16} = .75 \cdot 10_{16}^{-6}$). Hence the sixth digit is increased by one if the seventh digit is 8 or more but is left the same if the seventh digit is 7 or less. The error in representation due to rounding is called *roundoff error*.

When arithmetic is performed with numbers having roundoff errors, the error is propagated in the result and sometimes multiplied, as shown in the following example.

Example: Perform the addition

$$\begin{array}{r} 18.6 \\ + 19.8 \\ \hline 38.4 \end{array}$$

using System/360 floating-point representations for each of the numbers.

Solution. The floating-point representation of 18.6 is 4212999A, and the floating-point representation of 19.8 is 4213CCCD. In each case, the least significant digit has been rounded to the next highest digit. Perform the floating-point addition

$$42\ 13CCCD[0]$$
$$+\ \underline{42\ 12999A\ [0]}$$
$$42\ 266667\ [0]$$

Reversing the conversion process the decimal value of 4213CCCD is 19.800003, and the decimal value of 4212999A is 18.600006. In each case, the numbers have been represented by floating-point numbers that are larger than the original numbers. The error in the normalized fractions is less than $.75 \cdot 10_{16}^{-6}$ in each case. Verify that the errors are $.3 \cdot 10_{16}^{-6}$ and $.6 \cdot 10_{16}^{-6}$, respectively. Converting the floating-point result to decimal, we have 38.400009. Thus there is also an error in this representation. The floating-point representation of the true result (38.4) is 42266666. Note that this representation differs in the last digit from the sum above. Hence the sum differs from 38.4 by more than the normal roundoff error, and the error in the two original numbers has multiplied in their sum. If several numbers that have been rounded up in the last digit are added together, the error will mulitply, resulting in a loss of significant digits. But not all representations are rounded up to the next digit. If two floating-point numbers are added—where one fraction has been rounded up and the other has not—errors tend to cancel each other.

Example: Perform the addition

$$19.8$$
$$+\ \underline{\ \ 2.7}$$
$$22.5$$

using floating-point representations for each number.

Solution.   The floating-point representation of 19.8 is 4213CCCD (rounded up), and the floating-point representation of 2.7 is 412B3333 (no rounding). The floating-point sum is formed as follows:

$$42\ 13CCCD[0]$$
$$+\ \underline{42\ 01B333\ [3]}$$
$$42\ 1588000[3]$$

The result (42158000) in decimal is exactly 22.5. The errors in the floating-point numbers cancelled each other.

Thus roundoff errors may be propagated when operations are performed between numbers that are in error. When adding two floating-point numbers, the error in the sum is approximately equal to the sum of the errors in each number; when subtracting two floating-point numbers, the error in the result is approximately equal to the difference between the errors in each number; when multiplying two floating-point numbers, the error in the product is a sum of two errors with each error being a fraction of the errors in the original numbers; and when dividing two floating-point numbers, the error in the quotient is a difference of two errors with each error being a fraction of the errors in the original numbers. These errors are called *propagation errors.* Roundoff errors and thus propagation errors can be reduced by using the long form representation, where the difference between successive fractions is $.1 \cdot 16^{-14}$. Roundoff errors due to approximate representations are not the only errors that occur with floating-point numbers. For example, roundoff errors due to unnormalization before addition and subtraction occur when two numbers are added or subtracted whose exponents differ by more than the number of hexadecimal digits in the fraction. Errors also occur because large numbers and very small numbers with more significant digits (in decimal) than the number of digits in the fraction may be represented by the same floating-point number. Roundoff errors and their effects on mathematical calculations are studied in the branch of mathematics called *numerical analysis.*

We shall now turn our attention to how the basic forms of data representation can be used to form the more complex representations called data structures.

EXERCISES

1. Convert the following binary numbers to decimal.
   - (a) −10111
   - (b) 1010101
   - (c) 11001100
   - (d) 111.10101
   - (e) 1111000.1001
   - (f) .111

2. Convert the following octal numbers to decimal.
   - (a) 37
   - (b) 446
   - (c) −1172
   - (d) −24.247
   - (e) 31.4
   - (f) .762

3. Convert the following hexadecimal numbers to decimal.
   (a) ABC   (d) A.8
   (b) 1F73   (e) −2AF.333
   (c) −E1627   (f) .03F

4. Convert the following decimal numbers to binary.
   (a) 37   (d) 210.5
   (b) 172   (e) −75.75
   (c) −2741   (f) .3333

5. Convert the following decimal numbers to octal.
   (a) 206   (d) −.675
   (b) −75   (e) 29.75
   (c) 1024   (f) 210.88

6. Convert the following decimal numbers to hexadecimal.
   (a) 157   (d) 39.5
   (b) 2048   (e) −.875
   (c) −64   (f) 124.04

7. Convert the following octal and hexadecimal numbers directly to binary.
   (a) 214_8 (d) 202_{16}
   (b) ABC_{16} (e) -261_8
   (c) 22_8 (f) -261_{16}

8. Convert the following binary numbers directly to octal.
   (a) 1110110010   (d) 101011101
   (b) 1101   (e) 11101110011
   (c) 1111111   (f) 1101110111101

9. Convert the binary numbers in Exercise 8 directly to hexadecimal.

10. Convert each of the following decimal numbers to their 12-bit S/A binary representations.
    (a) 1234   (d) 562
    (b) −565   (e) −89
    (c) −2048   (f) 406

11. Form the 16-bit, two's-complement representation of each of your answers to Exercise 10.

12. Perform the following using two's-complement arithmetic (8-bit words).
    (a) 11001101 + 01101110
    (b) 01110000 + 00010001
    (c) 01011011 − 01110001
    (d) 11101111 + 11111111
    (e) 00010000 − 11101111
    (f) 10110111 − 00010111

13. Form the 36-bit, floating-point representations of the following decimal numbers.
    (a) 22.9   (b) −66.23

14. Form the short-form, System/360, floating-point representations of the following decimal numbers.
    (a) 22.9   (b) −.756

15. Determine the decimal values of the following System/360, short-form, floating-point numbers.
    (a) 43AAA550   (b) BFFA0000

16. Perform the subtraction

    19.7
    − 8.4

    using System/360 short form floating-point representation. Determine the roundoff error in the representation of each number and the propagation error in the result.

SELECTED REFERENCES

Cashman, Thomas J., and William J. Keys, *Data Processing and Computer Programming,* San Francisco: Canfield Press, 1971.

Gear, C. William, *Computer Organization and Programming,* New York; McGraw-Hill, 1969.

Hamming, Richard W., *Calculus and the Computer Revolution,* Boston: Houghton Mifflin, 1968.

Hassitt, Anthony, *Computer Programming and Computer Systems,* New York: Academic Press, 1967.

Hellerman, Herbert, *Digital Computer Systems Principles,* New York: McGraw-Hill, 1967.

IBM 1403 Printer Component Description, Form GA24-3073, IBM Corporation.

IBM 2501 Models B1 and B2 Component Description and Operating Procedures, Form A21-9026, IBM Corporation.

Maley, Gerald A., and Edward J. Skiker, *Modern Digital Computers,* Englewood Cliffs, N. J.: Prentice-Hall, 1964.

Ralston, Anthony, *Introduction to Programming and Computer Science,* New York: McGraw-Hill, 1971.

Schmidt, Richard N., and William E. Meyers, *Introduction to Computer Science and Data Processing,* (2nd ed.), New York: Holt, Rinehart and Winston, 1970.

Stark, Peter A., *Introduction to Numerical Methods,* New York: Macmillan, 1970.

Struble, George, *Assembler Language Programming the IBM System/360,* Reading, Mass.: Addison-Wesley, 1971.

Data Structures

The algorithms discussed in Chapters 2 and 3 used variable names to represent numerical information. These variables were assigned values either through calculation or through input, and the values remained constant until another input or calculation redefined the variables. Many problems require that all the values assigned to a variable be retained for use later in the algorithm, but the methods discussed previously retain only the last value assigned to a variable. We can overcome this limitation by defining a linear list to represent the data. From this point on, we shall assume that, unless otherwise stated, a *variable* in an algorithm is a *name for a word of computer storage.*

LINEAR LISTS

Structure and Basic Usage

A *linear list (vector array* or *singly-dimensioned array)* is a sequence of N (N > 0) contiguous words of storage that have been given a collective name. Individual words in the sequence are accessed by attaching a subscript to that name. For example, NAME(1)—pronounced "name sub one"—refers to the first word in the list; NAME(2), the second word in the list; and NAME(N), the Nth word in the list, where N has been previously defined. This subscript notation has the same meaning as the standard mathematical subscript notation (e.g., $NAME_1$, $NAME_2$, ..., $NAME_N$). The parenthetical notation has been chosen because of

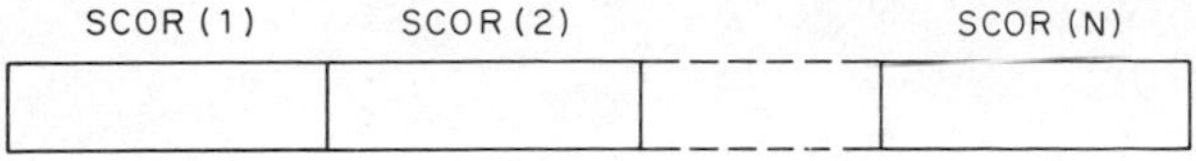

SCOR (1)   SCOR (2)   SCOR (N)

FIGURE 5.1   Linear List Representation

its relationship to the subscript forms found in programming languages. Figure 5.1 gives a pictorial representation of a linear list.

The basic rules of usage for a linear list are best understood through an example.

Example: Suppose we are requested to find the average of a list of N scores and then scale the scores to a standard average of 75. This problem requires that all the scores be retained, since each score must be modified after the average is computed.

Solution.   The algorithm in Figure 5.2 solves the problem by representing the scores as a linear list. The loop counter K serves two purposes in the algorithm: it counts the number of scores, and it simultaneously defines a subscript for the linear list SCOR. Since the value of K proceeds sequentially $(1, 2, 3, \ldots, N)$, the scores are stored sequentially at locations SCOR(1), SCOR(2), ..., SCOR(N). For exemplary purposes, assume we have the five scores 95, 87, 96, 68, and 77 to be used as input for this algorithm. The scores are stored in contiguous locations, as shown in Figure 5.3. Each score is placed in a unique storage location and can be used later in the algorithm simply by using the list name, SCOR, with a subscript attached. In the loop that computes the scaled scores, J is used as a loop counter and as a subscript for SCOR. Since J attains the values 1 through N, the same words of SCOR are accessed within this loop as in the initial loop.

It is unnecessary to define SSCOR as a linear list, since the value of a scaled score is no longer needed after it is printed. If the scaled scores are needed later in the algorithm, however, they can be stored in a linear list when they are defined. The scaling loop of the algorithm would then be written as shown in Figure 5.4. The loop index J defines a subscript value for each linear list, and the scaled scores are stored in SSCOR in corresponding positions to the original scores in SCOR. Now each of the scaled scores can be referred to later within the algorithm simply by using the name of the linear list, SSCOR, with a valid subscript attached.

Since we have all the scores available, we can define another section within the algorithm that will find the largest score in the

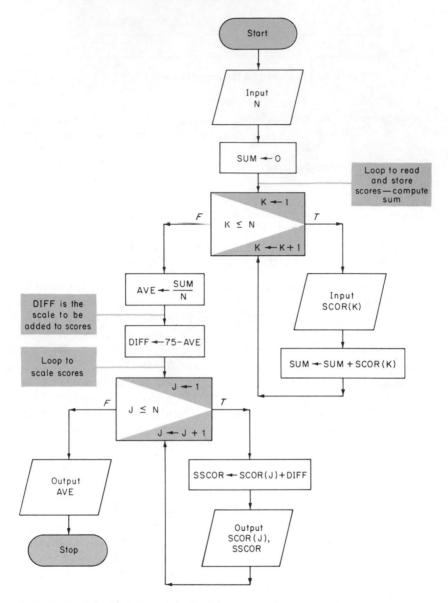

FIGURE 5.2   Algorithm to Scale Scores to an Average of 75

SCOR(1)	SCOR(2)	SCOR(3)	SCOR(4)	SCOR(5)
95	87	96	68	77

FIGURE 5.3   Sample Linear List

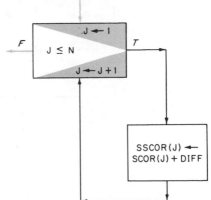

FIGURE 5.4
Scaling Loop that Stores Scaled Scores
in a Linear List

list. The technique for finding the largest entry in a linear list is described in flowchart form in Figure 5.5. Each score must be compared to the location BIG. An initial value is therefore assigned to BIG that forces the true branch to be followed after the first comparison is made. BIG is initialized at zero—an unlikely value for a maximum score! Using the same scores as in Figure 5.3, Figure 5.6 shows the different values assigned to BIG when the algorithm is executed. Note that the value of BIG changes only when a score is larger than the current value of BIG. Another

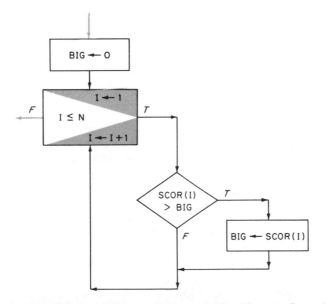

FIGURE 5.5   Algorithm Segment to Find Largest Score in the List

Old Value of BIG	Score to Be Tested	New Value of BIG
0	95	95
95	87	95
95	96	96
96	68	96
96	77	96

FIGURE 5.6

possibilty is to assign the value of SCOR(1) to BIG initially and then execute the comparison loop from 2 to N. This method allows the procedure to be used for a range of scores that includes zero as a valid entry. Figure 5.7 gives the flowchart for this alternate technique. In either case, the important point is that the variable that will eventually hold the largest value must be initialized prior to the testing loop. We shall now study some operations that can be performed on linear lists.

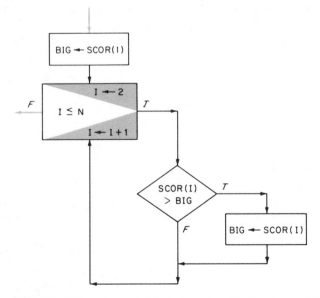

FIGURE 5.7   Alternate Technique for Finding Largest Score

Searching and Sorting

One of the most common operations performed on a list of information is a search for a particular item in the list. The

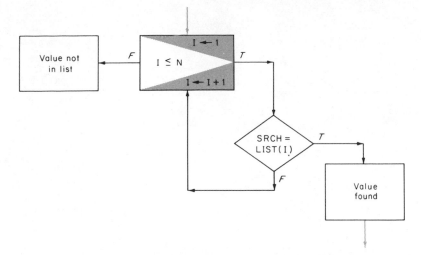

FIGURE 5.8 **Sequential Search for a Value in a Linear List**

algorithm for this operation will search a linear list, comparing the entries with a desired value until it is found or until the entries in the list are exhausted. The simplest method of searching a list is to start at the first element in the list and proceed sequentially, testing each entry in turn. The algorithm in Figure 5.8 illustrates this technique, where LIST is the linear list of N elements and SRCH is the value sought. This method is very efficient if the item sought is near the beginning of the list, but it becomes less efficient if the value is near the end of the list. For a list of N elements, an average of approximately N/2 comparisons will be required to find an element. As the value of N increases, the number of required comparisons increases proportionately. A more efficient method of searching, called the *binary search,* can be used, provided the list is *sorted* into ascending order. Hence we shall now turn to the study of algorithms for sorting lists.

One method of sorting uses the algorithm for finding the largest entry in a list as a base. The algorithm for this sorting technique appears in Figure 5.9, but a specific example will best illustrate the steps in the algorithm.

Example: Consider the list of five elements in Figure 5.10(a). The initial values of JBIG, BIG, and NTOP are shown in Figure 5.10(b). After the largest element is found, BIG and JBIG have the values shown in Figure 5.10(c). The value of JBIG indicates the position in the list where the largest element was found, and NTOP is the subscript associated with the last element in the list. In this case, NTOP equals five. The largest element and the element at the end of the list are interchanged, resulting in the

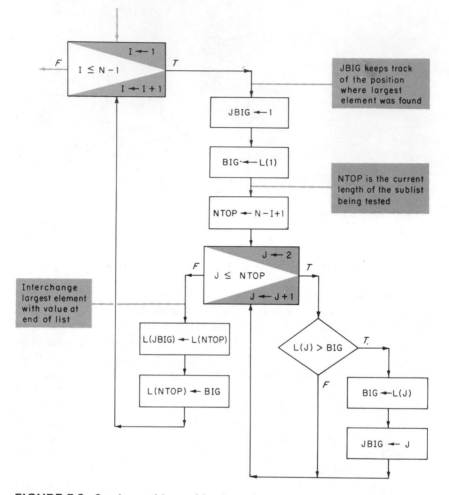

FIGURE 5.9 Sorting a Linear List into Ascending Order with Technique Based on Finding Largest Element

largest element in the fifth and last position. Next, the process of finding the largest element is repeated, but only the first four elements are tested. This second largest element found is placed in the fourth position in the list. The same procedure is repeated for the first three elements and then for the first two elements. Figure 5.10(d) shows the resultant lists after each pass through the loop controlled by the variable I.

In general, as the value of the loop counter I increases from 1 to N − 1, the value of NTOP decreases from N to 2. Each largest entry is placed at the current end of the list, as determined by the value of NTOP, and is eliminated from further processing by the

L(1)	L(2)	L(3)	L(4)	L(5)
87	72	67	94	86

(a) *Original linear list L*

JBIG	BIG	NTOP
1	87	5

(b) *Original values of JBIG, BIG, and NTOP*

JBIG	BIG
4	94

(c) *Values of JBIG and BIG after first largest element is found*

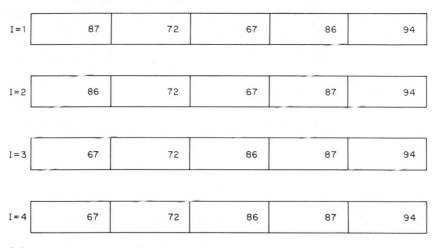

I = 1	87	72	67	86	94

I = 2	86	72	67	87	94

I = 3	67	72	86	87	94

I = 4	67	72	86	87	94

(d) *Transformations of list for each pass over the list*

FIGURE 5.10

fact that NTOP assumes a smaller value. The effective result is that the list is shortened by one element each time a largest entry is found. When the list is shortened to the first two elements and they are rearranged into the proper order, the algorithm terminates. To sort a list into descending (instead of ascending) order using this technique, the section of the algorithm that finds the largest entry in the list is replaced by steps that find the smallest entry.

Another method of sorting, called the *shuttle-interchange sort*, starts at the beginning of a list and checks the pairs: L(1) and L(2), L(2) and L(3), L(3) and L(4), etc. When the members of a pair are out of order, they are interchanged, and the preceding pairs are rechecked. The algorithm proceeds back from the point of interchange, comparing consecutive pairs and interchanging whenever necessary. The backward checking is halted when a properly ordered pair is found. At this time, all entries up through the first pair interchanged are in order. The algorithm then proceeds from the point of the first interchange, repeating the process just discussed until the entire list is in order. The algorithm for the shuttle-interchange sorting of a list, L, into ascending order appears in flowchart form in Figure 5.11. The index variable I controls the forward motion through the list, whereas J is used to control the backward motion through the list. Whenever the false branch is followed from the first decision diamond, the elements of a pair are interchanged. The variable T is necessary to preserve the values of the two entries of the pair. It is not possible to interchange the two entries with the single statement $L(J) \leftarrow L(J + 1)$, since the original value of L(J) is destroyed. The value of L(J) is therefore assigned to T, allowing L(J) to be redefined with the value of $L(J + 1)$. $L(J + 1)$ is then assigned the value of T, which is the old value of L(J). The two values have now been interchanged. The inner loop is then used to test the pairs preceding the pair just interchanged. The value of J is reduced by 1 and tested at the end of each execution of the loop to eliminate erroneous processing when J is less than one. In other words, there is no reason to process previous pairs after the first two entries of the list have been interchanged. The loop continues either until a pair is found in the proper order or until J becomes less than one. Figure 5.12 illustrates the shuttle-interchange sorting of a list into ascending order, using the first five elements of the list.

A popular method of ordering a list with N entries is called the *bubble sort*. Each entry is compared with its neighbor and then interchanged if they are in the wrong order. After $N - 1$ comparisons, the largest (or smallest) value will have "floated" to the Nth position in the list. The process is then repeated for the first $N - 1, N - 2, \ldots, 3, 2$ elements, thus resulting in an ordered list after $N - 1$ passes over the list. The bubble sort algorithm for sorting a list into ascending order appears in Figure 5.13. The

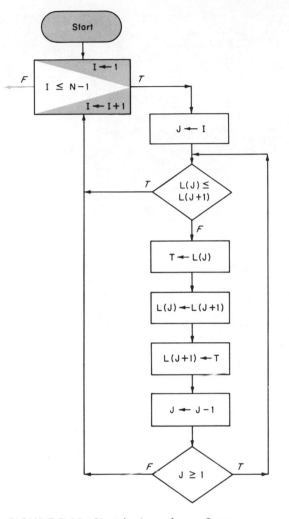

FIGURE 5.11   Shuttle–Interchange Sort

inner loop, indexed by J, compares consecutive pairs and interchanges them if necessary. Prior to executing this loop, a counter variable M is assigned the value zero. The variable T is a temporary location used when the elements of a pair are interchanged. Each interchange of consecutive pairs is accompanied by an increment of M. Upon completion of the inner loop, M is tested. A value of zero indicates no interchanges were made; consequently no further passes over the list are necessary. The index of the outer loop determines the number of comparisons to

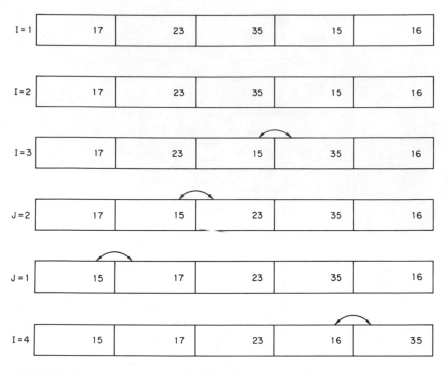

FIGURE 5.12   An Example of the First Few Steps of Shuttle—Interchange Sort

be made within the inner loop. As I increases from 1 to N − 1, N − I decreases from N − 1 to 1. As in the largest element method discussed previously, once a largest value is at the end of the list, the loop structure eliminates it from further processing. The outer loop also controls the necessary N − 1 passes over the list. Figure 5.14 shows the modifications of a linear list at each step of the bubble sort.

There are many other methods available for sorting lists of information, but these three methods are a sufficient introduction to sorting techniques. Since these three algorithms require essentially the same number of steps, there is no significant advantage in using one instead of another. We shall now return our attention to searching methods.

Each test for a particular value in a list with the *binary search technique* either finds the value or eliminates one-half of the remaining list from further testing. This technique requires that the list be stored in order. [The following discussion assumes ascending order.] The first test (probe) is made at the middle

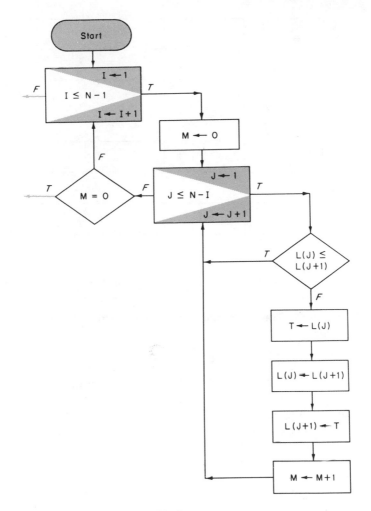

FIGURE 5.13   The Bubble Sort

entry in the list. If the entry is the value sought, we are finished. If the search value is less than the middle entry, we can confine our search to the partial list (sublist) consisting of the elements in the first half of the original list. If the search value is greater than the middle entry, we can confine our search to the sublist consisting of the entries in the second half of the list. In either case, we have shortened the list by a factor of two, thus eliminating one-half of the data. We now apply this technique to the sublist that *possibly* contains the value we are seeking. The process continues, testing the middle entry of each new sublist and forming still shorter sublists, until either the value is found or there is only one entry in

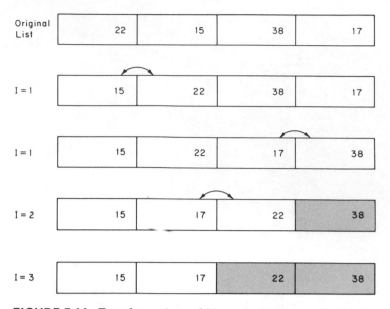

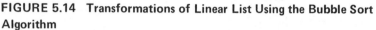

FIGURE 5.14   Transformations of Linear List Using the Bubble Sort Algorithm

a sublist and that entry is not equal to the search value. An algorithm for the binary search for the value X in the list L with N elements appears in Figure 5.15. In this algorithm, the variable J represents the average value of the first and last subscripts of the list. After each unsuccessful probe, the variable I or K is modified, defining either a new top or new bottom of a sublist. If I and K are equal after the modification, there is only one element left to test. If I is greater than K after the modification, all entries in the list have been tested.

Example: Now consider the list of ten elements shown in Figure 5.16(a). A search is to be made for the value eighteen using the algorithm of Figure 5.15. In this algorithm, the principles of integer division are assumed for the calculation of J; that is, the integral part of the quotient $(I + K)/2$ is assigned to J. This means that if the quotient is not a whole number, the remainder is dropped, and no rounding occurs. Using this principle, the first value of J is $(1 + 10)/2$ or 5. Thus the first probe is at L(5). Since the search value eighteen is larger than twelve, the search is confined to L(6) through L(10), as shown in Figure 5.16(b). The next probe is at L(8), which has the value nineteen. Since eighteen is less than nineteen, the search is confined to L(6) and L(7), as shown in Figure 5.16(c). The algorithm causes the next probe to occur at L(6), which has the value fifteen. Since the value sought

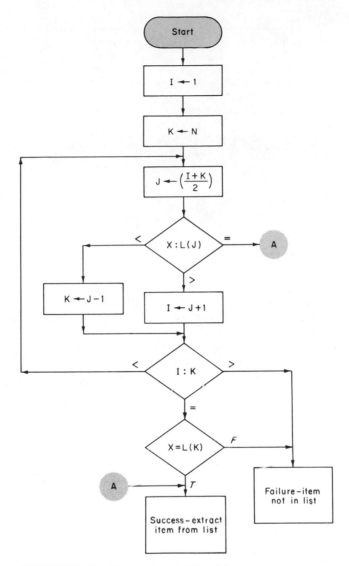

FIGURE 5.15   Binary Search Algorithm

is greater than fifteen, the value of I is increased by one, making it equal to K and leaving only one entry to test [see Fig. 5.16(d)]. The fourth and final test is made, and the search value has been located.

Since the effect of the binary search is to halve the remaining list after each probe, the total number of probes necessary can be related mathematically to a power of two. The maximum number of probes necessary—whether or not the value being sought is in

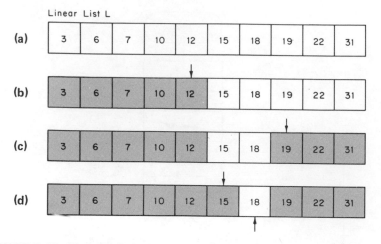

FIGURE 5.16   Pictorial Representation of Binary Search for the Value 18 in a Linear List

the list—is the smallest integer P such that $2^P \geq N + 1$, where N is the number of entries in the list. This can also be stated as the smallest integer P such that $P \geq \log_2 (N + 1)$. It is necessary to add one to N to assure that all positions are tested. For example, in a list with three entries, the first probe is at the middle entry. Assuming that the middle entry is not the value sought, one more test is required. The total number of comparisons necessary was two, and $2^2 = 4$ satisfies the relationship $2^2 \geq 4$. Note that the value N = 5 gives a value of P = 3, but if N is a power of two, it must be increased by one. If, in a list with four entries $[4 = 2^2]$, one is not added to N, the value of P is two. But a list with four entries could require three comparisons to find a value. To determine the number of comparisons needed, therefore, the relationship $P \geq \log_2 (N + 1)$ is used in all cases.

The following discussion presents another method of performing the binary search.

Example (optional): The number of probes that may be necessary is determined by finding the first power of two greater than or equal to N + 1. The exponent of the power of two is the maximum number of probes needed, and the power of two itself is used to modify the values of the subscripts used during the probes. The algorithm for this technique appears in Figure 5.17. The variable N1 represents the power of two, and the variable LIM represents the associated exponent. NP is the number of elements plus one. The initial loop in the flowchart generates the first power of two greater than or equal to NP. At the conclusion of this loop, N1 is divided by four; LIM is reduced by one; and the

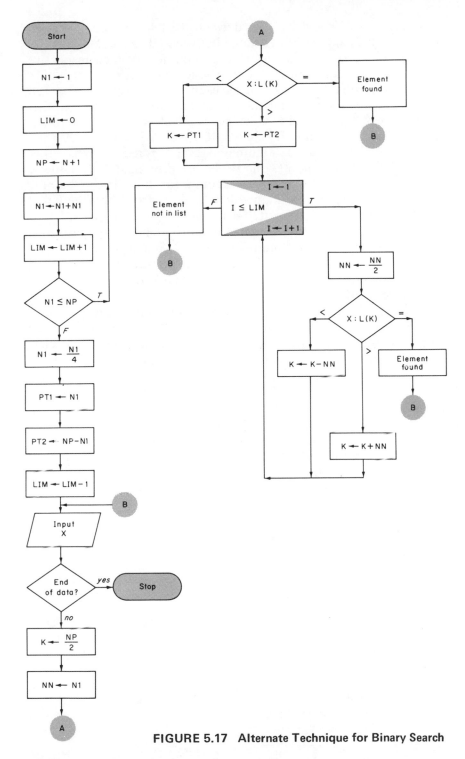

FIGURE 5.17 Alternate Technique for Binary Search

two variables PT1 and PT2 are defined. PT1 has a value between one and NP/2, and PT2 has a value between NP/2 and NP. If NP is a power of two, these values are the midpoints of their respective ranges. The steps just discussed are basic to the search procedure and their results are used during each search. Next, the search value X is determined, and the initial value of the subscript K is calculated. NN serves as a working value of N1. The first test is with the subscript value K = NP/2. If a match is not found, then one-half of the list can be eliminated, and K is redefined as either PT1 or PT2. At this point, one probe has been made; the value of LIM was reduced previously to account for this. The remaining steps of the search are contained in a loop controlled by the index variable I. The loop is executed a maximum of LIM times. NN is divided by two in the first step of the loop; then the comparison is made between the search and list values. NN is a power of two and represents the amount to be added to or subtracted from the value of the subscript K. NN assumes the value one for the final comparison within the loop.

We can illustrate the algorithm by again considering the list in Figure 5.16(a). There are ten entries in the list, meaning that NP equals eleven, N1 equals sixteen, and LIM equals four. Next N1 is reduced to four; PT1 is assigned the value four; PT2 is assigned the value seven $(11 - 4)$; and LIM is reduced to three. Assume that nineteen is input for X. The initial value of K is five, and NN assumes the value four. A comparsion is made between X and L(5). Since L(5) equals twelve and is smaller than X, K is assigned the value of PT2, which equals seven. The search loop is executed three times with the variables assuming the values shown in Figure 5.18. As the table indicates, the maximum number of searches is required to locate the value nineteen.

	I	NN	K	L(K)
Values for Probe at Middle Entry Prior to Loop		4	5	12
Values within Search Loop	1	2	7	18
	2	1	9	22
	3	0	8	19

FIGURE 5.18   Values of Variables in Search Loop of Algorithm in Figure 5.17

The basic differences between these two binary search techniques: the value of the subscript K is calculated differently in each case, and the maximum number of searches is predetermined in the second method but not in the first. Also, since the second technique requires several preliminary steps before the searching begins, it should be used only when several searches are to be made.

The binary search technique requires that two separate operations be performed on the list. The list was initially sorted; then it was searched for several desired values. But one operation can be eliminated if the original list is ordered at the same time it is structured. One technique for accomplishing this incorporates in part the principle of the shuttle-interchange sort, as seen in the algorithm in Figure 5.19. The list A is to be structured in ascending order. The first of N unordered elements is assigned to the first position in the list. As each successive element is input, it is compared to the element in the list position just prior to it. If the elements are in proper sequence, the loop continues with the input of the next item. Otherwise, a shuttle-interchange sort is applied, working back through the list until the element is in its proper position. Thus the value of each input item determines its placement in the list with reference to the items already stored. When all N elements have been input, the resulting list has been structured in ascending sequence.

Another method of searching a list is a combination of list structure and searching. When structuring the data into a list, the position of a datum is determined by performing a mathematical manipulation on the datum before it is stored. This method is called *hashing,* and the result of the mathematical manipulation of the datum is called the *hash code*. The hash code is an index into the list, thus determining the position in the list where the datum is to be stored. When searching for a datum, the same mathematical manipulation is performed on the search value before making a comparison. Two hashing algorithms will be discussed, both of which use modular arithmetic as the basis of the index computation. The mathematics involved requires only a few steps, resulting in an easily understood algorithm.

First, modular systems must be discussed. If a, b, and m are nonnegative integers, and b is greater than or equal to zero and less than m, $a \equiv b \bmod m$—read as "a is congruent to b modulo m"—means that there is an integer k such that $a - km = b$. In simpler terms, k is the integral (whole number) part of the

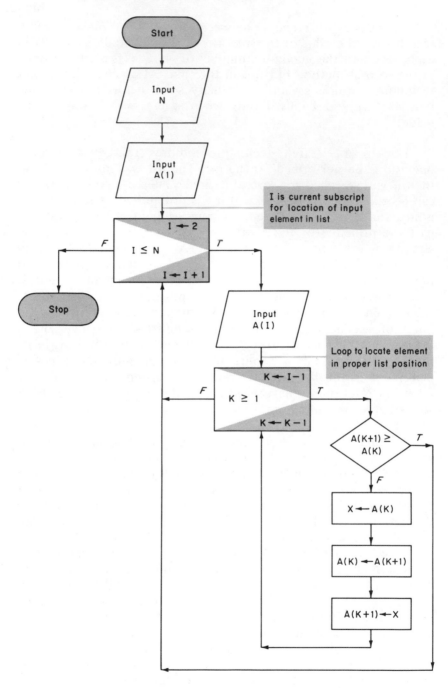

FIGURE 5.19 Constructing a List in Ascending Order, One Element at a Time

quotient a/m, and b is the remainder. Very often the terminology a mod m is used to describe b without really naming b explicitly. In other words, a mod m is a synonym for b.

Example: Applying the definitions to a specific example, 22 is congruent to 2 modulo 5 ($22 \equiv 2(\text{mod } 5)$), since there is an integral value of k such that $22 - k \cdot 5 = 2$. This value of k is the whole number part of the quotient 22/5, while 2 is the remainder. Therefore 22 mod $5 = 2$, and similarly, 17 mod $5 = 2$, 19 mod $12 = 7$, and 1 mod $41 = 1$. In the last three examples, k equals 3, 1, and 0, respectively.

In the first hashing technique, a value in the range 1 to N is derived from each datum, where N is the total number of spaces available in the list. If K is a datum to be stored in a linear list L with N possible positions, then the value K(mod N) plus one is a value between 1 and N. Also, N must be a prime number to avoid exact divisions which would result in several derived values equal to one. [A prime number is evenly divisible only by itself and one.] Figure 5.20 gives an algorithm for storing data in a linear list using the method just described. Unfortunately, any two or more data that differ from each other by a multiple of N cause the same value to be generated. For example, if N equals 31 and the data to be stored are 61 and 123, 61 mod 31 equals 30 and 123 mod 31 also equals 30. Note that 123 minus 61 equals $62 = 2 \cdot 31$. A provision is made in the algorithm to rectify this situation. The entire list is initialized at zero, under the assumption that zero is not a valid datum. But any value that is not a valid datum could be used. The values to be stored are input—one by one—and a value of NK is derived from each. The entry L(NK) is tested for value of zero. If it is zero, the value of K is stored at that location. If it is not zero, at least one other datum has generated the same value of NK. This situation is termed a *collision* of two data. The easiest way to rectify a collision is to proceed sequentially through the list until a zero is found. The counter M assures that no more than N − 1 attempts are made to store the datum. Note also that if the end of the list is reached, the sequential search for a zero continues from position one in the list. Collisions are the biggest problem with all hashing methods, and each new hashing method proposed purports to rectify collisions between data more efficiently. Once the list is stored, it can be searched applying the same hashing method to each search value, as shown in the algorithm in Figure 5.21.

This hashing technique is very rudimentary and not very

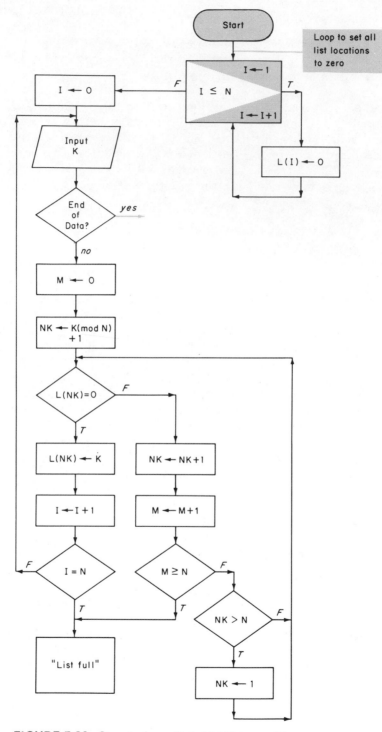

FIGURE 5.20 Structuring a Data List Using an Elementary Hashing Technique

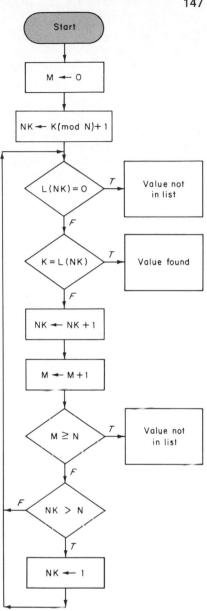

FIGURE 5.21 Search for a Value K Using Hashing Technique in Figure 5.20

efficient. As the list becomes filled, the chances of collisions are greater and the number of attempts necessary to find a zero, or match, increases. The list can be made longer to remedy these problems, but increased list size is not always possible when using a computer with limited storage capabilities.

Another hashing method, called the *linear-quotient hashing method* offers a significant improvement of the method just discussed. The technique is similar, but a more sophisticated technique is used to correct collisions. Instead of searching sequentially for an empty space in the list when a collision occurs, another subscript is derived from the subscript first computed. More subscripts are computed, each based on a mathematical manipulation of the previous subscript, until an empty space is found or the list is exhausted. The algorithm for structuring a list using linear-quotient hashing appears in flowchart form in Figure 5.22. For each datum to be stored, indices are generated until an empty space in the list is reached. Initially, the datum K is divided by N, the length of the list, assuming the rules of integer division. The result is stored at Q. As in the previous method, N must be a prime number. The first derived value is stored at NK and is equal to K mod N. The value of Q is used later and must not be congruent to zero(mod N). A test is therefore made, and Q is assigned the value one, if it is congruent to zero. The loop that generates the probes into the list appears next, and M counts the number of probes. Since the value of NK is between 0 and N − 1, the value of NK + 1 is assigned to KK in order to have a value between 1 and N. If the space at index KK is empty, K is stored at L(KK). If the space is full, a new value of NK is generated by computing (NK + Q) mod N. This computation generates a value that permits a probe to be made Q mod N places beyond the position determined by the value of KK.

Example: If the value of K is 14792 and the list has thirty-one possible spaces, then the value of Q is 477, and Q mod N equals 12. Figure 5.23 shows the first sixteen probes that could result when attempting to store this value of K in the list. Note that the modular arithmetic keeps the value of NK between 0 and 30. Instead of searching sequentially for an empty space in the list, therefore, probes are made in semi-random fashion. Once the list has been structured, it can be searched by applying the same algorithm to the search values. The resultant subscripts determine positions in the list to be tested, and the search continues until either a match or a zero is found. Assuming that the list is not completely filled, we do not have to count the number of probes, since a zero or a match will be found before the list is exhausted.

In fact, hashing techniques start to decrease in efficiency after the list is 80% full. To retain efficiency with a hashing method, therefore, more space must be allowed in the list than will ever be used.

All three searching methods discussed in this section have assumed simple entries in the list. Two-dimensional arrays that

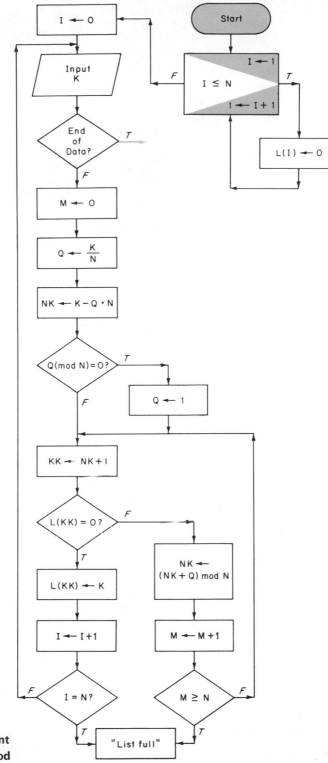

FIGURE 5.22
Linear Quotient
Hashing Method

Probe Number (M)	Value of NK	Value of KK
1	5	6
2	17	18
3	29	30
4	10	11
5	22	23
6	3	4
7	15	16
8	27	28
9	8	9
10	20	21
11	1	2
12	13	14
13	25	26
14	6	7
15	18	19
16	30	31

FIGURE 5.23 Sequence of subscripts generated during the first 16 probes attempting to store 14792 in a linear list with 31 possible positions

permit the extension of these techniques to lists with complex entries are discussed next.

TWO-DIMENSIONAL ARRAYS

The input data to and the output data from an algorithm are often best represented in a two-dimensional (tabular) form. The current inventory of a store, values of commonly used statistical data, and coefficients of a system of linear equations are all represented in tabular form on the printed page. It is therefore convenient to have a way of representing a table within an algorithm. The representation used is the matrix or two-dimensional array. For generality, the term *table* will be used to refer to matrix arrays in the following discussion, except when the examples are from linear algebra.

Tabular Structure and Notation

The entries of a table are represented by the name of the table with two subscripts attached: $T(R,C)$. The first subscript, R, represents the row of the table in which the entry resides, and the second subscript, C, represents the column. A table consisting of four rows and three columns of numbers is written as shown in Figure 5.24(a). The entries of the table are represented symbolically as shown in Figure 5.24(b). The unique pair of subscripts associated with an entry distinguishes it from all other entries. A

Columns

	1	2	3
1	3	12	4
2	21	6	10
3	37	72	51
4	4	8	212

Rows

$T(1,1)$	$T(1,2)$	$T(1,3)$
$T(2,1)$	$T(2,2)$	$T(2,3)$
$T(3,1)$	$T(3,2)$	$T(3,3)$
$T(4,1)$	$T(4,2)$	$T(4,3)$

(a) *Sample table*   (b) *Symbolic notation for a table*

FIGURE 5.24

particular entry from a table is used in an algorithm by specifying the table name, with the proper subscripts attached, in an expression, decision, or input/output (I/O) operation. Since computer storage is treated as if it were linear, tables are stored either *column after column* or *row after row*. The method of storage is dictated by the type of programming language used. The row-after-row method of storage will be assumed throughout the remainder of this chapter. The table in Figure 5.24(b) might be stored in a computer like that shown in Figure 5.25. Note that each entry requires one word of storage.

It is necessary to develop some conventions for the I/O of tables before looking at a specific problem requiring the table structure. The input of data into a table structure will be considered first. The simplest method of input is to present one entry of the table at a time for input. The order of input depends on the structure of the input loop. Figure 5.26(a) inputs the entries of each row—one at a time—until all the rows are filled. There are two loops necessary, and the index, J, of the inner loop attains all its values for each value of the outer loop index, I. This

$T(1,1)$	$T(1,2)$	$T(1,3)$	$T(2,1)$	$T(2,2)$	$T(2,3)$	$T(3,1)$	

FIGURE 5.25   Computer Storage of a Matrix or Table

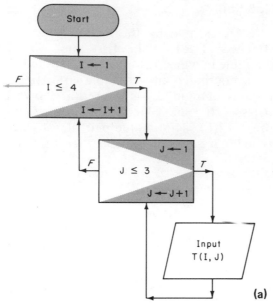

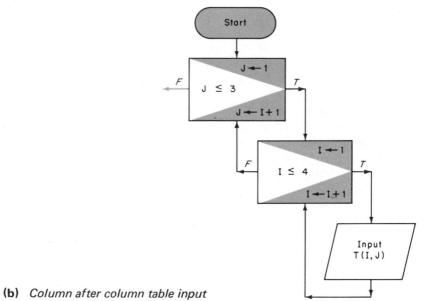

(a) *Row after row table input*

(b) *Column after column table input*

FIGURE 5.26

results in an input sequence T(1,1), T(1,2), T(1,3), T(2,1), T(2,2), etc. In other words, the column index, J, passes through all its values for each value of the row index, I. In Figure 5.26(b), the situation is reversed—the row index attains all its values for each value of the column index. The input sequence is then T(1,1), T(2,1), T(3,1), T(4,1), T(1,2), T(2,2), etc., or a column-after-column input. But tables are usually considered one row at a time or one column at a time—not one element at a time. The elements of a row or column are related to each other and are considered as a unit. There are various methods available in programming languages for accomplishing table input, but the flowchart symbol is kept simple, as shown in Figure 5.27(a). The comment associated with the input is to specify that T is a table. The output of tabular information can be represented similarly, as shown in Figure 5.27(b). The comment is necessary only to indicate that T is a table, since tables are usually presented for output in a row-by-row manner.

A specific example will illustrate the basic subscript manipulations associated with tables.

Example: ·The average daily high temperatures, the average daily low temperatures, and the average dew points have been computed for the metropolitan Boston area from readings of the past twenty-five years. An algorithm is needed that will allow towns in the area to compare their daily readings with the averages. For convenience, the comparisons will be made using data grouped by month. Specifically, the algorithm will determine the percentage of the total days in a month for which the daily low temperatures were below the average low temperatures, the percentage of the total days for which the daily high temperatures were above the

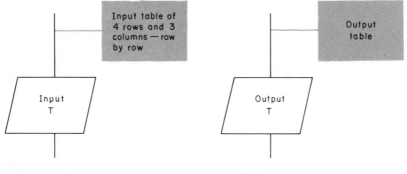

(a) *Table input symbol*   **(b)** *Table output symbol*

FIGURE 5.27

average high temperatures, and the percentage of the total days for which the dew points were above the average dew points. The input to the algorithm is separated into two distinct parts. First, the daily averages of a particular month must be received as input and retained since the information must be examined later in the algorithm. Next, the readings for the same month must be compared to the averages, one by one.

Solution. The algorithm in Figure 5.28 provides a solution to this problem. In the algorithm, the number of days in the month is represented by N, and the three averages for each day of a month are retained as the elements of rows in the table, AVES. The information is stored in order of ascending day number—that is, row one holds the information for day one, row two for day two, etc. The counters LOW, HIGH, and DP are used to count the number of times the questions posed in the problem are true. The daily readings are considered one group at a time. The day number, D, accompanies the readings and is used as a row subscript into the table AVES. The use of the day number as a row subscript value assures that a daily reading is compared with its counterpart in the averages table. The second subscripts in each decision diamond are constant, representing the average low, the average high, and the average dew point, respectively. Once the daily readings have been processed, the counts are converted to percentages and sent to output.

One important point to note about this algorithm is that although the daily readings are tabular in form, they were not stored as a table. There is no need to retain a set of daily readings once it is processed. Hence it would be wasteful of storage space to retain a second table. In keeping with the philosophy of Chapter 3, this algorithm can be generalized to process data from any number of towns for a given month without restarting the algorithm. Also, it could be further generalized to process any number of towns for up to twelve months. Since space does not allow such generalization here, they are left to the reader as exercises.

Elementary Matrix Manipulations

To further exemplify double subscript manipulation, algorithms that perform operations basic to linear algebra are now developed. It is sometimes necessary, especially in linear algebra, to interchange the rows and columns of a matrix or table. That is, row one becomes column one, row two becomes column two, etc., thus forming a new matrix. The result of this interchange is called the *transpose* of the original matrix. Figure 5.29(b) shows a 4 X 3 matrix and its transpose.

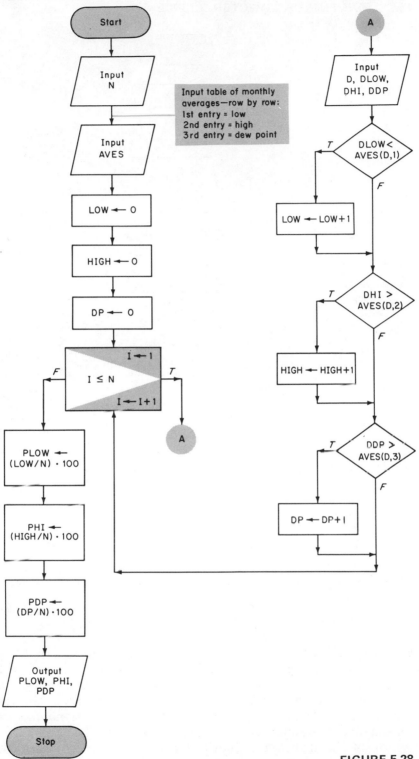

FIGURE 5.28

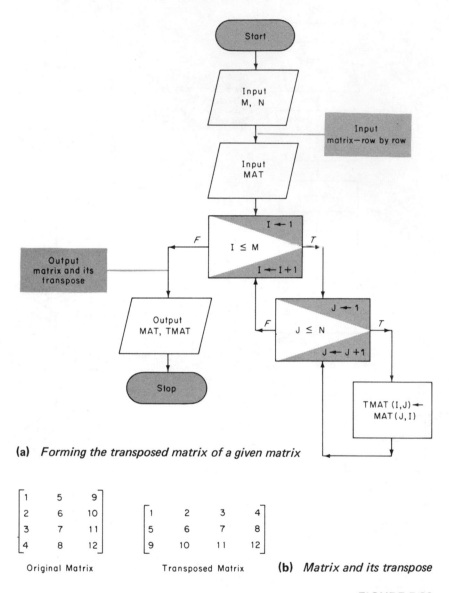

(a) *Forming the transposed matrix of a given matrix*

$$\begin{bmatrix} 1 & 5 & 9 \\ 2 & 6 & 10 \\ 3 & 7 & 11 \\ 4 & 8 & 12 \end{bmatrix} \qquad \begin{bmatrix} 1 & 2 & 3 & 4 \\ 5 & 6 & 7 & 8 \\ 9 & 10 & 11 & 12 \end{bmatrix}$$

Original Matrix   Transposed Matrix   **(b)** *Matrix and its transpose*

FIGURE 5.29

Example: If one is working with a matrix composed of three rows and four columns, called a 3 × 4 (three by four) matrix, the transpose will be a 4 × 3 matrix. An algorithm for forming the transpose of a matrix while retaining the original matrix appears in Figure 5.29(a). The variables M and N represent the number of rows and the number of columns, respectively. The processing section of the algorithm requires simply an assignment statement

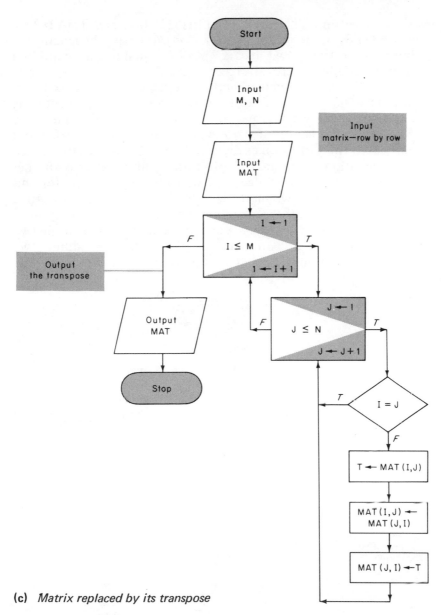

(c) *Matrix replaced by its transpose*

and a reverse in the order of the subscripts. For example, all the entries of row one are represented with the same first subscript. The symbolic form is MAT(1,J), where J ranges from one to the maximum number of entries in a row. The transposed matrix is TMAT. These entries form column one, which has a symbolic representation of TMAT(I,1), where I ranges from one to the number of entries in a *row* of MAT. Hence, for a 4 × 3 matrix,

MAT(1,1) becomes TMAT(1,1), MAT(1,2) becomes TMAT(2,1), and MAT(1,3) becomes TMAT(3,1). Consequently, the length of a column in the transposed matrix TMAT is equal to the length of a row in the original matrix MAT.

Figure 5.29(c) presents a method of replacing a matrix by its transpose. The additional test in the inner loop prevents the superfluous operation of replacing one of the diagonal elements by itself. The interchange of two matrix elements is carried out exactly as in the sort routines discussed earlier in this chapter.

The addition of two matrices to form a third matrix is another basic operation in linear algebra. The only requirement for this operation is that the two matrices to be added must have the same number of rows and the same number of columns. The addition is performed between elements in corresponding positions in the two matrices. Figure 5.30 presents an algorithm for adding two matrices. The variables M and N represent the numbers of rows

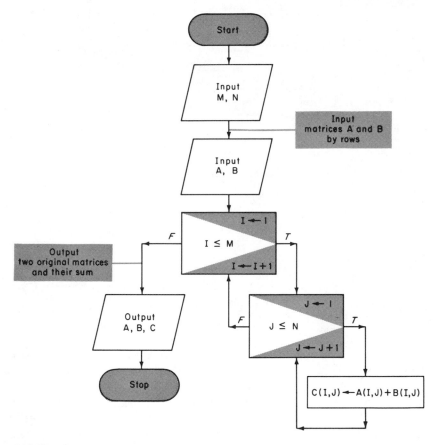

FIGURE 5.30

and columns, respectively. For each I and J, the sum A(I,J) + B(I,J) is formed, thus establishing a third matrix, C. Since the inner loop determines the column, the addition takes place sequentially through the rows; that is, the elements of the first rows are added together before the elements of the second rows are added, etc. As in the previous example, the algorithm can be rewritten to have the matrix sum replace one of the original matrices.

These examples serve only to set the stage for more complicated operations in linear algebra. Such operations will be left as exercises for the interested reader.

Lists with Complex Entries

The list representations studied in the first section of this chapter contained only single-item entries. But a single entry is often comprised of several related items. For example, list entries might consist of a student number and an examination score; a product number, a price, and the amount on hand; a flight number, a fare, the number of seats available, and a departure time; or a real number, its square, and its square root. The two-dimensional array can be used to represent list entries that have many items. Each row of a two-dimensional array is considered to be a single list entry, with the individual words of the row containing the elements that make up the entry. Such complex entries are often called *records*, and the elements that make up a record are called *fields*. It must be noted that certain fields within a record (e.g., character strings) require more than one word to represent them. The number of characters that can be stored in a word depends on the design of the computer being used.* To keep the following discussion general, *a single element of a row,* as determined by a pair of subscripts, will represent a field regardless of the type of data being stored.

The individual records of the list can be manipulated and searched in a manner similar to the single-item entry lists. Usually, one particular item in such complex entries distinguishes them from other entries in the same list. This item is used when searching the list and is called the record *key* of the list entry. In all previous discussions of searching, the data and the keys coincided.

Example: An algorithm is needed that will search a list of student records for desired information. The information retained for each student is the student number, the name, sex, class, cumulative grade point, and amount of financial aid received.

*Refer to Chapter 4, the second section, for details.

Solution. The rows of a two-dimensional array can be used to represent this information for each student. A single record is represented symbolically in the array RECDS in Figure 5.31. Each row contains six distinct fields, and the total number of rows needed is equal to the number of students. The student number is the best choice for the key, since it is the only unique item in a record. Since it is unlikely that two student names would be exactly the same, the student name could also serve as a key. But the student name cannot be stored in a single word of computer storage, whereas the student number can be stored in a single word, making it the better choice for the key. The algorithm is to be designed to search the list for a particular student number and then output the student number, student name, and the grade-point average. The binary search technique will be applied to the key of each record.

RECDS(I,1)	RECDS(I,2)	RECDS(I,3)	RECDS(I,4)	RECDS(I,5)	RECDS(I,6)
Student Number	Name	Sex	Class	Grade Point	Financial Aid

FIGURE 5.31   Record of Student Information

Usually, such a collection of information is kept in ascending order according to student number, but for exemplary purposes, a sorting algorithm will be included prior to the searching. The main difference between sorting a list with single-item entries is that the algorithm must provide for the interchange of an entire record of information—not just a single word. Figure 5.32(a) gives the sorting section of the algorithm using the bubble-sort technique. A loop is required to complete the interchange, since six fields must be moved. The loop index, K, controls which field is to be moved. The first binary search algorithm discussed [see Fig. 5.15] will be applied to this list. Figure 5.32(b) gives the search section of the algorithm. Note that the algorithm operates exactly the same as in the simple list and that the two-dimensional structure allows extraction of the desired information from the record easily.

As we saw in the sorting section of the algorithm, the sorting of records requires the movement of much more data than the sorting of single-item entries. It is possible to add an additional word to each record and reduce the data movement when sorting long records. Since the keys of the record are the only information that must be ordered, a technique is developed that sorts the keys but does not move the remainder of the records. The additional

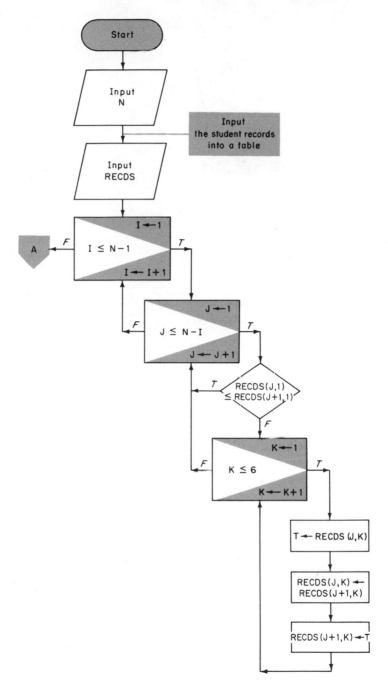

FIGURE 5.32   (a) *Sorting records within a complex list*

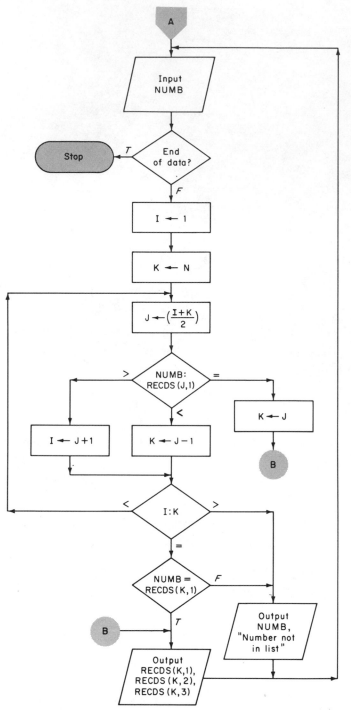

FIGURE 5.32   **(b)**   *Searching the records of a complex list*

word in each row is used to identify in which row the remainder of the record is stored. When the records are initially read and stored in rows of a two-dimensional array, the additional word is assigned the row number in which the record is stored. The contents of the additional word is called a *pointer*, since it points to the row in which the record is stored. During the sorting, whenever two keys are interchanged, the pointers are also interchanged. The remaining fields of the records remain stationary. A binary search can now be applied to the keys, and when a desired key is found, the accompanying pointer value determines which row holds the remainder of the record.

The problem of sorting and searching the records of student information, as described in Figure 5.31, is considered again, and pointers are added to the representation. Each row of the two-dimensional array that holds the records now has seven words. The first word holds the pointer value, and the remaining six words hold the record. An algorithm for reading and sorting the records appears in Figure 5.33(a). The first loop inputs each record into the last six words of a row and sets the first word of each row equal to the row number. The next two loops perform a bubble sort according to the record key (i.e., the student number). Whenever two keys are interchanged, the associated pointers are also interchanged. The key and pointer therefore remain side by side, and the pointer tells in which row the key originally appeared. Note that the interchange now requires only six steps compared to the eighteen steps in Figure 5.32(a). Also, only six steps are required regardless of the length of the record. The binary search can be applied to the keys exactly as in Figure 5.32(b). Since the key has been separated from the record, however, the output of information from the desired record is performed as shown in Figure 5.33(b). The additional step assigns the value of the pointer to K in order to output the information from the correct record. The other searching and sorting methods discussed can be easily modified for use with lists comprised of complex entries. Also, the hashing methods discussed can be similarly modified.

The important feature of the complex record is the key. The key can usually be represented as a single word, thus reducing the complex entry to a single-item entry. The key can appear anywhere in a record but must be in the same position in all records considered. The use of pointers with records to physically separate the key from the record increases the efficiency of sorting. The concept of the pointer becomes even more important in the next section, where structures are developed to overcome the limitations of the sequential nature of computer storage.

(a) *Storing and sorting a list of records with pointers*

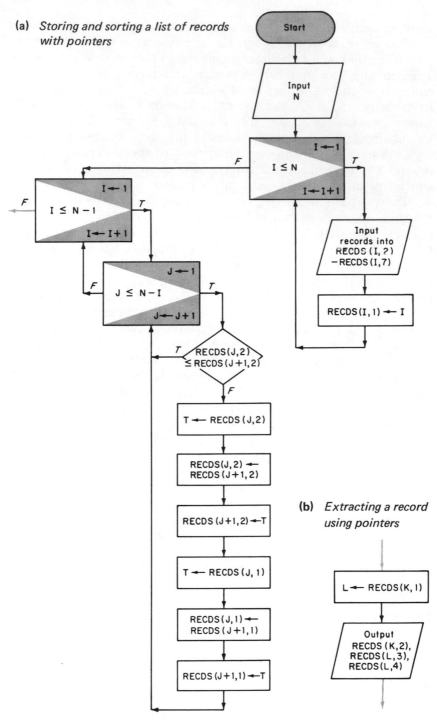

(b) *Extracting a record using pointers*

FIGURE 5.33

COMPLEX STRUCTURES

The Need for More Flexible Data Structures

Two more operations often performed on lists of information are the addition and deletion of data. To simplify the details of these operations, lists with single-item entries will be discussed first. The process of adding an entry to a linear list with N elements is very elementary. Simply increase the value of N by one and add the entry to the end of the list [see Fig. 5.34(a)] The deletion of an entry is nearly as elementary but is also very inefficient. Figure 5.34(b) gives an algorithm segment that deletes the Kth entry from a linear list with N elements. Since the removal of an entry requires that its space be filled, all the entries beyond the vacated entry must be moved up one word in the list. In a list with N entries, the removal of the Kth entry requires that N − K other entries be moved. A structure will be introduced later that will decrease the amount of data to be moved, but this is accomplished at the expense of some extra storage space. First, we shall study three special types of linear lists characterized by the addition and deletion of data always at the same point in the list.

(a) *Adding the value of the variable X to the linear list,* **LIST**

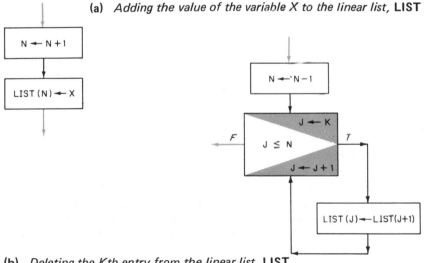

(b) *Deleting the Kth entry from the linear list,* **LIST**

FIGURE 5.34

Stacks, Queues, and Deques

A *stack* is a linear list characterized by the removal of data on a last in—first out (LIFO) basis. In other words, the last item added to the stack will be the first item removed. The stack structure can be likened to a stack of plates, since the last plate placed on top of the stack is normally the first one removed. There are two operations performed on stacks: adding an entry to the stack, called *pushing down* the stack, and removing an entry, called *popping* the stack. When an entry is removed from a stack, it is considered to be *physically* removed—just as with the stack of plates.

Example: Let the variable name STK represent a linear list that is a stack. The bottom of the stack is assumed to be in position STK(1), as shown in Figure 5.35. Since information is added and deleted, the stack changes in length. The top of the stack moves to different positions as these changes take place. An additional variable, called a *pointer*, is defined that holds the subscript value of the *next* available position in the stack. The variable PTR is the pointer in Figure 5.35. The value of the pointer is increased when the stack is "pushed down," and decreased when the stack is "popped."

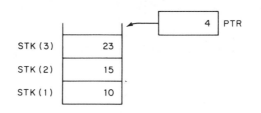

FIGURE 5.35   A Sample Stack

In Figure 5.36(a), a stack (STK) with three entries is shown with the pointer (PTR) variable set equal to four—the subscript value of the next available position in STK. The value of the variable M is to be added to the stack. The flowchart segment in Figure 5.36(b) presents the steps necessary for adding the value of M to the stack. The value of PTR is used as a subscript for STK to determine the position for M. The value of PTR is increased to point to the next available position in the stack after the addition. The results of pushing down the stack are shown in Figure 5.36(c).

In Figure 5.37(a), a stack (STK) with four entries is shown. The top of the stack is to be assigned to the variable N. The flowchart segment in Figure 5.37(b) presents the steps necessary for popping the stack. The value of the pointer must be reduced by one to point to the current top of the stack, since it normally points to the next available position in the stack. The pointer is then used as a subscript value for the stack. The result of popping

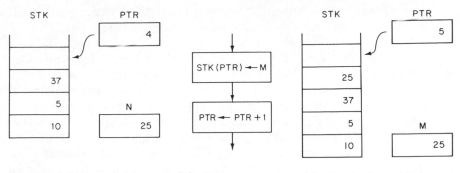

(a) *Stack before addition of value of M*

(b) *Steps necessary to push down stack*

(c) *Stack after addition of M*

FIGURE 5.36

the stack appears in Figure 5.37(c). Note that the value that was removed from the stack is still physically in the stack, but it is logically removed. The value of the pointer now points to the position holding this value. When a new value is added to the stack, the value in this newly available position is destroyed. The stack structure is used later as an aid in forming a more complex data structure.

A structure that is similar to the stack is the *queue*. As its name implies, the queue is a simulation of a waiting line, such as a school lunch line or a line of traffic at a stop light. The queue is represented by a linear list that has data added at one end and removed from the other. Since the queue is accessed at two different points, two pointers are necessary. One pointer gives the

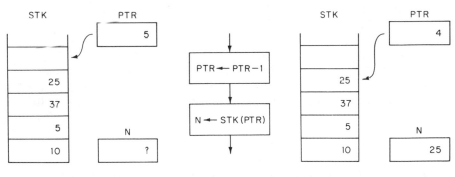

(a) *Stack before deleting top value*

(b) *Technique for "popping" the stack*

(c) *Stack after deleting top value*

FIGURE 5.37

current subscript value of the "head" of the queue, and other pointer gives the subscript value of the "rear" of the queue.

Example: In Figure 5.38(a), a queue (QUE) with five entries is shown. The variable HD points to the head of the queue, and the variable RR points to the rear of the queue. The flowchart sequence in Figure 5.38(b) presents the steps necessary for removing an entry from the head of the queue and placing it at the rear of the queue. The value at the head of the queue is assigned to the variable X, using the value of HD as a subscript. The value of HD is then increased by one to point to the new head of the queue. The value of RR is increased by one to point to the next available space in the queue, since RR normally points to the last used position in the queue. The value of RR is then used as a subscript for QUE, and the value of X is assigned to the resultant position in the queue. Figure 5.38(c) shows the resultant queue and the new values of the two pointers.

A structure related to the queue and stack—but with more flexible I/O properties—is the double-ended queue or *deque* (pronounced "deck"). The deque is similar to the queue, except additions and deletions may be carried out at either end. Some deques restrict additions to the deque to one end but allow deletions from either end. Such a deque is called an *input-restricted deque*. Similarly, *output-restricted deques* allow additions at either end but restrict deletions to one end. Two pointers are again needed, but each assumes a double role. The logic of an algorithm that uses a deque determines the operations to be performed with the pointers. The deque is really a generalization of the stack and the queue. A stack is a deque that is input-and output-restricted at one end. A queue is a deque that is input-restricted at one end and output-restricted at the other end.

The three structures just discussed provide a more efficient means of adding information to and deleting information from linear lists. But these three types of lists are special cases, and the operations performed on them do not apply to all uses of linear lists. A still more flexible structure is needed to represent a linear list that allows efficient addition and deletion of data.

Linked Lists

In the first part of this section, we mentioned that the deletion of data from a linear list required the movement of several entries in the list. Since the entries of a linear list are considered to be in consecutive storage locations (i.e., sequentially allocated) and are

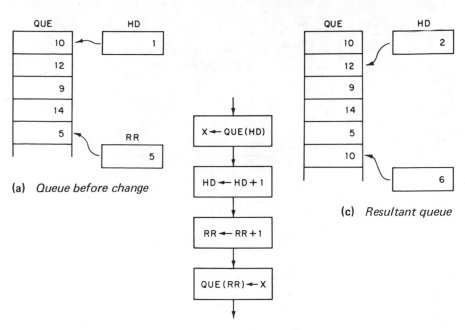

(a) *Queue before change*

(b) *Steps to place value at head of queue at rear of queue*

(c) *Resultant queue*

FIGURE 5.38 Sample Queue Operations

accessed by sequential subscript values, deleted entries must be physically removed by filling their positions with other entries in the list.

Singly Linked Lists. The restrictions of the linear list can be removed at the expense of extra storage space. The linear list still forms the basis of the representation, but two words of the list are needed for each entry. The first of the two words holds the datum (assuming single-item entries), and the second word contains the subscript value associated with the next entry in the list. This subscript value is called the pointer (link) to the next entry, and the resultant structure is called a *singly linked list*. Each entry looks like that shown in Figure 5.39(a). Each entry of the singly linked list contains a datum and structural information called a link. Whenever an entry of a data structure contains both data and structural information, it is called a *node*. The node is referenced using the subscript value associated with the datum in the node. The term *linked list* will be used to refer to singly linked lists in the following discussion.

All previous discussions of list entries required no mention of structural information, since the structures were bound to the physical characteristics of computer storage. The second entry

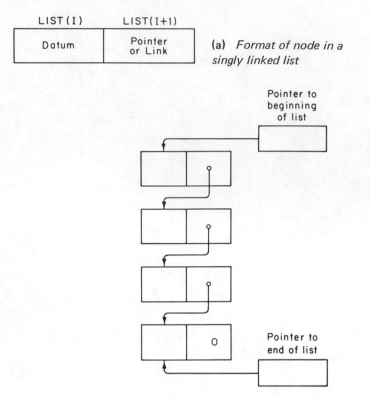

LIST (I)   LIST(I+1)

Datum | Pointer or Link

(a) *Format of node in a singly linked list*

Pointer to beginning of list

Pointer to end of list

(b) *Symbolic structure of singly linked list*

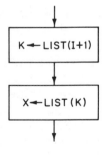

K ← LIST(I+1)

X ← LIST (K)

(c) *Steps required to proceed from node to node in linked list*

FIGURE 5.39 **Fundamental Properties of Linked Lists**

physically followed the first entry; the third entry physically followed the second entry; and so forth. This is not the case in linked lists. The entire linked list structure is represented symbol-ically in Figure 5.39(b). The nodes of the linked list may appear anywhere within the confines of the linear list. Their order of stor-age is unimportant, since movement from node to node is controlled by the links and not by the sequential nature of the linear list. Effectively, the linked list is a logical structure that frees the list elements from the physical characteristics of computer storage. Since the beginning of the logical list may be anywhere within the linear list, a pointer variable maintains the subscript value associated with the first node, as shown in Figure 5.39(b). Similarly, another pointer variable maintains the subscript value of the last node in the linked list. The sequence of operations necessary to proceed from the Ith node to the next node in the list as shown in Figure 5.39(c). The sequence may also be written as the single step, $X \leftarrow LIST(LIST(I + 1))$. In this case, one list element becomes the subscript for still another list element.

The initialization of the nodes in a linked list is easily carried out by inputting the data within a loop. The data are stored in positions with odd-valued subscripts. The links are generated from the loop index and are stored in the positions with even-valued subscripts.

Example: Figure 5.40(a) presents a flowchart segment for initializing a linked list called LIST with N data items. As in Figure 5.38(a), LIST (I) represents a datum, and LIST (I + 1) represents

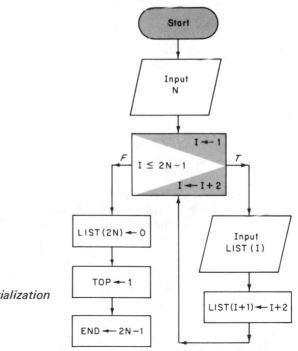

(a) *Linked list initialization*

FIGURE 5.40

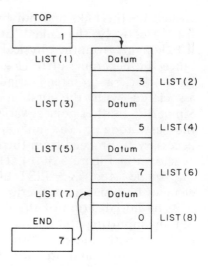

(b) *Initialized linked list with four data entries*

FIGURE 5.40 (Con't)

the link to the next node. Since two entries in the linear list are required to represent one node of the linked list, 2N entries of the linear list are filled. The value of LIST (2N), the link associated with the last node, is assigned the value zero to denote the logical end of the list. In this case, the pointer to the top of the list, TOP, is initialized at 1, and END, the pointer to the end of the list, is initialized at $2N - 1$. Figure 5.40(b) gives a pictorial representation of a linked list initialized with four nodes. The structure of the linked list after initialization looks very similar to the linear list representation of the same data—but with twice as many storage locations.

The distinction between the linked list and the linear list becomes more apparent when addition and deletion operations are performed on the linked list. To allow for additions to the linked list, more words of storage are allocated for the linear list than are necessary to initialize the linked list. A method must therefore be devised that keeps track of the empty spaces in the linked list. One method of keeping track of the available positions in the list is to place pointers to these positions in a stack. The pointers are the subscript values associated with empty data positions in the linked list. The stack is initialized, starting with the subscript value of the next to last position in the linear list (the very last position represents a link) and working backward toward the last entry used in the initialization of the linked list. This stack is called the *stack of available space*.

Example: Assume there are one hundred words available in a linear list for representing a linked list. If the linked list is initialized with forty-five data, only ninety positions in the linear list are used. Thus five more nodes can be added to the list, and pointers to them are placed on the stack of available space. Figure 5.41(a) presents the algorithm segment for initializing the stack of available space for the linked list just described, and Figure 5.41(b) shows the resultant stack. The variable N represents the number of data actually placed in the linked list; 50 is the number of data that can be placed in the linked list; and M therefore represents the number of unused spaces. PTR is the stack pointer, and K represents the pointers to available spaces in the linked list. The initial value of K is ninety-nine—the subscript associated with the next to last position in the linear list. Whenever an entry is to be made to the linked list, the pointer to an available position is taken from the top of the stack. Similarly, when a node is deleted from the linked list, the subscript value associated with the node is placed on top of the stack of available space. The mechanics of adding and deleting nodes are now considered in detail.

The deletion of a node from a linked list is a logical process. The node is not physically removed, but it is removed from the chain

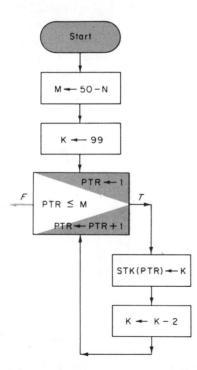

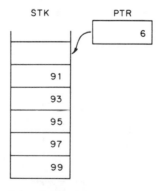

(b) *Stack of available space for linked list with data capacity of 50 but only 45 data entries filled*

(a) *Initialization of stack of available space*

FIGURE 5.41

of nodes that are linked together to form the linked list. In other words, no link associated with a datum will point to a deleted node. The first step in the process of deleting a node is to search through the list until the node is found. The subscript value associated with the node is placed on the stack of available space, and the link value in the node becomes the link within the previous node. This adjustment causes the previous node to contain a link to the node following the one being deleted. The process is represented pictorially in Figure 5.42, where the linked list is represented by the linear list named LIST. In reference to Figure 5.42, the transition from part (a) to part (b) consists of two steps:

1. placing the pointer associated with LIST(7), that is, the value of LIST(8), on the stack of available space, and
2. changing the value of LIST(8) to the value of LIST(12).

The node has not been physically deleted, but since its associated subscript value is on the top of the stack of available space, it will be the first position used when a node is added to the linked list. Additional operations are necessary when the node deleted is either the first or last node in the linked list. If the node to be deleted is currently the last node in the list, the pointer of the preceding node must be changed to zero, and the pointer to the

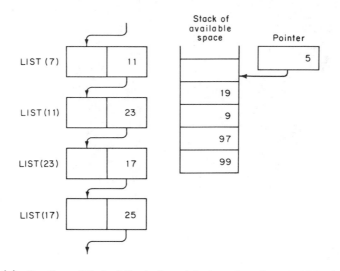

(a) *Section of linked list before deletion of node at* **LIST(11)**

FIGURE 5.42 Deleting Nodes from a Linked List

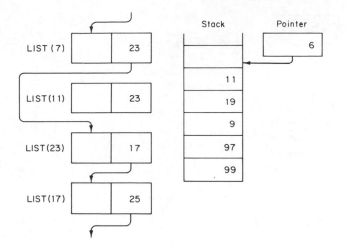

(b)   *Same section of linked list after deletion of node at* **LIST(11)**

end of the list must be changed to point to the preceding node. The deletion of the first node requires that the link value in the node replace the value of the pointer to the top of the list. The flowchart segment in Figure 5.43 presents the logic necessary to delete a node from a linked list that is represented by a linear list named LIST and a stack of available space named STK. The variable X represents the data value to be deleted, and the first loop contains the logic necessary to find the value in the list. The variable I is the index for the list nodes. It is initialized with the value of TOP–the pointer to the beginning of the linked list. The value of J is always the previous value of I, thus providing a method of "remembering" where the previous node is located. The variable END points to the end of the linked list. After each unsuccessful comparison, the value of I is replaced by the value of LIST(I + 1)–the subscript value of the next node in the list. The search continues until either the node is found or the value of I becomes zero, thus signaling the end of the list. If the node is found, the value of I is placed on the stack of available space. The mechanics of deletion are chosen depending on whether the node is the first node in the list (I = value of TOP), the last node in the list (LIST(I + 1) equals zero), or an interior node.

The process of adding a node to a linked list is much simpler than deleting a node. The node is always added to the logical end of the linked list, meaning that this node then becomes the new logical end of the list. The link part of the former logical end is changed from zero to point to the new logical end. The node is placed in the list at the position associated with the subscript on

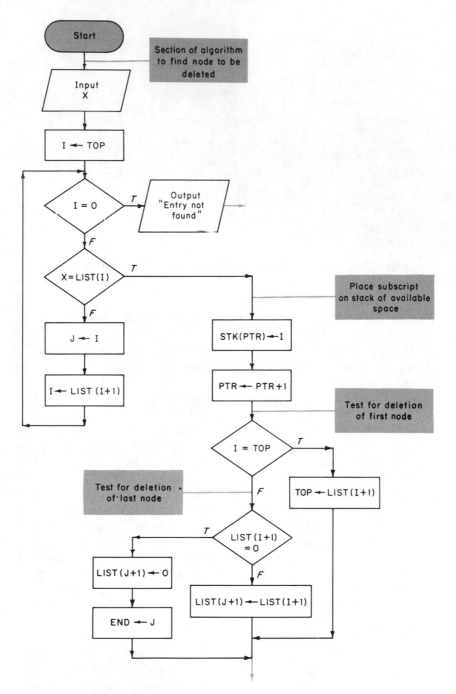

FIGURE 5.43   Deleting a Node from a Linked List

top of the stack of available space. The pointer to the end of the list is also updated to point to the new end. The logic necessary for adding a node to a linked list appears in Figure 5.44. LIST is the variable name of the linear list representing the linked list; STK is the name for the stack of available space; PTR is the stack pointer; END points to the logical end of the linked list; Y represents the value to be added; and I is the subscript associated with the list position where Y is to be added. As soon as a value is assigned to Y, I is assigned the value on the top of the stack. If the stack is empty, the list is full, and nothing can be added. If there is a value in the stack, Y is stored at LIST(I), and LIST(I + 1), the link portion of the node, is assigned a value of zero. LIST(END) is the former last datum in the list; therefore the associated pointer

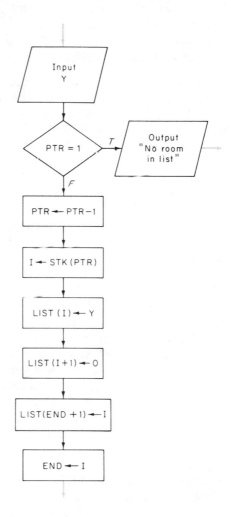

FIGURE 5.44 Adding a Node to a Linked List

stored in LIST(END + 1) must be changed to the value of I. Finally, END is assigned the value of I, since the value of LIST(I) is now the last datum in the linked list.

The use of the linked list to represent a list of information reduces the number of steps required to add or delete nodes. But the binary search cannot be applied to a linked list when searching for a value to be deleted, since the binary search requires the sequential word-after-word characteristics of the linear list. The sequential search must therefore be used to find a node in a linked list. The interested reader may attempt to remove this problem when using linked lists. One possible solution is to modify the linked list so that the data are in ascending order as the list is searched from node to node. Next, form a linear list having the link values of the nodes as entries. A binary search can be applied to this linear list, and the value of each probe can be used to reference a node in the linked list. Another solution is a data structure, discussed in the next section.

Doubly Linked Lists. A data structure that allows much easier deletion of nodes than the singly linked list is the *doubly linked list*. This list requires three words of storage to represent each node: one represents the datum (assuming single-item entries); one represents the link back to the previous node in the list; and one represents the link ahead to the next node in the list. These links are called the *backward link* and the *forward link*, respectively. A node is referenced using the subscript value associated with the datum in the node. Figure 5.45(a) shows a typical node in a doubly linked list that is represented by a linear list named LIST. As indicated in Figure 5.45(b), the first and last nodes have only one link: one to the next node and one to the previous node, respectively. Two additional words of storage are used: one to point to the first node in the doubly linked list and one to point to the last node. The resultant structure is represented in Figure 5.45(c).

The basic advantage of the doubly linked list over the singly linked list is that when a node is deleted, there is no need to keep track of the physical location of the previous node. This information is always the value of the backward-link portion of the node being deleted. Data can be structured as a doubly linked list in a manner similar to the construction of a singly linked list. The only difference is the addition of instructions to define the links to the previous nodes. A stack of available space is also constructed to manage the available space in the list. When a node is deleted from a doubly linked list, the backward link becomes the backward link of the next node in the list, and the forward

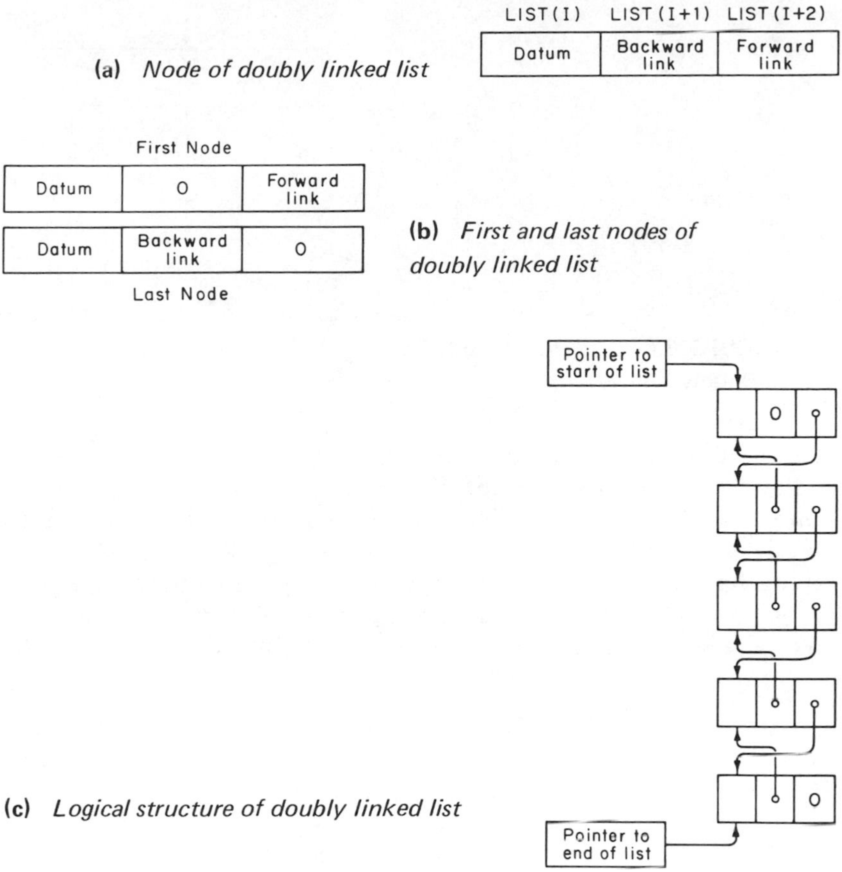

LIST(I)   LIST(I+1)   LIST(I+2)

Datum	Backward link	Forward link

(a) *Node of doubly linked list*

First Node

Datum	0	Forward link

Datum	Backward link	0

Last Node

(b) *First and last nodes of doubly linked list*

Pointer to start of list

Pointer to end of list

(c) *Logical structure of doubly linked list*

FIGURE 5.45 Structure of Doubly Linked Lists

link becomes the forward link of the previous node in the list. If DLIST is a linear list representing a doubly linked list, the steps necessary for the deletion of the node at DLIST(I) are shown in Figure 5.46. DLIST(I + 2) is the subscript value associated with the next node in the list, and (DLIST(I + 2) + 1) is the subscript value of the backward link portion of the next node in the list. The backward link of the node being deleted replaces the backward link of the next node in the list. Similarly, DLIST(I + 1) is the subscript value associated with the previous node in the list, and (DLIST(I + 1) + 2) is the subscript value of the forward link portion of the previous node in the list. The forward link of the node being deleted replaces the forward link of the previous node. Additional steps are needed when either the first or last nodes are deleted. A similar procedure is also required when adding a node

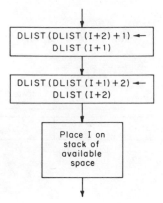

FIGURE 5.46   Deleting a Node from a Doubly Linked List

to a doubly linked list. As with the singly linked list, the node is added to the logical end of the list, requiring a change in the pointer to the end of the list. The former end-of-list node has its link to the next node changed to point to the new node. The new node's link to the previous node is set to point to the former end of list, and its link to the next node is set to zero to denote the end of the list. The details of these operations are left to the reader.

Linked Lists with Complex Entries. Earlier in this chapter, lists of data records were represented by two-dimensional arrays. The elements of each row of the two-dimensional array represented the fields of the records. The two-dimensional array can also be used to represent lists of records as linked lists. An additional word is added to each row to represent the link value. The link portion of each node points to the row in the array that represents the next node in the list.

Example: Letting the two-dimensional array TLIST with seven elements in a row represent a linked list of records, the nodes would look like the one in Figure 5.47. The stack of available space and the pointers to the beginning and end of the list are used exactly as with the linked list with single datum nodes. The initialization of a linked list with records of information is shown in Figure 5.48(a), where TLIST is a two-dimensional array representing the linked-list structure. There is room for M fields in each row and a maximum of two hundred records. N records,

TLIST(I,1)	TLIST(I,2)	TLIST(I,3)	TLIST(I,4)	TLIST(I,5)	TLIST(I,6)	TLIST(I,7)
Link to next node	R e c	o r d	o f	D a t a		

FIGURE 5.47   Node of singly linked list containing a record of information

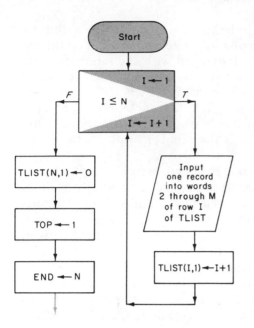

(a) *Initialization of linked list with nodes containing records*

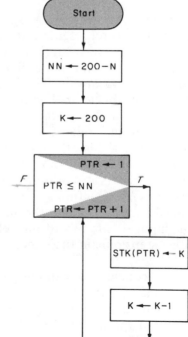

(b) *Initialization of stack of available space for linked list with capacity of 200 records*

FIGURE 5.48

where $N \leq 200$, are placed in the linked list. The variables TOP and END point to the beginning and the end of the linked list, respectively. The first word in each row used is assigned the number

of the next row in the array to be filled. The link value within the
last node is assigned the value of zero to denote the end of the list.
The stack of available space is initialized with the numbers of the
rows in the array that were not used. The logic necessary for initializing the stack appears in Figure 5.48(b). STK is the name of the
linear list representing the stack; PTR is the stack pointer; K represents the numbers of the available rows in the array that is representing the linked list; and NN is the number of places to be used
in the stack.

When deleting a node from a linked list of complex nodes
(records), the keys of the records are tested sequentially against a
desired key in the order determined by the links. Once a desired
record is found, the deletion process is exactly the same as with
linked lists with single datum nodes. The reader is urged to work
out the details for himself. But the addition of a node requires
additional steps that do warrant discussion. One method is to
input the record to be added into a linear list, determine a free
row from the stack of available space, and then copy the record
from the linear list into the row in the two-dimensional array.

Example: Let TLIST be a two-dimensional array, with M words
per row, that represents a linked list with complex entries; let STK
be the stack of available space with pointer PTR; let END be the
pointer to the end of the linked list; and let RCD be a linear list
with M − 1 locations. The steps necessary to add a node to the
linked list appear in Figure 5.49. The major difference between
these steps and the steps for adding a node to a linked list with
single datum nodes is that a loop is necessary to move the
component fields of the record into a row in the two-dimensional
array. If the logic of the algorithm using a linked list with complex
entries permits it, additions may be made directly into the linked
list, instead of defining the linear list RCD and copying it into the
linked list. The loop in the algorithm of Figure 5.49 is replaced by
the input of the record into elements 2 through M of row I. The
other steps remain the same.

To conclude our discussion of linked lists, we must note that
the singly linked list with a single datum per node can be
represented by a two-dimensional array with two elements per
row, and the doubly linked list with a single datum per node can
be represented by a two-dimensional array with three elements per
row. The links in each node then become row numbers in the
array rather than subscript values of individual words. The reader
should change some of the algorithms already discussed to utilize

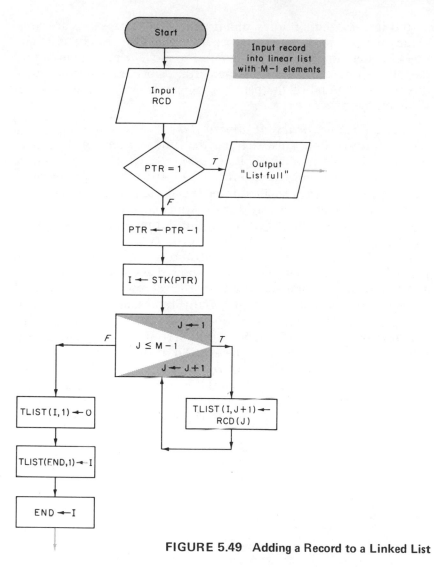

FIGURE 5.49 Adding a Record to a Linked List

these representations. We now turn our attention to a data structure that implicitly includes an ordering of the data in its representation.

Binary Tree Structures

The binary search technique provides an efficient method for finding a particular entry in a linear list. The major drawback of this technique is that once the linear list is initialized, it must be sorted into ascending order, and if additions or deletions are to be made, the list must retain its ordered structure. Hence not only does the deletion of a datum require the movement of many other data but so does the addition of a datum, since it cannot be added directly to the end of the list. The binary tree structure alleviates these problems.

Basic Characteristics of Binary Trees. The *binary tree* is a special form of linked list that has the fundamentals of the binary search technique implicit in its structure. Each node of a binary tree contains two links. The left link points to the first node of all nodes that have data smaller than the datum in the node being examined. Similarly, the right link points to the first node of all nodes that have data larger than the datum in the node being examined. Since each node has zero, one, or two branches associated with it, the entire structure can be represented pictorially as a tree. One node is designated as the *root* of the tree, and this forms the starting point for the representation. The most widely used convention for pictorially representing trees appears in Figure 5.50. Node A is the root of the tree. The section of the tree that contains all the nodes to the left of the root is called the *left subtree* of the root, and the section of the tree to the right of the root is called the *right subtree* of the root. In Figure 5.50, nodes B, D, J, and K form the left subtree of the root, and nodes C, E, G, F, H, and I form the right subtree of the root. It follows that any node in a binary tree is the root of some subtree. The

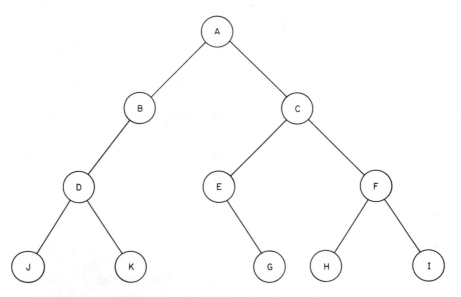

FIGURE 5.50 Pictorial Representation of a Binary Tree

number of subtrees of a node is called the *degree* of the node. A node of degree zero is called a *terminal node* (sometimes called a *leaf*), and a node with a nonzero degree is called a *branch node*. In Figure 5.50, nodes J, K, G, H, and I are terminal nodes, and node B has degree one and node C degree two. Note that the binary tree with node E as its root has a right branch but no left branch. The left branch is called a *null branch* and, in this case, means that no node in the right subtree of the root contains a datum smaller than the datum in node E. Similarly, a node may have a null right branch. A terminal node has both a left and a right null branch.

In a sense, the binary tree is a special case of a more general structure called a *tree*. The general tree structure does not distinguish between right and left subtrees. In fact, a node of a general tree may have more than two subtrees. We shall confine our discussion to binary trees, since they are used more frequently in applications and also form a basis for representing general trees.

Representation and Initialization of Binary Trees. Each node of a binary tree can be represented by three contiguous words of storage. The entire tree can be represented by a linear list with each set of three words representing a node or by a two-dimensional array with rows of three elements each representing a node. The latter method is used in the remainder of this section. Let a two-dimensional array named TREE with N rows and three columns represent a binary tree. Then the Ith node appears as shown in Figure 5.51(a). The first word is the pointer to the row that represents the root node of the left subtree. All data in the left subtree are smaller than the datum in the node containing the pointer. Similarly, the third word is the pointer to the row that represents the root node of the right subtree. All data in the right subtree are larger than the datum in the node containing the pointer. Word two contains the datum. Terminal nodes have both

TREE(I,1) TREE(I,2) TREE(I,3)

Left pointer	Datum	Right pointer

(a) *Two-dimensional representation of a branch node*

TREE(I,1) TREE(I,2) TREE(I,3)

0	Datum	0

(b) *Two-dimensional representation of a terminal node*

FIGURE 5.51

their pointers set to zero, as shown in Figure 5.51(b). When data are input to form a binary tree, the rows of the two-dimensional array are used in sequence. Since additions to and deletions from the tree will be made, however, a stack of available space is constructed after tree initialization to aid in data management. The binary tree is a specialized form of the singly linked list. The basic difference is that a branch node has two possible successors in the structure with a link pointing to each. As the tree is searched, the search value determines which pointer is to be used. If the search value is less than the datum in a node, the left link is used to acquire another node for testing. Conversely, if the search value is greater than the datum in a node, the right link is used.

The binary tree structure is best understood by studying an algorithm designed to structure a collection of data as a binary tree. For purposes of discussion, single word data are stored in the nodes. More complex nodes containing records of information will be studied later. The algorithm in Figure 5.52 represents such a method, where TREE is a two-dimensional array with a maximum of N rows and three elements per row. Each node is in the form shown in Figure 5.51(a). X represents the individual data items to be placed in the binary tree. All positions in the tree are set to zero to ensure that all links are initially zero. The first value of X is assigned to the root of the tree, and the placement of all other values of X is dependent initially on whether they are larger or smaller than the value at the root. Since the nodes are stored in sequential rows during tree initialization, a stack is not needed to keep track of the next row available for storage of a node. Note that as each value of X is input, it is compared with the nodes in the tree starting at the root. After each comparison with the datum in a node, the value of the left or right link is assigned to I, depending on whether the value of X is smaller or larger than the datum. If the left or right link is equal to zero, however, X can be added to the tree. A zero pointer indicates that no value exists in the tree that is larger or smaller than the datum in the node. The value of X is placed in the datum portion of the next available node, as determined by the value of J, and the value of J is assigned to the left or right link of the last node tested. Once all the data are placed in the tree, a stack of available space is created for use with additions and deletions. The stack contains the numbers of the rows that were not filled.

Example: Assume that the sequence of numbers 8, 4, 2, 6, 12, 10, 9, 11, 14, 1, 7, 5, 13, 15, and 3 is to be structured as a binary

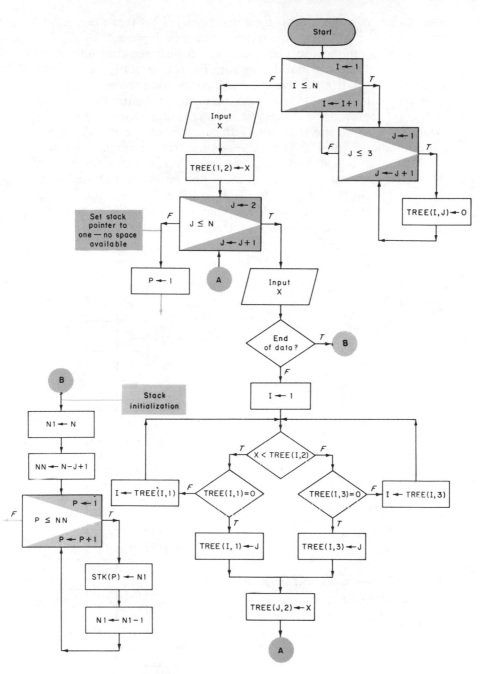

FIGURE 5.52   Binary Tree Initialization

tree, using the algorithm just discussed. The two-dimensional array, which represents the tree, appears in Figure 5.53(a). The relationships among the nodes are much more easily understood by looking at the schematic diagram of this tree in Figure 5.53(b). The numbers written above the lines connecting the nodes are the pointers that appear in the two-dimensional representation. An important feature of the tree just constructed is that it is *perfectly balanced;* that is, the right and left subtrees of the root have the same number of nodes. The balance of a tree becomes important when the tree is searched for a particular value. Since the root of the tree is the first node tested, more comparisons are required to find a value on the heavy side of an unbalanced tree than on the light side. With an unbalanced tree, therefore, the efficiency of the search decreases. An unbalanced tree of the same data as Figure

Row Number

1	2	8	5
2	3	4	4
3	10	2	15
4	12	6	11
5	6	12	9
6	7	10	8
7	0	9	0
8	0	11	0
9	13	14	14
10	0	1	0
11	0	7	0
12	0	5	0
13	0	13	0
14	0	15	0
15	0	3	0
16	0	0	0

(a) *Two-dimensional array configuration of initialized binary tree*

FIGURE 5.53   Initialized Binary Tree

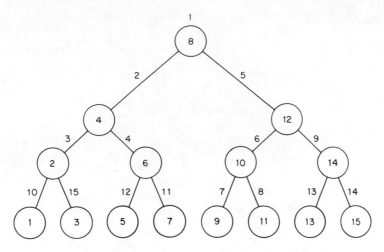

(b) *Pictorial representation of initialized binary tree*

FIGURE 5.53 (Con't)

5.53 appears in Figure 5.54(a). The worst possible case occurs if the tree is structured from a list that is in ascending order. The resultant tree looks like the one in Figure 5.54(b), and the search

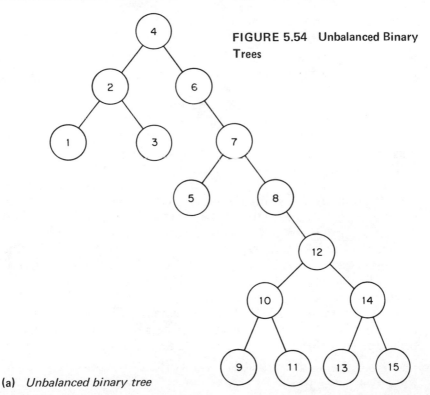

FIGURE 5.54   Unbalanced Binary Trees

(a) *Unbalanced binary tree*

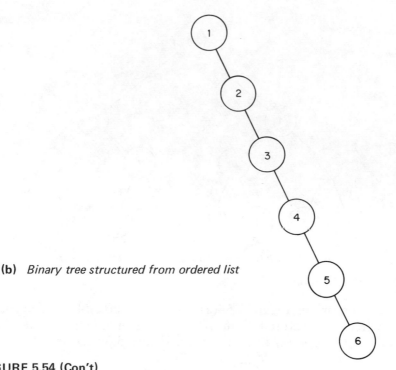

(b)   *Binary tree structured from ordered list*

FIGURE 5.54 (Con't)

technique degenerates to a sequential search of a singly linked list. Hence some caution is advisable when presenting data for placement in a binary tree.

Since the basic ideas behind the binary search are inherent in the binary tree structure, data that are to be deleted can be located very efficiently. Once a node is deleted, however, changes must be made that preserve the structure of the tree.* If the node to be delected is a *terminal* node, then the pointer to that node is set to zero, and an entry is made on the stack of available space. The deletion of a terminal node is symbolically represented in Figure 5.55(a). If the node to be deleted is an *interior* (branch) node, then using the node as the root of a subtree, the datum is replaced either by the largest datum in the left subtree or by the smallest datum in the right subtree. The links in the node are not changed, and the node remains in the tree. The node actually deleted is the one containing the largest or smallest datum. The deletion process is symbolically represented in Figure 5.55(b). The largest datum in the left subtree must be smaller than the datum being deleted in order to be in the left subtree originally.

---

*The following discussion of deleting nodes from a binary tree is restricted to perfectly balanced binary trees to reduce the complexity of the deletion algorithm.

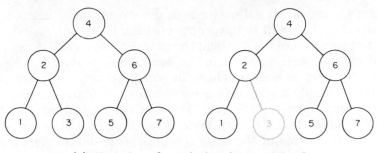

(a) *Deletion of terminal node containing 3*

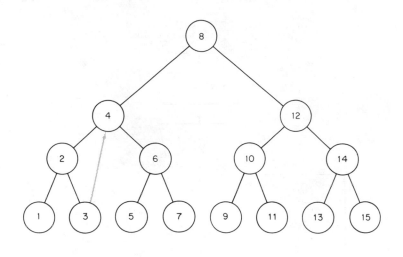

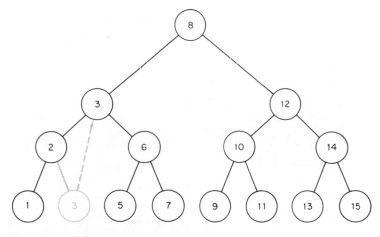

(b) *Deletion of branch node containing 4*

FIGURE 5.55   Deleting Nodes from a Binary Tree

Therefore when this datum replaces the datum being deleted, the resultant node is still in the proper position in the tree. All data in the left subtree are smaller than the new datum, and all data in the right subtree were larger than the new datum before the change. The reasoning is similar when the smallest datum in the right subtree is used. An algorithm for deleting data from a balanced binary tree appears in Figure 5.56. In this algorithm, a datum being deleted from a branch node is replaced by the largest value in the left subtree of the node containing the datum. The tree is represented by a two-dimensional array, named TREE, with three elements per row. ROOT is a pointer to the root of the tree, and X

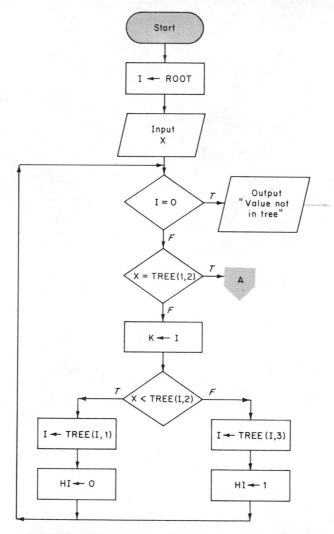

FIGURE 5.56   Deleting a Node from a Binary Tree

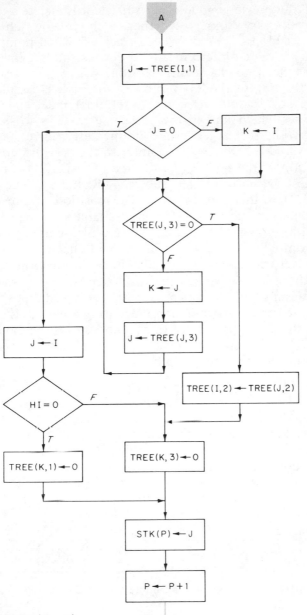

FIGURE 5.56 (Con't)

holds the value to be deleted. The first loop (with I as index) searches for the value of X in the tree. If the datum to be deleted is located in a terminal node, it is necessary to change the link to the node to zero. Since the link is held in the preceding node, the variable K is used to retain the old value of I. But knowing the position of the previous node is not sufficient to delete a terminal node. It is necessary to know whether to change the right or left link. The variable HI is used to keep track of which pointer is to be changed. A value of zero means to change the left link, and a value of one means to change the right link. Once the desired node is located, the link to the left subtree of the node is assigned to J. If the value of J is zero, the node is a terminal node. The value of HI determines which link in the preceding node is to be set to zero. Otherwise, the largest value in the left subtree is found. Again, the variable K retains the pointer to the previous node. The datum portion of the node to be deleted (TREE(I,2)) is replaced by the largest datum in the left subtree (TREE(J,2)). The pointer to TREE(J,2) is then set to zero. The position of the deleted terminal node is placed on the stack of available space.

The addition of nodes to a binary tree is essentially the same process as initializing the tree. Since deletions may have been made, however, the positions of added nodes are determined from the stack of available space. In other words, the positions of deleted nodes are refilled with new nodes before the positions at the physical end of the two-dimensional array are used. It must be noted that the addition and deletion of nodes disturbs the balance of the tree. After several additions and/or deletions, therefore, the tree should be restructured into a balanced tree.*

Doubly Linked Binary Trees. The problem of deleting nodes from a binary tree can be facilitated at the expense of extra storage space. By adding another word to each node, a link back to the preceding node can be maintained, resulting in a *doubly linked binary tree* structure. The problem of keeping track of the preceding node when nodes are deleted is therefore eliminated. A two-dimensional array with four elements per row is used to represent the tree, and each node looks like that in Figure 5.57.

TREE(I,1)	TREE(I,2)	TREE(I,3)	TREE(I,4)
Left link	Datum	Right link	Pointer to preceding node

FIGURE 5.57   Node of a Doubly Linked Binary Tree

An algorithm for structuring data in a binary tree with backward pointers appears in Figure 5.58. The only difference between this algorithm and the algorithm of Figure 5.52 is the definition of the pointer back to the previous node when a datum is added.

*Since the technique for balancing a tree is advanced, it is not covered in this text. So we shall assume that any additions or deletions do not seriously alter the balance of the tree.

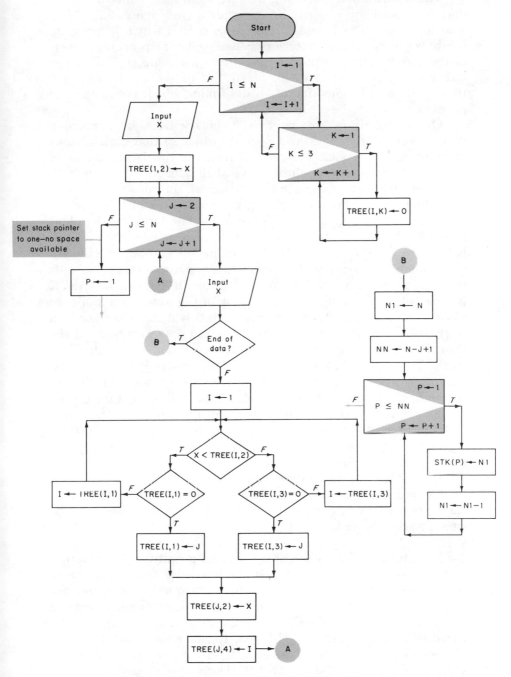

FIGURE 5.58 Initializing a Doubly Linked Binary Tree

The algorithm for deleting a node from a perfectly balanced doubly linked binary tree is presented in Figure 5.59. The additional variables K and HI [see Fig. 5.56], which help locate the previous node, are no longer needed, since the previous node is easily determined. If the node is a terminal node (i.e., J = 0), a direct comparison is made between the datum in the terminal node and the previous datum to determine which pointer in the previous node is to be set to zero.

Other algorithms associated with binary trees are concerned with traversing the trees in a specific order so that each node is encountered only once. The reasons for using the datum in a node depend on the problem solution. We shall concern ourselves with the problem of traversing the tree to get an output of the data in ascending order. This is called a *post order (symmetric)* traversal, and its algorithm appears in Figure 5.60. The term "post order" refers to the fact that the left subtree of a node is encountered before the right subtree. In the algorithm, the variable TREE is a two-dimensional array with three elements per row that represents the binary tree. I holds the pointers to the different nodes. ASTK is an auxiliary stack used to keep track of pointers to the nodes in various left subtrees. P is the pointer into this stack. The algorithm starts by searching for the smallest datum in the left subtree of the root. Pointers to the intervening nodes are placed on the auxiliary stack. The traversal starts from the node containing the smallest datum. Whenever a node is encountered with a nonzero right or left link, the value of the link is placed on the stack. Conversely, when a zero link is encountered, a link is taken from the stack, and the resultant datum is output. The reader should apply this algorithm to a particular binary tree to gain complete understanding of the technique.

It must also be noted that the nodes of a tree can be expanded to hold records of information simply by increasing the number of elements per row in the two-dimensional array that represents the tree. The details are left to the reader.

In summary, the linear list is the most primitive data structure and the most easily understood. It can be used as the basis of more complicated structures, and efficient techniques are available for locating data within them. But deletions of data cannot be carried out efficiently when data are represented in a linear list. The two-dimensional array—in addition to its application in linear algebra—allows representation of lists of records. But it has the same limitations as the linear list. The singly linked list allows efficient addition and deletion of data using either the linear list or two-dimensional array as the basis of its representation. Yet

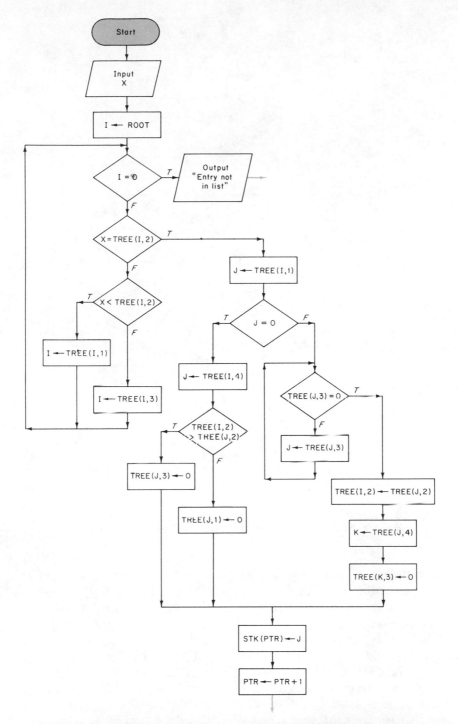

FIGURE 5.59 Deleting a Node from a Doubly Linked Binary Tree

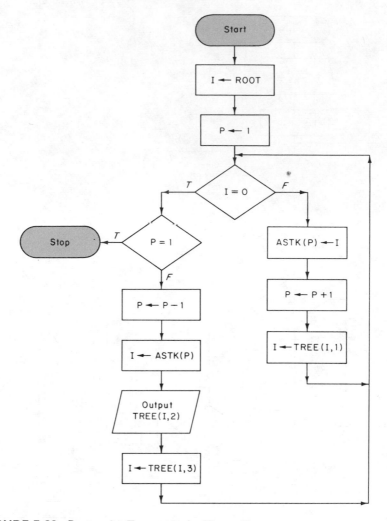

FIGURE 5.60   Post-order Traversal of a Binary Tree

searching for data in a linked list must be a purely sequential process and is therefore not very efficient. The doubly linked list allows even greater ease in deleting and adding data; otherwise it has the same advantages and limitations of the singly linked list. The binary tree structure has both the ability to locate data quickly and an efficient means of adding and deleting data. For these reasons, the binary tree is one of the most important data structures used in computer applications. Having studied how data can be represented and structured within a digital computer, we now turn our attention to the details of how a computer represents and executes the instructions that use these data.

EXERCISES

Define algorithms in flowchart form for each of the following problems.

1. Read and store a list of N integers and then count how many of the integers in the list are unique (i.e., appear only once in the list). Include the original list as part of your output.

2. A college student was recently married and suddenly realized that he no longer had enough money to pay all his bills. Rather than choose which of his creditors would get paid each month, he decided to rotate them each month so that the creditor he paid first this month would be placed at the end of the list for the following month and everyone else would move up one. Given a list of creditors, store them in a linear list and output the payment sequence for a twelve-month period.

3. Given the number of students that have taken a multiple-choice examination, the number of questions on the examination, the number of choices per question, the examination key, and each student's social security number, name, and answers to the questions, determine each student's score (percentage of 100) on the examination. Check the validity of the input data and output a table consisting of the social security number, student name, and exam grade on each line.

4. One method for approximating the real roots of a function $f(x)$ is known as *Newton's method* and is given by the recursion relation

$$x_{i+1} = x_i - \frac{f(x_i)}{f'(x_i)}$$

where x_i is the ith approximation of the root. Given an initial value x_1, this relationship may be used repeatedly until the difference between x_{i+1} and x_i is sufficiently small; that is, $|x_{i+1} - x_i| < \epsilon$, where $\epsilon > 0$ and ϵ is a small number.

This recursion relationship may be applied to polynomials of the form

$$f(x) = a_1 x^{n-1} + a_2 x^{n-2} + \ldots + a_{n-1} x + a_n$$

For efficient computation, polynomials of this form should be organized as follows:

$$f(x) = (\ldots ((a_1 x + a_2)x + a_3)x + \ldots + a_{n-1})x + a_n$$

$f'(x)$ may be coded similarly.

Given the coefficients of a polynomial of degree $n - 1$, initial guesses for the roots, and a value for ϵ, determine the real roots of the polynomial. Since, in some cases, convergence may not occur, a maximum number of iterations should be defined by input. Generalize the algorithm to process any number of polynomials and restrict the polynomials to degree less than or equal to five.

5. Given a list of numbers in ascending order, store them as a linear list and then rearrange them into descending order without making any comparisons between list elements.

6. Given two lists of numbers containing M and N elements, respectively, form one list of M + N elements that is sorted in descending order. First, sort each list into descending order and then merge the two lists into a new list by comparing corresponding elements of the two lists and putting the larger element in the new list.

7. The Abbe Tritheme developed a code consisting of the three digits 1-2-3 as follows:

A	111	J	211	S	311
B	112	K	212	T	312
C	113	L	213	U	313
D	121	M	221	V	321
E	122	N	222	W	322
F	123	O	223	X	323
G	131	P	231	Y	331
H	132	Q	232	Z	332
I	133	R	233	·	333

    Store the above letters and codes in two linear lists, each having 27 elements. Input messages in coded form and decode the messages using a binary search to locate the corresponding characters. Each decoded character is to be stored in a linear list of length 130. When the list is full, output the contents, fill the list with blanks, and continue the decoding process. The following information is necessary for proper decoding and should be tested on input: one period in the code means a blank is to be inserted between words; and two periods together in the code (e.g., 333333) mean an end to a sentence. If a complete word will not fit in the output list, put the entire word at the beginning of the next line.

8. Given an M X N matrix, determine whether the matrix is symmetric. An M X N matrix, A, is symmetric if $A(I,J) = A(J,I)$, for all I, J, where $I \neq J$. Generalize the algorithm to test any number of matrices.

9. Given a matrix of order N, compute its determinant. Perform row operations to zero the upper or lower triangle and then multiply together the elements of the main diagonal. Generalize the algorithm to process any number of matrices.

10. Given a matrix of order N, find its inverse. Append a unit matrix of order N to the right of the original matrix forming an N X 2N matrix. Perform row operations to reduce the original matrix to the unit matrix on each row of 2N elements. The inverse matrix will replace the appended unit matrix. Generalize the algorithm to process any number of matrices.

11. You have been chosen to analyze data gathered by a political poll.
     Each person polled answered thirty questions concerning a leading
     candidate's stands on major issues. A month later, the same people
     were polled again and answered the same thirty questions about the
     first candidate's strongest opponent. Each person polled has been
     assigned an identification number. The answers to the questions are
     coded as follows: 1 = agree, 2 = disagree, and 3 = no opinion. Given
     each person's identification number and his answers to the ques-
     tions, store the results of the first poll in a two-dimensional array.
     Compare each person's answers to the questions in the second poll
     with his stored answers to the questions in the first poll. Each time
     the answers to the same question are both 1 or both 2, add one to a
     counter; each time one answer is 1 and the other is 2, add one to
     another counter. After all answers have been compared, subtract the
     second counter from the first to determine a "choice" index.
     Assuming that an index below −15 indicates that the two candiates
     differ significantly, an index between −15 and +15, inclusively,
     indicates that differences may or may not exist, and an index greater
     than +15 indicates there is no significant difference between the
     candidates, determine the percentage of the people polled whose
     index fell in each of these three categories.

12. Referring back to Exercise 7, store the characters in a three-
     dimensional array using the digits in the code number as subscripts.
     For example, W with code 322 would be stored at the position in
     the array with subscripts 3, 2, and 2. Input messages in coded form
     and translate them to characters and then proceed as in Exercise 7.

13. Given the student number, student name, and cumulative grade
     point average for each student in a small university, store them in
     three linear lists. The positions in the linear lists where the
     information is to be stored will be determined by applying the linear
     quotient hashing method to the student number. The resultant
     subscript will be used for all three linear lists so that the related
     information is stored in the same position in each list. Once the lists
     have been initialized, input a list of student numbers (one at a time)
     and locate them in the student number list. If found, output the
     student number, the student name, and the grade point. If the
     student number is not found, output an appropriate error message.

14. Determine all the prime numbers between 2 and some integer N by
     using the *sieve of Erastosthenes* algorithm:
     (a) write down all the numbers in order from 2 to N;
     (b) cross out all multiples of the first uncrossed number in the
          list; and
     (c) repeat step (b) until the number being tested is greater than
          $\sqrt{N}$.

Example: Find all the primes between 2 and 17.

List: 2 3 4 5 6 7 8 9 10 11 12 13 14 15 16 17
Pass 1:   2 3 4 5 6̸ 7 8̸ 9 1̸0̸ 11 1̸2̸ 13 1̸4̸ 15 1̸6̸ 17
Pass 2:   2 3 4̸ 5 6̸ 7 8̸ 9̸ 1̸0̸ 11 1̸2̸ 13 1̸4̸ 1̸5̸ 1̸6̸ 17
Pass 3:   5 is greater than $\sqrt{17}$, so stop.

Represent the list of numbers as a singly-linked list and perform crossing out by deletion from the linked list.

15. Extend the algorithm given in Figure 5.56 for deleting nodes from a perfectly balanced binary tree to be valid for unbalanced trees.

16. Given a list of N numbers, store them as a linked list. Sort the list so that the data are in ascending order according to links. Next create an auxiliary linear list whose entries are the links to the successive nodes in the linked list. You are to search the linked list for a set of input values. Perform the search using the binary search technique applied to the linked list indirectly through the list of pointers.

17. Given a set of data in which each item consists of a driver's license number, the driver's name, and his age, store the information in an array sorted simultaneously by license number, name, and age. Output the sorted data in three columns:

License no. Name Age   License no. Name Age   License no. Name Age
  (ascending order by   (alphabetical order)   (ascending order by age)
    license number)

The array used for storage of the original data will contain three extra columns to be used for pointers. The first pointer column will be the license number pointer; the second will be the name pointer; and the third will be the age pointer. After all data items have been stored, they are to be output using the pointers. The pointers in the first row contain the row numbers of the first record in each of three possible orderings. [No record is stored in the first row.] The pointers in each of those rows contain the row numbers of the next record in each category, etc. In all cases, when a zero pointer is encountered, there are no more records to output.

18. The Registrar's Office needs an algorithm for processing adds and drops for all courses in the university. For each course, you are given the department number, the course number, the number of credits in the course, each student's name and number, and a one-digit code as follows: 1 = registered for credit, 2 = registered for pass/fail, and 3 = registered for audit. For each student who wishes to made a change of registration in a particular course, you are given the course number, department number, each student's name and number, and a one-digit code as follows: 0 = desires to drop, 1 = desires to register for credit, 2 = desires to change to pass/fail, and 3 = desires to change to audit.

Given this information, store the original enrollment in a course as a doubly-linked list. Process change of registration data for this course as follows: if the one-digit code is 0, delete the student from the list; if the code is 1, add the student to the list; if the code is 2 or 3, find the student in the list and change his enrollment code to 2 or 3. Include appropriate error messages for requests for codes 0, 2, and 3 by students who are not currently enrolled. Once all changes of registration have been made, sort the list by keying on the student number. Output the updated list.

SELECTED REFERENCES

Bell, James R., and Charles H. Kaman, "The Linear Quotient Hash Code," *Communications of the ACM*, Vol. 13, No. 11, (November, 1970).

Flores, Ivan, *Computer Sorting*, Englewood Cliffs, N.J.: Prentice-Hall, 1969.

Flores, Ivan, *Data Structure and Management*, Englewood Cliffs, N.J.: Prentice-Hall, 1970.

Gauthier, Richard, and Stephen Ponto, *Designing Systems Programs*, Englewood Cliffs, N.J.: Prentice-Hall, 1970.

Gear, C. William, *Computer Organization and Programming*, New York: McGraw-Hill, 1969.

Katzan, Harry Jr., *Advanced Programming: Programming and Operating Systems*, New York: Van Nostrand Reinhold, 1970.

Knuth, Donald E., *The Art of Computer Programming*, Vol. 3, "Sorting and Searching," Reading, Mass.: Addison-Wesley, 1972.

Kuo, Shan S., *Computer Applications of Numerical Methods*, Reading, Mass.: Addison-Wesley, 1972.

Martin, William A., "Sorting," *ACM Computing Surveys*, Vol. 3, No. 4 (December 1971), pp. 147-174.

Maurer, Ward Douglas, *Programming: An Introduction to Computer Techniques*, San Francisco: Holden-Day, 1972.

Meadow, Charles T., *The Analysis of Information Systems*, New York: John Wiley, 1967.

Price, C.E., "Table Lookup Techniques," *ACM Computing Surveys*, Vol. 3, No. 2 (June 1971), pp. 50-65.

Walker, Terry M., *Introduction to Computer Science: An Interdisciplinary Approach*, Boston: Allyn and Bacon, 1972.

Walker, Terry M., and William W. Cotterman, *An Introduction to Computer Science and Algorithmic Processes*, Boston: Allyn and Bacon, 1970.

Wegner, Peter, *Programming Languages, Information Structures and Machine Organization*, New York: McGraw-Hill, 1968.

Williams, Robin, "A Survey of Data Structures for Computer Graphics Systems," *ACM Computing Surveys*, Vol. 3, No. 1 (March, 1971), pp. 1-21.

6

Computer Organization

Different methods of representing information in a digital computer were discussed in Chapter 4. There we learned that the basic building blocks of all information representation in a digital computer are two binary digits; 0 and 1. *Bits* are grouped together to form larger units of information. Each computer has a minimum grouping of bits, called a *word*, that can be used for processing by the computer. The number of bits in a word depends on the design of the computer being used. The collection of all such words is called the *memory* of the computer. Associated with each word is a unique number, called its *address*. The computer uses these addresses to "find" information requested within a program. Devices, such as *card readers* and *line printers*, input information into the computer memory and output the results. *Magnetic tapes* and *magnetic disks*, discussed in the Appendix, are also used for input/output (I/O) and for extra storage space. All the algorithms discussed in the previous chapters involved manipulations of data and required that these manipulations be carried out in a specified order. A digital computer must therefore have a means of performing arithmetic and logical operations and a way of controlling these operations in addition to the memory unit and the I/O equipment.

The basic components of a digital computer are represented schematically in Figure 6.1. The *I/O devices* are responsible for the transmission of information to and from the *computer memory*. The *arithmetic and logic unit* operates on information that is stored in the memory. The *control unit* determines which operation on the contents of the memory is to be performed next.

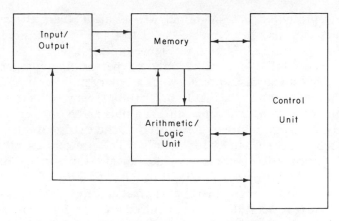

FIGURE 6.1 **Basic Components of a Digital Computer**

The control unit, however, must be given a list of commands to carry out this task. The list of commands is in the form of machine instructions. The machine instructions are stored in the memory along with the data on which they operate. This phenomenon is commonly called the *stored-program concept*. The control unit "fetches" the instructions (one at a time) from the memory, decodes them, and initiates the operation of other parts of the computer that are necessary to carry out the instruction. An algorithm for a problem must be converted into a list of machine instructions before it can be "executed" by a computer. This form of the algorithm is called a *program* or, more specifically in this context, a *machine language program*. To exemplify how a digital computer executes a program's instructions, we will develop a hypothetical computer. This hypothetical computer allows discussion of the basic operations of a digital computer without the need for understanding the idiosyncracies inherent in a particular computer. Two real computers are then discussed and compared to the hypothetical computer.

A HYPOTHETICAL COMPUTER—THE ES-EL/410

The Memory Unit

Since this computer will be concerned mainly with numerical processing, the memory is divided into words large enough to represent meaningful numbers rather than into bytes capable of representing single characters or very small numbers. The memory consists of $2^{15} = 32,768$ 24-bit words. Each word has associated with it a 15-bit binary number called its *address*. In decimal the addresses range from 0 to 32,767. Since each group of three bits can be represented as a single octal (base eight) digit, the range of addresses can also be expressed as 0 to 77777_8. The memory of the ES-EL/410 is represented in Figure 6.2(a).

This computer is capable only of performing integer arithmetic. Each integer is represented as a binary number in one word of memory, as shown in Figure 6.2(b). Bit 0 represents the sign of the number with a zero representing a plus and a one representing a minus. Negative numbers are stored as the two's-complement of the number. [See Chap. 4 for details.] The use of a 24-bit binary representation for numbers provides an allowable range of -2^{23} through $2^{23} -1$ or $-8,388,608$ through $8,388,607$. The internal form of numbers can also be represented externally as octal numbers. Eight octal digits are required to represent one word of storage. The range of allowable numbers in octal is 40000000 to 37777777. Remember that 40000000 is the two's-complement form of -2^{23}.

The Arithmetic/Logic Unit

The arithmetic/logic unit contains the necessary electronic circuitry for performing arithmetic and for testing the results of arithmetic operations. All arithmetic takes place between one word of memory and the contents of one or two special storage locations, called *registers*, that are located in the arithmetic/logic

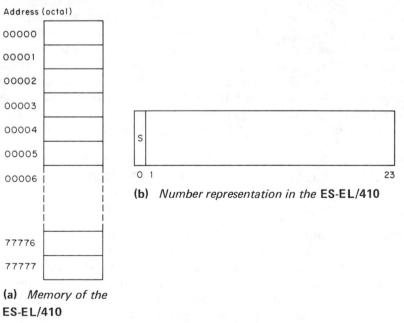

(b) *Number representation in the* **ES-EL/410**

(a) *Memory of the* **ES-EL/410**

FIGURE 6.2

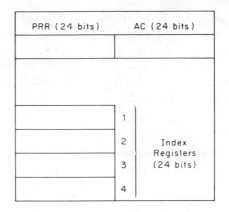

FIGURE 6.3   Arithmetic/Logic Unit of the ES-EL/410

unit. Each of these registers contains twenty-four bits. The arithmetic/logic unit is pictured in Figure 6.3. The *accumulator* (AC) is used in all four basic arithmetic operations, while the *product-remainder register* (PRR) is used only during multiplication and division. The results of all arithmetic operations remain in the AC, PRR, or both. The details of these operations—plus operations for loading numbers into the arithmetic/logic unit and storing results of arithmetic operations into memory—will be discussed later. The *index registers*, numbered 1 through 4, are used to modify memory addresses in machine instructions. Each register is twenty-four bits long. These registers will be used to implement the subscript notation that appeared in Chapter 5.

The Input/Output Units

The ES-EL/410 has very primitive I/O capabilities. A card reader is provided for input and a line printer for output.

The Card Reader. The card reader is capable of reading, under program control, a number punched in columns 1 through 8 of a card. The sign of the number must appear in column 1, and the least significant digit of the number must be in column 8. A + or a blank represents a positive sign, and a − represents a negative sign. The contents of the eight columns are stored, using BCD coding for the sign and digits, into storage locations 77776_8 and 77777_8. Recall that BCD coding requires six bits per character; thus two 24-bit words are necessary to represent the number. An instruction is available for converting data from BCD to binary. Invalid card punches cause the computer to discontinue processing of the program. The card reader also has a special reading mode for reading in and storing machine instructions.

The line printer. The printer is capable of printing the contents of words 77776_8 and 77777_8 whose contents are in BCD coding. An instruction is available for converting binary numbers to their corresponding BCD representation in these two storage locations. The printer automatically provides single spacing as successive numbers are printed.

The Control Unit

The control unit is responsible for interpreting machine instructions and engaging the proper circuity to carry out those instructions.

Machine Language Instructions. The format of all instructions in the ES-EL/410 is the same. As shown in Figure 6.4, an instruction is represented in one word of memory. Bits 0 through 5 are used to represent the *operation code* (OP code) in binary. Each instruction has a unique OP code. Bits 6 through 8 are used to represent the number of an index register. A value of zero means that no index register is to be used. Bits 9 through 23 represent one of the allowable machine addresses in binary. The address portion of each instruction determines either one of the numbers (operands) to be used in an arithmetic operation or a branch address to be used by a branching instruction. The memory address used during the execution of an instruction is determined by adding together the address specified in the instruction and the contents of an index register. The fifteen least significant bits of the sum form the *effective address*, used during instruction execution. If no index register is to be used, a zero is placed in the bits that represent the index register. The memory address used then is the address specified in bits 9 through 23 of the instruction. In the following discussions, the symbol XXXXX represents the octal address of one of the available memory locations; I represents one of the four index registers, numbered 1 through 4; c(XXXXX) denotes the contents of a word of memory; and c(I) denotes the contents of an index register. Also, c(XXXXX + c(I)) represents the contents of the storage location

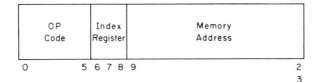

FIGURE 6.4   Instruction Format of the ES-EL/410

whose address is determined by adding a memory address and the contents of an index register. Letting CC represent any of the possible OP codes in octal, an instruction can be written symbolically as CCIXXXXX. A description of each of the available instructions for the ES-EL/410 appears in Figure 6.5.

Machine Language Programs. A program consisting of machine language instructions is another form of an algorithm for a particular class of problems. Two basic differences exist between the machine language program and the other forms of the algorithm: variable names become memory addresses, and computations and decisions become numerical codes that imply the manipulation of the contents of these storage locations.

Example: An algorithm for evaluating the expression

$$Y = \frac{A \cdot B - C \cdot D}{B + C}$$

for different values of *A, B, C,* and *D* will be coded in machine language.

Since the first instruction of the program will eventually be in location 0, the program is written using 00000 as the label for the first instruction. The complete program appears in Figure 6.6. The instructions in locations 00000 through 00002 read, convert, and store the number of sets of data. This value is then loaded into index register 4. Index register 4 controls the looping. The instructions in locations 00004 through 00023 read, convert, and store the values of A, B, C, and D. Locations 00024 through 00026 add B and C together and test the sum for a result of zero. If the sum is zero, the calculations are terminated, since (B + C) is the denominator of the expression. Otherwise, the value of the expression is stored temporarily. The instructions in locations 00030 through 00035 compute the numerator. The instruction in location 00036 completes the computation. Since the result is in the AC, it is converted to BCD and printed without storing it in a temporary location. The next instruction decrements index register 4 by one, and if the result is not equal to zero, a branch is made to repeat the processing; otherwise the program terminates.

Example: To exemplify the use of index registers, the algorithm that appears in Figure 5.2 for scaling a list of scores will be coded in machine language. The necessary linear list for retaining the scores consists of a sequence of contiguous storage locations. The individual words of the linear list are accessed by specifying the

Name of Instruction	OP Code (octal)	Description
Load AC (accumulator)	11	$c(AC) \leftarrow c(XXXXX+c(I))$—contents of the resultant memory location are loaded into the accumulator; contents of the memory location remain unchanged.
Load PRR (product-remainder register)	12	$c(PRR) \leftarrow c(XXXXX+c(I))$—contents of the resultant memory location are loaded into the product-remainder register; contents of the memory location remain unchanged.
Store AC	13	$c(XXXXX+c(I)) \leftarrow c(AC)$—contents of the AC are placed in the resultant memory location; $c(AC)$ remain unchanged.
Store PRR	14	$c(XXXXX+c(I)) \leftarrow c(PRR)$—contents of the PRR are placed in the resultant memory location; $c(PRR)$ remain unchanged.
Load Index	15	$c(I) \leftarrow c(XXXXX)$—index register specified is loaded with the contents of memory location XXXXX; $c(XXXXX)$ remain unchanged.
Load Address	16	$c(I) \leftarrow XXXXX$—memory address specified in the instruction is placed in the specified index register.
Store Index	17	$c(XXXXX) \leftarrow c(I)$—contents of the specified index register replace the contents of the word at the specified memory address; $c(I)$ remain unchanged.
Load Index from AC	20	$c(I) \leftarrow c(AC)$—contents of the specified index register are replaced by the contents of the AC; $c(AC)$ remain unchanged. Memory address portion of instruction ignored.
Add	21	$c(AC) \leftarrow c(AC)+c(XXXXX+c(I))$ —contents of the resultant memory location are added to $c(AC)$. Sum is

FIGURE 6.5   Instruction Repertoire of the ES-EL/410

Name of Instruction	OP Code (octal)	Description
		retained in AC. Contents of memory location remain unchanged.
Subtract	22	$c(AC) \leftarrow c(AC) - c(XXXXX+c(I))$ —two's complement of the word at the resultant memory address is added to the $c(AC)$. The result is retained in the AC. The word in memory remains unchanged.
Multiply	23	$c(PRRAC) \leftarrow c(AC) \cdot c(XXXXX+c(I))$ —the 48-bit product resulting from multiplying $c(AC)$ by a word of memory is stored in the combined PRR and AC registers. With smaller numbers, the entire product will be in the AC.
Divide	24	$c(AC) \leftarrow c(PRRAC)/c(XXXXX+c(I))$, $c(PRR) \leftarrow$ remainder—contents of the combined PRR and AC registers are divided by the contents of a word in memory. The quotient is placed in the AC, and the remainder is placed in the PRR. The word in memory remains unchanged. If the contents of the PRR is zero, it is automatically filled with copies of the sign bit in the AC. If it is nonzero, it is left unchanged.
Add to Index	25	$c(I) \leftarrow c(I) + XXXXX$—in this instruction, XXXXX is used to specify the amount to be added to the specified index register and *not* a memory address.
Unconditional Branch	31	The next instruction to be executed is found at location $c(I) + XXXXX$.
Branch on Negative	32	If the $c(AC) < 0$, the next instruction to be executed is at location $XXXXX + c(I)$; otherwise the next instruction in sequence is executed. $c(AC)$ remain unchanged.
Branch on Zero	33	If $c(AC) = 0$, the next instruction to be executed is at location $XXXXX + c(I)$; otherwise the next instruction in sequence is executed. $c(AC)$ are unchanged.

FIGURE 6.5 (Con't)

Name of Instruction	OP Code (octal)	Description
Branch on Positive	34	If the $c(AC) > 0$, the next instruction to be executed is at location XXXXX + c(I); otherwise the next instruction in sequence is executed. c(AC) are unchanged.
Branch on Index not Zero	35	$c(I) \leftarrow c(I) - 1$; if $c(I) \neq 0$, the next instruction to be executed is at location XXXXX; otherwise the next instruction in sequence is executed. The memory address is not modified by an index register.
Branch and Save	36	The next instruction to be executed is at c(AC); the address of the next instruction in sequence becomes c(I). The memory address portion of the instruction is ignored.
Branch to Index Register	37	The next instruction to be executed after this one is at c(I). The memory address portion of the instruction is ignored.
Input	41	Columns 1–8 of a card are read and stored in BCD coding in memory locations 77776_8 and 77777_8. The sign (+ or blank for positive and − for negative) must be in column 1, and the least significant digit of the number must be in column 8.
Output	51	The contents of memory locations 77776_8 and 77777_8, which are in BCD, are transferred to the line printer.
Convert to Binary	61	The contents of storage locations 77776_8 and 77777_8 are converted from BCD coding to binary and placed in the AC. The contents of the two memory locations remain unchanged. Index register and memory address portions of the instruction are ignored.

FIGURE 6.5 (Con't)

Name of Instruction	OP Code (octal)	Description
Convert to BCD	71	c(AC) are converted to BCD coding and placed in memory locations 77776_8 and 77777_8 . c(AC) remain unchanged. Index register and memory address portions of the instruction are ignored.
Halt	77	Computer terminates execution of instructions. Index register and memory address portions of instruction are ignored.

FIGURE 6.5 (Con't)

Location (octal)	Instruction (octal)	Comments
00000	41000000	Read number of sets of data.
00001	61000000	Convert number of sets of data to binary.
00002	13000051	Store value in memory.
00003	15400051	Load number of sets of data into index register 4.
00004	41000000	Read value of A.
00005	61000000	Convert to binary.
00006	13000046	Store value in memory.
00007	51000000	Print value of A.
00010	41000000	Read value of B.
00011	61000000	Convert to binary.

FIGURE 6.6   Sample Machine Language Program To Compute the Expression (A*B - C*D)/(B+C)

Location (octal)	Instruction (octal)	Comments
00012	13000043	Store value in memory.
00013	51000000	Print value of B.
00014	41000000	Read value of C.
00015	61000000	Convert to binary.
00016	13000045	Store value of C.
00017	51000000	Print value of C.
00020	41000000	Read value of D.
00021	61000000	Convert to binary.
00022	13000044	Store value of D.
00023	51000000	Print value of D.
00024	11000043	Load value of B into AC.
00025	21000045	Add value of C.
00026	33000041	Terminate calculation if denominator is zero.
00027	13000047	Otherwise, store value of B + C.
00030	11000045	Load value of C into AC.
00031	23000044	Multiply by D.
00032	13000050	Store product in memory.
00033	11000046	Load value of A into AC.
00034	23000043	Multiply by B.
00035	22000050	Subtract C*D.
00036	24000047	Divide by (B+C).
00037	71000000	Convert quotient to BCD for printing.

FIGURE 6.6 (Con't)

Location (octal)	Instruction (octal)	Comments
00040	51000000	Print the result.
00041	35400004	Branch to repeat loop.
00042	77000000	Halt.
00043		Storage for B.
00044		Storage for D.
00045		Storage for C.
00046		Storage for A.
00047		Storage for B+C.
00050		Storage for C*D.
00051		Storage for number of sets of data.

FIGURE 6.6 (Con't)

address of the first word in all instructions that need elements of the array and an index register whose contents are added to this address. The complete program appears in Figure 6.7. The original scores and scaled scores are printed separately because of the output limitations of the hypothetical computer. The instruction in location 00004 initializes index register 1 at zero, prior to the reading and summing loop. The instruction in location 00012 stores a score in the linear list. The address of the first word of the list and index register 1 are both specified in the instruction. The actual address where the score is stored is found by adding the contents of index register 1 to the specified memory address. Since index register 1 is incremented by one each time the loop is executed, the scores are stored in successive memory locations. The instructions in locations 00020 through 00033 compute the average. The remainder of the division of the sum of scores by the number of students is tested against the total number of students divided by two. If it is greater, the average is increased by one; otherwise, the average remains unchanged. The scaling loop uses the index register in a similar way.

Location (octal)	Instruction (octal)	Comments
00000	41000000	Read number of scores.
00001	61000000	Convert to binary.
00002	13000053	Store in memory.
00003	15400053	Load number of scores into I4.
00004	15100055	Load zero into I1 (linear list index register).
00005	11000055	Load zero into AC.
00006	13000054	Initialize sum at zero.
00007	41000000	Read a score.
00010	51000000	Print the score.
00011	61000000	Convert score to binary.
00012	13100063	Store score in linear list.
00013	21000054	Add sum to score.
00014	13000054	Store updated sum.
00015	25100001	Increase index register 1 by one.
00016	35400007	Loop to read another score.
00017	12000055	Clear the PRR for division.
00020	24000053	Calculate average (sum still in AC).
00021	13000057	Store quotient.
00022	14000060	Store remainder.
00023	11000053	Load number of students into AC.
00024	12000055	Clear PRR for division.
00025	24000061	Calculate N/2.
00026	22000060	Subtract remainder of average from N/2.

FIGURE 6.7 Scaling a List of Scores

Location (octal)	Instruction (octal)	Comments
00027	32000034	Branch if remainder is less than N/2.
00030	33000034	Branch if remainder is equal to N/2.
00031	11000057	Otherwise, load average.
00032	21000062	Add one to average, rounding to next higher integer.
00033	13000057	Store average.
00034	11000056	Load constant 75.
00035	22000057	Subtract average.
00036	13000060	Store difference.
00037	15100055	Load index register 1 with zero.
00040	15400053	Load index register 4 with number of scores.
00041	11100063	Load a score.
00042	21000060	Add difference to get scaled score.
00043	71000000	Convert to BCD.
00044	51000000	Print the scaled score.
00045	25100001	Increase index register 1.
00046	35400041	Continue looping.
00047	11000057	Load average.
00050	71000000	Convert to BCD.
00051	51000000	Print average.
00052	77000000	Halt.
00053		Storage for number of scores.
00054		Storage for sum.

FIGURE 6.7 (Con't)

Location (octal)	Instruction (octal)	Comments
00055	00000000	Constant zero.
00056	00000093	Constant 75 (in octal).
00057		Storage for average.
00060		Temporary storage for remainder & storage for average—remainder of N/2.
00061	00000002	Constant two.
00062	00000001	Constant one.
00063		Storage for first score in linear list.

FIGURE 6.7 (Con't)

The one thing these two machine language programs have in common is that the instructions appeared in memory prior to the storage of data. The computer executes instructions in sequence, unless a branch instruction alters the order of execution. In any case, if constants are intermixed with instructions without branching instructions to avoid them, a word of data could be mistaken as a computer instruction, with unpredictable results. The basic steps the control unit carries out when executing machine instructions are now considered in detail.

Execution of Machine Language Programs. The execution of a machine language instruction is carried out in two cycles: the *fetch cycle* and the *execute cycle*. Special registers in the control unit are used for determining which instruction is to be executed next and for retaining a copy of this instruction for decoding. The control unit is represented schematically in Figure 6.8. Machine language instructions are punched in columns 1 through 8 as eight octal digits. When a special button on the card reader is pushed, the instructions are read and stored starting at location 0. Each digit of an instruction is converted to a 3-bit representation as it is stored, meaning that the instructions are in the correct internal format. When the last instruction card has been read (data cards are loaded separately), the *control counter* (CC) in the control unit is set to zero. Data cards are placed in the card reader, and program execution may begin. A "start" button initiates the program execution. The CC "tells" the control unit where the next instruction to be executed is stored. The control unit causes

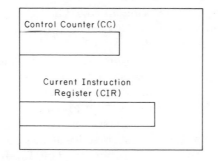

FIGURE 6.8   Control Unit of the ES-EL/410

the instruction to be "fetched" from this memory location and placed in the *current instruction register* (CIR). The OP code is decoded, and if it is a valid code, the CC is incremented by one. If the OP code is invalid, the computer terminates processing of the instruction and the program. This sequence of operations is the *fetch cycle*. The effective memory address is calculated by adding together the contents of bits 9 through 23 of the CIR and the contents of an index register, if one is specified. If the index register specification is zero, the memory address specified in the instruction is not modified. If the instruction requires the use of a word of memory, the effective address is used to locate the word, and its contents are then stored in the arithmetic/logic unit. The arithmetic process is then executed. If the instruction is a branching instruction, the CC is modified according to the logic shown in figure 6.9. Figure 6.9(a) indicates that the effective address in the instruction replaces the contents of the CC. The next instruction executed is fetched from the new location, which is now in the CC. The conditional branching instruction [see Fig. 6.9(b)] is similar except that the CC is replaced by the effective address only if the condition tested is true. Otherwise, since the

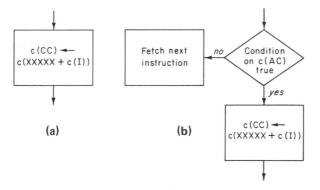

FIGURE 6.9   Execution of Branching Instructions

CC was incremented by one during the fetch cycle, the next instruction in sequence is fetched. The preceding steps are carried out during the *execute cycle*.

More specialized instructions, such as branch on index and branch and save, are executed similarly. A fetch cycle and an execute cycle are still necessary, but the actual internal steps required to complete the instruction are more complicated. Since instructions are fetched in sequence unless a branch instruction is detected, it is imperative that storage locations containing data not be in the main flow of the program. The fetch cycle does not distinguish between instructions and data; thus if a program inadvertantly causes a piece of data to be fetched, an invalid OP code will most likely terminate the program. But if the first six bits of a datum are the representation of a valid OP code, the remainder of the word is interpreted as bits 6 through 23 of a machine instruction. The results of such an error are unpredictable.

Reading the steps of a machine language program, in light of the fetch and execute cycles, gives an accurate picture of the execution of a program by a digital computer. But the construction of a program consisting of strings of octal digits is tedious and prone to many errors. To alleviate the problems associated with machine language programming, symbolic languages have been developed.

ASSEMBLER LANGUAGE

To exemplify a symbolic language for the ES-EL/410, we must assume the following conditions: instructions are available for processing character data in BCD form; the card reader can read all eighty columns of a card; the line printer can print an 80-column line; and a card punch is attached to the computer. With these extended options, a program can be written that accepts a *symbolic* (mnemonic) representation of machine language programs as input and that produces a correct machine language program as punched output. Programs of this type are available for all computers and are called *assemblers.* The mnemonic representation of the machine language is called the *assembler language,* and the actual translation process (i.e., execution of the assembler) is called an *assembly.*

An assembler language, called SAL (Sample Assembler Language), will now be defined for the ES-EL/410. This language provides a symbolic form for each of the machine language instructions defined in the first section. To keep the programming simple, the extended features of the computer that were necessary to develop the assembler will not be made available to the programmer. Assembler language instructions are mnemonic representations of machine language instructions. Pseudo-operations are commands to the assembler. Each statement in SAL is divided into three parts. A statement may have a symbolic address consisting of one to four alphanumeric characters (i.e., letters and digits), the first of which must be alphabetic. A symbolic OP code or a pseudo-operation must appear in each statement. Finally, operands pertinent to the instruction stated are specified. An instruction may have zero, one, or two operands. Instructions in which memory addresses are not needed have no operands. All other instructions either specify a symbolic memory address, an index register, or a symbolic memory address and an index register. If SSSS represents a symbolic address and I represents an index register, the following would be the standard operands for a machine instruction: SSSS; SSSS,I; and I. In addition to these forms, it is possible to modify a symbolic address by adding or subtracting a constant. For example, SSSS + 1 represents the address of the word that is one word beyond SSSS, and SSSS − 2 represents the address of the word that is two words before SSSS. These simple expressions may also appear as operands when index registers are used. SSSS + 4,1 is therefore a valid operand form. The basic format of a SAL statement is shown in Figure 6.10. If a symbol is used, it must begin in column 1. OP codes begin in column 7, and operands begin in column 12. Comments may be placed on the card beginning no earlier than column 20. The symbolic OP codes are defined in Figure 6.11. SSSS represents any symbolic address; NNNNN represents a 5-digit decimal number; and I represents one of the numbers 1, 2, 3, or 4.

The first instruction in a SAL program is always the STRT pseudo-operation, and it must have a symbolic address stated. The symbolic address is the name of the program. The last instruction is always the END pseudo-operation, and it must *not* have a symbolic address. All other instructions may or may not have a symbolic address. The logic of the program determines when they

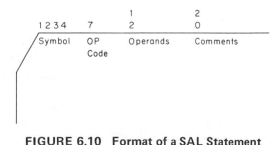

FIGURE 6.10   Format of a SAL Statement

(a) Symbolic machine instructions

Name of Instruction	Octal OP Code	Symbolic OP Code	Form of Symbolic Operands
Load AC	11	LOAD	SSSS; SSSS,I; or I
Load PRR	12	LPRR	SSSS; SSSS,I; or I
Store AC	13	STOR	SSSS; SSSS,I; or I
Store PRR	14	SPPR	SSSS; SSSS,I; or I
Load Index	15	LDX	SSSS,I
Load Address	16	LDA	SSSS,I
Store Index	17	STX	SSSS,I
Load Index from AC	20	LACX	I
Add	21	ADD	SSSS; SSSS,I; or I
Subtract	22	SUB	SSSS; SSSS,I; or I
Multiply	23	MPY	SSSS; SSSS,I; or I
Divide	24	DIV	SSSS; SSSS,I; or I
Add to Index	25	ADX	I,NNNNN (number not a symbol)
Unconditional Branch	31	BR	SSSS or SSSS,I
Branch on Negative	32	BN	SSSS or SSSS,I
Branch on Zero	33	BZ	SSSS or SSSS,I
Branch on Positive	34	BP	SSSS or SSSS,I
Branch on Index not Zero	35	LOOP	SSSS,I
Branch and Save	36	LINK	I
Branch to Index	37	BRI	I
Input	41	READ	None
Output	51	PRNT	None
Convert to Binary	61	BIN	None
Convert to BCD	71	BCD	None
Halt	77	HALT	None

(b) SAL pseudo-operations

Name of Pseudo-operation	Symbolic OP Code	Allowable Operands	Result of Assembly
Start Assembly	STRT	None	Assembly begins
Define constant	DCON	Constant in allowable range	Constant converted to binary and stored

FIGURE 6.11   Assembler Language for ES-EL/410.

(b) (Con't)

Name of Pseudo-operation	Symbolic OP Code	Allowable Operands	Result of Assembly
Define storage	DSTR	Number of words of storage to be reserved	Space reserved
Define internal address constant	ACON	Symbolic address in program	Binary address stored
Define external address constant	XCON	Symbolic name of subprogram	Binary address of first instruction of subprogram stored when program is loaded
End assembly	END	None	Assembly terminates

FIGURE 6.11 (Con't)

are necessary. Comments may be placed throughout the program on cards that have a + punched in column 1. The SAL form of the machine language program of Figure 6.6 appears in Figure 6.12.

This program is much easier to read and follow than its machine language counterpart. The programmer is able to work with symbols that are independent of numerical machine addresses. The machine language version of the program is still necessary, however, if the computer is to execute the steps of the program. The SAL program must be submitted as input to the SAL assembler program, which produces the corresponding machine language version. The SAL assembler, like most assemblers, makes two passes over the SAL program. As the SAL program is read during pass one, the assembler maintains a pseudo-control counter that is updated whenever a symbolic OP code, constant definition, or storage allocation command appears on the card. The detection of a symbolic OP code or a constant definition causes the CC to be updated by one. A storage allocation command (DSTR) causes the CC to be updated by the number of words specified in the operand field. For example, the statement DSTR 5 results in the addition of five to the CC. Each time a symbol is encountered in the symbol field of a SAL statement, an entry is made in a *symbol table*. The entries of the symbol table are pairs of the form: symbol/address, where the address associated with a symbol is the current value of the assembler's CC. The program is read until the END statement is encountered. The entries are made in the

```
+    PROGRAM TO COMPUTE (A*B - C*D)/(B+C)
EXPR   STRT
       READ                 READ NO. OF SETS OF DATA
       BIN                  CONVERT TO BINARY
       STOR NO              STORE VALUE AT NO
       LDX   NO,4           LOAD NUMBER AT NO INTO INDEX REGISTER 4
FRST   READ                 READ VALUE OF A
       BIN                  CONVERT TO BINARY
       STOR A               STORE AT A
       PRNT                 PRINT VALUE OF A
       READ                 READ VALUE OF B
       BIN                  CONVERT TO BINARY
       STOR B               STORE VALUE AT B
       PRNT                 PRINT VALUE OF B
       READ                 READ VALUE OF C
       BIN                  CONVERT TO BINARY
       STOR C               STORE VALUE AT C
       PRNT                 PRINT VALUE OF C
       READ                 READ VALUE OF D
       BIN                  CONVERT TO BINARY
       STOR D               STORE VALUE AT D
       PRNT                 PRINT VALUE OF D
       LCAD B               LOAD B INTO AC
       ADD   C              ADD C TO B
       BZ    NEXT           BRANCH TO NEXT IF C(AC)=0
       STOR BC              STORE C(AC) AT BC
       LOAD C               LOAD C INTO AC
       MPY   D              MULTIPLY BY D
       STOR CD              STORE PRODUCT AT CD
       LOAD A               LOAD A INTO AC
       MPY   B              MULTIPLY BY B
       SUB   CD             SUBTRACT C(CD) FROM A*B
       DIV   BC             DIVIDE RESULT BY C(BC)
       BCD                  CONVERT ANSWER TO BCD
       PRNT                 PRINT THE ANSWER
NEXT   LOOP FRST,4          BRANCH TO FRST IF C(I4) IS NOT EQUAL TO ZERO
       HALT
B      DSTR 1               STORAGE FOR B
D      DSTR 1               STORAGE FOR D
C      DSTR 1               STORAGE FOR C
A      DSTR 1               STORAGE FOR A
BC     DSTR 1               STORAGE FOR B+C
CD     DSTR 1               STORAGE FOR C*D
NO     DSTR 1               STORAGE FOR NO OF SETS OF DATA
       END
```

FIGURE 6.12   SAL Program To Compute (A*B - C*D)/(B + C)

symbol table either sequentially or by using a hashing method. If they are stored sequentially, the table must be sorted alphabetically before the second pass. During pass two, the symbolic OP codes are replaced by their numerical equivalent. The assembler maintains a table of symbolic OP codes and numerical OP codes. A table look-up procedure, such as the binary search, is used to locate the symbolic OP codes in the table. The symbolic addresses appearing in the operand field are replaced by their numerical equivalents by searching the symbol table that was created during pass one. The instructions are assembled into the correct format and punched on cards. All constants are converted to binary and punched on cards. The resultant deck can then be loaded into the computer and executed. The machine language program in Figure

6.6 looks exactly like the assembler output would look after the translation of the program in Figure 6.12.

We shall conclude this section by presenting assembler language versions of algorithms that were presented in earlier chapters.

Example: Our first example is the assembler language version of the algorithm for finding the factorial of a nonnegative integer. The flowchart appears in Figure 3.27, and the corresponding program appears in Figure 6.13. In this program, the comments on each line serve as an explanation of the overall processing. But some of the techniques used require further explanation.

In line (7) index register 2 is loaded with the value of the number of sets of data. The LOOP instruction in line (32) uses index register 2 to control the outer loop of the algorithm. Lines

```
(1)   FCTR   STRT
(2)          READ              READ NUMBER OF SETS OF DATA
(3)          BIN               CONVERT TO BINARY
(4)          BN    ERR1        TEST VALIDITY OF VALUE OF NUMBER OF
(5)          BZ    ERR1        SETS OF DATA
(6)          STOR  NSET        STORE VALUE AT NSET
(7)          LDX   NSET,2      LOAD VALUE INTO INDEX REGISTER 2
(9)          BIN               CONVERT TO BINARY
(8)   L1     READ              READ AN INTEGER
(10)         BN    ERR2        TEST FOR POSITIVE OR ZERO
(11)         STOR  NUMB        STORE VALUE AT NUMB
(12)         SUB   ONE         SUBTRACT ONE
(13)         BP    GT1         TEST FOR VALUE GREATER THAN 1
(14)         LOAD  ONE         LOAD A ONE INTO AC
(15)         BR    ONCE        BRANCH TO PRINT FACTORIAL
(16)  GT1    LOAD  NUMB        RELOAD NUMBER INTO AC
(17)         STOR  FACT        INITIALIZE FACTORIAL
(18)         STOR  N           INITIALIZE WORKING VALUE OF NUMBER
(19)  L2     SUB   ONE         REDUCE NUMBER BY ONE
(20)         BZ    OUT         IF NUMBER EQUALS ONE, FACTORIAL IS COMPLETE
(21)         STOR  N           STORE REDUCED NUMBER
(22)         MPY   FACT        MULTIPLY BY CURRENT VALUE OF FACT
(23)         STOR  FACT        STORE UPDATED FACTORIAL
(24)         LOAD  N           RELOAD WORKING VALUE OF NUMBER
(25)         BR    L2          BRANCH TO CONTINUE MULTIPLYING
(26)  OUT    LOAD  FACT        LOAD FACTORIAL INTO AC
(27)  ONCE   PRNT              PRINT ORIGINAL NUMBER WHICH IS STILL IN MEMORY
(28)         BCD               CONVERT FACTORIAL TO BCD
(29)         PRNT              PRINT FACTORIAL
(30)         BR    INC         BRANCH TO INDEX INCREMENT INSTRUCTION
(31)  ERR2   PRNT              PRINT BAD INPUT VALUE
(32)  INC    LOOP  L1,2        LOOP TO READ MORE DATA
(33)         HALT              TERMINATE PROGRAM
(34)  ERR1   PRNT              PRINT INVALID NUMBER OF SETS OF DATA
(35)         HALT              TERMINATE PROGRAM
(36)  TWO    DCON  2           CONSTANT 2
(37)  ONE    DCON  1           CONSTANT 1
(38)  NSET   DSTR  1           STORAGE FOR NUMBER OF SETS OF DATA
(39)  NUMB   DSTR  1           STORAGE FOR NUMBERS
(40)  N      DSTR  1           WORKING STORAGE FOR VALUE AT NUMB
(41)  FACT   DSTR  1           STORAGE FOR FACTORIAL
(42)         END
```

FIGURE 6.13 SAL Program for Finding N!

(12) and (13) determine whether the value of an input is greater than one. Since the contents of the AC can be tested only for positive, negative, or zero values, comparisons must be accomplished by subtracting the desired value from the value in the AC. If the result of the subtraction in the AC is zero, the desired value and the test value are equal. If it is negative, the test value is less than the desired value. If it is positive, the test value is larger than the desired value. In line (17) and (18), the value of the number whose factorial is to be computed is stored at locations that hold the factorial and the working value of the number. The loop in lines (19) through (25) contains the instructions necessary to compute the factorial. In lines (19) through (21), the value of the number is reduced by one, tested for a value of one, and then stored. If the value is one, the factorial has been computed and a branch is made to OUT. Otherwise, the number is multiplied by the current value of the factorial, and the result is stored back in the location holding the factorial. The reduced value of the number stored in line (21) is loaded into the AC, and the loop is continued. The instructions in lines (27) through (29) are used for printing the original number and its factorial. The physical characteristics of the machine require that two lines of printout be used. Lines (31) and (34) are used to print the values of invalid input, as determined by lines (4) and (5) or line (10).

Example: The program in Figure 6.14 reads and stores a set of data as a linear list, sorts the list into ascending order using the bubble sort [see Fig. 5.13], and then prints the sorted list.

The instructions in lines (2) through (6) read, convert, test, and store the number of entries to be placed in the list. The instructions in lines (7) through (13) contain the necessary instructions for reading and storing the data. Index register 4 is used to modify the address of LIST in the store instruction in line (11). The index register is initialized at zero and is incremented by one in line (12)—just before the body of the loop is executed again. The use of the index register allows the data to be stored in contiguous locations starting at LIST. Index register 1 initially contains the number of data and is used to control the looping in the LOOP instruction in line (13). In line (14) the number of elements in the list is loaded into index register 4. Since the outer loop of the bubble-sort algorithm is executed $N - 1$ times, where N is the number of elements in the list, the index register is reduced by one. The LOOP instruction is used because of its decrementing property, and a branch is made to the next statement. This technique saves the steps of loading the value of N

```
(1)   BUBL   STRT
(2)          READ            READ NUMBER OF ELEMENTS IN LIST
(3)          BIN             CONVERT TO BINARY
(4)          BN    ERR1      TEST IF VALUE IS NEGATIVE OR
(5)          BZ    ERR1      ZERO
(6)          STOR  N         STORE VALUE AT N
(7)          LDX   ZERO,4    INDEX REGISTER 4 IS USED TO INDEX INTO LIST
(8)          LDX   N,1       LOAD VALUE AT N INTO I1 FOR LOOPING
(9)   INPT   READ            READ A NUMBER
(10)         BIN             CONVERT TO BINARY
(11)         STOR  LIST,4    STORE VALUE IN LIST
(12)         ADX   4,1       ADD ONE TO INDEX REGISTER FOUR
(13)         LOOP  INPT,1    BRANCH BACK TO READ MORE DATA
+
+     SORTING SECTION OF PROGRAM
+
(14)         LDX   N,4       LOAD VALUE OF N INTO INDEX REGISTER 4
(15)         LOOP  NEXT,4    DECREMENT I4 BY ONE AND BRANCH TO NEXT INSTRUCTION
(16)  NEXT   STX   IND,4     STORE REDUCED VALUE OF N AT IND
(17)         LDX   IND,3     LOAD VALUE OF IND INTO I3 TO CONTROL INNER LOOP
(18)         LOAD  ZERO      LOAD A ZERO INTO AC
(19)         STOR  M         INITIALIZE SORTED-LIST INDICATOR M AT ZERO
(20)         LDX   ZERO,2    INDEX REGISTER 2 IS USED TO INDEX INTO LIST
(21)  TEST   LOAD  LIST,2    LOAD LIST(I) INTO AC
(22)         SUB   LIST+1,2  SUBTRACT LIST(I+1)
(23)         BZ    OK        ENTRIES IN ORDER IF RESULT IS
(24)         BN    OK        LESS THAN OR EQUAL TO ZERO
+
+     SECTION TO INTERCHANGE LIST ENTRIES
+
(25)         LOAD  LIST,2    LOAD LIST(I) INTO AC
(26)         STOR  T         STORE AT T
(27)         LOAD  LIST+1,2  LOAD LIST(I+1) INTO AC
(28)         STOR  LIST,2    STORE AT LIST(I)
(29)         LOAD  T         LOAD VALUE AT T INTO AC
(30)         STOR  LIST+1,2  STORE AT LIST(I+1)
(31)         LOAD  M         LOAD VALUE AT M INTO AC
(32)         ADD   ONE       UPDATE BY ONE
(33)         STOR  M         STORE UPDATED VALUE OF M
(34)  OK     ADX   2,1       INCREMENT INDEX REGISTER 2 BY 1
(35)         LOOP  TEST,3    LOOP TO CONTINUE TESTING
(36)         LOAD  M         LOAD VALUE AT M INTO AC
(37)         SUB   ZERO      SUBTRACT ZERO FROM VALUE OF M
(38)         BZ    SRTD      LIST IS SORTED IF M IS ZERO
(39)         LOOP  NEXT,4    LOOP TO SCAN LIST AGAIN
+
+     SECTION OF PROGRAM TO PRINT SORTED LIST
+
(40)         LDX   N,4       LOAD VALUE OF N INTO INDEX REGISTER 4
(41)         LDX   ZERO,1    INDEX REGISTER 1 WILL INDEX INTO LIST
(42)  OUT    LOAD  LIST,1    LOAD LIST(I) INTO AC
(43)         BCD             CONVERT TO BCD FOR PRINTING
(44)         PRNT            PRINT LIST ELEMENT
(45)         ADX   1,1       INCREASE INDEX REGISTER 1 BY 1
(46)         LOOP  OUT,4     LOOP TO CONTINUE PRINTING
(47)         HALT            TERMINATE PROCESSING
(48)  ERR1   PRNT            PRINT INVALID LENGTH OF LIST
(49)         HALT            TERMINATE PROCESSING
(50)  ZERO   DCON  0         CONSTANT ZERO
(51)  N      DSTR  1         STORAGE FOR LENGTH OF LIST
(52)  IND    DSTR  1         TEMPORARY STORAGE LOCATION
(53)  LIST   DSTR  200       STORAGE FOR A LIST WITH 200 ELEMENTS
(54)  T      DSTR  1         TEMPORARY LOCATION FOR INTERCHANGE
(55)  M      DSTR  1         STORAGE FOR M, SORTED-LIST INDICATOR
(56)  ONE    DCON  1         CONSTANT ONE
(57)         END
```

FIGURE 6.14   SAL Program To Perform the Bubble Sort

into the accumulator, subtracting one, storing the result, and then loading the result into the index register. The value of index register 4 is stored at the beginning of the loop in line (16). This value is loaded into index register 3 and is used to control the number of executions of the inner loop. The value of the sorted-list indicator M is initialized at zero in lines (18) and (19). The inner loop is executed $N - I$ times, where I is the index of the outer loop. Since the contents of index register 4 are reduced by one for each execution of the outer loop, the values assumed are $N - 1$, $N - 2$, $N - 3$, etc. These values are exactly the number of times the inner loop is to be carried out for successive executions of the outer loop. Note that all loop counters are decremented from the maximum value down to zero rather than from a value of one up to the maximum, as stated in the flowchart. Index register 2 is used to index the list within the inner loop. Lines (21) through (24) contain the instructions necessary to compare two successive elements in the list. The instructions in lines (25) through (30) perform the interchange of two elements. The value of M is incremented by one in lines (31) through (33). Lines (35) and (39) contain the looping instructions for the inner and outer loops, respectively. The value of M is tested in lines (36) through (38), and a branch is made out of the outer loop if the value at M is zero. This implies that no interchanges were necessary within the inner loop; thus the list is sorted. Lines (40) through (46) print the sorted list. Note that two-hundred words of storage are reserved for the linear list.

THE PDP-8/E AND THE IBM SYSTEM/360

This section will present basic descriptions of two computers that are widely used today. The PDP-8/E is classified as a minicomputer, and the IBM System/360 is a series of computers ranging from small to large scale systems. Our discussion of these computers will allow the reader to compare them to our hypothetical computer with respect to memory and addressing structure, the arithmetic/logic unit, instruction sequencing, instruction formats, and assembler language. Additional features are mentioned briefly.

The PDP-8/E

The PDP-8/E programmed data processor is a small, fast, and inexpensive general purpose digital computer manufactured by Digital Equipment Corporation (DEC) of Maynard, Massachusetts. The PDP-8/E is pictured in Figure 6.15.

FIGURE 6.15   A PDP-8/E

The Memory Unit.   There are 4096 12-bit words in the memory of PDP-8/E. Each word of memory has associated with it a 12-bit address in the range 0 to 4095 or 0 to 7777_8. To effect memory addressing without requiring that an entire word of memory be used to specify a memory address, the memory is divided into 32 fixed-length blocks, called *pages*, each containing 128 words. The pages are numbered 00 to 37_8, and the locations within each page are in the range 000 to 177_8. The memory of the PDP-8/E is shown schematically in Figure 6.16(a).

Words of memory are referenced by specifying a 5-bit page address and a 7-bit location-within-page address, as shown in Figure 6.16(b). The control unit changes the memory address from the page/location-within-page representation to a 12-bit absolute memory address. A programmer is required to specify only the location-within-page address (seven bits) in machine instructions that reference words of memory. The basic format of a memory reference instuction appears in Figure 6.17(a). Bit 4 determines whether the page address is on the current page (i.e., on the same page as the instruction) or on page zero. If bit 3 is zero, then the referenced word is used directly either from the

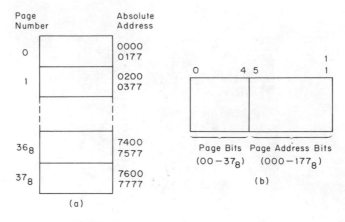

FIGURE 6.16   Memory of PDP-8/E

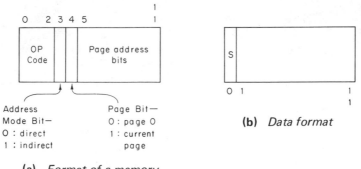

(a) *Format of a memory reference instruction*

(b) *Data format*

FIGURE 6.17

current page or from page zero, depending on bit 4. If bit 3 is one, the contents of the referenced memory location are used as the effective memory address. In other words, the content of the word addressed is a "pointer" to the desired word. This technique is termed *indirect addressing* and is the only means the programmer has for referencing a memory location that is not on page zero or on the current page. This technique allows a programmer to place all his program instructions on one page and his data on a different page. The pointers to these data can be conveniently maintained on page zero; hence all data would be addressed indirectly through page zero.

Locations 0010_8 through 0017_8 on page zero are used for indexing operations. When one of these locations is addressed *indirectly*, its contents are automatically incremented by one *before* being used as an operand. These eight locations are called *autoindex registers*. Indexing into a list of information can be accomplished by storing the address of the memory location that immediately precedes the beginning of the list in one of the autoindex registers. The first indirect reference to the autoindex register used will cause the address stored there to be incremented by one, thus making it equal to the address of the first word in the list. Subsequent indirect references to this register will generate the addresses of the list elements in sequence.

The basic unit of data is a 12-bit binary integer, as shown in Figure 6.17(b). Bit 0 represents the sign, with a zero indicating a positive number and a one indicating a negative number. Negative numbers are stored in two's-complement form.

The Arithmetic/Logic Unit. The arithmetic/logic unit contains a 12-bit AC and a 1-bit register, called the *link*, that is used to extend the arithmetic facilities of the AC. Two basic operations are possible between the contents of the AC and a word of memory. The contents of a word of memory may be added to the contents of the AC, leaving the result in the AC. [The rules of two's-complement arithmetic are inherent in the instruction.] The logical AND may be performed between the contents of a word of memory and the contents of the AC. Instructions are available to complement the contents of the AC, to load values into the AC, to store the contents of the AC into memory, and to rotate the contents of the link and the AC, either right or left. These instructions, plus a special looping instruction, can be used to program other arithmetic instructions and logic instructions. Subtraction can be performed by complementing and adding, multiplication by successive additions, and division by successive subtractions.

The *extended arithmetic element* (EAE) option permits additional instructions such as multiplication, division, and shifting to be specified in a program. These operations utilize another 12-bit register in the arithmetic/logic unit called the *multiplier-quotient register* (MQ). The MQ may also be used as a temporary storage register.

Instruction Formats and Instruction Sequencing. There are eight basic instructions in the PDP-8/E. These instructions are divided into two types: *memory reference instructions* and *augmented instructions.* One word of storage is required to represent an instruction of either type, and bits 0 through 2 represent the OP code in each case. The format of a memory reference instruction, explained previously, is represented in Figure 6.17(a). Operation codes 0 through 4 represent memory reference instructions.

There are two augmented instructions: the *operate instruction* (OP code 7) and the *I/O transfer instruction* (OP code 6). The operate instruction is used to test and modify the contents of registers in the processing unit. The action carried out by the operate instruction depends on the settings of bits 3 through 11 in the word containing the instruction. The operate instruction consists of three groups of instructions specified by a single bit. These instructions are called *microinstructions*. Bits 3 and 11 are used to determine a group, and bits 4 through 10 are used to specify microinstructions within a group. The format of the operate instruction appears in Figure 6.18(a). Group-one micro-instructions are used to manipulate the contents of the AC and the link. A zero in bit 3 of the instruction indicates a group-one operate instruction. The remaining bits are used to specify the individual microinstructions within the group. For example, if bit 3 is zero and bit 11 is one, the octal representation of the instruction is 7001, which means increment the contents of the AC by one. Similarly, if bit 3 is zero and bit 4 is one, the octal representation is 7200, which means clear the AC. The binary representation of this instruction is shown in Figure 6.18(b). Group-two microinstructions permit the testing of the AC and link and the skipping of the next instruction in sequence, depending on the result of the test. These instructions are usually followed by an *unconditional branch (jump) instruction*. If the condition is met, the next instruction after the unconditional branch instruction is executed; otherwise the branch is taken to another location in memory. These instructions are identified by a one in bit 3 and a zero in bit 11. If bit 3 is one, bit 11 is zero, and bit 5 is one, the octal representation of the instruction is 7500. The instruction means skip the next instruction in sequence if the number in the accumulator is negative. The binary representation of this instruction is shown in Figure 6.18(c). Group-three microinstructions are used to manipulate data between the MQ and AC registers. Available operations are the interchanging of the contents of AC and MQ (clearing both registers) and the performing of a logical OR between the contents of the MQ and AC. Group-three microinstructions are identified by a one in *both* bit 3 and bit 11. Operate microinstructions may be *microprogrammed* (combined) to form composite instructions. For example, if bits 4, 5, and 6 are all one in a group-two operate instruction, the next instruction in sequence is skipped if the contents of the accumulator are less than or equal to zero. The AC is cleared after testing.

The I/O transfer instruction allows communication to take place between the processor and peripheral equipment.* The

---

*A detailed discussion of I/O operations is beyond the scope of this text.

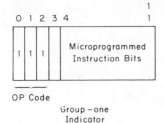

(a) *Format of the operate instruction*

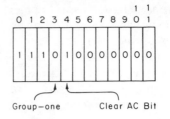

(b) *Clear AC operate instruction*

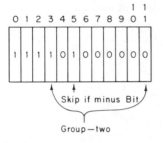

(c) *Skip on negative accumulator instruction*

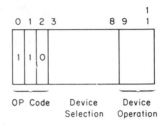

(d) *Format of the input/output transfer instruction*

FIGURE 6.18

format of this instruction is shown in Figure 6.18(d). Another instruction, called the *housekeeping (jump) instruction* (OP code) 5), permits an unconditional branch to any location within a program.

Instructions are fetched from memory, starting at the address in the *program counter* (PC), during the *fetch cycle*. The 3-bit OP code is placed in the *instruction register* (IR). If the instruction is a jump, operate, or I/O transfer instruction, it is executed immediately. If the instruction is a memory reference instruction, the associated memory address is computed, and the *execute cycle* begins. During the execute cycle, the operation is performed between the contents of the AC and the contents of the specified memory address. If the instruction specifies indirect addressing, the computer enters the *defer state*. During this cycle, the effective memory address is obtained indirectly from the current page or page zero. Following the address acquisition, an execute cycle is performed. Instructions are fetched sequentially, unless a jump instruction or group-two operate instruction is encountered. These instructions can modify the address in PC.

Assembler Language. There are several symbolic assemblers available for the PDP-8/E, but we shall consider only the first and most basic assembler language, PAL-III (Program Assembly Language version three). The PAL-III assembler is a two-pass assembler that translates programs written in PAL-III source code into machine language and punches it onto a paper tape using binary representation. The resultant tape is then loaded into memory for execution using a loader program. The format of a PAL-III statement is shown in Figure 6.19.

| LABEL, | OPCODE | OPERAND | /COMMENTS |

FIGURE 6.19   Format of a PAL-III Statement

PAL-III statements are normally entered via a teletype connected to the PDP-8/E and are format free. There are no column restrictions as there are with many card-oriented assemblers. A PAL-III statement must contain one of the four entries and may contain all four. Statement labels may contain any number of letters and numbers—the first must be a letter—but the assembler only retains the first six characters. So the programmer might as well restrict himself to six characters. The label must be immediately followed by a comma. The symbolic OP code may immediately follow the comma after the label, if a label is used. The operand must be separated from the OP code by at least one blank. A slash denotes the end of a statement, and information following the slash is considered to be a comment. Normally, the programmer sets standards for himself concerning the placement of the different fields in a statement. Such standardization yields a more readable program.

Example: A PAL-III program for performing the bubble sort (ascending order) on a list of fifty numbers appears in Figure 6.20. The first column of numbers represents the memory locations of each instruction in octal, and the second column contains the machine instructions in octal. We shall assume that the list has been initialized with the list elements and that the list is stored starting at memory location 3000_8.

The instruction *300 is a pseudo-operation that instructs the assembler to start assigning instructions to memory at address 300_8. The CLA CLL sequence in location 300_8 is a composite group-one operate instruction that clears the AC and the link. The TAD instruction in location 301_8 adds the contents of location N to the AC. Since the AC was previously cleared, this results in loading the value at N into the AC. In location 302_8 the two's complement of N is formed in the AC, and in location 303_8 it is incremented by one to form $-(N-1)$. The DCA instruction in

```
        / PAL-III VERSION OF THE BUBBLE SORT ALGORITHM TO SORT
        / A LIST INTO ASCENDING ORDER.  THE LIST IS STORED
        / STARTING AT LOCATION 3000(OCTAL).
                        *300
0300  7300            CLA CLL              /CLEAR  AC AND LINK
0301  1345            TAD N                /LOAD VALUE OF N INTO AC
0302  7041            CIA                  /FORM 2'S COMPLEMENT OF AC
0303  7001            IAC                  /ADD 1 TO AC TO GET -(N-1)
0304  3346            DCA CNT1             /STORE TO CONTROL OUTSIDE LOOP
0305  1346    PASS,   TAD CNT1             /LOAD REDUCED VALUE OF N INTO AC
0306  3347            DCA CNT2             /STORE TO CONTROL INSIDE LOOP
0307  1350            TAD ALIST            /LOAD ADDRESS OF LIST INTO AC
0310  3351            DCA INDEX1           /STORE FOR INDEXING INTO LIST
0311  1350            TAD ALIST            /LOAD ADDRESS OF LIST INTO AC
0312  7001            IAC                  /ADD ONE TO GET ADDRESS OF
                                           /NEXT ELEMENT
0313  3352            DCA INDEX2           /STORE AT INDEX2
0314  3354            DCA M                /INITIALIZE SORTED-LIST INDICATOR
0315  1752    TEST,   TAD I INDEX2         /LOAD LIST(J+1) INTO AC
0316  7041            CIA                  /COMPLEMENT TO GET NEGATIVE
0317  1751            TAD I INDEX1         /FORM LIST(J)-LIST(J+1)
0320  7710            SPA CLA              /SKIP NEXT INSTRUCTION IF C(AC)>0
                                           /AND CLEAR AC
0321  5333            JMP OK               /BRANCH TO SKIP INTERCHANGE
0322  1751            TAD I INDEX1         /LOAD LIST(J) INTO AC
0323  3353            DCA T                /STORE IN TEMPORARY LOCATION
0324  1752            TAD I INDEX2         /LOAD LIST(J+1) INTO AC
0325  3751            DCA I INDEX1         /STORE AT LIST(J)
0326  1353            TAD T                /LOAD ORIGINAL LIST(J) INTO AC
0327  3752            DCA I INDEX2         /STORE AT LIST(J+1)
0330  1354            TAD M                /LOAD VALUE OF M INTO AC
0331  7001            IAC                  /INCREMENT BY ONE
0332  3354            DCA M                /STORE UPDATED VALUE OF M
0333  2351    OK,     ISZ INDEX1           /ADD 1 TO INDEX1
0334  2352            ISZ INDEX2           /ADD 1 TO INDEX2
0335  2347            ISZ CNT2             /ADD 1 TO COUNTER OF TEST LOOP
0336  5315            JMP TEST             /CONTINUE TESTING PAIRS IF NOT ZERO
0337  1354            TAD M                /LOAD VALUE OF M INTO AC
0340  7710            SPA CLA              /TEST VALUE OF M AND CLEAR AC
0341  5344            JMP SRTD             /LIST IS SORTED IF VALUE OF M=0
0342  2346            ISZ CNT1             /INCREMENT OUTSIDE LOOP COUNTER
0343  5305            JMP PASS             /PASS OVER LIST AGAIN IF NOT ZERO
0344  7402    SRTD,   HLT                  /OTHERWISE, HALT
0345  0062    N,      62           /CONSTANT 50 = 62(OCTAL)
0346  0000    CNT1,   0000         /STORAGE FOR OUTSIDE LOOP COUNTER
0347  0000    CNT2,   0000         /STORAGE FOR INSIDE LOOP COUNTER
0350  3000    ALIST,  3000         /ADDRESS(OCTAL) OF BEGINNING OF LIST
0351  0000    INDEX1, 0000         /STORAGE FOR ADDRESS OF LIST(I)
0352  0000    INDEX2, 0000         /STORAGE FOR ADDRESS OF LIST(I+1)
0353  0000    T,      0000         /TEMPORARY STORAGE LOCATION
0354  0000    M,      0000         /STORAGE FOR SORTED-LIST INDICATOR
```

FIGURE 6.20   PAL-III Version of Bubble Sort Algorithm

location 304_8 stores the result at location CNT.1 and also clears the AC. The value at CNT1 is used in location 342_8; the number at CNT1 is increased by one; and if the result of the addition is zero, the next instruction in sequence is skipped. By placing a jump instruction (unconditional branch) immediately after the ISZ instruction, a loop can be constructed. The location used by the ISZ instruction must be initialized with the negative of the number of times the loop is to be executed, since one is *added* each time the instruction is executed. The counter for the inside loop contains the successive values of the outside loop counter for each execution of the outside loop (locations 305_8 and 306_8). Location ALIST contains the address of the beginning of the list. This address and the address of the second word in the list are stored in locations INDEX1 and INDEX2 (locations 311_8 through 313_8), respectively. These locations are used for indirect addressing into the list. The sort-list indicator M is initialized at zero in location 314_8. The I in the instruction in locations 315_8 and 317_8 means that indirect addressing is to be used. The contents of location INDEX1 and INDEX2 are used as addresses of entries in the list. The difference between LIST(I) and LIST(I + 1) is formed in locations 315_8 through 317_8. The composite instruction in location 320_8 skips the next instruction if the value in the AC is positive and clears the AC. A positive value means that the list entries are out of order, and a skip is made to the interchange section (locations 322_8 through 327_8). In locations 330_8 through 332_8, the value of M is incremented by one to denote that an interchange has taken place. If the value is negative or zero, the next instruction in sequence causes an unconditional branch to the end of the inside loop in location 333_8. The ISZ instructions in locations 333_8 and 334_8 are used to increment the addresses stored at INDEX1 and INDEX2 to compare the next pair of list elements during another execution of the testing loop. These values will not become zero because they started as positive numbers. The instructions in locations 335_8 through 343_8 control the passes through the two program loops. The value of M is tested in locations 337_8 through 341_8; if it is zero, a branch is made to terminate the program. Location 344_8 contains the halt instruction. Locations 345_8 through 354_8 are used for defining constants and storage. Constant definitions are assumed to be in octal. Finally, the $ at the end of the program is used to indicate the end of the assembly.

The IBM System/360

The System/360 is a family of computers consisting of different model sizes. The different models possess *upward compatibility*, meaning that a program that runs on a small model can be run on a larger model with little or no modification. All models have a common machine language and appear logically the same to the programmer. The basic difference between models is the technology employed to implement the instructions. The basic models of System/360 that possess upward compatibility are the 30, 40, 50, 65, and 75. Other specialized models exist at both ends of this range, but they possess some incompatibilities with the basic models. A System/360 model 50 is pictured in Figure 6.21.

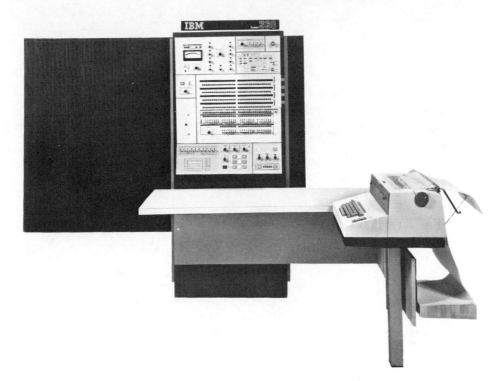

FIGURE 6.21   An IBM System/360 Model 50

The Memory Unit. The basic unit of memory in the System/360 is an 8-bit byte [see Fig. 6.22(a)]. The main memory of a System/360 can contain between 8,192 and 1,048,576 bytes. Bytes are combined together to form larger units of information to be used in arithmetic operations. Two bytes form a *half-word* (sixteen bits); four bytes form a *full word* (thirty-two bits); and eight bytes form a *double word* (sixty-four bits). Half-words and full words are used to represent fixed-point integers in two's complement form, as shown in Figure 6.22(b) and 6.22(c). Floating-point numbers are represented in a full word with a 1-bit sign, a 7-bit exponent field, and a 24-bit fraction field [see Fig. 6.22(d)]. Double-precision, floating-point numbers are represented in a double word with a 1-bit sign field, a 7-bit exponent field, and a 56-bit fraction field [see Fig. 6.22(e)]. The details of these representations were covered in Chapter 4. Although the System/360 uses several other data formats*, we shall examine only the two types just discussed.

*The interested reader may obtain additional information from the *Principles of Operation* manual for the System/360.

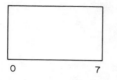

0   7

(a) *One byte*

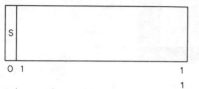

0 1   1
                                    1

(b) *Half-word integer*

0 1   3
                                                                    1

(c) *Full word integer*

0 1   7 8   3
                                                                    1

(d) *Short form floating-point*

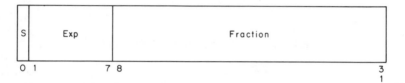

0 1   7 8   6
                                                                   4

(e) *Long form floating-point*

FIGURE 6.22   Data Formats in System/360

The System/360 hardware provides for a 24-bit address for each byte of memory. Half-words, full words, and double words are addressed using the address of their leftmost byte. The address of a half-word must be divisible by two, the address of a full word divisible by four, and the address of a double word divisible by eight. The technique employed for addressing memory cannot be explained without a brief description of part of the arithmetic/

logic unit. The arithmetic/logic unit contains sixteen 32-bit registers (accumulators). They are called *general purpose registers*, since they are used for both fixed-point arithmetic and memory addressing. To conserve space within machine instructions, a memory address is specified by the 4-bit address of a general register (0000 to 1111_2) and a 12-bit displacement. The effective machine address is computed by adding the *contents* of the specified register and the 12-bit displacement. The register used is called the *base register*, and the addressing technique is called *base-displacement addressing*. In Figure 6.23(a) the address portion of an instruction and the associated computation is shown in hexadecimal. The base register is general register 10, and the displacement is $01C_{16}$. The displacements in each program are computed relative to some fixed location and are comparable in use to the absolute addresses generated by the PAL-III assembler. However the base register is loaded with the absolute memory address of the fixed location. Since each displacement is modified by the contents of the base register, the net result is to relocate each instruction in the program by an amount equal to the contents of the base register; thus the program is *relocatable*, meaning that it will work anywhere in memory without changing

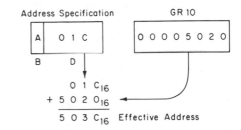

(a) *Base-displacement address computation*

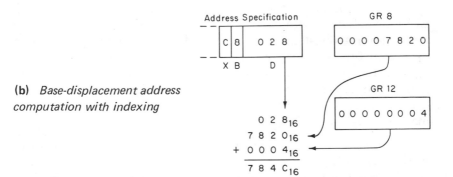

(b) *Base-displacement address computation with indexing*

FIGURE 6.23 System/360 Address Calculation

any memory addresses. Loading the base register with the proper value is the only step necessary to relocate the program.

Some machine instructions allow another register to be specified as an index register. The effective memory address is found by adding together the contents of the base register, the contents of the index register, and the displacement. Figure 6.23(b) shows the computation of an address using general register 8 as a base register and general register 12 as an index register. In each case, the programmer is responsible for loading the proper values into the specified registers.

The Arithmetic/Logic Unit.   The arithmetic/logic unit of the System/360 contains sixteen general purpose 32-bit registers and four 64-bit, floating-point registers, as shown in Figure 6.24. The four basic arithmetic operations are carried out between the contents of a general register and a full word of storage for 32-bit integers and between the contents of a general register and a half-word of storage for 16-bit integers. In addition to these instructions, operations may be performed between the contents of two general registers without any reference to memory. Instructions are available for loading the contents of a half-word or full word of memory into a general register, for storing the contents of a general register in a half-word or full word of memory, for copying the contents of one register into another register, and for loading the address of an instruction operand into a general register.

The four basic arithmetic operations are performed between the contents of a word of memory and the first thirty-two bits of a floating-point register for single precision floating-point numbers and between the contents of a double word and an entire 64-bit, floating-point register for double-precision, floating-point numbers. Operations may also be performed between two floating-point registers using either precision. Instructions are available for loading the contents of a floating-point register from either a full word or double word, for storing the first thirty-two bits of a floating-point register into a full word, and for storing the entire sixty-four bits of a register into a double word. One floating-point register may be loaded with the contents of another floating-point register. Since there are multiple accumulators (registers) for each type of data, it is necessary to specify register addresses within machine instructions.

Instruction Formats and Instruction Sequencing.   Instructions in the System/360 may occupy one, two, or three half-words. The instructions for operating on fixed- and floating-point numbers are of two types: *register-to-register* (RR) *instructions* occupy one half-word, and *register-to-storage* with index (RX) *instructions*

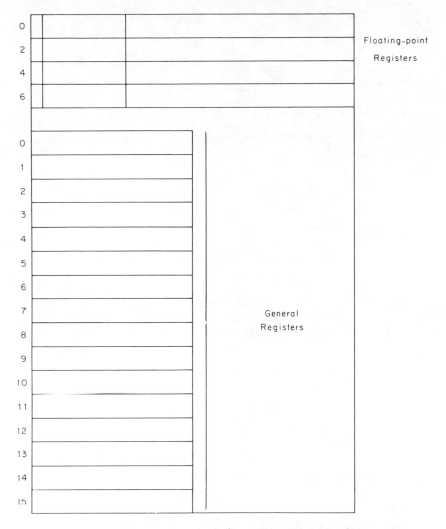

FIGURE 6.24   Arithmetic/Logic Unit of System/360

occupy one full word of memory, as shown in Figure 6.25. In each case, the OP code occupies the first eight bits of the instruction. The RR instructions are used for performing operations between registers. For example, the OP code for performing addition between two fixed-point registers is $1A_{16}$, and the instruction for adding the contents of register 10 to the contents of register 7 is $\boxed{1\,A}\boxed{7\,A}$, expressing each four bits as a hexadecimal digit. The sum is retained in register 7. Similarly, the instruction for loading the contents of register 9 into register 12 would be $\boxed{1\,8}\boxed{C\,9}$, where 18_{16} is the OP code for the load register instruction. The instruction for multiplying the contents of floating-point register 2

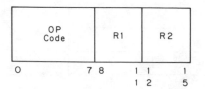

(a) *Format of register-to-register (RR) instructions*

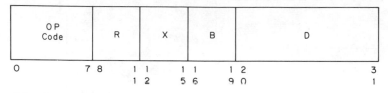

(b) *Format of RX instructions*

FIGURE 6.25   System/360 Instruction Formats

and floating-point register 4 in single precision is $\boxed{3\ \text{C}\ 2\ 4}$. The result is placed in floating-point register 2. The OP code determines whether fixed- or floating-point registers are to be used.

The RX instructions are used for performing operations between a word of memory and a register. Bits 8 through 11 of the instruction specify the address of the register to be used in the operation; bits 12 through 15 specify an index register; bits 16 through 19 specify the base register; and bits 20 through 31 specify the displacement. If indexing is not desired, a zero is placed in the bits that specify the index register. An instruction that loads register 4 from the address, found by adding the contents of general register 7 and a displacement of 038_{16}, is written as $\boxed{1\ 8\ 4\ 0\ 7\ 0\ 3\ 8}$.

Instructions are fetched and executed in sequence, unless a branch instruction is encountered. The address of the next instruction to be executed is determined by bits 40 through 63 of a special double word called the *program status word* (PSW). The fields of the PSW are indicated in Figure 6.26, but only the fields to be discussed here are labelled.* Bits 32 and 33 determine the length of the current instruction in half-words, that is, one (01_2), two (10_2), or three (11_2) half-words. Bits 34 and 35 represent the condition code. The results of some arithmetic operations and all compare instructions cause the condition code to be set in a particular way. The possible settings are 00, 01, 10, and 11. The condition code is tested by a branch on condition instruction, which causes branching to occur if a desired condition is met;

*The use of the remaining fields are specialized and beyond the scope of this discussion.

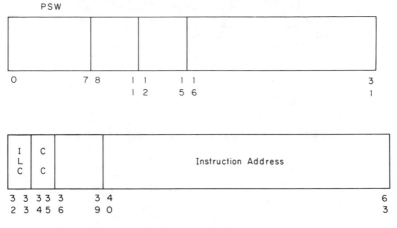

FIGURE 6.26   Program Status Word of System/360

otherwise the next instruction in sequence is executed. For example, the instruction $\boxed{1\ 9\ \text{A}\ 4}$ compares the contents of general register 10 with the contents of general register 4. The condition code will be set to 00_2 if the contents of the two registers are equal, to 01_2 if the contents of register 10 are less than the contents of register 4, and to 10_2 if the contents of register 10 are greater than the contents of register 4. If the contents of general register 10 are less than the contents of general register 4 and the next instruction is $\boxed{4\ 7\ \text{C}\ 0\ 5\ 0\ 1\ 8}$, a branch would be made to the address found by adding the contents of general register 5 to 018_{16}. Bits 8 through 11 of the branching instruction represent the code for testing the condition code for a setting of zero or one.

Assembler Language. The assembler language for the System/360, called BAL (Basic Assembly Language), is translated into relocatable machine language code by a two-pass assembler. Each symbol used is translated into a base-displacement type address. The programmer specifies the point from which all displacements are calculated and also specifies which register the assembler is to use as a base register. The translated program is stored temporarily on magnetic disk and is then stored into memory by a loader program for execution. The format of a BAL statement is shown in Figure 6.27.

A statement may have a symbol consisting of one to eight alphanumeric characters—the first must be a letter. Symbols must start in column 1. The next field contains the symbolic OP code, and only one blank is necessary between the symbol and the OP code. If no symbol is used, the OP code must not start in column 1. The operands field must be separated from the OP code by at

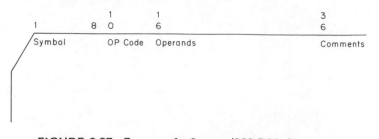

FIGURE 6.27   Format of a System/360 BAL Statement

least one blank, and the comments field must be separated from the operands field by at least one blank. Comments may not extend beyond column 71. A comment card is indicated by placing an asterisk (*) in column 1. The format shown in Figure 6.27 shows the column margins that have been adopted by many BAL programmers.

We shall now conclude the discussion of the System/360 with the BAL version of the bubble sort routine, previously programmed in PAL-III and SAL.

Example: The program for this example appears in Figure 6.28. As before, we shall assume that the list has been read and stored in memory. Line (7) in the program contains the START pseudo-operation, indicating the beginning of the assembly process. The symbol BUBBLE is retained as the name of the program. The instruction in line (10) stores the contents of registers 14, 15, 0, 1, . . . , 12, starting at the memory address found by adding 12_{10} to the contents of register 13. System/360 computers are controlled by a series of complex programs called an *operating system* [see Chapter 9]. The operating system initiates the execution of every job, and control must be returned to the operating system when a job terminates. The purpose of the instruction in line (10) is to save the contents of the registers as they existed just prior to the initiation of the job by the operating system. The operating system provides the address of a save area in register 13. The USING pseudo-operation in statement (11) instructs the assembler to calculate all displacements relative to the location named BUBBLE and to use register 3 as the base register when replacing each symbolic address by a base and displacement. In line (12) the contents of register 15 are loaded into the base register (register 3). When the operating system transfers control to a program, the address of the first instruction in the program is in register 15. This register therefore contains the absolute memory address of location BUBBLE. Loading this value into register 3 sets the base register for the program. In line (13) the contents of register 13 are stored in memory.

```
LOC     OBJECT CODE  ADDR1 ADDR2  STMT  SOURCE STATEMENT

                                  1   * ************************************************
                                  2   *     SYSTEM/360 BAL VERSION OF THE BUBBLE SORT ALGORITHM  *
                                  3   *     TO SORT A LIST INTO ASCENDING ORDER.                 *
                                  4   *                                                          *
                                  5   * ************************************************
                                  6   ************************************************
000000                            7   BUBBLE  START
                                  9   *       STANDARD ENTRY SEQUENCE
000000  90EC 000C          00000C  10         STM   14,12,12(13)     SAVE CONTENTS OF REGISTERS
000000                            11         USING BUBBLE,3          DECLARE GR3 AS BASE REGISTER
000004  183F                      12         LR    3,15              LOAD ENTRY ADDRESS INTO GR3
000006  50D0 3050          00050  13         ST    13,SAVE13         SAVE C(GR13)
                                  15  *       INITIALIZATION FOR SORTING SECTION
00000A  5850 3054          00054  16         L     5,N               LOAD VALUE OF N INTO GR5
00000E  5850 3058          00058  17         S     5,ONE             REDUCE C(GR5) BY ONE
000012  1B88                      18  PASS   SR    8,8               ZERO GR8 FOR INDEXING
000014  1828                      19         LR    2,8               GR2 CONTAINS VALUE OF M
000016  18A5                      20         LR    10,5              LOAD GR10 TO CONTROL INNER LOOP
000018  5868 305C          0005C  21  TEST   L     6,LIST(8)         LOAD LIST(I) INTO GR6
00001C  5878 3060          00060  22         L     7,LIST+4(8)       LOAD LIST(I+1) INTO GR7
000020  1967                      23         CR    6,7               COMPARE LIST(I) WITH LIST(I+1)
000022  4700 3032          00032  24         BNH   OK                BRANCH TO END LOOP IF LIST(I) IS
                                                                     LESS THAN OR EQUAL TO LIST(I+1)
                                  26  *       INTERCHANGE SECTION
000026  5068 3060          00060  27         ST    6,LIST+4(8)       STORE VALUE OF LIST(I) AT LIST(I+1)
00002A  5078 305C          0005C  28         ST    7,LIST(8)         STORE VALUE OF LIST(I+1) AT LIST(I)
00002E  4122 0001          00001  29         LA    2,1(2)            INCREASE VALUE OF M BY ONE
000032  4188 0004          00004  30  CK     LA    8,4(8)            INCREMENT GR8 BY FOUR
000036  46A0 301B          0001B  31         BCT   10,TEST           BRANCH ON COUNT TO TEST
00003A  1222                      32         LTR   2,2               TEST VALUE OF M
00003C  4780 3044          00044  33         BZ    SORTED            IF ZERO, LIST IS SORTED.
000040  4650 3012          00012  34         BCT   5,PASS            BRANCH ON COUNT TO PASS
                                  36  *       STANDARD EXIT SEQUENCE
000044  58D0 3050          00050  37  SORTED L     13,SAVE13         RESTORE REGISTER 13
000048  98EC 000C          0000C  38         LM    14,12,12(13)      RELOAD THE REGISTERS FROM SAVE AREA
00004C  07FE                      39         BR    14                BRANCH TO THE ADDRESS IN GR14
                                  41  *       CONSTANTS AND STORAGE
000050                            42  SAVE13 DS    F                 SAVE AREA FOR GR13
000054  00000032                  43  N      DC    F'150'            VALUE OF N
000058  00000001                  44  ONE    DC    F'1'              CONSTANT ONE
00005C                            45  LIST   DS    200F              STORAGE FOR LIST
000000                            46         END   BUBBLE
```

FIGURE 6.28   BAL Version of the Bubble Sort Algorithm

The value of N is loaded into register 5 and reduced by one in lines (16) and (17). Register 5 is used to control the necessary $N-1$ passes through the outer loop. The *branch-on-count instruction* (BCT) in line (34) is the last instruction in the outer loop. The value of register 5 is decreased by one, and if the result is not equal to zero, a branch is made to PASS; otherwise the next instruction in sequence is executed. In line (18) register 8 is cleared by subtracting it from itself. Register 8 is used as an index register into LIST. Register 2 is initialized at zero and contains the value of the sorted-loop indicator M. Register 10 is used to control the passes through the inner loop. The BCT instruction in line (31) decrements and tests register 10. The contents of register 5 are loaded into register 10 in line (20). Register 5 contains the successive values $N-1, N-2, \ldots, 3, 2, 1$, as the outer loop is repeatedly executed. The symbol LIST is the address of the first word of the list of numbers, and the symbolic expression LIST + 4 represents the address of the second word in the list. A four is added to LIST because addressing is carried out in terms of bytes, and there are four bytes in a full word. These two symbols are indexed, using register 8 in lines (21) and (22), when loading two consecutive elements into registers 6 and 7. The two list elements are compared in line (23), and a branch is made if the elements are in order [line (24)]. Otherwise, the two list elements are interchanged in lines (27) and (28). Since both elements are in registers, they are interchanged simply by storing each at the other's memory location. The instruction in line (29) is a special usage of the *load address* (LA) *instruction*. The contents of register 2 and the constant one are added together and retained in register 2. The effective result is to update index register 2 by one, thus increasing the value of M. The LA instruction is used again in line (30) to update the index register by four—the number of bytes in a full word. The current value of M, the sorted-list indicator, is tested prior to the reexecution of the outer loop in line (32). If it is zero, the list has been sorted, and a branch is made out of the outer loop.

The instructions in lines (37) through (39) return control to the operating system. Register 13 is restored to its original value, and the remaining registers are then reloaded with the values stored in line (10). The instruction in line (39) causes a branch to the address contained in register 14. The address in register 14 is the return point in the operating system. The pseudo-operations in lines (42)–(45) reserve storage for symbols and, in two cases, also define constants. In line (42) the symbol SAVE13 is assigned to one full word of storage. The constant 50 is stored as an integer in a full word in line (43). Two-hundred full words are reserved at

LIST in line (45). Finally, the END pseudo-operation in line (46) terminates the assembly.

Many features of the two computers discussed were omitted intentionally, since their study is beyond the scope of this text. The features presented were chosen to show the similarities and differences between two existing computer systems and to give the reader a chance to compare these features to the hypothetical computer developed in the beginning of the chapter. Additional features of the PDP-8/E and PAL-III assembly language can be found in two DEC publications: the *PDP-8/E Small Computer Handbook* and *Introduction to Programming*. Additional features of the System/360 computers and BAL can be found in two IBM manuals: *System/360 Principles of Operation* and *System/360 Assembler Language*.

EXERCISES

1. What is meant by the *stored-program* concept?

2. Describe the structures of the memory unit, arithmetic/logic unit, I/O units, and the control unit of the ES-EL/410.

3. How is addressing implemented in the ES-EL/410?

4. Write an ES-EL/410 machine language program to evaluate

$$Y = \frac{[(A + B)/(C - D)]^2}{(E \cdot F)^3}$$

5. Distinguish between the fetch and execute cycles.

6. How does the ES-EL/410 implement branch instructions?

7. Describe the operation of the two-pass assembler.

8. Write a SAL program to determine prime numbers between any two given positive even integers [see Chapter 3, Exercise 15].

9. Write a SAL program to structure a list of data using the hashing technique illustrated in Figure 5.20 and then search for a given number of input values [see Fig. 5.21].

10. Write a SAL program that will convert any given decimal integer to its octal representation.

11. Compare and contrast the addressing techniques implemented in the ES-EL/410, the PDP-8/E, and the System/360.

SELECTED REFERENCES

Barron, D.W., *Assemblers and Loaders,* New York: American Elsevier, 1969.

Bergman, Samuel, and Steven Bruckner, *Computers and Computer Programming,* Reading, Mass,: Addison-Wesley, 1972.

Cole, R. Wade, *Introduction to Computing,* New York: McGraw-Hill, 1969.

Computers and Automation, Computer Directory and Buyers' Guide Issue, Vol. 20, No. 6B (June 30, 1971), pp. 27-54.

Gear, C. William, *Computer Organization and Programming,* New York: McGraw-Hill, 1969.

Hull, T.E., *Introduction to Computing,* Englewood Cliffs, N.J.: Prentice-Hall, 1966.

IBM System/360 Operating System Assembler Language, Form C28-6514, IBM Corporation.

IBM System/360 Principles of Operation, Form A22-6821, IBM Corporation.

Introduction to Programming, PDP-8 Family Computers, Maynard, Mass.: Digital Equipment Corporation.

PDP-8/E Small Computer Handbook, Maynard, Mass.: Digital Equipment Corporation.

Programming Languages, PDP-8 Family Computers, Maynard, Mass.: Digital Equipment Corporation.

Walker, Terry M., *Introduction to Computer Science: An Interdisciplinary Approach,* Boston: Allyn and Bacon, 1972.

7

Algorithms and Flowcharts — Subalgorithms

Complete generalization of some algorithms requires a design that is flexible enough to represent a solution to a class of problems that are themselves subproblems of a larger class of problems. Such generalization extends beyond the construction of a procedure capable of handling any number of data items or sets of data items. The task is to develop a method for performing a procedure two or more times with one or more variable names altered for each execution. The demands of generalization might even require multiple part algorithms, where each part is designed by a different person, but the final version of the algorithm is composed of all the assembled parts. Any algorithm whose structure permits either type of usage is called a *subalgorithm*.

CONCEPT OF SUBALGORITHMS

Consider the flowchart form of the algorithm for finding the factorial of a nonnegative integer stated in Figure 3.19. Let us assume that the solution to a given problem requires that the input of several data items—all with different variable names—be followed by the computation of the factorial of each of those input values. The steps in the factorial algorithm would have to be included in the solution of the main problem, appearing as many times as the number of variables that are input. Yet, in each case, the only change in the factorial algorithm would be the replace-

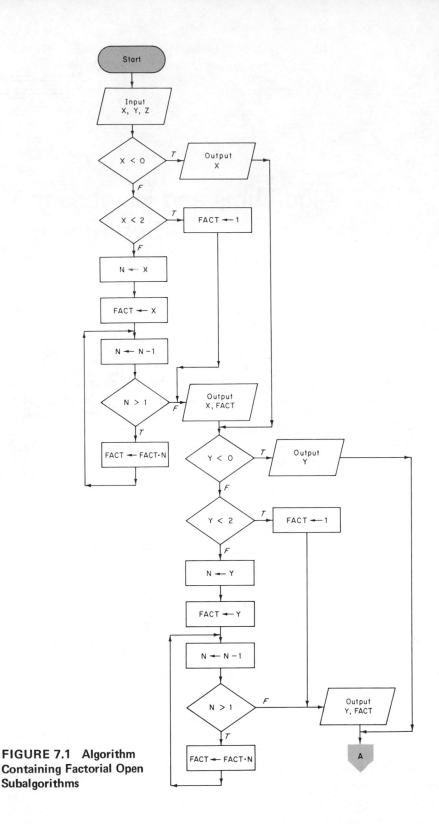

FIGURE 7.1 Algorithm Containing Factorial Open Subalgorithms

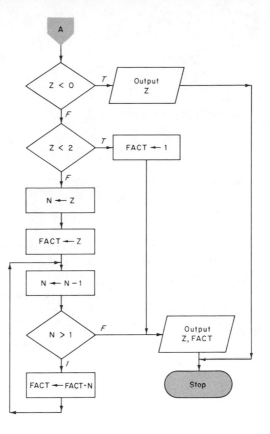

FIGURE 7.1 (Con't)

ment of the variable name NUMBER by the new input variable name. The result would be an algorithm like the one in flowchart form in Figure 7.1. Each occurrence of the factorial algorithm constitutes an *open subalgorithm*.

Obviously, such a technique becomes overwhelmingly redundant for a large number of different variables. The alternative is to make the open subalgorithm, which requires multiple execution, independent of the main algorithm. The factorial algorithm has already been developed as a separate entity. All that remains is to find a method that keeps it separate from yet affords a link to the main algorithm, when necessary. The desired structure is schematically illustrated in Figure 7.2, where the factorial algorithm now constitutes a *closed subalgorithm*.

The process involves a branch from one algorithm to the other. Whenever a step in the main algorithm necessitates the calculation of the factorial of a positive integer, a branch to the factorial subalgorithm takes place. The subalgorithm is executed, followed by a return to the main algorithm. The procedure is repeated at any other step in the main algorithm that requires a factorial

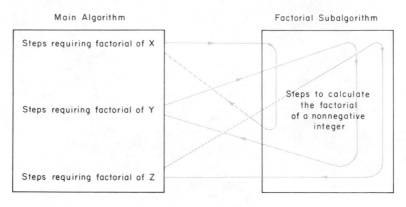

FIGURE 7.2

value. The main algorithm is termed the *invoking procedure*, and
the subalgorithm becomes the *invoked procedure*. The step in the
invoking algorithm that calls for the use of a subalgorithm is
referred to as the *point of invocation*. Following execution of the
subalgorithm, it is necessary to return to the point of invocation.
The step in the subalgorithm to which control is transferred is
labeled the *entry point*. A subalgorithm may have more than one
entry point. A main algorithm can invoke several subalgorithms in
the course of execution, and each subalgorithm can in turn invoke
other subalgorithms. Subalgorithms are classified as either *implicit*
or *explicit*, depending on the manner in which they are invoked.
In the first case, the use of a subalgorithm is implied in an
assignment statement that requires a function to be performed on
a given variable, returning the functional value to the invoking
algorithm. This type of subalgorithm is also called a *function
subalgorithm*. In the second case, the use of a subalgorithm is
explicitly stated as a predefined process to be performed from
which values may or may not be returned to the invoking
algorithm. A subalgorithm in this classification is often referred to
as a *subroutine*. Both of these types of subalgorithms will be
discussed in greater detail in the following section.

Clearly, the invoking of a subalgorithm and the consequent
return to the invoking algorithm necessitate the transfer of key
information to and from each algorithm. In the algorithms
developed in previous chapters, the communication of information
was primarily restricted to connecting the outside world with the
algorithm. The use of subalgorithms requires the development of
methods for communicating information among algorithms and
subalgorithms.

COMMUNICATION AMONG
ALGORITHMS AND SUBALGORITHMS

Algorithms and subalgorithms must be linked to each other by the communication of certain key information. First, the process of invoking a subalgorithm implies that the subalgorithm can be found or located by the main algorithm. This is accomplished by assigning a name to the subalgorithm, usually at the point of entry. This name appears in the main algorithm in any step requiring the invoking of the subalgorithm, and the transfer of control is thereby established. The second aspect of communication is considered with reference to Figure 7.2. It is apparent that each time the factorial subalgorithm is invoked, a value of a different variable in the main algorithm must be made available to the subalgorithm. This value must be assigned to a variable in the subalgorithm in such a way that it is duplicated, thus leaving the value of the variable in the main algorithm unaltered. Such a transfer of information is accomplished through an *argument* or *parameter list*. Within the invoking algorithm, the list is referred to as the *actual* parameter list, while in the invoked subalgorithm, it is referred to as the *formal* parameter list. [The latter is sometimes called a dummy argument list.] The correspondence of variables between the two lists is one-to-one. Any variables in a subalgorithm not present in either parameter list are considered to be *local* variable names. Any change in the value of a local variable does not transfer to any other algorithm. Applying the discussion specifically to the factorial problem, the actual parameter list for the first invoking of the subalgorithm consists of X; for the second invoking, it consists of Y; and for the final invoking, it consists of Z. In each case, the formal parameter list for the subalgorithm consists of NUMBER.

Finally, a method for making information from a subalgorithm available to the invoking algorithm must be determined. The return of a value or set of values depends on whether an invoked algorithm is implicit or explicit. If an algorithm is implicitly invoked as a function, its name will appear in the main algorithm in an expression. A functional value of some expression is calculated by the invoked algorithm, and this value is returned to the main algorithm via the name of the invoked algorithm. When an algorithm is explicitly invoked as a subroutine, however, the process to be performed may or may not return values to the invoking algorithm. No functional evaluation is indicated, and the invoking of the subalgorithm is not part of an assignment statement. Consequently, both the transfers of values (if any) from the subalgorithm are accomplished via the parameter list.

The communication of information among algorithms therefore involves three items:

1. a name for each subalgorithm,
2. an actual parameter list (invoking algorithm) and a formal parameter list (invoked algorithm), and
3. a method for returning values to the invoking algorithm.

Parts (a) and (c) of Figure 7.3 illustrate the method for indicating these items when an algorithm invokes a function subalgorithm. The main algorithm contains a process symbol, indicating the name of the subalgorithm, followed by the actual parameter list in parentheses. The variable to the left of the arrow will be assigned the functional value that is returned. The subalgorithm flowchart contains a notation symbol at the point of entry that indicates the name and the formal parameter list. In addition, it is necessary to

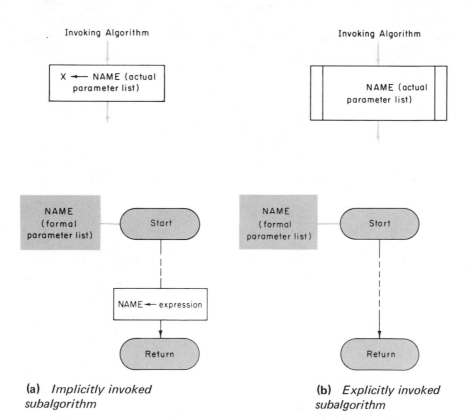

(a) *Implicitly invoked subalgorithm*

(b) *Explicitly invoked subalgorithm*

FIGURE 7.3   Flowchart Forms for Invoking Subalgorithms

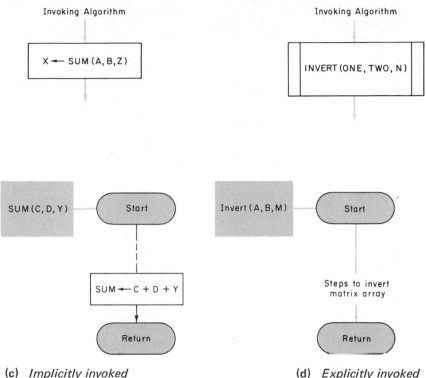

(c) *Implicitly invoked subalgorithm*

(d) *Explicitly invoked subalgorithm*

FIGURE 7.3   (Con't)

have a step in the subalgorithm in which the calculated functional value is assigned to the name of the subalgorithm. The RETURN symbol is used to indicate the termination of processing in the subalgorithm, resulting in the transfer of control back to the point of invocation in the main algorithm. In parts (b) and (d) of Figure 7.3 the flowchart representation for invoking a subroutine subalgorithm uses a *predefined process* symbol in the main algorithm. The name of the invoked subalgorithm is indicated within this enclosure, followed by the actual parameter list in parentheses. The flowchart for the invoked subalgorithm contains the notation symbol at the point of entry as well as a RETURN symbol at the end of the flowchart. Note that there is no assignment of value to the subalgorithm name, since any values returned will be transferred via the parameter list.

Example: The full flowchart version of the factorial problem utilizing the subalgorithm concept is given in Figure 7.4. The invoking of FACT occurs three times, and in each case, the actual argument list consists of the value of one variable. This value is

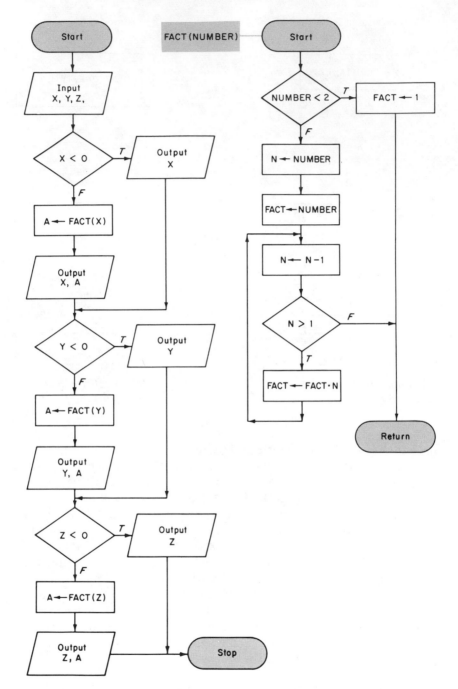

FIGURE 7.4   Factorial Subalgorithm

transferred to the formal argument list in FACT that contains the single variable NUMBER. The steps within FACT do not alter the value of NUMBER during execution; while N is by definition a local variable. The returned value of the factorial is transferred via the subalgorithm name FACT and is assigned to a variable A in the main algorithm. Note that the validity tests for the input have been placed in the invoking algorithm. Previously, in Figure 3.19, such values caused termination of the algorithm. If such a termination step were included in the subalgorithm in Figure 7.4, however, no return would take place; consequently there would be no way to calculate the factorial for any other values.

In Chapter 5, Figure 5.9 illustrated an algorithm for sorting a linear list into ascending order. This algorithm is now presented in Figure 7.5 as an explicitly invoked subalgorithm.

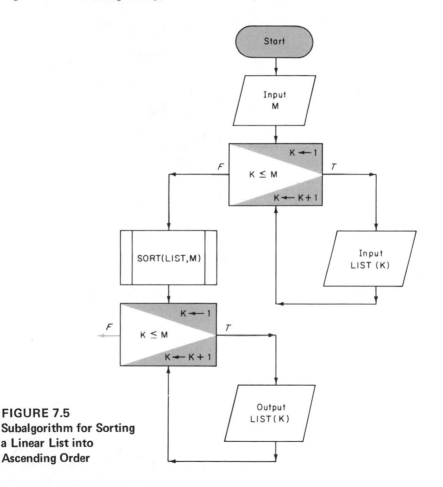

FIGURE 7.5
Subalgorithm for Sorting
a Linear List into
Ascending Order

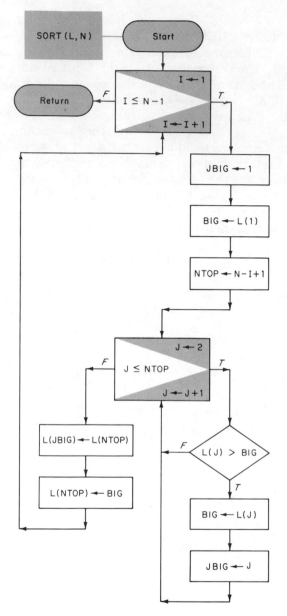

FIGURE 7.5 (Con't)

Example: A linear list identified as LIST, consisting of M
elements, is input in the main algorithm. The subalgorithm, SORT,
is then invoked in the predefined process symbol, and the actual

parameter list indicates that the values of LIST and the value of M are to be made available to the subalgorithm. The formal parameter list for SORT indicates that these values will be assigned to L and N, respectively. Execution of the subalgorithm causes the elements in L to be sorted, thereby producing the same result in LIST. Note that the value of M remains the same, since subalgorithm SORT did not alter the value of N; thus the correct number of elements of LIST are output in the main algorithm. Any other variable names in either the main algorithm or the subalgorithm are considered to be local.

The type of subalgorithm selected for any given problem obviously depends on the task to be performed. A function subalgorithm is applicable when a series of steps is necessary to produce a single value. The actual parameter list can contain more than one value, but only one value can be returned to the invoking algorithm. The use of subroutine subalgorithms is justified when the solution to a problem requires either the alteration of given values or the creation of new values for variables not yet assigned values in the main algorithm. However the utilization of subalgorithms as an essential part of the solution to a problem is a valid generalization only if a series of instructions must be executed several times at different points in the main algorithm with possibly different variable names. Further examples of the use of function and subroutine subalgorithms are illustrated in the final section of this chapter. We now turn to a discussion of the computer instructions and techniques used when linking algorithms and subalgorithms for execution.

MACHINE IMPLEMENTATION OF SUBALGORITHMS

The assembler language developed for the ES-EL/410 machine in Chapter 6 enabled algorithms to be stated in program form. Since subalgorithms can also be stated in program form, our discussion of linkage between programs and subprograms in a machine can be accomplished by referring to the techniques used by the ES-EL/410.

The concept of *addressing* is the key to the transferral of information between programs. First, an argument list must be created within the invoking program. Consider the following set of SAL instructions in a program that calls the subroutine SORT(A,N), where A is the name of a list with N elements.

```
            LDA    A,1
            STX    ARGS,1
            LDA    N,1
            STX    ARGS + 1,1
              .
              .
              .

ARGS    DSTR   2
A       DSTR   200
N       DSTR   1
```

The first instruction loads the address of location A into index register 1. This address is then stored in the first word at location ARGS. The next two instructions similarly store the address of N in the second word at location ARGS. The argument list is now established, since the address of the first element in list A and the address of the value of N can be found in ARGS. The argument list is therefore a list of addresses. Note that the construction of the argument list is dynamic in the sense that it enables the subroutine to be called more than once and also makes it possible for any named list to be passed as an argument. The following two instructions indicate an alternate form for the argument list that is useful if the subroutine is invoked only once with a specific list.

```
        ARGS   ACON   A
               ACON   N
```

The load and store instructions would not be necessary in this case.

The name of the subprogram to which control is transferred must be made available to the main program. This is accomplished by declaring an external constant within the calling program that contains the address of that name. The first instruction of the invoked subprogram can thus be located. Finally, proper return to the invoking program must occur at the address of the instruction immediately following the invoking instruction. This address must therefore be made available to the subprogram.

We now identify a calling sequence for a program that invokes the subroutine SORT.

```
            LDA    ARGS,1
            LOAD   ENTR
            LINK   2
              .
              .
              .

ENTR    XCON   SORT
ARGS    DSTR   2
```

The first statement indicates that index register 1 is loaded with the address of the argument list. The accumulator is then loaded with the address of the entry point of the subroutine. Finally, a Link instruction causes the address of the next instruction in the calling program to be stored in index register 2, followed by a branch to the address in the AC.

Since essential information relating to the linkage of the two programs exists in the index registers, it must not be destroyed. But the subprogram must have these registers available during execution. The first set of instructions in the subprogram therefore saves the contents of the index registers, as indicated in the following sequence of instructions.

```
SORT   STRT
       STX    SAVE,1
       STX    SAVE + 1,2
       STX    SAVE + 2,3
       STX    SAVE + 3,4
            .
            .
            .

       SAVE   DSTR   4
```

The contents of the index registers are stored in four words starting at SAVE—one register per word. The address of the argument list is stored at SAVE, while the address of the point of return in the main program is stored at SAVE + 1. The index registers can now be used without destroying critical linkage information. When processing in the subprogram is complete, the original contents of the registers are restored before returning to the main program, as the following sequence illustrates.

```
LDX   SAVE,1
LDX   SAVE + 1,2
LDX   SAVE + 2,3
LDX   SAVE + 3,4
BRI   2
```

The last instruction results in a branch to the address contained in index register 2—namely, the instruction in the invoking program to which control is returned.

Example: Figure 7.6 illustrates the SAL version of the flowchart given in Figure 7.5. The invoking program, called PRGM, first creates an argument list (steps 7 − 10) and then stores M elements of the linear list LIST (steps 13 − 17). Steps 18 − 20 make up the calling sequence for invoking the sorting subroutine named SORT. Within the subprogram SORT, after saving the registers, the first

```
(1)  PRGM  STRT
(2)        READ              READ NO. OF ELEMENTS IN LIST
(3)        BIN               CONVERT TO BINARY
(4)        BN    ERR         TEST VALIDITY OF VALUE OF
(5)        BZ    ERR         NO. OF ELEMENTS IN LIST
(6)        STOR  M           STORE NO. OF ELEMENTS AT M
 +   CREATE ARGUMENT LIST TO ENABLE INVOKING OF ROUTINE SORT
(7)        LDA   LIST,1      LOAD ADDRESS OF LIST INTO INDEX REGISTER 1
(8)        STX   ARGS,1      STORE CONTENTS OF INDEX REGISTER 1
 +                          IN FIRST WORD OF ARGS
(9)        LDA   M,1         LOAD ADDRESS OF M INTO INDEX REGISTER 1
(10)       STX   ARGS+1,1    STORE CONTENTS OF INDEX REGISTER 1
 +                          IN SECOND WORD OF ARGS
(11)       LDX   ZERO,4      INDEX REGISTER 4 USED TO INDEX INTO LIST
(12)       LDX   M,1         INDEX REGISTER 1 USED TO CONTROL LOOPING
(13) INPT  READ              READ AN ELEMENT OF LIST
(14)       BIN               CONVERT TO BINARY
(15)       STOR  LIST,4      STORE VALUE IN LIST
(16)       ADX   4,1         ADD ONE TO INDEX REGISTER 4
(17)       LOOP  INPT,1      BRANCH BACK TO READ NEXT VALUE
 +   CALL SORT ROUTINE
(18)       LDA   ARGS,1      LOAD ADDRESS OF ARGUMENT LIST INTO INDEX REGISTER 1
(19)       LOAD  ENTR        LOAD ADDRESS OF ENTRY POINT OF SORT INTO AC
(20)       LINK  2           INDEX REGISTER 2 CONTAINS ADDRESS OF NEXT INSTRUCTION
 +   RETURN FROM SUBROUTINE
(21)       LDX   ZERO,4      INDEX REGISTER 4 USED TO INDEX INTO LIST
(22)       LDX   M,1         INDEX REGISTER 1 USED TO CONTROL LOOPING
(23) OUT   LOAD  LIST,1      LOAD LIST(I) INTO AC
(24)       BCD               CONVERT TO BCD
(25)       PRNT              PRINT ELEMENT
(26)       ADX   1,1         INCREASE INDEX REGISTER
(27)       LOOP  OUT,4       BRANCH TO CONTINUE PRINTING
(28)       HALT              TERMINATE PROCESSING
(29) ERR   PRNT              PRINT INVALID VALUE OF NO. OF ELEMENTS
(30)       HALT              TERMINATE PROCEDURE
(31) ZERO  DCON  0           CONSTANT ZERO
(32) M     DSTR  1           STORAGE FOR NO. OF ELEMENTS IN LIST
(33) LIST  DSTR  200         STORAGE FOR LIST
(34) ARGS  DSTR  2           ARGUMENT LIST STORAGE
(35) ENTR  XCON  SORT        EXTERNAL ADDRESS OF SUBROUTINE SORT
(36)       END
```

FIGURE 7.6

address of the argument list is used to store the address of LIST at
location L (steps 6 and 7). The second address of the argument list
is used to load the value of M into the accumulator(steps 8 − 11).
Index register 4 is assigned the value of M, since it will be used as
the index of the outer loop. This value also becomes the maximum
number of times the inner loop is perfomed and is therefore stored
at MTOP for proper exchange of list values upon completion of
the inner loop. Step 16 is thus equivalent in purpose to the step in
the flowchart that initialized NTOP at $N - I + 1$. The address of
the first element of L is stored at JBIG in step 18, and the value of
that element of L is stored at BIG (steps 19 and 20). The
comparison of each consecutive value of L with the current value
of BIG is accomplished in steps 21 and 22, with a branch to OK if
the difference is zero or positive. Otherwise, the address of L(J) is
stored at JBIG (step 25), and the value of L(J) is stored at BIG
(steps 26 and 27). Upon completion of the inner loop, the value of
L(MTOP) is stored at the address of L(JBIG) in steps 29 through
32. The value of BIG is stored at the address of L(MTOP) (steps

```
( 1)   SORT  STRT
( 2)         STX   SAVE,1   SAVE CONTENTS OF
( 3)         STX   SAVE+1,2 INDEX REGISTERS
( 4)         STX   SAVE+2,3 (NOT NECESSARY TO
( 5)         STX   SAVE+3,4 SAVE CONTENTS OF AC)
( 6)         LOAD  1        ADDRESS OF ARGUMENT LIST STORED IN AC
( 7)         STOR  L        STORE ADDRESS AT L
( 8)         ADX   1,1      ADD ONE TO INDEX REGISTER 1
( 9)         LOAD  1        LOAD SECOND ADDRESS IN ARGUMENT LIST INTO AC
(10)         LACX  4        LOAD ADDRESS OF M INTO INDEX REGISTER 4
(11)         LOAD  4        LOAD VALUE OF M INTO AC
(12)         LACX  4        LOAD VALUE OF M INTO INDEX REGISTER 4
(13)         LOOP  NEXT,4   DECREASE INDEX REGISTER 4 BY ONE, GO TO NEXT
+        OUTER LOOP TO CONTROL NO. OF ELEMENTS SCANNED IN EACH PASS OF LIST
(14)   NEXT  STX   MTOP,4   STORE VALUE OF M-1 AT MTOP
(15)         LDX   MTOP,3   LOAD REDUCED VALUE OF M INTO INDEX REGISTER 3
(16)         LDX   L,1      LOAD ADDRESS OF LIST INTO REGISTER 1
(17)         STX   JBIG,1   STORE ADDRESS OF L(1) AT JBIG
(18)         LOAD  1        LOAD VALUE OF L(1) INTO AC
(19)         STOR  BIG      STORE VALUE OF L(1) AT BIG
+        LOOP TO LOCATE BIGGEST VALUE AND CORRESPONDING SUBSCRIPT
(20)   TEST  ADX   1,1      INCREASE INDEX REGISTER 1 BY ONE
(21)         SUB   1        SUBTRACT L(J) FROM CURRENT VALUE OF BIG
(22)         BZ    OK
(23)         BP    OK
(24)         STX   JBIG,1   STORE ADDRESS OF LIST ELEMENT AT JBIG
(25)         LOAD  1        LOAD L(J) INTO AC
(26)         STOR  BIG      STORE AT BIG
(27)   OK    LOOP  TEST,3   CONTINUE INNER LOOP
+        INTERCHANGE LAST ELEMENT WITH CURRENT LARGEST ELEMENT
(28)         LOAD  JBIG     AC NOW CONTAINS ADDRESS OF L(JBIG)
(29)         LACX  2        LOAD ADDRESS OF L(JBIG) INTO INDEX REGISTER 2
(30)         LOAD  1        LOAD VALUE OF L(MTOP) INTO AC
(31)         STOR  2        VALUE OF L(MTOP) STORED AT L(JBIG)
(32)         LOAD  BIG      VALUE OF BIG STORED IN AC
(33)         STOR  1        VALUE OF L(MTOP) REPLACED BY VALUE OF BIG
(34)         LOOP  NEXT,4   CONTINUE OUTER LOOP
+        RETURN TO INVOKING ROUTINE
(35)         LDX   SAVE,1   RESTORE ORIGINAL CONTENTS
(36)         LDX   SAVE+1,2 OF INDEX REGISTERS
(37)         LDX   SAVE+2,3
(38)         LDX   SAVE+3,4
(39)         BRI   2        BRANCH TO ADDRESS IN INDEX REGISTER 2
(40)   SAVE  DSTR  4        INDEX REGISTER SAVE AREA
(41)   L     DSTR  1        STORAGE FOR ADDRESS OF LIST
(42)   MTOP  DSTR  1        STORAGE FOR CURRENT TOP OF LIST
(43)   JBIG  DSTR  1        STORAGE FOR ADDRESS OF BIGGEST ELEMENT
(44)   BIG   DSTR  1        STORAGE FOR BIGGEST ELEMENT
(45)   ZERO  DCON  0        CONSTANT ZERO
(46)         END
```

FIGURE 7.6 (Con't)

33 and 34), and the outer loop continues. After the sorting routine is completed, return to the main program occurs, as explained earlier. Steps $21-27$ in PRGM output the sorted list. Note that the restoring of index registers permits register 1 to be used for indexing into LIST, since the first address of the argument list is stored in that register.

The invoking of function subprograms is identical to the procedure just discussed, except that in the ES-EL/410 the value of the function is returned in the AC. It is therefore necessary to load the value into the AC before returning to the invoking program. When subprograms invoke other subprograms, the same calling sequence applies. In those cases where the argument lists are identical, however, it is not necessary to create new argument lists. The process of saving and restoring registers must still be performed. In general, the use of subprograms necessitates the use of a *loader program*. The function of a loader program is to store machine language programs into memory consecutively. Normally, machine language versions of subprograms are placed in memory following the main program. When the assembler translates SAL programs, all addresses are determined relative to zero. Assuming that main programs are loaded into memory starting at location 0, the addresses of the entry points of any subprograms are no longer equal to zero. Since memory addresses used within each subprogram were originally determined relative to the beginning of the subprogram, however, these addresses must be modified by adding the new entry point address of the subprogram to each of them. It is the responsibility of the loader to modify these addresses and to provide the proper entry point addresses for all XCON statements that appeared in the main program and the subprograms.

FUNCTION AND SUBROUTINE SUBALGORITHMS

We now present three examples of the use of function and subroutine subalgorithms. The first incorporates the binary search technique introduced in Chapter 5 [see Fig. 5.15].

Example: The flowchart in Figure 7.7(a) represents the steps in the invoking algorithm. After input of the elements of LIST, the subroutine SORT [see Fig. 7.5] is invoked, causing the elements of the linear list to be arranged in ascending order. The second loop provides for input of K values—one at a time. The function subalgorithm [see Fig. 7.7(b)] is then invoked, resulting in a binary search of LIST. If the value of Y is in the list, the subscript value is returned via the subalgorithm name BIN and assigned to NUM in the main algorithm. A value of zero is returned, however, if Y is not found in the list. Following the test, the appropriate output occurs, and the loop execution continues.

Figure 7.8 illustrates the flowchart form of a subroutine subalgorithm for traversing a binary tree.

Example: The name of the subroutine is TRAVRSE, and the formal parameter list indicates that TREE and ROOT are passed to the subalgorithm. In this case, the invoking algorithm would have already accomplished the construction of the binary tree. Neither the elements of TREE nor the value of ROOT are altered by this subalgorithm. Output of the values stored in TREE occurs entirely within the subalgorithm. A return to the main algorithm consequently leaves all values preserved.

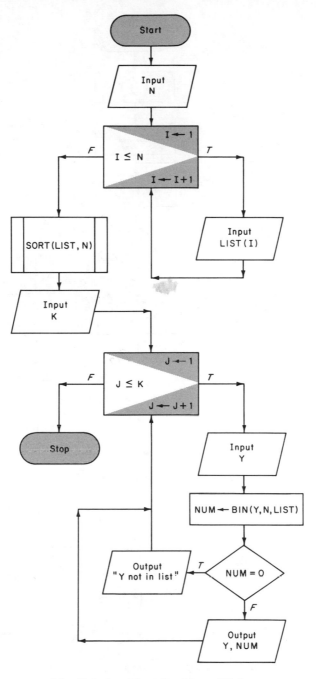

(a) *Main invoking algorithm utilizing subalgorithms* **SORT** *and* **BIN**

FIGURE 7.7

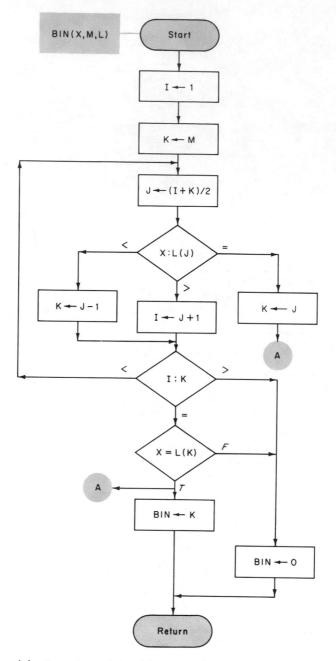

(b) *Function subalgorithm to perform binary search*

FIGURE 7.7   (Con't)

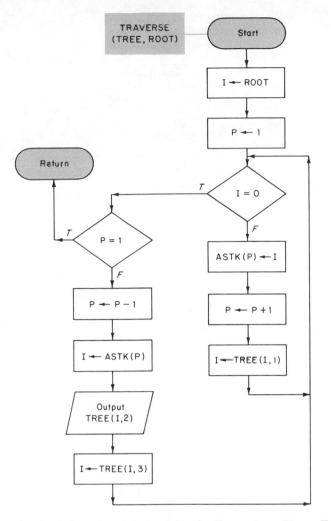

FIGURE 7.8 Subroutine Subalgorithm for Traversing a Binary Tree

As stated earlier, subalgorithms can invoke other subalgorithms. This is illustrated in Figure 7.9, utilizing two function subalgorithms and a subroutine subalgorithm.

Example: The problem for which this group of algorithms forms a solution requires the calculation of the mean, median, and standard deviation of a set of N values. It is assumed that the list of N values has already been sorted into ascending order. The *mean* is found by summing the values in the set and dividing by

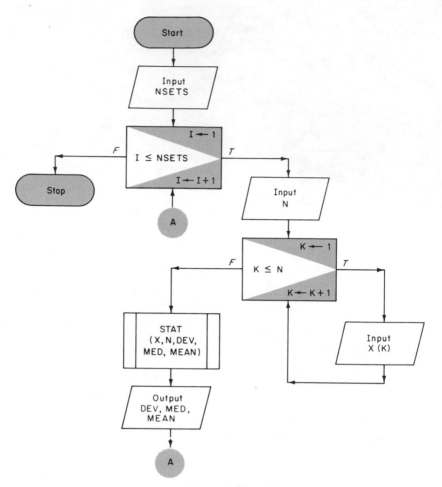

FIGURE 7.9 (a) *Main invoking algorithm*

the number of values. The *standard deviation* is given by the formula

$$S = \sqrt{\frac{N \cdot \sum\limits_{i=1}^{N} x_i^2 - \left(\sum\limits_{i=1}^{N} x_i\right)^2}{N \cdot (N-1)}}$$

where the numerator of the fraction is N times the sum of the squares of the values minus the square of the sum of the values. The *median* can be defined in two ways.

    1. If the number of values in the set is odd, the median is the value of the middle element.
    2. If the number of values is even, the median is the mean of the two middle values.

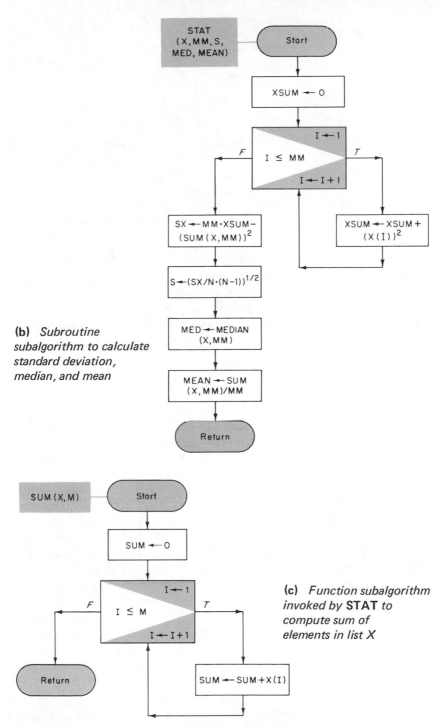

(b) *Subroutine subalgorithm to calculate standard deviation, median, and mean*

(c) *Function subalgorithm invoked by* **STAT** *to compute sum of elements in list X*

FIGURE 7.9   (Con't)

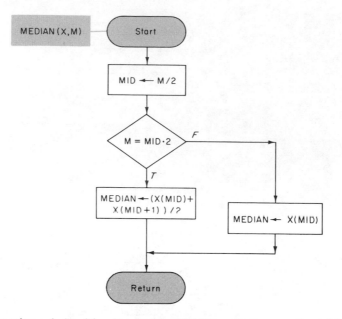

(d) *Function subalgorithm invoked by* **STAT** *to calculate median of list X*

FIGURE 7.9   (Con't)

The flowchart for the main algorithm is presented in Figure 7.9(a). The set of ordered values are input and stored in a linear list X. The subroutine subalgorithm STAT is invoked, with the actual parameter list containing X and N (already assigned values), and DEV, MED, and MEAN, which will be assigned values in STAT. The subroutine subalgorithm [see Fig. 7.9(b)] first calculates the sum of the squares of the values in the list X and assigns this value to XSUM. Following the loop, the next step evaluates the required numerator in the standard deviation formula, utilizing the function subalgorithm SUM. The actual parameters are the variables in STAT—not the ones from the main algorithm. The function returns to STAT a value of the sum of the values in X, which is then squared. After the square root of the quotient is determined and assigned to S, the median is found by invoking the function subalgorithm MEDIAN. Note that the function makes use of integer division to determine if the number of elements in X is odd or even. The appropriate course of action is followed, resulting in the median value. Upon return to the subalgorithm STAT, the mean is determined by again invoking SUM. Since MM is the formal parameter corresponding to the actual parameter N, the sum of the elements is divided by the number of elements, and the result is assigned to MEAN. The return to the main algorithm results in the return of values for the standard deviation, median, and mean from the subalgorithm via S, MED, and MEAN. These values are identified in the main algorithm by DEV, MED, and MEAN. Note: The use of identical names in both parameter lists is permitted since values are located by address and not by the name of the variable. Consequently, the output of the required information is valid.

The structuring of algorithms as functions or subroutines affords the maximum flexibility in problem-solving, when a main algorithm is little more than a series of statements that invoke subalgorithms. If all input, output, and processing of information is performed by subalgorithms, the main algorithm serves to direct control to each procedure where required. Within such a framework rests the complete generalization of algorithms.

EXERCISES

1. Distinguish between an open subalgorithm and a closed subalgorithm.

2. What are the significant differences between implict and explicit subalgorithms?

3. Describe the method of communication of information among algorithms and subalgorithms.

4. Define a function subalgorithm to compute the greatest common divisor of two positive integers [see Chapter 3, Exercise 13].

5. Define function subalgorithms, SIN and COS, that will determine the sine and cosine, respectively, of an angle $x(-1.2 \leq x \leq 1.2)$ given in radians. Approximate the sine using the series

$$\sin(x) = x - \frac{x^3}{3!} + \frac{x^5}{5!} - \frac{x^7}{7!} + \cdots$$

Given the first term $t_1 = x$, successive terms $t_i, i = 2, 3, \ldots$ can be determined by the formula

$$t_{i+1} = -t_i \cdot \frac{x^2}{(2N-1)(2N-2)}$$

where $N > 1$ is the number of the term being computed. Terminate the approximation when the next term to be added or subtracted is less than .000001. Similarly, approximate the cosine using the series

$$\cos(x) = 1 - \frac{x^2}{2!} + \frac{x^4}{4!} - \frac{x^6}{6!} + \cdots$$

Given the first term $t_1 = 1$, successive terms $t_i, i = 2, 3, 4, \ldots$ can be determined by the formula

$$t_{i+1} = -t_i \cdot \frac{x^2}{(2N-3)(2N-2)}$$

where $N > 1$ is the number of the term being computed.

6. A projectile is fired from a launcher with an initial velocity of v_0 at an angle of inclination θ. Assuming that the projectile is in nonpowered (free) flight, the equations of motion giving its theoretical position in the x - y plane at time t are

$$x = (v_0 \cos \theta)t$$
$$y = (v_0 \sin \theta)t - (\tfrac{1}{2})gt^2$$

where $0° < \theta < 90°$ and $g = 32$ ft/sec^2.

Define a subroutine subalgorithm that will compute the theoretical x - y coordinates of a projectile at 1 sec intervals when given the initial angle of inclination, the length of the flight (i.e., time), and the initial velocity. Store these coordinates in a matrix. Use the subalgorithms developed in Exercise 5 to compute the sine and cosine of θ. Given the actual x - y positions of a projectile at 1 sec intervals and the initial velocity and angle of inclination, describe a main algorithm that computes first the distance between the theoretical coordinates (determined by invoking the above subalgorithm) and the true coordinates, using the distance formula [see Chapter 3, Exercise 5], and then the average distance between those two sets of coordinates.

7. Describe the method of communication between a SAL main program and a SAL subprogram.

8. Write a SAL subroutine subprogram that will input data and then store it in a linear list, using the linear-quotient hashing method. Write a SAL function subprogram that will search a list that has been constructed by using the linear-quotient hashing method. Write a SAL main program that will store a list of data, using the above subroutine, and then input a list of data and search for them, using the above function.

9. Given this year's Form 1040, develop a set of function and/or subroutine subalgorithms that will compute a taxpayer's income tax.

SELECTED REFERENCES

Bergman, Samuel, and Steven Bruckner, *Computers and Computer Programming.* Reading, Mass.: Addison-Wesley, 1972.

Flores, Ivan, *Computer Programming,* Englewood Cliffs, N.J.: Prentice-Hall, 1971.

Forsythe, A.I., T.A. Keenan, E.I. Organick, and W. Stenberg, *Computer Science: A First Course*, New York: John Wiley, 1969.

Gear, C. William, *Computer Organization and Programming*, New York: McGraw-Hill, 1969.

Knuth, Donald E., *The Art of Computer Programming*, Vol. 1, "Fundamental Algorithms," Reading, Mass.: Addison-Wesley, 1968.

Maurer, Ward Douglas, *Programming: An Introduction to Computer Techniques*, San Francisco: Holden-Day, 1972.

Walker, Terry M., *Introduction to Computer Science: An Interdisciplinary Approach*, Boston: Allyn and Bacon, 1972.

Programming Languages

The far-reaching utilization of computers is based firmly on the premise that a means of communication must exist between the user and the computer, and the more natural the form, the better the communication. Throughout the rapid development of computers, this problem of communication has been of major importance. Although machine languages afford a direct method of supplying instructions to and receiving information from a computer, they cannot be read or understood without an extensive familiarity with the internal structure of the particular machines. Such languages exist as purely numerical coding. Symbolic assembler languages are an improvement, but their instructions are still very much tied to individual machine instructions. Programs written in such languages must account for every detailed operation a computer is to perform. Thus, the language of a solution looks far different from the language used to state the problem. Consequently, higher level languages, called *programming languages*, have been developed to close the gap between the user and the computer.

CHARACTERISTICS OF PROGRAMMING LANGUAGES

The original intent in developing higher level languages was to eliminate the machine dependency made necessary by the use of machine or assembler languages. A programmer should be able to express an algorithm more naturally in a standardized language that can be "understood" by any computer. But in the end, the fact could not be ignored that a machine can execute only those instructions presented in its own machine language. The development of a programming language therefore required a method whereby statements written in the language could be translated into the machine language of a computer. This is done by a program called a *compiler*. There must be a compiler for each language utilized by a computer. Since computers differ in their internal structures, there are many different compilers for any one language. The ideal situation exists when the compiler takes care of all peculiarities associated with the use of the language on all computers. The programmer is then free to write a program in a language and know that it can be executed on any computer with no alterations.

A programming language is easier to learn than a machine language. It is more natural to read and write, and it is also easier to correct for errors (debug). Such a language usually exhibits a problem-oriented notation in the sense that it is closer in text to the original problem than machine code would be. Programs written in higher level languages are called *source programs*, and the result of translation by a compiler is called the *object program*. The computer actually executes only the object program. Conversion to other computers is therefore made possible, and programs become machine-independent. But there are sacrifices that have to be made when using such languages. More time is used either in compiling and executing a program than would be used in executing a pure machine-language program or in assembling and executing an assembler language program. Without a good working knowledge of the internal structure of a computer, inefficient programming can occur, and this results in an inefficient machine code. Some things, such as manipulating bits or dynamically allocating storage, cannot be done by certain higher level languages. Yet, in the long run, the development of programming languages has enormously expanded the potential of the computer.

Higher level languages can be further characterized by describing various classifications. It should be noted that these classifications are not all mutually exclusive. *Procedure-oriented languages* are those in which the user specifies a set of operations that can be executed one at a time in sequence. The application of such languages is completely general. *Application-oriented languages* are those written for specialized use in specific areas such as engineering or economics. *Problem-oriented languages* are used with a restricted class of problems. The solution of problems is stated in a language very similar to that of the problem itself. Many languages of this type simply define the input and output of information without requiring the user to generate the steps in the problem solution. The elimination of the sequential nature of program steps produces a *nonprocedural language*. Form is not as important as the information that must be supplied in detail about a problem and its method of solution. *Problem-defining* is a term sometimes applied to such languages. Of course, languages may be designed as one type and then later used in an entirely different manner.

Any programming language can exist in three forms, although at present only the ALGOL language exhibits all three forms. The *reference language* is used to define the characteristics and structure of the language. It is not necessarily easy to read, nor does it necessarily have a form suitable for computer input. The *publication language* is used in various journals or publications to express algorithms written in the language and is easy to communicate on the printed page. The *hardware language* is a transformation of the reference language into input form for use with a computer. This is the form actually used for machine input.

Programming languages also possess *dialects* in the sense that modifications in use may occur from computer to computer. When a language works on a certain computer, it is said to be *implemented* on that computer. There are some languages whose implementation is nonexistent or extremely limited.

GENERAL STRUCTURE OF PROGRAMMING LANGUAGES

When programming languages came into general use, they were accompanied by a shift in emphasis. Computer details were not as important as such language details as punctuation, vocabulary, grammar, usage, and syntax. A very identifiable structure has developed that every programming language exhibits. First, the language must be able to describe and handle data. Then, there are various operators that are defined for computation ($+$, $-$, $\times$, $\div$), relation ($<$, $>$, $\leq$, $\geq$, $\neq$, $=$), and logic (AND, OR, NOT). Commands, or statements, must be constructed that can define actions to be performed on the data using these operations. Punctuation in the form of commas, periods, semicolons, or colons must be supplied. Blanks, parentheses, ampersands, and many other symbols may be assigned specific tasks within the framework of the language.

Languages require words, and words require characters for their formation. Each programming language therefore defines a character set, usually consisting of the letters of the alphabet, all the digits 0 to 9, and some special characters. "Less than," for example, may be represented as $<$, .LT., or LESS THAN, depending on the language. Identifiers are defined so that program units can be labeled. Statements are defined by combinations of letters, constants, and variable names. Some programming languages need to reserve certain words for key operations, and these key words cannot be used as variable names. Finally, the language is structured into units, such as loops, subprograms, blocks, or groups. Some languages are even structured so that they can interact with other languages after translation.

Each programming language makes use of variables, and the type of data represented by those variables must be characterized for each language. The most common type of data variable is arithmetic, consisting purely of numbers that can be manipulated according to the rules of algebra. Logical data variables can be used, possessing values of T for true and F for false, or 1 and 0, repectively. Nonnumeric data variables may be allowed, and they are referred to as character data. The language may accept complex numbers for processing. Strings, consisting of combinations of letters and numbers that can be connected (concatenated), are becoming more frequent as a data type. The programming language may be powerful enough to allow the user to refer to the internal location of a data item—in which case, he makes use of list or pointer variables. Data variable types are usually either stated specifically by the user within the program or are defined by default within the design of the language.

The type of arithmetic a programming language is designed to perform is also important. A number may be an integer (230) or a mixed number (32.45). It can be expressed as floating-point number with an exponent and fraction ($13.145 = .13145 \times 10^2$). If a number is complex, it has a real and an imaginary part ($24 + 6i$). Logical data may require arithmetic of a Boolean nature, which makes use of values such as T or F and 0 or 1. In some cases, both decimal and binary arithmetic may be performed. Each programming language must therefore clearly indicate the type of arithmetic it performs and the type of results from such operations. Restrictions may be due to many factors, including the internal structure of the machine on which the language is implemented.

The environment within which a programming language exists determines other characteristics in the structure of the language. Input and output operations can be defined to cover a wide range of interaction with many types of physical devices, such as card readers, tapes, disks, and line printers. Some languages may have extensive libraries that are located in an auxiliary storage and are available to the user of the language. These libraries contain routines already programmed that cover a wide variety of specialized algorithms, such as sort routines, trigonometric functions, or statistical routines. Some languages have excellent debugging facilities that are available to assist the user in better utilization of the language and the computer.

The remainder of this chapter is devoted to a brief survey of some of the programming languages in use today. This survey is not designed as a complete course in any of the languages. Highlights of each language are presented to provide a better appreciation of the variety found in programming languages. Each description is accompanied by an algorithm written in that particular language.

NUMERICAL/SCIENTIFIC PROBLEM LANGUAGES

FORTRAN

Although as early as 1952 a programming language called SHORT CODE had appeared for use with the UNIVAC computer, it was not until 1957 that the first widely accepted scientific programming language appeared. FORTRAN (from FORmula TRANslator) was introduced at this time for use on the IBM 704. It was followed in 1958 by FORTRAN II and in 1962 by FORTRAN IV. By 1963 almost all manufacturers of computers had committed themselves to providing implementation of some version of FORTRAN. The original intent of IBM was to design a language that would be capable of expressing any problem of numerical computation. As a result, the language is computation-oriented, works with words of data, and has a limited number of data types. FORTRAN can be classified as a procedure-oriented, problem-solving language. At first there was no machine independence, but the version known as FORTRAN IV made this independence and integral feature of the language.

The program in Figure 8.1 will serve as a model for futher discussion of the FORTRAN language. The original algorithm appeared in flowchart form in Figure 3.30.

Example: The basic format of this FORTRAN program is that all statements are punched on cards starting in column 7 and continuing to column 72. Only one statement is allowed per line. Statement labels (which are numbers in FORTRAN) are punched in columns 1 through 5. Column 6 is reserved for a continuation code, if any statements are longer than the allocated space on one card. A "C" in column 1 is used to indicate the beginning of a comment, and such information is not translated into machine language. Data is input by use of a READ statement, which

```
C   THIS PROGRAM CALCULATES THE NTH ROOT OF ANY POSITIVE NUMBER X,
C   SATISFYING A SPECIFIED DEGREE OF ACCURACY, E.
C
C   THE ORIGINAL FLOWCHART FORM OF THE ALGORITHM APPEARS IN FIGURE 3.30.
C
      DOUBLE PRECISION X,Y,Q
C
C   INPUT NUMBER OF SETS OF DATA FROM CARD READER.
C
    1 READ(5,2)NSETS
    2 FORMAT(10X,I4)
      IF(NSETS.LE.0)GO TO 55
C
C   OUTPUT TITLES ON LINE PRINTER
C
      WRITE(6,6)
    6 FORMAT(12X,5HINDEX,15X,4HBASE,19X,4HROOT//)
C
C   SET UP OUTER LOOP
C
      DO 80 M=1,NSETS
C
C   INPUT VALUE OF INDEX (N), BASE (X), AND SPECIFIED ACCURACY (E).
C
    5 READ(5,3)N,X,E
    3 FORMAT(I3,2X,D15.6,1X,F6.4)
C
C   VALIDITY CHECKS FOLLOW
C
      IF(N.LE.1)GO TO 50
      IF(X.LE.0.0)GO TO 60
      IF(E.GE.1.0)GO TO 70
      Q=X/N
C
C   IN THE NEXT STATEMENT, 'FLOAT' IS A FORTRAN BUILT-IN FUNCTION
C   THAT CHANGES N-1 FROM INTEGER TO REAL
C
      XN=FLOAT(N-1)
C
C   ITERATION TO OBTAIN REQUIRED ACCURACY FOR NTH ROOT MAKES UP
C   INNER LOOP.
C
   10 Y=(XN*Q+X/Q**XN)/N
      IF((Y-Q)/Y.LE.E)GO TO 20
      GO TO 30
   20 IF((Y-Q)/Y.GE.-E)GO TO 40
   30 Q=Y
      GO TO 10
C
C   OUTPUT INDEX, BASE, AND REQUIRED ROOT ON LINE PRINTER.
C
   40 WRITE(6,4)N,X,Y
    4 FORMAT(1H ,10X,I4,9X,F15.6,10X,F12.5)
      GO TO 80
   50 WRITE(6,7)N
    7 FORMAT(24H N HAS INVALID VALUE OF ,I4)
      GO TO 80
   60 WRITE(6,8)X
    8 FORMAT(24H X HAS INVALID VALUE OF ,F12.5)
      GO TO 80

   70 WRITE(6,9)E
    9 FORMAT(24H E HAS INVALID VALUE OF ,F7.4)
   80 CONTINUE
   55 STOP
      END
```

INDEX	BASE	ROOT
5	1001.889000	3.98257
E HAS INVALID VALUE OF	1.2400	
3	10941.048000	22.20000
2	1523002.810000	1237.33657
N HAS INVALID VALUE OF	-4	
3	0.000008	0.02000
X HAS INVALID VALUE OF	-7.45000	
4	81.000000	3.00000

FIGURE 8.1

indicates the input device by use of a logical unit number, followed by a format statement number. The specification codes in the format statement indicate the types of data as well as information regarding spaces to be skipped. For example, statement 1 indicates that NSETS is to be input from the card reader according to the FORMAT in statement 2, which specifies that after skipping ten spaces, the item is to be accepted as an integer from card columns 11 through 14. The output of data is accomplished by a WRITE statement, having characteristics similar to the READ statement—printer, line, and page control are also included in the associated format statement. Other data types include F for floating-point and D for double-precision floating-point. The language also allows for complex and logical data and a limited character data type. FORTRAN permits explicit declarations of data type, as in the DOUBLE PRECISION statement for X, Y, and Q. Note that the titles of columns were output by using the Hollerith code, which in some versions of FORTRAN has been replaced by enclosing the character string in quotes.

Arithmetic operations are indicated by +, −, * (for Multiplication), / (for division), and ** (for exponentiation). Parentheses, commas, and periods are the most common punctuation, but no punctuation is required at the end of statements or following statement labels. Logical comparisons are performed with the use of operators such as .LE. (less than or equal) and .EQ. (equal). Variable names are allowed to have as many as six characters. The DO statement corresponds to the special flowchart symbol used for a loop structure and indicates the range of the loop by statement number, the loop counter, the initial value, and the maximum value. In this case, the increment is understood to be 1. GO TO statements allow for transfer of control—either conditional (following an IF) or unconditional. The control passes to the statement whose number is indicated. The program also uses a built-in function called FLOAT, which causes an integer value to be expressed as a real number. Additionally, the language has a provision for working with arrays, although none were used in this program. The DIMENSION statement is used to identify variables that are array names, along with their dimensions, and reserves the proper amount of storage for each array. For example, DIMENSION X(20), ABLE(3,5), BOSTON(36) would identify X as a linear list of length 20, ABLE as a matrix array of 3 rows and 5 columns, and BOSTON as a linear list of 36 elements. When such arrays are used, their subscripts can be indicated specifically or by variables, such as A(5) or ABLE(I, J + 1).

Although FORTRAN was originally designed for a specific area of problem-solving, it has proved useful in other areas. The language possesses built-in functions, such as sine and cosine, and also allows for user-defined functions and subprograms. It cannot be applied well in areas such as character string manipulation or list-processing. Yet it has undergone steady improvement and satisfactorily meets the needs of a great number of users.

ALGOL

In 1958 an international committee presented a language they hoped would become a universal standard for describing computational processes. It was called ALGOL (ALGOrithmic Language), and it is the only language to exist in all three forms of representation, namely, reference, publication, and hardware. Since it was widely supported by scientists in both Europe and the United States and (unlike FORTRAN) was not dominated by a major company, ALGOL was soon adopted as an excellent medium in which algorithms could be described. In fact, since 1960, the *Communications of the ACM* (Association for Computing Machinery) has used the ALGOL 60 version of the language to represent algorithms submitted for publication. The major drawback in the United Sates, however, is that ALGOL has a very limited implementation on computers. Adapting the language to various machines tends to produce incompatible versions of the language due to differences in hardware representation. ALGOL can be said to be compatible only through the use of its reference language. The lack of clearly defined input or output procedures, along with an inability to handle alphanumeric information and certain complex forms of data structures, has caused ALGOL to be criticized. Yet it is definitely a procedure-oriented, problem-solving language that does allow for a good formal language description of an algorithm.

ALGOL does have a limited number of data types: integer, real, and Boolean. It was the first language to use the concept of block structure to define the scope of variables. Essentially, the scope of a variable determines whether the declared characteristics and meaning of a variable will hold true for an entire program or just for the smaller units of a program. The closest thing to a block in FORTRAN is the DO group. Furthermore, ALGOL makes use of the concept of a procedure that is roughly equivalent to the program unit in FORTRAN. Whereas the block is used for iteration and control purposes, the procedure is used to delimit the scope of identifiers in the program. The language permits the definition and use of *recursive functions*—functions that can call themselves. The factorial problem would be the best example of such a function.

ALGOL is usually written in a publication form different from that used for implementation on a particular computer. So before proceeding to the hardware version of an algorithm, we should examine some features of ALGOL based on the publication version.

Example: As an illustration of the publication form, consider the algorithm for the nth root of any positive number originally stated in Figure 3.30. If it were written in ALGOL, it would appear as shown in Figure 8.2. The first thing to note is the structure of the language itself, which utilizes **begin** blocks and procedures. Data-type declarations in ALGOL are made within a block, do not hold outside that block, and specify the nature of the variable as real, integer, or Boolean (logical values of T or F). The procedure in this case is labeled "root" and is actually imbedded within the text of the main program that utilizes it. The main program itself is delineated as a block by the use of a **begin** coupled with an **end**, found in the last statement of the program after the label "stop." In fact, every block in ALGOL must be concluded with **end**. In the case of the procedure, the **end** statement includes the name of the procedure.

The second important feature of the program is found in examining the words printed in **bold** type. Although these would normally be considered key words for implementation purposes, they are defined as single characters in the ALGOL reference language. Such words include **begin**, **procedure**, **end**, **integer**, **real**, **boolean**, **array**, **if**, **then**, **else**, **goto**, **step**, **until**, **and**, **or**, and **do**, an well as many others. The **if-then** clauses may be followed by a transfer of control (**goto**) or coupled with an **else**, which describes the alternate action to be taken if the original condition is false. Many such clauses may be grouped together. The **for** statement corresponds to the flowchart loop symbol, identifies the loop variable, indicates the initial value, and defines the increment (**step**) and the maximum value (**until**). The **do** is followed by a single statement, which may be a compound statement, and is executed as the main body of the loop.

Finally, the written form of the language permits the indentation of statements as well as multiple statements on each line, since the semi-colon (;) indicates the end of a statement and the colon (:) indicates a label. Other delimiters include **begin**, **end**, the comma (,) and the colon-equal (: =). It is customary to write either the reference or the publication language in lowercase letters. Wide variation of I/O procedures does not allow for any standard keyword representation of such operations, although **inreal** and **outreal** are sometimes used. Assignment of values to variables is indicated by : = and multiplication by X. Exponentiation is indicated by a raised exponent, and relational operators are

```
begin
      procedure root(n,x,e,y); real x,e,y; integer n;
            begin
                  if n ≤ 1 then output error message for "n"
                  else
                  if x ≤ 0 then output error message for "x"
                  else
                  if e ≥ 1 then output error message for "e"
                  else begin real q;
                      q: = x/n;
                    loop: y: = ((n–1) q + x/q^(n–1))/n;
                          if (y–q)/y ≤ e and (y–q)/y ≥ -e then goto
                          endit; q: = y; goto loop;
                        endit: end;

      end root;
integer nsets;
input nsets;
if nsets ≤ 0 then goto stop
    else begin integer m,nn; real xx,ee,yy;
        output titles "index, base, root";
        for m: = 1 step 1 until nsets do
            begin input nn,xx,ee;
            root(nn,xx,ee,yy);
            output nn,xx,yy;
            end;
        end;
stop: end
```

FIGURE 8.2

used exactly as they would appear in algebraic representations. Symbols for logical operations are ∧ (and), ∨ (or), ≡ (equivalence) and ⌐ (negation).

Although no arrays were used in this particular algorithm, the declaration and use of such structures in ALGOL is worth mentioning. If a linear list X of length 20, a matrix array ABLE consisting of 3 rows and 5 columns, and a vector array BOSTON of length N were used in a program, they would be declared in the block

real array X[1:20], ABLE[1:3,1:5], BOSTON[1:n];

Note that the declaration includes the first and last subscript value and that such values may be variable. The brackets are standard subscript enclosures, even when the array elements are used in a program statement.

The hardware version of this ALGOL program appears in Figure 8.3. It exhibits a few of the alterations necessary when using an available hardware form of ALGOL.

Example: Capital letters have replaced the lowercase letters in all instances, but punctuation remains the same as does the free form. Although ALGOL permits variable names to be a character string of any length, hardware implementations usually consider only the first six characters. Relational operations such as "less than or equal" become $<$ =; multiplication is indicated by $*$ and exponentiation is represented by $\uparrow$. Input is achieved by using the word READATA, where the first item in the parentheses indicates the device used for input was the teletype. Output is accomplished by using the PRINT statement with literal information in quotes. The results can be compared to those from the FORTRAN program output in Figure 8.1. The question mark preceding each line of ouput simply indicates that the system was querying the user for input from the terminal. Comments are indicated by COMMENT followed by any number of words, provided the entire comment is ended with a semicolon. Such comments may be used anywhere in the program, except in the middle of a statement.

ALGOL is used more in Europe than in the United States, but it is interesting to note that many of the later improvements in FORTRAN derived from the desirable features already existing in ALGOL. Although inconsistent in different implementations, it is a powerful programming tool. By formally defining a standardized language, creating three separate language forms, and introducing the concept of block structure, ALGOL greatly enhanced the world of programming languages. The creation of several new languages has resulted because of ALGOL, but even more important is the development of new and better implementation techniques for programming languages in general. The contribution to the fields of standardization and future development of programming languages are the enduring hallmarks of ALGOL.

BASIC

One philosophy regarding the purpose of programming languages holds firm to the belief that languages should be simple to learn, easy to translate, and easy to use. This philosophy was combined with the development known as *time-sharing* and resulted in a language called BASIC (Beginner's All-purpose Symbolic Instruc-

```
LIST

ALGO1     14 MAR 72  10:09

100 BEGIN
111 COMMENT
112       THIS IS AN ALGOL VERSION OF THE ALGORITHM PRESENTED
113       IN FLOWCHART FORM IN FIGURE 3.30 FOR FINDING THE
114       NTH ROOT OF ANY POSITIVE NUMBER "X" WITHIN A
115       SPECIFIC DEGREE OF ACCURACY "E".
116
117       THE PROCEDURE "ROOT" CONTAINS THE CALCULATION OF
118       THE DESIRED VALUE OF THE ROOT, WHICH IS THE INNER
119       LOOP.  THE MAIN BODY OF THE PROGRAM CONTAINS
120       ALL INPUT AND OUTPUT OF KEY VALUES, AS WELL AS THE
121       OUTER LOOP. ;
122
130 PROCEDURE ROOT(N,X,E,Y); REAL X,E,Y; INTEGER N;
200       BEGIN
210       IF N<=1 THEN PRINT ("INVALID VALUE FOR N IS",N)
220     ELSE
230       IF X<=0 THEN PRINT("INVALID VALUE FOR X IS",X)
240     ELSE
250       IF E>=1 THEN PRINT("INVALID VALUE FOR E IS",E)
260     ELSE BEGIN REAL Q;
300       Q:=X/N;
310       LOOP: Y:=((N-1)*Q+X/Q↑(N-1))/N;
320       IF(Y-Q)/Y<=E AND (Y-Q)/Y>=-E THEN GO TO ENDIT;
330       Q:=Y;  GO TO LOOP;
340       ENDIT: END;
350 END ROOT;
500 INTEGER NSETS;
510 READATA(TTY,NSETS);
520 IF NSETS<=0 THEN GOTO STOP
600       ELSE BEGIN INTEGER M,NN; REAL XX,EE,YY;
610         PRINT("  INDEX            BASE                ROOT");
620         FOR M:=1 STEP 1 UNTIL NSETS DO
630           BEGIN READATA(TTY,NN,XX,EE);
640           ROOT(NN,XX,EE,YY);
650           PRINT(NN,XX,YY);
660           END;
670       END;
680 STOP: END;
READY


RUN ALGOL

ALGO1     14 MAR 72  10:11


DARTMOUTH ALGOL

? 8
  INDEX          BASE              ROOT
? 5,1001.889,.0005
  5              1001.89           3.98257
? 8,111.034,1.240
INVALID VALUE FOR E IS          1.24
  8              111.034           3.98257
? 3,10941.048,.001
  3              10941.            22.2
? 2,1523002,.10
  2              1523002           1237.34
? -4,11.345,.001
INVALID VALUE FOR N IS          -4
  -4             11.345            1237.34
? 3,.000008,.003
  3              0.000008          0.02
? 2,-7.45,.0045
INVALID VALUE FOR X IS          -7.45
  2              -7.45             0.02
? 4,81.00,.0001
  4              81                3

0.327 SEC.  15 I/O
READY
```

FIGURE 8.3

tion Code), which was implemented on a GE 235 as an interactive, conversational, on-line system. Developed at Dartmouth College the system has been operational since 1964 and is known as the DTSS (Dartmouth Time-Sharing System). The BASIC language was designed to afford undergraduate students at a college-algebra level the opportunity to quickly learn a language that would provide the means for easy communication with the computer. The system itself was designed to service several users simultaneously via teletype machines on a time-sharing basis, thus producing an interactive and conversational environment with a certain element of immediacy.

BASIC was the first language designed specifically for use from a time-sharing terminal. It is a formula translation language similar to FORTRAN but much more streamlined in structure. Input and output are simplified. Variable names are limited to a single letter or a letter followed by a single digit. Arithmetic is performed using a single data type, namely, real numeric, although constants can be integers, mixed numbers, or floating-point numbers. Data is supplied to a program by the user from a terminal and can be defined within the program or accepted by query when the program is executed. String variables can be defined that may contain up to fifteen characters. The language is easily read and understood when used in problem-solving, as illustrated in Figure 8.4. This BASIC version of the algorithm in Figure 3.26 will serve as a basis for further discussion of the language.

Example: BASIC allows one statement per line, with each statement numbered. Statement numbers must be in the range 1 to 99999. The five arithmetic operators are $\uparrow$ (exponentiation), / (division), * (multiplication), + (addition), and $-$ (subtraction). Relational operators are =, <, ≤, >, ≥, and <> (which represents ≠). Input is accomplished in two ways. The first method uses the word INPUT and indicates that the terminal user is to enter data in a conversational manner. In the second method, READ is associated with a DATA statement within the body of the program. The DATA statement provides a list of data elements that is matched with the list of variables in the READ statement. Output is accomplished by PRINT, which is used to print strings or numbers or to skip lines. GO TO is used for unconditional transfer of control. IF-THEN provides the conditional transfer of control by indicating a statement number to branch to if the condition is true. Variables are assigned values by using a LET statement, where the equal sign takes on the meaning "be replaced by the value of." The FOR statement corresponds to the loop flowchart symbol by defining a loop variable, initializing it,

```
BASIC5     14 MAR 72   10:24

010 REM THIS IS A BASIC VERSION OF THE PRINCIPAL AND INTEREST
020 REM ALGORITHM PRESENTED IN FLOWCHART FORM IN FIGURE 3.26.
100 PRINT "TYPE THE NUMBER OF INVESTMENTS TO BE PROCESSED."
110 INPUT N1
115 REM OUTER LOOP STARTS HERE
117 PRINT "TYPE THE RATE OF INTEREST DESIRED."
118 INPUT R
120 FOR  J=1 TO N1
130 PRINT "TYPE THE MAXIMUM PRINCIPAL DESIRED."
140 INPUT M1
150 PRINT "TYPE THE AMOUNT TO BE INVESTED."
160 INPUT P1
170 IF P1<1000 THEN 250
180 LET Y1=0
190 LET P=P1
195 REM INNER LOOP STARTS HERE, CALCULATES PRINCIPAL
196 REM TO PRESCRIBED MAXIMUM.
200 LET  I=R*P
210 LET Y1=Y1+1
220 LET P=P+I
225 IF P<M1 THEN 200
230 PRINT Y1; I; P
240 GO TO 260
250 PRINT "INITIAL INVESTMENT TOO SMALL."
258 REM THE NEXT STATEMENT CAUSES THE INCREMENT OF OUTER LOOP COUNTER.
260 NEXT J
270 END
READY


RUN

BASIC5     14 MAR 72   10:26

TYPE THE NUMBER OF INVESTMENTS TO BE PROCESSED.
? 3
TYPE THE RATE OF INTEREST DESIRED.
? .06
TYPE THE MAXIMUM PRINCIPAL DESIRED.
? 40000
TYPE THE AMOUNT TO BE INVESTED.
? 2500
 48   2319.89   40984.7
TYPE THE MAXIMUM PRINCIPAL DESIRED.
? 8500
TYPE THE AMOUNT TO BE INVESTED.
?  650
INITIAL INVESTMENT TOO SMALL.
TYPE THE MAXIMUM PRINCIPAL DESIRED.
? 8500
TYPE THE AMOUNT TO BE INVESTED.
? 6500
 5   492.366   8698.47

0.192 SEC   00 I/O
READY
```

FIGURE 8.4

and defining a maximum value. The extent of the loop is indicated by the NEXT statement, which causes the increment to occur. If the increment is not 1, a STEP phrase is included at the end of the FOR statement. Comments (remarks) are indicated by placing REM at the beginning of the statement (as in this program) or by a single quote.

Arrays are identified by a DIM statement, which performs the proper allocation of storage space. For example, DIM S2(100,150), X(150) would identify S2 as a matrix array of 100 rows and 150 columns, and X as a linear list of length 150. Subscripts in the program can be numbers, variables, or variable expressions. Moreover, BASIC provides several MAT commands, which are built-in for manipulation of matrix arrays. MAT READ S2 and MAT A = INV(S2) are examples of this feature, where the first expression inputs an array and the second inverts S2 and stores the inverse in A. There are also built-in functions for square root, sine, cosine, absolute value, etc. User-defined functions require a statement such as DEF FNA(X) = X ↑2, and user-defined subroutines are indicated by a GOSUB followed by the statement number indicating the beginning of the subroutine.

Over a dozen versions of BASIC exist today, implemented in some form on just about every major computer. Extensions to the language have introduced new data types, new statements, string manipulations, use of data files, and new I/O conventions. Some versions have come close to destroying the simple design and intent of the original BASIC language. Yet the power of BASIC in a time-sharing environment has done much to enhance the field of programming languages, providing a useful tool that is in great demand today. DTSS alone handles more than 150 terminals on the Dartmouth campus with another seventy remote terminals in or near the New England area. The usage of these terminals involves thousands of accounts, which is strong testimony to the utilization of both the language and the time-sharing concept.

APL

The final language that qualifies for examination in this numerical–scientific category is also a time-sharing language, but it differs radically from BASIC. APL (A Programming Language) was developed in 1962 by Dr. Kenneth Iverson and was further developed by him and Adin Falkoff for implementation on the System/360. APL is designed to perform in a time-sharing environment, using a terminal that has a special character set required by the language. Operating on information set down in arrays, the language is well suited for a wide range of problems. Emphasis is placed on defining operations or groups of operations in a functional format. APL statements are actually interpreted on a line-by-line basis; thus the language can handle very complex statements. There is no set of reserved words, no hierarchy of operations, no dimensioning or formatting, and no need to distinguish among types of numeric data. APL works directly with vectors and matrices, and many functions useful in working with such structures have been defined and given a single character notation in APL. There are forty-five operators (called functions) contained in the language. Even the symbols that normally represent such operations as multiplication or division are considered functions in APL. Sine, cosine, tangent, arcsin, arccos, and arctan exist as built-in functions, along with such others as logarithms.

The best way to continue a discussion of APL is to individually examine a few of the unique characteristics. The basic character set is:

$$A\ B\ C\ D\ E\ F\ G\ H\ I\ J\ K\ L\ M\ N\ O\ P\ Q\ R\ S\ T\ U\ V\ W\ X\ Y\ Z$$
$$1\ 2\ 3\ 4\ 5\ 6\ 7\ 8\ 9\ 0$$

There are fifty-two special characters, including

$$+ - \times \div * \lceil \ \lfloor \ \top \bot \wedge \vee = \neq < > \leq \geq \ | \rightarrow \leftarrow ^- \circ : \Delta \nabla$$

The method by which basic functions are represented by the use of special characters is best understood by defining some of the symbols.

$\leftarrow$ used for assignment of values to variables; means replacement of value.

$\times$ multiplication.

$\div$ used for division or reciprocal notation.

$*$ exponentiation.

$\lceil$ used to denote maximum of two values, or next integer greater than or equal to a single value.

$\lfloor$ used to denote minimum of two values, or next integer smaller than or equal to a single value.

$|$ for absolute value, or remainder when second value is divided by first.

, concatenation symbol.

Since these symbols can be used monadically (with one variable) or dyadically (between two variables), there are dual definitions for their usage, as in the case of $\div$ or $\lceil$. The relational functions include $<$, $\leq$, $=$, $\geq$, $>$, and $\neq$; all appear in exactly this form in APL programs. Logical functions include $\wedge$ (and), $\vee$ (or), $\sim$ (nand), and $\sim$ (nor). Lowercase Greek letters such as ρ and ι define other more specialized functions, which will be described later.

Although it is impossible in this brief description of APL to present all its features, a few illustrations will provide a look at some of the more interesting applications.

Example: If a vector is defined as $X \leftarrow 2\ 3\ 5\ 7\ 11$, then $+/X$ defines the sum of all the elements of X, and $\times/X$ defines the product of all the elements. Thus the following sequence of instructions will find the area of a triangle using Hero's formula, if the sides measure 3, 4, and 5.

$$L \leftarrow 3\ 4\ 5$$
$$P \leftarrow +/L$$
$$S \leftarrow P \div 2$$
$$(S \times \times /S - L) *.5$$

In the last statement $S-L$ represents a new vector consisting of the three values $S-3$, $S-4$, and $S-5$.

Defined as a function, the program would be entered from a terminal in this form:

$$\triangledown\ R \leftarrow AREA\ L$$
[1] $P \leftarrow +/L$
[2] $S \leftarrow P : 2$
[3] $R \leftarrow (S \times \times /S - L) *.5$
[4] $\triangledown$

When executed, a typical input would be

$$V \leftarrow 3\ 4\ 5$$
$$AREA\ V$$

and the answer returned would be 6. The use in the program of the symbol $\triangledown$, called del, marks the beginning and the end of the function definition. R is to carry the result of the functional evaluation of L, the variable. $AREA$ is the name of the function. Statement numbers are enclosed in brackets, and statements may have labels followed by a colon. In statement [3] note that the statement is read from left to right but is evaluated from right to left, starting with the parenthetical expression first. $S-L$ actually represents a vector of three elements, each of which is the difference between the semi-perimeter and the measure of a side of a triangle. The product of the elements is found first and is then multiplied by S. The whole quantity is raised to the one-half power.

Example: Branching in a program is accomplished by using any one of three methods.

$\rightarrow$s.n. provides an unconditional branch to the statement number indicated.

$\rightarrow$s.n.$\times$ (logical comparison) will cause a conditional branch, since the parenthetical expression will yield a 1 for true or a 0 for false. The product thus results in the statement number or in zero, and a branch to 0 stops the program, since there is no 0 statement number. Finally, $\rightarrow$ (logical comparison)/s.n. will provide a branch to the statement number indicated if the expression is true, or a continuation to the next statement in sequence if the expression is false.

The area function can utilize this feature as follows:

$$\nabla \ R \leftarrow AREA \ L$$
[1] $P \leftarrow +/L$
[2] $\rightarrow (P=0)/0$
[3] $S \leftarrow P \div 2$
[4] $R \leftarrow (S \times \times /S-L)*.5$
[5] ∇

Example: Two special Greek symbols provide interesting results when applied to vectors or matrices. ρQ (read as "rho of Q") will return the number of elements in a vector. It can also be used to reshape a vector, as in $7 \, \rho A$. If $A \leftarrow 1 \ 2 \ 3$, then $7 \, \rho A$ yields 1 2 3 1 2 3 1. If a variable represents a scalar, its rho value is an empty vector. Additionally, ιN (read as "iota of N") forms a vector of the first N integers in order; therefore, $\iota 7$ is 1 2 3 4 5 6 7. $A \iota B$ (referred to as the A-index of B) is defined as the locations in A (by count) where the value of B or each of the values of B can be found. For example, if $STRING \leftarrow 'ABCDEFGHI'$ and $B \leftarrow 'BABE'$ then $STRING \iota B$ would be the vector 2125.

Consider the following function definition for evaluating a polynomial with coefficients C evaluated at the point X.

$$\nabla Z \leftarrow C \ POL \ X$$
[1] $Z \leftarrow +/C \times X* ^-1 + \iota \rho C$
[2] ∇

If the polynomial is $3 + 5x + 4x^2 + x^3$ and the point X is 2, then $C \leftarrow 3 \ 5 \ 4 \ 1$. ρC is 4; so $\iota \rho C$ is 1 2 3 4. $^-1+$ has the effect of producing 0 1 2 3, since a negative 1 is added to each element of the vector. The powers of X have therefore been generated. X is raised to each of these powers, producing a vector 1 2 4 8. C multiplies this vector (element by element), and the sum (37) is stored in Z.

Example: ! is a function that calculates the factorial of any nonnegative integer to which it is applied. If A is an integer, $!A$ is defined as $\times / \iota A$.

Example: To sort a set of elements, such as student grades, into ascending order, the following function program could be written. Each step is explained directly after the statement.

$\nabla A \leftarrow SORT \ X$
[1] $A \leftarrow \iota 0$ A is blanked out.
[2] $A \leftarrow A ,(X=L/X)/X$ A is replaced by A concatenated with the minimum value of X.

[3] $X \leftarrow (X \neq \lfloor /X)/X$ X is replaced by all the remaining values of X.

[4] $\rightarrow 2 \times 0 \neq \rho X$ Control returns to statement [2], if the length of X is not zero. Otherwise,

∇ processing stops and A contains the sorted vector.

But APL has two function symbols ($\triangle$ and $\triangledown$), used to provide sorting into ascending and descending order, respectively. Given a numerical vector X consisting of the values 3537, $\triangle X$ gives the indices necessary to arrange the vector in ascending order (in this case, 1324). Therefore, $A \leftarrow X[\triangle X]$ means that A is replaced by the vector 3357.

Example: Matrices are formed by using a dimensioning feature applied to a vector. $D \rho X$ will yield a matrix of dimension D whose elements in row-by-row order are the elements of vector X. If $D \leftarrow 3\ 4$ and $X \leftarrow \iota 12$, then $M \leftarrow D \rho X$ produces

$$
\begin{array}{cccc}
1 & 2 & 3 & 4 \\
5 & 6 & 7 & 8 \\
9 & 10 & 11 & 12
\end{array}
$$

$M[3;4]$ selects an element of the matrix. $M[;3]$ yields a whole column (the third one); $M[2;]$ yields a whole row; and $M[;2\ 3]$ yields a matrix of the second and third columns. $M+.\times N$ is used to denote the matrix product of M and N. Of course, vectors may also be subscripted using a single value enclosed in brackets.

Example: As a final illustration of APL, consider the program in Figure 8.5(a), which finds the nth root of a given number. The flowchart that illustrates this method was given in Figure 3.30. The symbol $\square$ indicates input or output on the terminal. Note that all three values N, X, and E are stored as elements of a vector and are selected by use of subscripts. Statement [5] calculates Y in a form somewhat different than has previously been used, but this is due to the right-to-left evaluation of expressions in APL. Statement [9] outputs all the input values concatenated with the value of Y; so the output is a vector of length one more than SET. Error messages and validity checks have been eliminated, since the conversational mode of input permits easy checking and correction of data before transmitting for program use. Figure 8.5(b) illustrates an alternate form of the program in which $NSETS$ is a functional value and the statements are more compact in notation.

APL has the potential of becoming the foremost time-sharing language, although at present, its implementation is not very

```
      ∇ROOT[□]∇


      ∇ ROOT
[1]     NSETS←□
[2]     M←1
[3]     SET←□
[4]     Q←SET[2]÷SET[1]
[5]     Y←((Q×SET[1]-1)+SET[2]÷Q*SET[1]-1)÷SET[1]
[6]     →((((Y-Q)÷Y)≤SET[3])∧(((Y-Q)÷Y)≥(-SET[3])))/ENDIT
[7]     Q←Y
[8]     →5
[9]     ENDIT:□←SET,Y
[10]    →3×(NSETS≥M←M+1)
      ∇


      ROOT
□:
      5

□:
      5 1001.889 .0005
5  1001.889  0.0005  3.982574658
□:
      3 10941.048 .001
3  10941.048  0.001  22.20000013
□:
      2 1523002 .10
2  1523002  0.1  1237.336232
□:
      3 .000008 .003
3  8E⁻6  0.003  0.02
□:
      4 81 .0001
4  81  0.0001  3




      ∇NEWROOT[□]∇


      ∇ NEWROOT NSETS
[1]     M←1
[2]     L1:E←⁻1↑SET←□
[3]     Q←(X←SET[2])÷N←SET[1]
[4]     L2:Y←(÷N)×((N-1)×Q)+X÷Q*N-1
[5]     →((|(Y-Q)÷Y)≤E)/ENDIT
[6]     Q←Y
[7]     →L2
[8]     ENDIT:□←SET,Y
[9]     →L1×(NSETS≥M←M+1)
      ∇


      NEWROOT 2
□:
      4 81 .0001
4  81  0.0001  3
□:
      3 .000008 .003
3  8E⁻6  0.003  0.02
```

FIGURE 8.5

widespread. The future of APL will finally depend on its acceptance by a substantial number of users who are convinced that it is a better programming tool than any other available language.

BUSINESS DATA-PROCESSING PROBLEM LANGUAGES

COBOL

Early in the development of programming languages, it became apparent that there was a need for a language suited to the specific requirements of business applications. The basic demand was that any such language should be capable of handling problems that involved large files of information requiring fairly simple processing. Furthermore, the language should be English-like, containing natural words for operations and data manipulation. Early in 1955, FLOW-MATIC was developed for implementation on the UNIVAC computer, and in 1961 GECOM (GEneral COMpiler)* was developed for the GE 225 computer. Although other languages have also been designed, the only one to receive major use as a business-oriented programming language was COBOL (COmmon Business Oriented Language). Consequently, this language will be the only one examined in this section.

In 1959 the Department of Defense organized a Conference on Data Systems Languages (CODASYL) with forty representatives from users, government installations, computer manufacturers, and other interested parties. A group called the Short Range Committee of CODASYL was given the task of developing a business-oriented language, and in 1960 COBOL appeared. The first implementations of the language were carried out by Remington Rand on the UNIVAC II and by RCA on its 501 computer. Eventually, every major computer firm implemented COBOL, since it became a requirement attached to contracts involving purchase or rental of computers for government purposes. The CODASYL COBOL committee has remained responsible for maintaining the language, and documentation is still carried out by this group through the Government Printing Office.

COBOL has a character set consisting of twenty-six uppercase letters, ten digits, and the symbols

$$+ - * / = \$ < > . ; : " ( )$$

as well as the blank. Identifiers can have a maximum of thirty characters, including hyphens. There is a substantial set of reserved words in the language, and key words, such as ADD or READ, are called *verbs* or required words. Along with the usual four arithmetic operators, COBOL uses three relational ones (GREATER THAN, LESS THAN, and EQUAL TO), each of which can be preceded by the word NOT. The language can handle arithmetic and alphanumeric data, but all arithmetic numbers are

*This language resembled elements of ALGOL and COBOL.

either integers or real numbers. Furthermore, data can be expressed in internal form (specified as COMPUTATIONAL), BCD form (DISPLAY), or a form utilized to index tables (INDEX). The word PICTURE is used to describe the format characteristics of data items, such as the number of characters, whether an item is positive or negative, the placement of decimal points, or the placement of a dollar sign.

The structure of a program written in COBOL exhibits its unique form. First, there are four major classifications called *divisions* and defined as follows:

IDENTIFICATION—used to specify name, author, date and other remarks pertinent to the documenting of the program.

ENVIRONMENT —containing information about the hardware on which the program is to be compiled or executed.

DATA —files and records are described, as well as the data that the object program is to manipulate or create.

PROCEDURE —used to specify the steps the user wants the computer to follow, that is, the actual executable statements that make up the program.

Furthermore, the syntax of the language provides for statements, sentences, paragraphs, and sections. Working from the smallest unit, variables are called *nouns*, and several in sequence are separated by commas. Statements, such as the type IF-THEN-ELSE, use a semicolon to separate clauses, while sentences made up of a sequence of statements end with a period. A paragraph is the smallest grouping of sentences and statements that can be named (i.e., labeled), while sections must be named and consist of groups of paragraphs. Assignment statements in COBOL are preceded by the verb COMPUTE. Alternately, the MOVE verb is used to indicate the location where the value of a variable or constant is to be placed. Statements such as ADD A B GIVING C are also used to assign values to variables. Since data exist in the form of records, level numbers are used to delineate records or groups from other less inclusive groups in the data. For example, a record may have the name PAYROLL, subdivided into groups called NAME, HOURLY-RATE, and DEDUCTIONS, with the latter further divided into INCOME-TAX, SOC-SEC, and HEALTH INSURANCE. Subroutines (procedures) appear as paragraphs or sections, which are activated by a PERFORM command. There is no provision for functions in COBOL. The PERFORM command also affords one method of looping—the other is the IF-THEN statement combined with the GO TO statement.

Figure 8.6 illustrates a COBOL version of the sort and search algorithm presented in Figure 5.31. In addition to exhibiting the use of those features of the COBOL language already presented, the program affords the opportunity to observe other characteristics of this language.

Example: The source program is punched on cards in a prescribed form. Columns 1 through 6 are used for statement numbers; column 7 is for continuation purposes; and columns 8 through 72 are used for COBOL statements. Although several statements can occupy one line, there are two margins that must be observed. The A-margin starts in column 8 and is reserved for statement labels and procedure names. The B-margin starts in column 12 and is used for all sentences or clauses.

Input data is associated with three files: STUDENT-INFO-FILE, RECORD-NUMBER, and ST-NMBR. Output is associated with two files: SPECIAL-LINES to handle titles and PRINTER-FILE to handle all other output data. The description of the data itself is found in the FILE SECTION under each specific file name. Further data descriptions occur in the WORKING STORAGE SECTION, used for data that are either generated within the program or are assigned values at certain steps in the program. Linear lists and arrays in COBOL are structured by using the OCCURS statement, usually in the WORKING STORAGE SECTION. This is illustrated in Figure 8.6, where REKORDS is dimensioned for a maximum of 50 elements. Due to the grouping feature of COBOL, however, REKORDS assumes a structure that in some languages would appear in a row-by-column configuration.

The PROCEDURE DIVISION starts with the opening of an input file and an output file, thus preparing them for use in processing. The READ statement indicates the action to be taken when the end of the file is reached. Information is moved from the working storage section into an output file, which is then printed as indicated. The opening of the file named STUDENT-INFO-FILE indicates the point at which all student records will be input. This is done by a procedure called RDSTART, which is performed N times. The procedure A is performed next, using the sort procedure called PSORT. Finally, a file of student numbers is input—one at a time—and the sorted file is searched to locate the required numbers. When the search is complete, the program is terminated by the STOP RUN located in the statement labeled THE-END.

Two types of comparison operators have been used in this

1

```
00001    001010 IDENTIFICATION DIVISION.
00002    001020 PROGRAM-ID. 'STUDENTS'
00003    001030 INSTALLATION. UNIV OF NH
00004    001040 DATE-WRITTEN. 09/10/71
00005    001050 DATE-COMPILED. MAR 16,1972
00006    001060 REMARKS. THIS IS A COBOL VERSION OF THE ALGORITHM
00007    001070    PRESENTED IN FIG 5.31.
00008    001080
00009
00010    001100 ENVIRONMENT DIVISION.
00011    001110 CONFIGURATION SECTION.
00012    001120 SOURCE-COMPUTER. IBM-360 H50.
00013    001130 OBJECT-COMPUTER. IBM-360 H50.
00014    001140 INPUT-OUTPUT SECTION.
00015    001150 FILE-CONTROL.
00016    001160    SELECT STUDENT-INFO-FILE ASSIGN 'STUIN' UTILITY.
00017    001170    SELECT PRINTER-FILE ASSIGN 'PRNTR' UTILITY.
00018    001171    SELECT RECORD-NUMBER ASSIGN 'SYSIN' UTILITY.
00019    001172    SELECT ST-NMBR ASSIGN 'STUNC' UTILITY.
00020    001174
00021    001200 DATA DIVISION.
00022    001210 FILE SECTION.
00023    001220 FD  STUDENT-INFO-FILE,
00024    001230    LABEL RECORDS ARE OMITTED, DATA RECORDS IS RECDS,
00025    001231    RECORDING MODE IS F, RECORD CONTAINS 80 CHARACTERS.
00026    001250 01  RECDS PICTURE X(80).
00027    001370 FD  PRINTER-FILE,
00028    001380    LABEL RECORDS ARE OMITTED, DATA RECORD IS OUT,
00029    001382    RECORDING MODE IS F, RECORD CONTAINS 80 CHARACTERS.
00030    001400 01  OUT PICTURE X(80).
00031    001500 FD  RECORD-NUMBER,
00032    001510    LABEL RECORDS ARE OMITTED, DATA RECORDS IS COUNT,
00033    001520    RECORDING MODE IS F, RECORD CONTAINS 80 CHARACTERS.
00034    001530 01  COUNT.
00035    001531    02 N PICTURE 9999.
00036    001532    02 FILLER PICTURE X(76).
00037    001540 FD  ST-NMBR, LABEL RECORDS ARE OMITTED,
00038    001550    DATA RECORD IS NUMBER-LIST, RECORDING MODE IS F,
00039    001555    RECORD CONTAINS 80 CHARACTERS.
00040    001561 01  NUMBER-LIST.
00041    001562    02 NUMBER PICTURE X(7).
00042    001563    02 FILLER PICTURE X(73).
00043    002010 WORKING-STORAGE SECTION.
00044    002020 77  I PICTURE S9999 COMPUTATIONAL.
00045    002030 77  J PICTURE S9999 COMPUTATIONAL.
00046    002040 77  K PICTURE S9999 COMPUTATIONAL.
00047    002041 77  NN PICTURE S9999 COMPUTATIONAL.
00048    002042 77  JJ PICTURE S9999 COMPUTATIONAL.
00049    002043 77  JP PICTURE S9999 COMPUTATIONAL.
00050    002044 77  IIN PICTURE S9999 COMPUTATIONAL.
00051    002050 77  T PICTURE X(56).
00052    002100 01  HEADING-LINE-ONE.
00053    002110    02 FILLER PICTURE X(26) VALUE SPACES.
00054    002120    02 FILLER PICTURE X(27) VALUE 'STUDENT INFORMATION REQUEST'.
00055    002130    02 FILLER PICTURE X(27) VALUE SPACES.
```

FIGURE 8.6

2

```
00056   002140 01   RECRDS.
00057   002141      02 REKORDS OCCURS 50 TIMES.
00058   002142         03 STUDENT-NUMBER PICTURE X(7).
00059   002143         03 FILLER PICTURE X.
00060   002144         03 NAME PICTURE X(30).
00061   002145         03 FILLER PICTURE X.
00062   002146         03 SEX PICTURE X.
00063   002147         03 FILLER PICTURE X.
00064   002148         03 CLASS PICTURE X(2).
00065   002149         03 FILLER PICTURE X.
00066   002150         03 CUM-GR-PT-AVG PICTURE 9V99.
00067   002151         03 FILLER PICTURE X.
00068   002152         03 FIN-AID-RECVD PICTURE 9999999V99.
00069   002153         03 FILLER PICTURE X(23).
00070   002160 01   OUTDATA.
00071   002161      02 FILLER PICTURE X(3) VALUE IS SPACES.
00072   002162      02 STUDENT-NUMBER-OUT PICTURE X(7).
00073   002163      02 FILLER PICTURE X(5) VALUE IS SPACES.
00074   002164      02 NAME-OUT PICTURE X(30).
00075   002165      02 FILLER PICTURE X(5) VALUE IS SPACES.
00076   002166      02 SEX-OUT PICTURE X.
00077   002167      02 FILLER PICTURE X(5) VALUE IS SPACES.
00078   002168      02 FIN-AID-OUT PICTURE $Z,ZZZ,ZZZ.99.
00079   002200 01   HEADING-LINE-TWO.
00080   002210      02 FILLER PICTURE X(3) VALUE SPACES.
00081   002220      02 FILLER PICTURE X(7) VALUE 'STUDENT'.
00082   002230      02 FILLER PICTURE X(13) VALUE SPACES.
00083   002240      02 FILLER PICTURE X(7) VALUE 'STUDENT'.
00084   002250      02 FILLER PICTURE X(19) VALUE SPACES.
00085   002260      02 FILLER PICTURE X(3) VALUE 'SEX'.
00086   002270      02 FILLER PICTURE X(4) VALUE SPACES.
00087   002280      02 FILLER PICTURE X(13) VALUE 'FINANCIAL AID'.
00088   002290      02 FILLER PICTURE X(11) VALUE SPACES.
00089   002300 01   HEADING-LINE-LAST.
00090   002310      02 FILLER PICTURE X(3) VALUE SPACES.
00091   002320      02 FILLER PICTURE X(6) VALUE 'NUMBER'.
00092   002330      02 FILLER PICTURE X(15) VALUE SPACES.
00093   002340      02 FILLER PICTURE X(4) VALUE 'NAME'.
00094   002350      02 FILLER PICTURE X(30) VALUE SPACES.
00095   002360      02 FILLER PICTURE X(8) VALUE 'RECEIVED'.
00096   002370      02 FILLER PICTURE X(14) VALUE SPACES.
00097   002380
00098   002400 PROCEDURE DIVISION.
00099   002402      NOTE -- INPUT NUMBER OF RECCRDS,OPEN OUTPUT FILE.
00100   002403
00101   002410      OPEN INPUT RECORD-NUMBER OUTPUT PRINTER-FILE.
00102   002420      READ RECORD-NUMBER AT END CLOSE RECORD-NUMBER.
00103   002425
00104   002431      NOTE -- WRITE TITLES.
00105   002432
00106   002440      WRITE OUT FROM HEADING-LINE-ONE AFTER ADVANCING 2 LINES.
00107   002460      WRITE OUT FROM HEADING-LINE-TWO AFTER ADVANCING 3 LINES.
00108   002480      WRITE OUT FROM HEADING-LINE-LAST AFTER ADVANCING 1 LINES.
00109   002485
00110   002487      NOTE -- THE FILE OF STUDENT RECORDS IS INPUT
00111   002488      (USING PROCEDURE RDSTART) AND SORTED (USING PROCEDURE PSORT).
00112   002489
```

FIGURE 8.6 (Con't)

3

```
00113    002490    OPEN INPUT STUDENT-INFO-FILE.
00114    002491    SUBTRACT 1 FROM N GIVING NN.
00115    002500    PERFORM RDSTART VARYING J FROM 1 BY 1 UNTIL J > N.
00116    002510    PERFORM A VARYING I FROM 1 BY 1 UNTIL I > NN.
00117    002600    CLOSE STUDENT-INFO-FILE.
00118    002610    OPEN INPUT ST-NMBR.
00119    002611
00120    002613    NOTE -- THE SECTIONS LABELLED SEARCH-IT, LOOP, AND PASS
00121    002614    PERFORM THE BINARY SEARCH OF THE TABLE OF RECORDS FOR EACH
00122    002615    STUDENT NUMBER THAT IS INPUT.
00123    002616
00124    002620 SEARCH-IT. READ ST-NMBR AT END GO TO THE-END.
00125    002700    MOVE 1 TO I. MOVE N TO K.
00126    002701
00127    002710 LOOP.
00128    002711    ADD I K GIVING J.
00129    002720    DIVIDE 2 INTO J GIVING J.
00130    002730    IF NUMBER = STUDENT-NUMBER (J) THEN MOVE J TO K,
00131    002735-   PERFORM TEST2, GO TO WRIT
00132    002740    ELSE IF NUMBER > STUDENT-NUMBER (J) THEN GO TO PASS
00133    002750    ELSE IF NUMBER < STUDENT-NUMBER (J) THEN SUBTRACT 1 FROM J
00134    002751-   GIVING K.
00135    002770    GO TO TEST.
00136    002771
00137    002775 PASS. ADD 1 J GIVING I.
00138    002776
00139    002780 TEST. IF I < K THEN GO TO LOOP
00140    002790    ELSE IF I = K THEN PERFORM TEST2, GO TO WRIT
00141    002800    ELSE DISPLAY NUMBER, ' NUMBER NOT IN LIST', GO TO SEARCH-IT.
00142    002801
00143    002803    NOTE -- IF STUDENT NUMBER MATCHES ONE IN FILE,
00144    002804    IT IS OUTPUT AND THE NEXT NUMBER IS CHECKED.
00145    002806
00146    002810 WRIT. WRITE OUT FROM OUTDATA AFTER ADVANCING 2 LINES,
00147    002811-   GO TO SEARCH-IT.
00148    002812
00149    002820 THE-END. CLOSE ST-NMBR, PRINTER-FILE. STOP RUN.
00150    002821
00151    003100 RDSTART. READ STUDENT-INFO-FILE AT END GO TO EXIT-RDSTART.
00152    003105    MOVE RECDS TO REKORDS (J).
00153    003108 EXIT-RDSTART. EXIT.
00154    003110
00155    003111 PSORT. ADD 1 J GIVING JP.
00156    003200    IF STUDENT-NUMBER (J) IS GREATER THAN STUDENT-NUMBER (JP)
00157    003210    THEN PERFORM EXCHANGE.
00158    003220 EXIT-PSORT. EXIT.
00159    003225
00160    003240 EXCHANGE. ADD 1 J GIVING JJ.
00161    003241    MOVE REKORDS (J) TO T. MOVE REKORDS (JJ) TO REKORDS (J).
00162    003250    MOVE T TO REKORDS (JJ).
00163    003251 EXIT-EXCHANGE. EXIT.
00164    003255
00165    003260 TEST2. IF NUMBER IS NOT EQUAL TO STUDENT-NUMBER (K) THEN
00166    003270    DISPLAY NUMBER, ' NUMBER NOT IN LIST', GO TO SEARCH-IT
00167    003280    ELSE MOVE STUDENT-NUMBER (K) TO STUDENT-NUMBER-OUT.
00168    003290    MOVE NAME (K) TO NAME-OUT.
00169    003300    MOVE SEX (K) TO SEX-OUT.
```

FIGURE 8.6 (Con't)

4

```
00170    003310    MOVE FIN-AID-RECVD (K) TO FIN-AID-OUT.
00171    003320 EXIT-TEST2. EXIT.
00172    003325
00173    003512 A.   COMPUTE IIN = N - I.
00174    003513       PERFORM PSORT VARYING J FROM 1 BY 1 UNTIL J > IIN.
00175    003514 EXIT-A. EXIT.
```

STUDENT INFORMATION REQUEST

STUDENT NUMBER	STUDENT NAME	SEX	FINANCIAL AID RECEIVED
3247654	BLAK, SMOKEY T.	M	$ 2,500.50
1234567	BROWN, CHARLES	M	$ 10,111.90
8654321	WHATS-HIS-NAME	F	$ 444.43
8765432	PERILOUS, PAULINE	F	$ 1,250.90
1107642	CONTRARY,MARY Q.	F	$ 500.00

```
9999999 NUMBER NOT IN LIST
0010035 NUMBER NOT IN LIST
3334445 NUMBER NOT IN LIST
2313213 NUMBER NOT IN LIST
```

FIGURE 8.6 (Con't)

program. The first form involves the symbols $<$, $>$, or =, and the second form uses such phrases as IS GREATER THAN. For assignment purposes, both the COMPUTE statement and statements of the type ADD-GIVING have been used. Special messages are output using the DISPLAY verb with the information enclosed in quotes. Comments are indicated by the reserved word NOTE, which permits such comments to be either complete paragraphs or individual statements.

COBOL is not a succinct language, but it is English-like. This characteristic affords a form of documentation to all who might read a program written in the language. There is no problem with dialects, since the language was defined by a broadly based group that has maintained responsibility for its standardization. COBOL does not easily lend itself to applications beyond those for which it was designed, and there are languages in existence that incorporate its best features in a more general form. Nevertheless, it is a firmly entrenched tool in the world of programming languages.

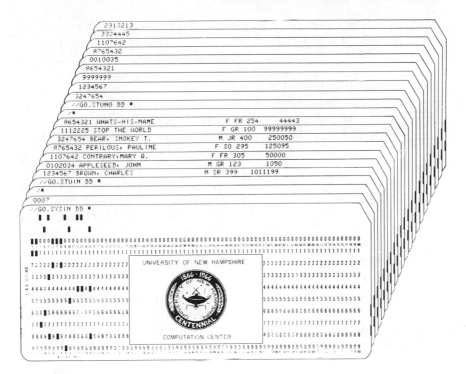

FIGURE 8.6 (Con't)

STRING- AND LIST-PROCESSING LANGUAGES

Often, a solution to a problem requires the input of substantially large amounts of data that must be stored in tables. The length and structure of the tables may change throughout the program. It is therefore impossible for the user to know ahead of time how much space is needed for each table. Great flexibility is required in dealing with such data, since storage must be dynamically altered in response to the demands of the program. This is accomplished by structuring the data in lists so that each data item has associated with it the location of the next item in logical sequence. Programming languages that are specifically designed to handle data in this manner are called *list-processing languages*. They are most often utilized for proving theorems, writing compilers, or investigating artificial intelligence.

LISP

LISP is a list-processing language whose development was started in 1959 at MIT by the Artificial Intelligence Group. A version called LISP 1.5 was presented in a programming manual published in 1960 by John McCarthy. There is also a LISP 2 version, which has a source language based on ALGOL. LISP is primarily a language for expressing functional relationships and is well suited for general symbol manipulation. Frequently, it is applied to symbolic mathematics, such as the examination of well-formed formulas, propositions, and logical expressions.

Unlike algebraically oriented programming languages in which a data element is a numerical value, LISP makes use of data elements that are lists. The basic data element in LISP is the *atom*. An atom is either an identifier (called an *atomic symbol*) or a number. An identifier consists of a string of letters or numbers, the first of which must be a letter. A, AB, XYZQ125, and THISISTHEEND are all atoms. LISP can be stated in its hardware language (which uses symbolic expressions called *S-expressions*) or in its reference language (which uses meta expressions called *M-expressions*).

S-expressions are the data for a LISP program. An S-expression is either an atomic symbol or a combination of two S-expressions indicated as (X.Y). S-expressions can be built from other S-expressions; for example,

    B
    (A.B)
    (A.(B.C))
    (((A.B).C).D)

If an S-expression is not an atomic symbol such as B, then it can be defined as the node of a binary tree in which both branches are other S-expressions. Figure 8.7 illustrates the representation of two different S-expressions as binary-tree structures. NIL is a special atomic symbol used as a terminator. The S-expression in Figure 8.7(b) is given in *list notation*, which is equivalent to

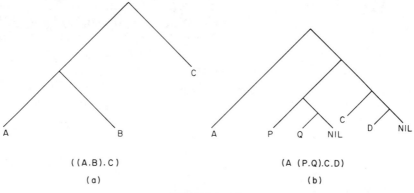

((A.B).C)

(a)

(A (P.Q).C.D)

(b)

FIGURE 8.7

(A. (P. (Q.NIL)) .(C. (D.NIL))); however Figure 8.7(a) is represented in list notation as ((A B).C), since the expression terminates
with an atom other than NIL.

When implemented on a computer, the S-expression becomes a
memory address. If the S-expression is an atom, then the address is
a pointer to the list of storage locations that contain information
about the atom (e.g., whether the atom is defined as a function
name or as a variable). When the expression is not an atom,
however, the address points to a memory location that contains
two addresses—one for each S-expression contained as the
branches of the binary-tree node. In the early development of
LISP, these two addresses were contained in an *address register*
and a *decrement register*. Consequently, the first half of a
nonatomic S-expression is known as the CAR (for Contents of
Address Register), while the second half is known as the CDR (for
Contents of the Decrement Register). The use of CAR and CDR
will be illustrated later in the discussion.

Languages such as FORTRAN have a program structure that is
composed of sequential lines of instructions. These instructions
specify the operations to be performed on numerical values. The
structure of a LISP program, however, is identical to its data
structure. This permits a program either to generate another
program, which can then be executed, or to modify itself during
execution. A LISP program consists of a sequence of S-expressions, called *forms*. A form is input and evaluated, and the result is
output. The process is then repeated for the next form. A form is
defined as follows:

```
        FORM
          |
        is a
          |
  VARIABLE:   a single atom whose value is the S-expression
          |           assigned to that variable.
        or a
          |
FUNCTION CALL:   a list whose first element is a
                 FUNCTION and whose remaining elements are ARGUMENTS
                    |                                          |
              FUNCTION NAME (an atom)                        FORMS
                    |                                          |
                  or a                                         or
                    |                                          |
        FUNCTIONAL EXPRESSION (most common is        S-expressions
                    |              LAMBDA type)
                  or a                  |
                    |           (LAMBDA (var.list)(form))
                  FORM
```

Two examples will illustrate the application of forms in LISP programs. LISP statements are written either as *composite functions* or as *conditional expressions*.

Example: The first type of statement is shown in Figure 8.8(a) for both reference and hardware languages. The composite function is evaluated starting from the innermost expression. The function *cdr* in LISP produces the second part of the composite argument (X.Y.Z.A.) or, in this case, (Y.Z.A). The function is applied again to produce (Z.A). Finally, the function *car*, which produces the first part of a composite argument, yields Z. Since LISP allows an entire composite function to be indicated by a simple composite name, the expression in Figure 8.8(a) can be represented as *caddr*[x].

Example: The use of conditional expressions in LISP is illustrated in Figure 8.8(b) by a recursive function that calculates the factorial of N. The M-expression is interpreted in the following manner:

If n = 0 is true, then the functional value is 1; otherwise the functional value is n(n−1)!

This results is a recursive procedure, as indicated in the following calculation of 2!

$$2! = [2=0 \rightarrow 1; T \rightarrow 2*(2-1)!] = 2*1!$$
$$= 2*[1=0 \rightarrow 1; T \rightarrow 1*(1-1)!] = 2*1*0!$$
$$= 2*1*[0=0 \rightarrow 1; T \rightarrow 0*(0-1)!] = 2*1*1$$
$$= 2$$

The S-expression defines the function named FACTORIAL. The word LAMBDA indicates that the function is operating on N. The conditional phrase is identified by COND, which first indicates that the value of FACTORIAL is 1 if N=0. Otherwise, the function will be called again with N=N−1. In LISP arithmetic computations are performed using forward Polish notation. For example, $A*B+C$ becomes $+*ABC$ and is stated in LISP as (PLUS (TIMES A B) C). This accounts for the strange appearance of the quantity N(N−1)! in the S-expression.

In general, a LISP program consists of pairs of arguments that are processed by the LISP interpreter, using special routines that are themselves functions. The language is difficult to read and write because of the massive use of parentheses or brackets. It does express functional relationships in a symbolic form that is well suited to specific applications of the language. LISP is

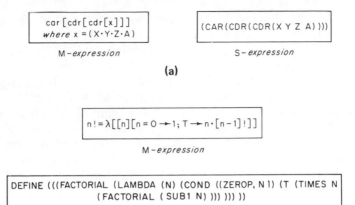

car[cdr[cdr[x]]]
where x = (X·Y·Z·A)

M-*expression*

(CAR(CDR(CDR(X Y Z A))))

S-*expression*

(a)

n! = λ[[n][n = 0 → 1; T → n·[n−1]!]]

M-*expression*

DEFINE (((FACTORIAL (LAMBDA (N) (COND ((ZEROP, N 1) (T (TIMES N
(FACTORIAL (SUB1 N)))))))))

M-*expression*

(b)

FIGURE 8.8

machine independent but lacks standardization; consequently it is implementation dependent. A full discussion of LISP is beyond the scope of this text, but this brief survey serves as a contrast to the second type of specialized programming language, which completes the remainder of this section.

The data associated with a problem must sometimes be represented as a sequence of characters that vary in length. Such a sequence is referred to as a *string*, and languages that manipulate data of this type are called *string-processing languages*. Lists and strings are closely related, since strings are one kind of information that can be represented internally in a computer by lists. The need for string-processing is found in problems dealing with pattern searching, handling of text material, or character transformation.

SNOBOL

SNOBOL is a string-processing language developed at Bell Telephone Laboratories in 1962. It is a problem-oriented language that is especially useful for pattern-matching and string-handling. Integer and real number arithmetic are also available. Variable names in SNOBOL may be assigned "values" that are character strings, such as BETA='XYZ'. The length of strings can be determined by the SIZE function so that SIZE(BETA) is evaluated as 3. Combining this function in an expression such as SIZE(BETA) +   1   12 /   4 results in an answer of 43. The quantity to the left of the blank yields 4; the quantity to the right yields 3; and the blank itself causes concatenation of the two strings for a final result of 43.

Statements in SNOBOL can be labeled, and the last statement in every program is END. Logical comparisons can be made between strings that determine transfer of control or assign new values to variables. A statement such as M = .GT(M,27) M + 1 tests the value of M, and if it is greater than 27, M is incremented by 1. If a statement containing a test is followed by a :S(label), the result is a branch to the statement in the program containing that label if the condition is satisfied. Similarly, :F(label) results in a branch if the condition fails. Unconditional branching is accomplished by :(label).

Functions in SNOBOL are identified by statements of the form DEFINE ('function name (list of variable names)', 'label of entry point'); thus a factorial function can be designated by DEFINE('FACT(N)','COMPUTE'). Such a function includes the following statements:

    COMPUTE   FACT = N
        GO   FACT = FACT * (N −   1)
             N = .GT(N,2) N − 1   :S(GO)F(RETURN)

Another feature of SNOBOL is that strings of characters can be examined for patterns, and variables assigned values if the pattern matches the string. For example, if LINE is a variable consisting of 'NOW IS THE TIME' and WHEN is a variable with the value 'TIME', the statement LINE WHEN = 'HOUR' will cause LINE to be scanned for an occurrence of the value of WHEN. If a match is made, the value to the right of the equals sign replaces the matched pattern. In our example, LINE assumes the value 'NOW IS THE HOUR'. More complex pattern matchings can be realized by providing alternate patterns or the concatenation of two or more patterns.

SNOBOL and LISP are not the only two programming languages designed to permit the manipulation of strings and lists, but they do illustrate the attempts to provide methods for handling data that no other language discussed so far can adequately provide. The next section describes a language that incorporates many of the best features of all these languages.

MULTIPURPOSE LANGUAGES

The basic criterion for classifying a language as *multipurpose* is that it be designed specifically for solving problems in two or more distinct areas equally well. While languages such as FORTRAN and

COBOL may be applied to problems that they were not originally designed to handle, there is a degree of awkwardness in some of those applications. Most languages were written in response to particular programming needs and then later expanded in an attempt to provide wider usage. Multipurpose languages initially assume a wider utilization in problem-solving. Formula ALGOL (1963) extends ALGOL to operations in formal algebra, list-processing, and string-manipulation. LISP2 (1964) extended LISP1.5 to an ALGOL-like structure, including improvements in numerical computations, interpretation, and notation. At the same time, the application areas were increased to such fields as pattern recognition, game-playing, and algebraic manipulation. This section is concerned primarily with a language called PL/I, the most ambitious effort in the field of multipurpose languages.

PL/I

In 1963 a joint committee was set up by two organizations, SHARE (a scientific users' group) and GUIDE (a commercial users' group). Their purpose was to develop a programming language that would satisfy the needs of both groups, thus making communication between the two types of users much easier. They examined the best features of such existing languages as ALGOL, COBOL, and FORTRAN, and the result of their work was a high-powered language called PL/I (Programming Language One). The language was designed for third generation computers, which are general purpose machines; thus it interacts well with an operating system. The first official manual was issued by IBM in 1965, and in 1966 the first System/360 PL/I compiler was released. Although difficulties were encountered with early versions of the language, it soon became apparent that PL/I was a versatile programming tool with applications in commercial, scientific, textual and symbolic problem-solving areas. Virtually all the excellent features of other major languages were included in PL/I, and although the full version of the language is hard to implement due to storage size requirements, it is easy to read and write. In fact, PL/I is easy enough for beginning programmers to use, but it is also a powerful tool for advanced programmers (due to its facilities for dynamic storage allocation, text-editing of a program, and list-processing).

A PL/I program consists of the basic elements illustrated in Figure 8.9. The block concept is fundamental in PL/I, since all PL/I programs are made up of at least one procedure, termed a MAIN procedure, that can contain other procedures or blocks. These blocks can be nested (internal) or adjacent (external). PL/I is designed so that algorithms can be programmed in modules,

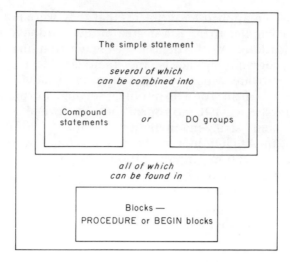

FIGURE 8.9   Basic Elements Constituting a PL/1 Program

which can be compiled separately and later combined to form one large program.

PL/I makes use of either a 48- or 60-character set, depending on the particular implementation. The full character set includes all uppercase letters of the alphabet, the 10 digits, and 21 specialized characters such as $<$, $>$, Γ, $|$, $;$, $:$, and $\%$. Arithmetic types include decimal and binary, floating-point and fixed-point, real and complex, while string operations can be performed on both characters and bit-string data. Data used for program control can also be identified, as in the case of labels. Input/output is performed using either LIST (unformatted I/O), EDIT (formatted I/O), or DATA (in which both the variable name and its value are indicated). These are combined with PUT and GET for I/O statements. Data are assumed to exist in a continuous stream (whether for input or output) and are associated with files and records. Record-oriented I/O makes use of READ and WRITE statements, such as READ FILE(PAYROLL) INTO (STORE) or WRITE FILE(STUDENTS) FROM (WORKAREA). Such I/O permits rapid transmission of entire records of data.

The physical structure of a PL/I program using card format requires statements to be punched in columns 2 through 72. No statement numbers are necessary. Since more than one statement is allowed per card, the semicolon is used as a delimiter for such statements. There are no restrictions regarding the column in which a statement is started, thus providing maximum flexibility in designing an easily read program. Comments may be inserted anywhere, including the middle of a statement, provided they start with /* and end with */. Statement labels are delimited with a colon, and statements may have more than one label. Identifiers can have as many as 31 characters.

Transfer of control is indicated by GO TO followed by a label name, and it becomes conditional through the use of IF—THEN—ELSE clauses. Loops are indicated by a DO statement that can increment or decrement to a set value and use positive or negative values for loop variables, and that includes a WHILE clause that can be used for early termination of the loop upon encountering a prescribed condition. An example would be DO I=−1 TO 2 BY .3 WHILE(X<6). If the DO statement contains no loop information, the group of statements is executed only once. In either case, each DO group is associated with an END statement that may contain the name of an optional label on the DO statement. Subroutines and functions are also classified as procedures and may be internal or external. Functions can be defined as recursive, and many built-in functions such as SIN or COS are available.

Other features of PL/I are best illustrated by referring to Figure 8.10, where the algorithm for building and traversing a binary tree is presented in program form.

Example: The first block of statements indicates the manner in which variables are typed using the DECLARE statement. Furthermore, TREE has been declared as a structure, which is subdivided into levels—each containing the data to be associated with the structure. Only the sub-levels can have data types declared. Structures in PL/I are an extremely useful means of forming aggregates of data items that may be of different types but logically related. The declaration of STACK illustrates the standard method of stating the dimension of a linear list, which in this case contains ten elements. Matrix arrays are similarly identified, while all dimensioned variables may use subscripts that are negative, zero, or positive. The arithmetic type declared for DATA includes a parenthetical expression called the *precision factor*. This allows the user to state the total number of significant digits to be associated with a data item as well as the number of decimal places to be maintained—if any.

The POINTER declaration in this program is used to identify certain variables as carriers of a special type of data, namely, a storage-location address. In addition, storage is allocated so that a base pointer can be set as a starting point; later, when a FREE statement occurs, this starting point becomes available. It is therefore unnecessary to carry the data associated with the binary tree in contiguous storage locations (e.g., an array), since the pointers indicate where the data items are to be found. The right-pointing arrow symbol in expressions such as Q−>DATA

```
/*   PL1 VERSION OF BINARY TREE AS STATED IN FLOWCHART (FIG. 5.52) */


             /*   PL1 VERSION OF BINARY TREE AS STATED IN FLOWCHART (FIG. 5.52) */
 1        PTRTEST: PROC OPTIONS(MAIN);
 2           DCL 1 TREE BASED(P),
                2 DATA BINARY FIXED(13,4),
                2 POINT1 POINTER,
                2 POINT2 POINTER;
 3           DCL STACK(30)POINTER;
 4           DCL BEG PCINTER;
 5           ALLOCATE TREE;
 6           BEG=P;   POINT1,POINT2=NULL;
 8           ON ENDFILE(SYSIN)GO TO END;
          /*
          CONSTRUCT BINARY TREE USING POINTERS TO INDICATE LOCATIONS IN
          STORAGE OF EACH ITEM
             */
10               GET FILE(SYSIN)LIST(P->DATA);
11               PUT FILE(SYSPRINT)LIST('ORIGINAL INPUT LIST FROM DATA CARDS');
12               PUT FILE(SYSPRINT)SKIP(2) LIST(P->DATA);
13        BEGIN: ALLOCATE TREE SET(Q);
14               GET FILE(SYSIN)LIST(Q->DATA); PUT FILE(SYSPRINT)LIST(Q->DATA);
16               P=BEG;   Q->POINT1,Q->POINT2=NULL;
          /*
              THIS LOOP PLACES ITEM IN PROPER LOCATION AND SETS
              APPROPRIATE POINTERS
          */
18        LOOP: IF Q->DATA<=DATA THEN IF POINT1=NULL THEN DO;
21               POINT1=Q; GO TO BEGIN; END;
24            ELSE DO;
25               P=POINT1; GO TO LOOP; END;
28            ELSE DO;
29               IF POINT2=NULL THEN DO; POINT2=Q; GO TO BEGIN; END;
34            ELSE DO; P=POINT2; GO TO LOOP; END;   END;
39         END: FREE Q->TREE;
          /*
               TRAVERSE BINARY TREE TO OUTPUT VALUES IN ASCENDING ORDER
               AS GIVEN IN FLOWCHART FIG. 5.59
          */
40        PUT FILE(SYSPRINT)SKIP(2) LIST('RESULTS FROM TRAVERSING THE TREE');
41        PP=1; P=BEG;
43        LOOP2: DO WHILE (P¬=NULL);
44               STACK(PP)=P; PP=PP+1; P=P->POINT1; END;
48            IF PP=1 THEN GO TO STOP; ELSE
50               PP=PP-1; P=STACK(PP);
52               PUT FILE(SYSPRINT)SKIP EDIT(P->DATA)(COLUMN(50),F(8,2),X(70));
53               P=P->POINT2; GO TO LOOP2;
55        STOP: END PTRTEST;
```

```
ORIGINAL INPUT LIST FROM DATA CARDS

      41.00              26.00      13.00       2.00        42.00
      27.00              18.00      54.00       5.00        12.00

RESULTS FROM TRAVERSING THE TREE
                                      2.00
                                      5.00
                                     12.00
                                     13.00
                                     18.00
                                     26.00
                                     27.00
                                     41.00
                                     42.00
                                     54.00
```

FIGURE 8.10

means that the address stored in Q points to the location of DATA. This specialized technique, illustrating a higher level programming technique in PL/I, is ideally suited to the particular demands of the original problem and solution, as stated in Chapter 5.

Although a user of PL/I is faced with choosing from among the many capabilities offered by the language, he can also choose to ignore many of them and simply operate under the default conditions that exist in PL/I. The language is strongly diagnostic and affords the user the opportunity of making system error conditions work to his advantage. These conditions, such as an end-of-file or division by zero, might otherwise cause termination of execution. An awareness of the particular implementation available at the user's installation is essential, and varying specifications can make the use of the language more difficult than is necessary. Some people make the claim that since other programming languages have expanded their capabilities to cover those areas in which they were deficient, there is no need to turn to PL/I to bridge the gap. Restricted implementation and poor standardization techniques have further restrained potential users from converting to PL/I. Despite these difficulties, PL/I remains a rich programming language that is an outstanding example of a truly general purpose language.

The programming languages discussed in this chapter are indicative of the rapid growth in the communication between men and machines. This is a small step toward a full appreciation of the wealth of experimentation found in the entire category of languages in existence today. Yet, even in such a selective presentation, one can sense the rapid progress being made to produce better programming languages with less limited areas of application and more freedom for the programmer.

EXERCISES

1. What is a compiler? What is its function?

2. Identify and describe three classifications of higher level programming languages.

3. Using a programming language of your choice, parallel its structure with the structure of a spoken language, such as English, with respect to punctuation, words, sentences, etc.

4. List the advantages and disadvantages of using a higher level programming language instead of an assembler language.

5. Describe the method used by the languages described in this chapter to identify arrays.

6. State five specific differences between APL and any of the other scientific languages.

7. Identify and describe the use of the DATA DIVISION and the PROCEDURE DIVISION sections of a COBOL program.

8. What is unique about the structure of a LISP program?

9. Prepare an in-depth report on any one of the programming languages in this chapter and—if possible—define an algorithm in that language and execute it on a computer.

SELECTED REFERENCES

Berry, Paul, *APL/360 Primer*, Form GH20-0689-1, New York: International Business Machines Corporation, 1970.

Blatt, John M., *Introduction to Fortran IV Programming Using the Watfor/Watfiv Compilers*, Pacific Palisades, Calif.: Goodyear, 1971.

Galler, B. A., *The Language of Computers*, New York: McGraw-Hill, 1962.

Griswold, Ralph E., James F. Poage, and Ivan P. Polonsky, *The SNOBOL4 Programming Language*, (2nd ed.), Englewood Cliffs, N.J.: Prentice-Hall, 1971.

Gross, Jonathan, and Walter S. Brainerd, *Fundamental Programming Concepts*, New York: Harper and Row, 1972.

IBM System/360 Operating System American National Standard COBOL, Form GC28-6396-2, IBM Corporation.

IBM System/360 Operating System FORTRAN IV(G and H) Programmer's Guide, Form GC28-6816-2, IBM Corporation.

IBM System/360 Operating System PL/I(F) Programmer's Guide, Form GC28-6594-6, IBM Corporation.

Iverson, K. E., *A Programming Language*, New York: John Wiley, 1962.

Katzan, Harry Jr., *Advanced Programming: Programming and Operating Systems*. New York: Van Nostrand Reinhold, 1970.

Kemeny, J. G., and T. E. Kurtz, *Basic Programming (2nd ed.)*, New York: John Wiley, 1971.

McCarthy, John, et. al., *LISP 1.5 Programmer's Manual*, Cambridge, Mass.: M. I. T. Press, 1969.

Naur, Peter (editor), "Revised Report on the Algorithmic Language ALGOL60," *Communications of the ACM*, Vol. 6, No. 1 (January, 1963), pp. 1-17.

Neuhold, Erich J., and Harold W. Lawson, Jr., *The PL/I Machine: An Introduction to Programming*. Reading, Mass.: Addison-Wesley, 1971.

Rosen, S., *Programming Systems and Languages*, New York: McGraw-Hill, 1967.

Sammet, Jean E., *Programming Languages: History and Fundamentals*, Englewood Cliffs, N.J.: Prentice-Hall, 1969.

Stern, Nancy B., and Robert A. Stern, *COBOL Programming*, New York: John Wiley, 1970.

Wegner, Peter, *Programming Languages, Information Structures, and Machine Organization*. New York: McGraw-Hill, 1968.

Software Systems

The principles of the stored program computer were developed by Dr. John von Neumann in 1946 and were realized in the EDSAC computer in 1949. Since then, computer programming has been characterized by the coding of algorithms in a form "understandable" to computers. Initially, computer programs were written in an external representation of machine language, as exemplified in Chapter 6. Later, standard programs such as assemblers and compilers were developed. The complete computer system could then be divided into two distinct parts: the physical equipment or *hardware*, such as readers, printers and processing units, and the standard programs or *software*, which allowed the programmer to express his algorithms in a more readable form. This development of hardware and software has continued to progress from 1956 to the present. Certain features originally introduced through software were later implemented in the hardware of newer computers, and some features, which existed as "hard-wiring," were replaced by programs to reduce the cost of the hardware. We shall now trace the development of software, making reference to hardware improvements whenever necessary.

MANUAL JOB-AFTER-JOB PROCESSING

The first stored program computers were controlled manually in the sense that each user was responsible for loading his "job" into the computer and operating the hardware. Machine language

314

programs were either punched on cards and input into the computer memory using a card reader or entered directly via a computer console typewriter. The entire hardware facilities were dedicated to satisfying the requirements of a single user's program, although only a fraction of the time spent by the user in the computer room was devoted to actual processing. Much of the time was spent loading cards or debugging the program. The debugging process was characterized by the user pressing buttons causing the computer to "single cycle"—execute one instruction for each push of the button. The contents of key memory registers resulting from execution of an instruction were displayed in lights on the computer console. Of course, whenever an error was detected, corrections were made, and the corrected program was again loaded into the computer. Depending on the size of the local computer-user population, a programmer might have had almost unlimited time to develop his program, or at worst, each user signed a schedule for a slot of time.

The advent of assemblers [see Chapter 6] made programming easier for computer users, while simultaneously complicating the operation of the computer. First, the assembler program was loaded into the computer memory. The user's symbolic program was loaded next and was accepted as input by the assembler. The assembler produced an equivalent machine language program that was punched on cards. If errors in syntax were made in the coding of the symbolic program, the assembler detected them and the programmer had to make corrections and reinitiate the assembly process. Eventually, the machine language program was loaded and executed, as explained previously. Hence the time spent in the computer room running one job most likely increased, but the amount of time spent computing useful output remained essentially static. The use of symbolic statements, however, afforded the programmer greater flexibility in programming and relieved the tedium of preparing lists of numerical instructions. This resulted in more complex algorithms and, consequently, more use of the processing power of the computer.

The development of compiler languages (e.g., FORTRAN) allowed algorithms to be expressed in an algebraic form rather than in the cryptic notation of assembler language. It was no longer necessary to be skilled in machine language to use a computer, and the number of computer users increased significantly. The procedure required to use the computer remained the same. First, the compiler was loaded into memory, followed by the source program as input. The result was an *object deck* (a punched machine language deck). As the compiler languages became more complex, more steps were added to the compilation process. The compiler first produced an intermediate output that became a second input to the compiler. Initially, the intermediate output was stored on cards; later it was stored temporarily on magnetic tape.

The concept of a subroutine added still another dimension to the operation of a computer. Since language translators assigned the first instruction of each program translated to location zero, it was necessary to provide a means for modifying addresses in subroutine instructions. This was necessary because subroutines were loaded into memory following the main program. *Loader programs* were developed for this purpose. Initially, instructions for loading were produced by the language translators as the first instructions in the object deck of the main program. This form of the loader was responsible for loading the main program (followed by subroutines) into contiguous storage locations, for changing the instructions in the subroutine by adding the address of the first instruction in each subroutine to the memory address portions of each instruction, and for providing the entry address of each subroutine to the main program. Eventually, loaders became separate programs that had to be stored in memory. The composite object deck, consisting of the object decks for the main program and subroutines, was submitted as input to the loader.

These advancements in programming computers provided the programmer with a means to improve and simplify his programs, while computer operations became increasingly inefficient. The casual user of a computer center who was not well skilled in computer operations spent much more time than was necessary running his programs. Consequently, computer centers placed the running of programs under the control of a trained computer operator. The programmer was banned from the machine room. Programs were submitted to a clerk, who in turn passed them on to the computer operator for processing, and the programmer eventually received his completed run from the clerk. This arrangement provided for a more efficient computer operation and allowed the programmer to spend time on other projects. Another consequence was that programmers, for the most part, became more careful when writing programs, since the time between computer runs was lengthened. But the job-to-job transition was still manual, and the processing unit remained idle, while decks were loaded and tapes were mounted.

BATCH-PROCESSING

As computer hardware components improved in speed, their cost also increased. Manual operating procedures became intolerable, since the processing unit—the most expensive component of the computer—still had to sit idle much of the time. *Monitor programs* that mechanized many of the manual operations were developed to control the job-to-job sequencing. The first widely used monitor system was FMS (FORTRAN Monitor System), which was developed in 1958 for the IBM 709 computer. The processing programs described in the previous section (e.g., assemblers, compilers, loaders) were stored on a magnetic tape, called the *systems library tape*. Library programs (i.e., standard user programs maintained at the computer center) were also stored on tape. Monitor programs reside permanently in memory, and all programs to be processed are collected in a "batch" and placed in the card-reader hopper. The monitor program controls the job-to-job sequencing and loads the appropriate processing programs and library programs needed by the user's program.

Since each user's requirements differ with respect to compilers or assemblers needed, the monitor program must be told the sequence of programs to load. Languages, called *job-control languages*, were developed to allow the user to communicate with the monitor program. A sample job set-up appears in Figure 9.1. The $JOB card signifies the beginning of a new job and serves to

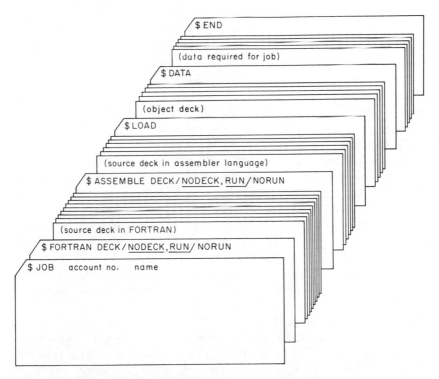

FIGURE 9.1 Sample Control Language

identify the user by account number. Part of the monitor program is required to keep track of the amount of time used for each account number so that the user can be billed. The $FORTRAN card means that a FORTRAN source program follows and the services of the FORTRAN compiler are needed. The options on this job-control card indicate whether an object deck is to be punched or the resultant machine language is to be executed—or neither, or both. The underlined options are the default values, meaning that if no options are specified, the underlined values are assumed. For example, if the card $FORTRAN DECK is used, the resultant object program is punched on cards and also written on a magnetic tape, called the *execution tape*. If FORTRAN errors are present, nothing is written on the tape, and no cards are punched. The $ASSEMBLE card implies that assembler-language routines follow and causes the monitor to load the assembler program into memory. The options are treated exactly as with FORTRAN. If the assembler language coding is a subroutine to be used with a FORTRAN main program, the object program is copied onto the execution tape. If all programs to be used are in object form, the $LOAD card is placed immediately after the $JOB card, and the cards for using the FORTRAN compiler and the assembler are not needed. If no object decks are included as part of the job, the $LOAD card is unnecessary. The $DATA card is a signal to the monitor to load the loader program into memory. The loader reads the object programs from the execution tape into memory, modifying addresses in instructions whenever necessary, and resolves external references in each routine. Moreover, whenever a standard library routine is referenced, the loader searches the library tape for the required routine and loads it into memory. If the job requires data cards, they are placed after the $DATA card and are read by the loaded program.

Since the monitor program causes indirect communication with a computer and also requires some of the physical resources that the programmer uses (e.g., memory space and tapes), the nature of computer programs has changed. Programs can no longer issues a HALT instruction but must return control to the monitor program when processing is complete. The library tape, the execution tape, and the tapes used by compilers and assemblers for intermediate storage are permanently mounted and cannot be used by the programmer. To prevent inadvertent or malicious halting of the computer or use of the system tapes, standard subroutines have been developed. The user is required to utilize these subroutines to return control to the monitor and to perform all I/O operations. The use of these subroutines was accomplished by providing new commands in compiler languages such as

FORTRAN, which were translated into calls to the appropriate subroutines. Assembler-language programs had to provide the code for invoking these routines. Program errors, such as dividing by zero or overflow, have to be detected by the monitor so that an error message can be printed and processing continued with the next job in the batch. Probably the most serious problem associated with early batch processing monitors was the over-writing of the monitor's instructions by incorrect instructions in a user's program. Such action "brought the system down" and required the monitor program to be reloaded into memory. Hardware improvements, which are discussed later, helped allevi-ate this problem.

As programs became longer and produced a greater number of lines of output, the card reader and printer became inadequate, since the reading of cards and the printing of lines took an inordinate amount of time. To decrease the amount of time necessary to process a batch of jobs, *off-line operations* were introduced. A smaller, less expensive computer is used to transcribe the entire batch of jobs, including control language, onto a magnetic tape. This tape, called the *system input tape*, becomes the primary input to the computer that normally processes user's jobs. The user jobs direct all their output to a *system output tape*. The system output tape is then carried to the smaller computer for printing. Hence the larger, more powerful computer was no longer slowed by card readers and printers. The major drawback of this technique, however, is that two computers are required. Further improvements in software systems were related to hardware improvements, which are discussed next.

HARDWARE DEVELOPMENTS

Prior to the early 1960s, peripheral equipment, such as card readers, printers, and magnetic tapes, were directly controlled by the computer's arithmetic and control units, collectively called the *central processing unit* (CPU). During each I/O operation, there-fore, the computer's CPU had to give its undivided attention to a particular peripheral unit. Since the peripheral devices are electro-mechanical they do not come close to approaching the speed of the completely electronic CPU. Hence the CPU spent much time waiting for the completion of reads and writes. During the idle time, the CPU could have executed several machine instructions. For example, if a card reader reads 600 cards/min and average instruction execution time of the CPU is 25 μsec (microsecond or millionth of a second), 4000 instructions can be executed in the time it takes to read a single card. Similarly, if an eighty-byte record (the equivalent of one card, called a card image) can be read from magnetic tape in .0013 seconds, 52 machine instructions can be executed by the CPU in the same length of time. Although faster peripherals such as magnetic disks and drums were developed, simultaneous improvements in CPUs left the computer system with the same inefficiency. Assume that the average instruction time has decreased to 5 μsec and that magnetic disks can transfer a card image in 260 μsec (.00026 sec). The CPU could then execute 52 instructions in the length of time that one 80-byte block can be read from disk. Since the number of read operations necessary at a particular point in a program is usually greater than one and since data are usually read from magnetic tapes and disks in blocks greater than eighty bytes, the idle processor time due to I/O is a multiple of the times cited in the previous examples. To alleviate the problem of inefficient use of the CPU during I/O operations, additional hardware was added to control these operations.

Input/Output Channels and Interrupts

In the System/360, peripheral devices are connected to the computer indirectly through I/O channels. A *channel* is a small computer-like device complete with registers, an instruction repertoire, and a control counter (CC). The commands that a channel is to execute, called a *channel program*, are stored in the main memory of the computer. The CPU initiates the operation of a channel by placing the address of the first instruction of the required channel program into the channel's CC. The channel begins transferring characters either from memory to an output device or into memory from an input device. Once the channel has been initiated by the CPU, it runs in parallel with the processing unit. When the channel completes its program, it signals the CPU that it is finished. The input and output of information can therefore be overlapped with processing, thus allowing the CPU to operate at greater efficiency. Several units may be attached to a single channel. One channel, called the *multiplexor channel*, has the slow speed devices such as card readers, card punches, and printers attached to it. This channel can send or receive information in an interleaved manner to or from several of these devices at a time. Other channels may have several units of the same type attached, (e.g., tape drives or disk drives), but the channel is capable of communicating with only one of these high speed devices at a time. A schematic representation of a computer with channels appears in Figure 9.2. The configuration shown has a

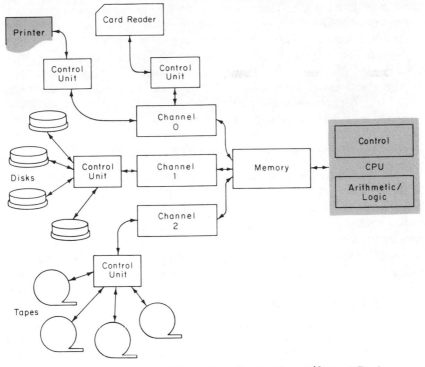

FIGURE 9.2 Computer with Channels to Control Input/Output Devices

card reader and printer on channel 0—the multiplexor channel—each with its own device control unit. Channel 2 has four tape drives. The units on these channels share a common device control unit, since only one drive can communicate with the channel at a time.

Any condition that causes the processing unit to suspend execution of the instructions is called an *interrupt*. Program errors, such as overflow, dividing by zero, and illegal instructions, are automatically detected by the hardware, and the condition that caused the interrupt is placed in a coded form in a special interrupt condition register. Interrupts are normally processed by a section of the monitor program called the *interrupt handler*. In addition to setting the interrupt condition register when an interrupt is detected, the hardware also causes a branch to a fixed location in memory. A branch instruction to the first instruction of the interrupt handler is stored in this location. The interrupt handler determines the type of interrupt and initiates the proper corrective action. The signal from a channel that its program has been completed is also processed as an interrupt by the hardware. The interrupt handler directs control to the proper I/O routine in this case. The basic difference between I/O interrupts and program interrupts is that I/O interrupts are external to the user's program. The user expects either corrective action or an error message for program interrupts, but none for I/O interrupts. Also, since interrupts of different types may occur in succession, the information concerning all interrupts must be retained, while the monitor program uses a built-in priority scheme to determine the order in which the interrupts are to be processed.

Automatic Relocatability and Memory Protection

To facilitate the loading of programs running under a monitor system, the addressing techniques in computers have been improved so that a program can be loaded anywhere in memory and executed without physically changing each reference to a memory address. In System/360, memory addresses are specified in instructions by indicating the number of a special register, called the *base register*, and a displacement. The *effective* memory address is determined by adding the contents of the base register and the displacement. Addresses used in a program can therefore be relocated to any position in memory simply by changing the contents of the base register. Language translators still assign the first instruction in the program to location 0, but such addresses become the displacement associated with a base register. Once the base register is loaded with the memory address of the first instruction in the program, its contents remain constant, and the displacements determine different addresses within the program.

The addition of memory-protection hardware helped alleviate the problem of a user overwriting the monitor program. Memory is broken into standard blocks of a fixed number of words; either each block is given a protection key, or special registers contain upper and lower limits for acceptable addresses. Whenever a user program attempts to write into a storage location that is not in a standard block of storage assigned to his job, an interrupt occurs, and the monitor program terminates the job.

These hardware developments, plus others to be mentioned later, could not be fully exploited without more complex software systems.

OPERATING SYSTEMS

As hardware developments appeared, new programs were developed to utilize these improvements. The development of I/O channels required a program to allow the programmer to effectively perform input/output, and the development of hardware interrupts required programs to process these interrupts. Thus the monitor program that controls the job-to-job sequencing has to be accompanied by these additional routines. Control programs like these, along with such processing programs as assemblers, compilers, and loaders and their associated libraries, are designed to maximize the overall operating effectiveness of the computer hardware. These programs are collectively known as an *operating system*. Those control programs that remain in memory at all times are called the resident operating system, the nucleus, or the *resident supervisor*.

To assure that a user cannot inadvertantly use an I/O device not assigned to his job, computers are designed so that certain instructions, such as initiating I/O channels, cannot be executed by the user's program but only by the resident supervisor. I/O operations are requested from the supervisor, and these instructions are executed in the *supervisor state*. The standard instructions in a user's program run in the *problem state*. The standard instructions of a user's program takes place at two distinct levels within the computer system.

The early operating systems (called monitor systems at that time) were concerned mainly with improving the operating efficiency of the hardware rather than the overall processing efficiency. The advent of channels permitted the user, via managing software routines, to design programs that allowed overlap between processing and I/O operations. The I/O routines provide for reading input into memory locations, called *buffers*, prior to the time they are needed. When a user requests input via an I/O routine, the routine initiates the proper input unit, and a buffer is filled. When the buffer is full, its contents are moved into the user's designated storage area. The input unit transmits information, until a fixed number of buffers are full. The I/O routine is responsible for causing the buffers to be refilled. Output requests are handled similarly. A line of output from a user's program is placed in an output buffer, and when all available buffers are full, the I/O routine initiates the output from a buffer to a specified output device. The assembler-language programmer is afforded more flexibility in programming the I/O operations by being able to use routines to initiate the physical I/O transfers and to perform his own buffering. Compiler-language programs are translated assuming the use of the more automatic technique just discussed.

Since channels provide an indirect connection between I/O devices and the CPU, I/O routines communicate with the channels, and the channels communicate directly with an I/O unit. Channels send information to memory in the same manner, regardless of the type of I/O unit being used. The programmer interface with I/O routines are therefore standardized, and special program instructions are not needed for different I/O units. Programmers no longer need special instructions for each different I/O unit—only a standard input and output statement. The assignment of specific devices for use by a program is deferred until execution time, and the devices are requested from the resident supervisor through job-control language statements. A programmer might direct his output to the printer during one run and to a disk during another run of the same program. The only change required is in the job-control language.

Although overlap of I/O operations with processing is possible under an operating system, few programs utilize this option with maximum efficiency. Most programs require more data at one time than can be held in one or two buffers; hence the CPU still has to sit idle waiting for the completion of I/O operations. Compiler languages often use routines that wait for the completion of input/output and thus do not make effective use of the overlap capabilities. Since memory protection and automatic program relocatability are available, operating systems have now been developed that retain more than one job in a state of activity at one time within the computer memory.

Multiprogramming

The term *multiprogramming* refers to the seemingly simultaneous execution of two or more user programs by one computer. The memory of the computer is divided into *partitions* (regions). Partitions in memory may be of fixed size, and the user decides in which partition his job will fit and indicates this in his job control language. Partitions may also be allocated dynamically just prior to loading of the job. Under this scheme, the user estimates the amount of storage required for his job and places it on a job-control card. The supervisor allocates that amount of storage to his job. The priority associated with a given job is determined by the supervisor, based on a user-assigned priority number and the length of time a job has awaited execution. The program with the highest priority is executed, until it generates an I/O interrupt. After the I/O operation is initiated, the supervisor saves specific control information about the job and switches to the job with the next highest priority. This job executes, until an I/O interrupt occurs signaling the completion of an I/O request or until it requests an I/O operation. At this time a new job or else a job which has had its current I/O request serviced is initiated, depending on job priorities. The supervisor checks that no job waits an inordinate length of time for the use of the processor and changes job priorities continuously. As soon as a job finishes execution, another job is loaded in its place. The switching between jobs is an attempt to maximize usage of the CPU. I/O waits in one program are now filled in with execution of another program. To avoid the problem of one program tying up the processing unit with many computations, some multiprogramming systems assign a maximum amount of time, called a *time slice*, to each job. When a job exceeds its time slice, a timer interrupt occurs, execution of the job is suspended temporarily, and another job is initiated. Time-slicing allows the shorter jobs to finish quickly, instead of waiting for the longer job to finish.

To further maximize processor utilization and to service all programs, jobs are continuously read into the system by a *resident-reader routine* and placed in a job queue on disk, while other jobs are processing. The supervisor loads jobs from the queue for execution. The output from these programs is directed to an output queue on disk, and this queue is emptied continuously by a *resident-writer routine*. The reader and writer routines allow the supervisor to service all I/O requests for card input or printed output in user programs utilizing faster magnetic disks rather than slower card readers and printers. The simultaneous operation of standard I/O devices via resident programs and execution of user programs is called SPOOLing (Simultaneous Peripheral Operation On-Line). Spooling operations read ahead far enough and maintain a backlog of work to be printed so that no job has to await completion of I/O on the card reader or printer. This method is analogous to earlier off-line operations, except the former off-line operations now become a transfer to and from disk at the same time that programs are executed. Note also that now only one computer, instead of two, is needed. Figure 9.3 presents a schematic diagram of a multiprogrammed computer system with a fixed number of partitions. Note that all I/O in a user's program is directed either to disk or tape, and no direct communication exists between a user's program and the card reader or printer.

Multiprogramming systems available on IBM System/360 computers are greatly enhanced by a program named HASP (Houston Automatic Spooling and Priority System), which was developed at IBM, Houston. HASP, as its name implies, takes over some of the functions of the reader and writer programs and directly controls others. It provides for a more efficient spooling of jobs, a more efficient method of time-slicing, improved dynamic priority changing, and the capability of entering jobs into

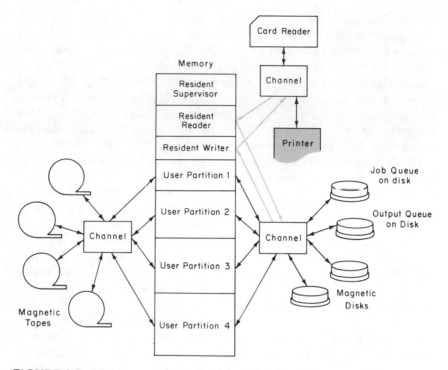

FIGURE 9.3   Multiprogramming System with a Fixed Number of Partitions

the job queue from a variety of remote stations (*remote job entry*).

Multiprocessing

The term *multiprocessing* refers to the existence of replicate hardware within the processing unit that allows truly simultaneous execution of more than one instruction at a time. The simultaneous operation of I/O channels and the CPU is considered to be one form of multiprocessing.

Another form of multiprocessing is the attached support processor system (ASP), which connects two computers in order to increase the overall efficiency of processing jobs. The support processor is usually a medium-scale computer whose function is to schedule jobs for execution by the main processor and to spool all I/O for the low-speed card readers and printers. The main processor, a high-speed computer, performs I/O only with high-speed I/O devices, such as tapes and disks. The two computers are connected to each other, using channel-to-channel adapters, so that each processor considers the other processor to be a very high-speed channel. The support processor maintains the job

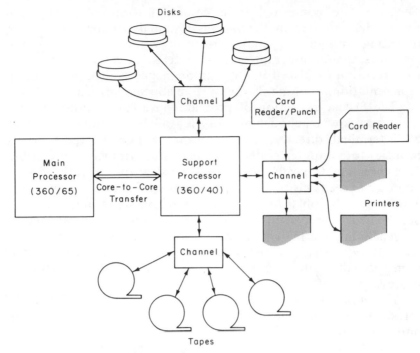

FIGURE 9.4   ASP System

queue and schedules each job for execution by the main processor. Jobs requiring tapes or disks to be mounted are preceded by mounting instructions to the operator so that the main processor is not kept waiting. When a job's turn for execution arrives, it is passed to the main processor via the core-to-core channel, and any output from the program which will eventually be printed is sent back to the support processor via the core-to-core channel. The support processor then spools it to the output queue. The main processor executes one program at a time, while the support processor is multiprogrammed to handle simultaneous job scheduling and spooling. Current improvements in this system provide for multiprogramming on the main processor also. An ASP system, using an IBM 360/40 as support processor and an IBM 360/65 as main processor, appears in Figure 9.4.

Time-Sharing

The term *time-sharing* refers to the simultaneous use of a computer by several users from remote terminals. Time-sharing systems are designed to give the user his results quickly and provide him with the illusion that he has the entire computing system at his disposal. The remote terminals are typewriter-like devices connected to the computer via the telephone-line network.

The lines are connected to a communications controller that routes the input from the various terminals to the time-sharing operating system. Depending on the workload and available resources, a user program may be entered directly into memory for execution or placed in a queue on magnetic disk. A schematic representation of a time-sharing system appears in Figure 9.5.

The fastest execution of programs in a time-sharing environment occurs when enough memory is available to store input from each terminal directly. The addition of LCS (Large Capacity Storage) to computer systems has made this arrangement feasible. Each program typically is given a time slice for execution. When one user exceeds his time slice or requests I/O, control is passed to another user's job. The sequence in which users are serviced is determined by a system-scheduling algorithm. A popular method of scheduling is known as *round robin scheduling.* Users are serviced sequentially in the order they entered the system, and all users get the same amount of time allocated to them for processing.

If memory resources are limited, a *swapping technique* is used for switching from one job to another. If the system can process only one job at a time, program A is written in auxiliary storage when the time slice allocated to it ends. Program B is read in from auxiliary storage to take its place. The availability of more than one partition in memory greatly enhances program swapping. While one program is being read in from auxiliary storage, another program is being written on auxiliary storage, and a third program can be executing.

Since time-sharing systems receive their primary input from slow-speed terminals and since each user does not continuously

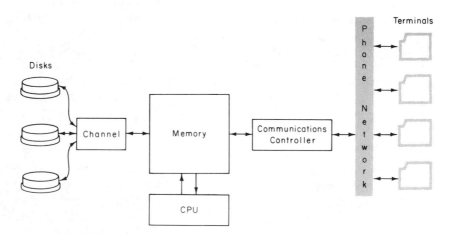

FIGURE 9.5 Time-Sharing System

interact with the system, there is much idle processor time. To alleviate this inefficiency, many time-sharing systems operate batch-processing simultaneously with interactive terminal I/O. The batch-processed jobs are low-priority jobs and are considered *background work*. The jobs being entered from terminals are high-priority jobs whose interrupts are serviced immediately. These jobs are termed the *foreground work*. The background work consists of long jobs that do not have to be completed at any special time and therefore can be interrupted frequently. The introduction of the background work keeps the computer busy when it is not servicing a user at a terminal.

The speed of a computer system, compared with the speed at which a person enters a program and a terminal's data transfer rate, makes it possible for a time-sharing system to service several users simultaneously and to give each user the illusion that he alone has all the resources of the system at his disposal. Time-sharing systems provide a means for editing and debugging of source programs without long waits between trial runs. Thus a user can often get a short program working during one "sitting" at a terminal, compared with three or four trial runs in a batch-processing environment.

Virtual Memory

Conventionally, the computer user must limit the size of his programs to physically fit within the confines of the computer's memory or, in larger computer systems, within the amount of memory available to him for processing. Increasingly, larger programs must either be run individually on larger computer systems or be broken into several smaller programs to obtain the desired results. *Virtual memory systems* provide the user with a logical memory that is much larger than the physical memory available in the computer system. The user's logical memory is maintained on auxiliary storage, such as magnetic disk, and he writes his program as if he had an amount of physical memory equal in size to his logical memory. That part of the user's program which is necessary for execution to begin is loaded from the user's virtual memory into real memory, and virtual addresses are translated to real memory addresses by a combination of hardware and software facilities. Since only a small part of real memory is used by a segment of one user's program, parts of several other users' programs may be maintained in memory simultaneously.

Virtual memory is divided into fixed-size units called *pages*. Addresses in virtual memory consist of two parts: a page number and a displacement relative to the beginning of the page. Memory is allocated to a user's programs in page size units, and the virtual addressing format does not require that the physical realization of successive pages of virtual memory be in consecutive real storage locations. A hardware feature called *dynamic address translation* converts virtual memory addresses into real memory addresses. A table, called a *page table*, is maintained for each job in the system. The entries of the table consist of either a page number and its beginning address in real memory or an indication that it is not in memory. The dynamic translation of the virtual addresses into real addresses is accomplished by a table look-up implemented in hardware. If a reference is made to a location in a page and the page is not in memory, an interrupt occurs, and the necessary page is brought into memory. During the time that the page is being loaded, control can be switched to another user's program.

A basic problem with the use of page tables is that an entry must exist for each page whether or not it is in real memory. Hence, if the user's program fits in one or two pages of memory, the additional entries in the page table are superfluous. A method of alleviating this problem appears in the design of IBM's TSS/360 system. Each user's virtual memory is divided into segments, and these segments are subdivided into pages. A virtual address now contains an additional component, namely, the segment number shown in Figure 9.6(a). The dynamic address translation now takes place indirectly through two tables. Each job has a segment table, and a page table exists for each segment used. The segment table is created by the supervisor, and its entries are pointers to the page tables associated with the segments. The page table is designed as discussed previously. A special register, the segment-table register, contains the memory address of the beginning of the segment table associated with the currently active job. The address translation process can be represented schematically, as shown in Figure 9.6(b). The contents of the segment-table register are added to the segment number, found in the high-order bits of the virtual address, to create an address within the segment table. The word referenced in the segment table contains the address of the beginning of the page table associated with the segment. The page number in the virtual address is added to the beginning address of the page table to extract the physical address of the page. The location within page portion of the virtual address is added to this physical address to obtain the effective memory address. This design requires page tables only for those segments of the virtual memory that are actually used and not for the entire user's virtual memory.

Virtual memory systems were initially designed for use with

Segment Number	Page Number	Location within Page

(a) *Virtual address format*

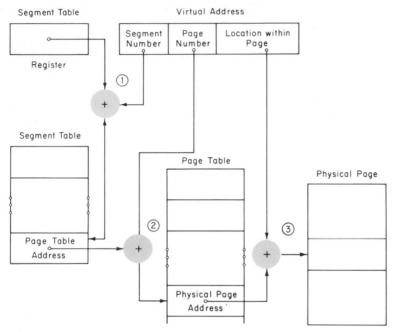

(b) *Schematic diagram of dynamic address translation*

FIGURE 9.6 Virtual Memory Addressing

time-sharing systems, but many computer manufacturers are developing new hardware and associated multiprogramming systems that permit the use of virtual memory in a batch-processing environment.

Virtual Machines

Virtual memory provides the user with a logical version of a large memory. Although the user has essentially unlimited memory space available for running programs, he is still restricted in his programming to the services and facilities provided by the operating system. A *virtual machine* provides the user with a logical version of an entire hardware system on which he can run operating systems of his own choosing. The user program's requests are serviced by this operating system—just as they are under the one operating system-one machine combination. Part of the operating system remains resident in the user's virtual memory and is responsible for loading processing programs into virtual memory and servicing interrupts. But it would be difficult—if not impossible—for several different operating systems to run in the supervisor state and to control alternately the allocation of the physical resources of the hardware over a period of time without a means for communication among them. This difficulty is overcome by a *virtual machine system* that supplies a resident control program to allocate physical resources as they are requested by users' operating systems. The control program runs in the supervisor state, and the users' operating systems are subservient to the control program and run in the problem state. Each user program, in turn, is subservient to the user-chosen operating system, resulting in three distinct levels of operation. User program requests from an operating system are serviced by *virtual interrupts*, which are programmed simulations of real interrupts. Since interrupts are detected by the hardware, all interrupts must be first processed by the control program. The control program reflects the interrupt back to the appropriate user operating system. The user operating system either performs corrective action or requests a service from the control program in the form of a real interrupt. Since both the user program and the user operating system reside in virtual memory, each may be paged. In other words, the control program retains only those pages of the user program and user operating system in real memory that are necessary to effect execution. Figure 9.7 illustrates the three levels of operation in a virtual machine system. A virtual machine system can be utilized by computer installations as well as by individual users. A computer center could provide its user population with a choice of two or more operating systems on its hardware system. For example, a large time-sharing system and a large batch-processing system could be made available simultaneously by providing a virtual machine for each system and by restricting the users to one of the two systems. A virtual machine system, CP-67/CMS (Control Program-67/Cambridge Monitor System), has been developed and implemented on an IBM 360/67 at the IBM Cambridge Scientific Center in Cambridge, Massachusetts. Under this system, it is possible to create virtual machines to run the different operating systems available on System/360.

In summary, the development of software systems has improved the operational and computational efficiency of computer systems, thereby facilitating better communication between

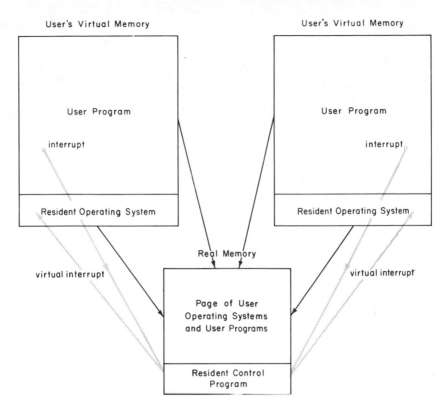

FIGURE 9.7   Levels of Control in a Virtual Machine System

the user and the computer. In the beginning, the user had to
specify each storage location he intended to use in his program
and had to manually load his program into memory. The
development of translators aided in program writing, but the user
still had to load his program. The use of trained operators
separated the user from the operational aspects of executing a
program, and the development of batch-processing techniques
lessened the tasks of the operator. Input/output channels and
multiprogramming provided for more efficient use of central
processor time by allowing overlap between I/O for one program
and execution of another program. Time-sharing has brought the
computer to the user via remote terminals. Finally, the development of virtual systems has transformed the resources of a
computer system into logical rather than physical entities. The
user, who once had to plan his programs with all the physical
constraints of a computer in mind, can now, in a sense, create his
own computer to meet his individual needs.

EXERCISES

1. Distinguish between hardware and software.

2. How did the use of batch-processing monitor programs improve the operation of a computer system?

3. What are off-line operations?

4. What is an operating system?

5. How do multiprogramming systems exploit the I/O-compute overlap made possible by the development of I/O channels?

6. Distinguish between multiprogramming systems and multiprocessing systems.

7. How is maximum utilization of a computer system made possible in a time-sharing environment?

8. How is virtual memory realized in the computer hardware?

SELECTED REFERENCES

Denning, Peter J., "Virtual Memory," *ACM Computing Surveys*, Vol. 2, No. 3 (September, 1970), pp. 153-190.

Denning, Peter J., "Third Generation Computer Systems," *ACM Computing Surveys*, Vol. 3, No. 4 (December, 1971), pp. 175-216.

Gibson, C. T., "Time-Sharing in the IBM System/360: Model 67," *Proceedings, SJCC, 1966*, Montvale, N.J.: AFIPS Press, 1966.

Katzan, Harry Jr., *Advanced Programming Techniques*, New York: Van Nostrand Reinhold, 1970.

Hassitt, Anthony, *Computer Programming and Computer Systems*, New York: Academic Press, 1971.

Rosen, Saul, *Programming Systems and Languages*, New York: McGraw-Hill, 1967.

Rosin, Robert F., "Supervisory and Monitor Systems," *ACM Computing Surveys*, Vol. 1, No. 1 (March, 1969).

Sayers, Anthony P. (Editor), *Operating Systems Survey*, Princeton, N.J.: Auerbach Publishers, 1971.

Wegner, Peter, *Programming Languages, Information Structures, and Machine Organization*, New York: McGraw-Hill, 1968.

10

Reflections on Computer Technology

The origin of computing is found far back in human history—the first time man responded to the need for a system of counting. Even before the existence of formal symbols, objects such as stones or sticks were used to establish a crude counting method that was nothing more than a physical one-to-one correspondence. For example, a herdsman would have a pile of stones, one for every sheep he owned. When the sheep returned from pasture, he allowed them to enter the pen, one at a time, while he removed stones from the pile one at a time and placed them into a second pile. If all the stones were removed from the first pile, the herdsman knew that all his sheep were safe. In fact, the word *calculate* derives from the Latin word *calculus*, a stone. Even after the development of formal written number systems, stones were still used in business transactions. They were placed on boards, called *counters*, and used to represent amounts of money during bartering sessions. The word counter survives to this day, and the concept of counters has been a key factor in the development of mechanical and electronic devices.

MECHANICAL CALCULATORS

The search for increasingly faster and more efficient means of calculating and computing gained momentum in direct proportion to the introduction and development of mechanical devices. The oldest calculating machine still in use today appeared several thousand years ago. Known as an *abacus* [see Fig. 10.1], it consists of a series of beads strung on rods that are set in a rectangular frame. A horizontal bar divides the beads into two groups. Each bead in the bottom set represents one unit, while each bead in the top set represents five units. The rods represent place values, such as tens and hundreds. The setting in Figure 10.1 illustrates the position of beads representing the number 581,120.64, if the decimal point is placed as indicated by the arrow. A skilled operator of an abacus can add, subtract, multiply, and divide numbers at a speed equal to that of an operator of a desk calculator. The abacus is a *digital* device, since it is based on a formal system of counting. Some calculators are *analog* devices, which measure uniformly varying physical quantities. Sundials, thermometers, and slide rules are examples of analog devices. Both devices are found in an automobile, where the odometer is digital and the speedometer is analog.

The development of modern computing procedures was further enhanced by the invention of logarithms, credited to John Napier. In 1617 he invented a device known as *Napier's Rods* (Napier's Bones) to be used in performing multiplications. The principle is very basic, as seen in Figure 10.2. Each surface of a rod contains an index number on the top, followed by the multiples of that number; each multiple is entered as a two-digit numeral with the digits separated by diagonal lines. One rod serves only as an index. To multiply 145 × 692, the 6, 9, and 2 rods

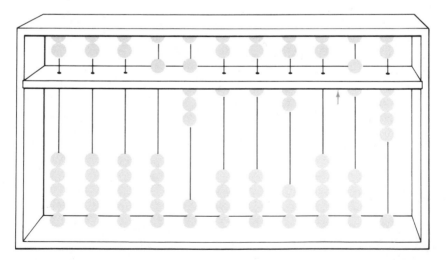

FIGURE 10.1 The Abacus — A Digital Device

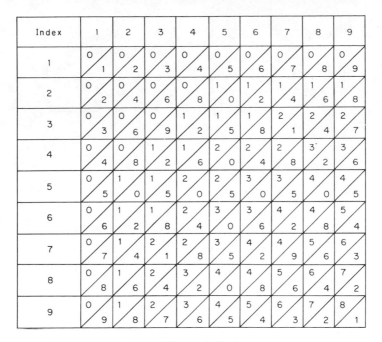

Index	1	2	3	4	5	6	7	8	9
1	0/1	0/2	0/3	0/4	0/5	0/6	0/7	0/8	0/9
2	0/2	0/4	0/6	0/8	1/0	1/2	1/4	1/6	1/8
3	0/3	0/6	0/9	1/2	1/5	1/8	2/1	2/4	2/7
4	0/4	0/8	1/2	1/6	2/0	2/4	2/8	3/2	3/6
5	0/5	1/0	1/5	2/0	2/5	3/0	3/5	4/0	4/5
6	0/6	1/2	1/8	2/4	3/0	3/6	4/2	4/8	5/4
7	0/7	1/4	2/1	2/8	3/5	4/2	4/9	5/6	6/3
8	0/8	1/6	2/4	3/2	4/0	4/8	5/6	6/4	7/2
9	0/9	1/8	2/7	3/6	4/5	5/4	6/3	7/2	8/1

FIGURE 10.2   Principle of Napier's Rods

would be placed in sequence next to the index rod [see Fig. 10.3]. Multiplication is then performed by adding along the diagonals, starting at the right. The units digit of each sum is written down, with any carry taken to the next diagonal. The final sequence of digits is the required product.

The first geared mechanical calculating device was developed in 1642 by Blaise Pascal, a French philosopher and mathematician. At the age of nineteen, he invented a small machine consisting of a number of toothed wheels mounted in a box. The notable feature of this machine [see Fig. 10.4] was the concept of an automatic carry, which occurred when each wheel tooth changed from position 9 to position 0. A stylus was used to operate the calculator, and the machine was not much larger than a shoe box. By 1672 Gottfried Leibniz, a German mathematician, improved Pascal's machine. He designed a *desk calculator* that could multiply and divide; the former operation used a series of additions and the latter used a series of subtractions. Leibniz's motivation was undoubtedly based on his belief that mathematicians should be relieved from the drudgery of performing arithmetic calculations by hand. Such machines were not dependable in performing the basic arithmetic operations well enough for

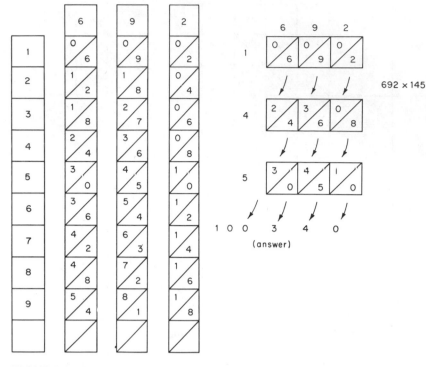

FIGURE 10.3   Illustration of Multiplication Using Napier's Rods

FIGURE 10.4   Pascal's Calculator (*Bettmann Archives*)

commercial use, however, until C. X. Thomas of Alsace made further improvements in the design. These developments eventually led to desk calculators similar to the ones in use today.

The calculators discussed so far all exhibit a common characteristic: there was no way to alter the task that the machine performed without mechanically altering the machine. The concept of programmed machines, capable of performing a variety of different tasks upon receiving the proper instructions, was still a long way in the future. But the advent of the *punched card* was a major development that opened the door to that future. As early as 1741, the concept of the programmed machine was applied in the weaving industry in France. Jacques de Vaucanson invented an automatic loom for weaving silk, with designs established by a prescribed pattern of punched holes in a metal drum. Mass-produced woven patterns became a fact of life in 1804, when Joseph Marie Jacquard adapted the idea for use with heavier materials such as rugs and tapestries. The controls for Jacquard's loom [see Fig. 10.5] consisted of stiff paper cards that were punched with holes and could be changed very easily. The cards controlled both the lifting of warp threads and the movement of the shuttle that controlled the woof threads. As might be expected, the relatively rapid output of duplicated woven patterns produced a cry of protest from the union of weavers in France,

FIGURE 10.5 Jacquard's Loom
(*Bettmann Archives*)

but the machine survived, and the weaving industry moved into a new era.

The first serious attempt to construct a truly general-purpose sequential calculator is attributed to the dedicated work of Charles Babbage, whose labors for more than fifteen years resulted in failure to produce a real machine. Yet the theory that formed the basis of his work has since been proven sound. His failure was due only to the lack of mass production of precision parts and the nonexistence of interchangeable machine parts. In 1820 this English mathematician began work on a *difference machine* to be used in evaluating functions.. He hoped to develop a machine capable of handling numbers with twenty-six significant figures and output differences to the sixth order. After spending ten years with no real results, he was forced to abandon the project in 1833, when government support was withdrawn. Babbage then developed plans for an *analytical machine* [see Fig. 10.6]. The machine had a *store* for retaining numbers; a *mill* that served as a central arithmetic unit for calculating; and an *operator* to direct the operation of the machine. The sequencing of operations was to be controlled by punched cards. Results would be output on copper plates, and answers could be automatically fed back into the

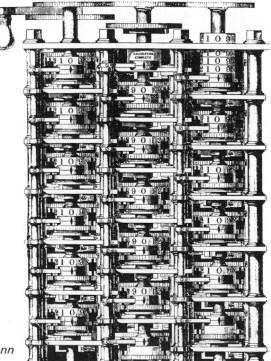

FIGURE 10.6 Portion of Babbage's Machine (*Bettmann Archives*)

machine so that additional calculations could be performed without further action by the operator. The concept of branching was included in the design simply by advancing or backing up a certain number of cards. Numbers were to be accurate to fifty places, while the machine's memory unit would hold 50,000 digits. The speed of the machine was indicated by the specification that addition could be performed in one second, and a 50-by-50 digit product would take approximately one minute. Unfortunately, the machine was never completed, although parts of it were built and still exist in museums. Even after technology reached a level where construction of the machine was possible, the size of the finished product would have been too large to make it of any practical use. The important contribution to the future of computers is found in comparing Babbage's concept of data storage, sequential control through programming, and automatic output with the implementation of these basic elements in modern computers. More than fifty years after his death, his theories became a definitive reference in the field of computer technology.

The invention of electrical devices enabled the use of punched cards to be combined with the use of electric impulses, resulting in a rapid system for counting. Herman Hollerith was a key figure in this development. His work in the U.S. Bureau of Census during the 1880 census count made him aware of a startling fact. Since that census had taken seven years to count, the 1890 census might take as long as twenty years to tabulate. Future census counts would be even more time consuming. In 1882 he developed a card on which all pertinent information about a person could be represented by a combination of punched holes. The card was divided into 240 areas and the holes were punched by using an ordinary conductor's punch. Hollerith also built a Census Machine [see Fig. 10.7], which "read" these punched cards and tabulated the results. The process involved a series of pins—one for each hole—that could be punched on the card. When a handle was pulled, the pins went through the holes into a cup of mercury, causing an electrical circuit to be completed. This in turn activated one of forty counters, increasing it by one. A sorting box accompanied the machine, and the same electrical impulse opened the proper slot of the box so that the card could be placed in the correct bin after processing.

This development was of major importance for two reasons. First, the census of 1890 took only one-third the time previously required. Secondly, it was the first application of the *unit record system*. Data could be stored as units on cards in such a form that they could be used separately for tabulating a variety of requested information. In 1894 Hollerith redesigned the card into its present

FIGURE 10.7   Hollerith's Census Machine (*Bettmann Archives*)

eighty-column form. In 1896 he formed the Tabulating Company, which was later sold and became the International Business Machines Corporation.

The first working application of the ideas of Charles Babbage emerged from the discovery of the relationship of relay switching devices to the concepts of Boolean Algebra—the mathematics of symbolic logic. It became apparent that electromechanical relays could be used to represent logical functions. The development of the first general purpose digital computer soon followed. In 1937 Professor Howard Aiken of Harvard University entered a joint enterprise with the IBM Corporation for the purpose of constructing such a computer. The first product was placed in operation in 1944 and was known as the *Harvard* Mark I *Automatic Sequence Controlled Calculator*. While some of the operating functions of the Mark I were accomplished by wiring a plugboard similar to a telephone switchboard, programming was basically accomplished by Jacquard-type punched paper tape. Also incorporated in the Mark I were pieces of equipment already in use in IBM tabulating machines, such as relays, counters, typewriters, card feeds, and card punches. The Hollerith accumulator became the calculating element for the Mark I, with seventy-two of these devices serving as arithmetic registers. Sixty manual switches were used for setting the values of constants in the machine.

The Mark I [see Fig. 10.8] was capable of a precision factor of twenty-three places, and in addition to performing the four basic arithmetic operations, it could reference tables containing previously computed results. Addition and subtraction took exactly 0.3 sec; multiplication required about 4 sec; and a maximum of 16 sec was required for division. The Mark I weighed about 5 tons and measured 51 ft in length and 8 ft in height. During the fifteen years it was in operation, the computer produced a great many important mathematical tables that were widely utilized in science and engineering. A second and more improved model of the Mark I was constructed in 1948 for use at the Naval Proving Grounds in Dahlgren, Virginia. The Mark I was the merged result of Babbage's theories and the machine technology available in the 1930s.

From 1944 to 1947, four types of relay computers were used in scientific problem-solving. The Mark I, the Mark II, and the IBM Pluggable Sequence Relay Calculator did not differ substantially in performance. But the *Bell Telephone Laboratories Relay Computer* deserves mention for several reasons. Known as the Complex Computer because it could handle square roots of negative numbers, the machine could be used from three different and separate operating stations. In fact, it was operated remotely over a teletypewriter circuit, a development that was to have its impact

FIGURE 10.8 Mark I Computer (*Crupt Photo Lab, Harvard University*)

in later computer technology. An equally important difference related to error checking. The Mark I and II machines left the task of checking the accuracy of results and operations performed by the machine to the programmer. Bell Labs designed their computer to be self-checking, with the result that the machine would stop rather than make a numeric mistake. Such developments may seem trivial by today's standards, but they stand as major contributions to the advancement of computer technology.

The increasingly rapid advances in computer technology from 1940 to the present are often described in terms of generations. Developments in both hardware and software are used when classifying computers in this manner. The span of time between generations has steadily decreased—witnessed by the changes in technology, usage, and cost requirements. At times, the line separating one generation from the next is blurred or even arbitrary; yet the method of classification still proves useful in any comparative discussion of computers.

THE FIRST GENERATION

The use of *vacuum tubes* in place of electromechanical relays in switching circuits and memory units is the primary hardware development that identifies a machine as a first generation computer. With regard to the processing of information, computers of this generation are all *batch-oriented* and *card-oriented*. It would therefore appear that the Mark I and related models should be placed in this category. But our classification of generations of computers is restricted to purely electronic machines. Furthermore, software developments associated with the first generation include the concept of subroutines. While the Mark I eventually contained a collection of special prewritten instructions that were incorporated within a more elaborate set of instructions, it did not make generalized use of this concept. Finally, the stored-program concept provided such a unique transition in the development of computers that it serves as an ideal means for identifying the advent of the first generation.

The ENIAC (Electronic Numeric Integrator and Calculator) is the first electronic digital computer that can be classified in this generation. The project started in 1943 under the direction of Dr. John Mauchly of the University of Pennsylvania and J. Presper Eckert, a graduate student at that university's Moore School of Electrical Engineering. The machine was developed in response to a need for ballistics tables by the U.S. Army Ordinance Department. In fact, World War II was responsible for many of the rapid developments in computer technology at this time. Electronic circuitry and design theory had advanced due to military demands. By 1945 the ENIAC was operational, performing at speeds up to one thousand times faster than the Mark I.

The only moving parts in the ENIAC [see Fig. 10.9] were the input and output devices. The machine used 19,000 vacuum tubes instead of electromagnetic relays, thus enabling relay switching to be performed at electronic speeds. Twelve vacuum tubes were used to store one decimal digit, so that the storage capacity was limited to twenty 10-digit numbers. In one second, 5000 additions could be performed, enabling 20 hours of human computing to ʿbe compressed into 30 seconds of computer time. ENIAC had 30 units, occupied over 15,000 ft² of floor space, and weighed more than 30 tons. The working units were not permanently wired together. Instead, they were brought out to plugboard connections where they could be patched together in certain patterns to solve a given problem. This required time—anywhere from a few hours to a full day. Consequently, ENIAC did not classify as a general purpose computer. Yet the machine did have the capability of performing several operations simultaneously, and it also made the first use of the subroutine.

In the late 1940s, ENIAC's wiring was made permanent; its function tables were utilized to store instructions rather than functional values; and the remainder of the machine was wired in a standard form that did not need to be altered. It was thus adapted

FIGURE 10.9 ENIAC Computer (*Sperry Rand Corporation*)

to the stored-program technique. The instructions did have to be manually set on the function-table switches, however, so that the programs were not really internally stored. ENIAC operated from 1947 to 1955 at the Aberdeen Proving Grounds, where it was retired from service. On February 4, 1964, records show that U.S. Patent Number 3,120,606 was issued to ENIAC.

The progress made with ENIAC attracted the attention of John von Neumann, who was working on the development of a stored-program computer. His theories were published in the late 1940s, including such ideas as the storage of instructions as well as data in numerical form inside a machine. Similar operations would be applied to both data and instructions for purposes of modification. He also suggested the use of binary numbers to economize computer operations. With earlier computers, once the instructions were coded on punched tape or cards, the individual operations could only be changed externally. The work of von Neumann allowed the machine to internally alter its operations and instructions. His theories of parallel processing also advanced the state of computer technology by permitting words of information to be processed as units rather than digit by digit. Finally, he introduced the concept of flowcharting to pictorially represent the solution of a problem.

The first computer to apply the stored program concept fully was the EDSAC (Electronic Delay-Storage Automatic Computer), built at Cambridge University. It was placed in operation in 1949 and was the first machine to make substantial use of subroutines. The feature of delayed storage was further implemented in EDVAC (Electronic Discreet Variable Computer), the second machine developed at the University of Pennsylvania. This computer was operational by 1952, and contained one-sixth the number of tubes required by ENIAC. A main-memory storage of 1024 words was made possible by using mercury delay lines for the storage of numbers. Since data could be transmitted through the mercury at the speed of sound, it was slower in operation than the rest of the computer, and the result was a temporary storage capacity. Magnetic-core storage would later replace this type of storage, but it is significant because delayed storage enabled EDVAC [see Fig. 10.10] to apply fully the stored-program principle. The instructions for the computer consisted of four addresses and an OP code. Auxiliary storage with a capacity of 20,000 numbers consisted of magnetic wire. This was an adaptation of the wire-recording techniques widely used at the time. This usage was later replaced by magnetic-tape systems.

In 1950 Remington Rand bought the Eckert-Mauchly Computer Corporation, which had already contracted for the construc-

FIGURE 10.10   EDVAC Four Front Panel Covers Removed (*University of Pennsylvania News Bureau*)

tion of a computer for the U.S. Bureau of Standards. This machine became the first large-scale electronic computer to be commercially marketed. Known as the UNIVAC-I (Universal Automatic Computer), it was a stored-program computer containing 5000 vacuum tubes. Addition could be performed in 2 μsec (millionths of a second), while multiplication took 10 μsec. There were forty-five instructions for operations, with large-scale use of magnetic tapes for I/O. One of the newest features was the capacity of the machine to process alphabetic and special symbols as well as numbers. Eventually forty-eight UNIVAC machines were built, the first of which was installed at the Bureau of Census to edit data from the 1950 census. It is interesting to note that sixty years earlier, Herman Hollerith had applied his new machines in the same bureau for the same purpose. Although limited in distribution, the UNIVAC [see Fig. 10.11] played a vital role in

FIGURE 10.11   UNIVAC-I Computer (*Sperry Rand Corporation*)

assisting the development of the important software component known as the programming language. This received wide application in computers from 1955 to 1965 and formed one of the distinctive elements of the second generation.

Other scientific computers rapidly appeared in the 1950s. The IBM 701 (1953) was developed as a result of demands of the Korean War and was originally called the Defense Calculator. The 701 had an accounting machine printer as well as card reader and card-punch units. Magnetic tape and drum were used for auxiliary storage. About nineteen of these machines were put into operation. In response to requests for small and medium-size machines, IBM released its 650 computer in 1954. Although slow by most standards, it was a popular machine, as evidenced by more than one thousand installations. The 650 was a stored-program, vacuum-tube, drum-memory machine. It possessed an extensive program library. Early programming of the machine was done in 650 machine language, but use of higher-level language was eliminated due to lack of facilities. The IBM 704, first installed in 1955, did much to foster wide acceptance of FORTRAN among users from 1957 to 1959. Users of the 704 computers formed the organization known as SHARE, which was responsible for many of the later software developments.

THE SECOND GENERATION

Vacuum-tube machines exhibited several drawbacks that became major concerns as time progressed. Large amounts of space were required to install these machines, and they generated large amounts of heat, making sizeable air-conditioning systems a necessity. The limitations of these machines with regard to speed in processing, application of programming languages, and cost factors had to be considered. Assembler languages and compilers were developed, and the use of subroutines increased. Yet most software advances could not be implemented before machine obsolescence occurred. The IBM 650 and 704 did assist these developments, since they remained in active use for substantial amounts of time. But the arrival of *solid-state technology* along with *increased use of magnetic-storage elements* drastically altered the face of computer technology, and the second generation appeared.

As early as 1948, Bell Telephone Laboratories had announced the invention of the *transistor* [see Figure 10.12]. This device consists of a three-layer crystal of solid material called a *semiconductor*. When wired into an electrical circuit, the transistor

FIGURE 10.12 SLT "Chip" Transistors and Transistor (*IBM Corporation*)

can control a flow of current in the same way as a vacuum tube. But the transistor is much smaller; consequently it takes less space and uses less power. It is also electrically stable and mechanically rugged. The operation of such devices depends on the properties of matter in a solid form; hence these components are often referred to as *solid-state*. By 1954 solid-state components were in wide use. At the same time a gradual improvement in computer performance was taking place. Machines were becoming sophisticated, and programming systems were being given new importance in the utilization of computers. In 1959 RCA marketed a solid-state core-memory machine, the 501, which was also its first commercial venture in the field of computers. The same year, IBM introduced the 7090, a scientific computer that was also solid-state, while Remington Rand produced the 1107. Development of new and better machines followed rapidly, but the main emphasis in the second generation was focused on two separate types of computer systems. One type of computer was designed for scientific and mathematical computation, while the second type was primarily for use in business applications. The reason for following such a path was the fact that solving business problems required the processing of massive amounts of input and output but relatively little internal calculating. Scientific requirements were just the opposite. Internal calculating speed and precision were necessary, since more "thinking" had to be performed with very little I/O in many cases. As a result, second generation computers suffered from a lack of compatibility in terms of internal structure and operation. The IBM 1620 and 1401 [see Fig. 10.13] models appeared in 1960, and both were widely used and are still in existence today. The former was primarily for scientific use, whereas the latter found wide acceptance in business. The 1401 finally exceeded 6000 installations, establishing a record for the number of commercial computers sold or rented to that date.

The second generation of computers was still batch-oriented, but *tape* was the basic medium for auxiliary storage, compilers, and even monitor systems. Channels were made available for controlling input and output, leaving the CPU free to process other information. The use of multiplexors relieved the CPU from this task by controlling the flow of information to and from main memory. The development of interrupt methods permitted the channels to indicate completion of tasks by signalling the CPU. The processor would then temporarily cease its activity, service the I/O requests, and return to execution of the program at the point where processing had been interrupted. The use of higher level languages proliferated during the years from 1955 to 1965,

FIGURE 10.13   IBM 1620 CPU, Model 1 (*IBM Corporation*)

most of which fall within the boundaries of the second generation. Development of hardware and software continued at an ever increasing rate, and by 1964 the next generation appeared.

THE THIRD GENERATION

Several expectations on the part of users defined the framework of the third generation of computer technology. There was *a demand for a single computing system* that would be capable of processing both business and scientific problems. *Upward compatibility* was required so that instructions written for use on a small computer would be understood by a larger computer. *Large, high-speed storage capabilities* were also necessary to meet the increasing demands for rapid processing of information. Finally, *the improvement of remote-terminal communications* would have to be implemented so that the use of computers would not remain dependent on physical proximity to a machine.

The major hardware development identified with this generation of computers is the *monolithic integrated circuit* [see Fig. 10.14]. Small chips of silicone are metallized to form an

FIGURE 10.14   Solid Logic Technology (*IBM Corporation*)

electronic circuit. One integrated circuit is equivalent to more than 150 electronic components. Smaller in size than a paper clip, such circuits make the transfer of information extremely rapid while reducing the size of machines. In 1964 IBM introduced the System/360 as a third generation computer [see Fig. 10.15]. It exhibited a high-speed core memory, high-speed I/O devices, and modular construction that permitted peripheral devices to be arranged in a variety of ways so that installations could grow as needs increased. Sperry Rand developed the 9000 series of computers and progressed effectively in the use of large magnetic drums and real-time computing. RCA chose to compete directly with IBM by developing the Spectra 70, which was compatible with the 360 but lower in price.

The third generation implemented a major development in the processing of information by the use of *multiprogramming*. Although computers remained batch-oriented for the most part, several different jobs could now be executed concurrently. Subsequently, *multiprocessing* was introduced, using two or more CPUs to execute jobs simultaneously. The sharing of computer

FIGURE 10.15   System/360 Model 40 with 2401 s and 1403 N1, (*IBM Corporation*)

facilities by many jobs was extended to remote access through time-sharing systems such as the one at Dartmouth College. Real-time capabilities were developed for third generation computers, enabling immediate response to incoming data. Applications in transportation control, space projects, and simulation soon followed. Progress in all these areas was due to the addition of high-speed peripheral devices such as disks, plotting units, and graphic display units.

Machines were now utilized with operating systems that contained sophisticated supervisory control programs. More and more operating speed in the CPU and main memory was combined with a refining of performance to enable maximum productivity of the high-cost CPU. Programming was extended beyond telling the system what to do by the development of *microprogramming* —a means by which a system's storage and logic elements can be controlled. Consequently, a programmer can tell a system or a device how to do a particular operation. A microprogrammable system thus becomes a flexible tool that can be modified without the conventional and high-cost physical modifications of hardware. With such impressive developments in the third generation, the question naturally arises as to whether there is any need for improvement.

THE FOURTH GENERATION

In 1970 IBM presented their 370 computer with the announcement that the fourth generation was here. It has been argued that although this may be true with regard to hardware, software development is not yet available to support the claim. Part of the difficulty is the lack of a clear definition of a fourth generation computer. But some guidelines do seem valid.

Processing of input data in a real-time mode will be the rule rather than the exception. Communication between systems will most likely increase. Computer networks will be used to interconnect machines. Large-scale integration (LSI) will merge logic, systems, and devices enabling systems designers to create new structures. Large read-only memories, multiple shift registers, and new logic elements will be combined with user-applied microprogramming, resulting in new and more flexible computer systems. New advances in technology will no longer cause obsolescence, since systems will be readily updated by altering the modular design of the hardware. For example, a multiplex control unit could use plug-in elements for the channel unit, data control unit, and power unit. Such hardware—when applied to communication and control features—will reduce the use of software control programs. Consequently, software systems will no longer remain device oriented. Data will be processed in line more and more by means of on-line units so that data can be collected at its source. More people will be able to use computer terminals as communication is made less difficult through the elimination of the vagaries of programming languages. Delays and resulting costs from down-time will be reduced by diagnostic routines that are compatible with existing I/O routines. Thus hardware and software facilities can be differentiated. In general, the gap between what computers have the capacity to do and what computers actually do will narrow. User needs will be of primary importance, since computer frameworks will no longer be designed as general tools for all applications; instead they will be a flexible tool to be dynamically utilized in specific applications.

Perhaps the fourth generation will only be a period of transition—an experimentation with new machine capabilities combined with a more efficient utilization of existing technological and software advances. The fourth generation might well be a breathing space on the way to actual implementation of a fifth generation. By 1975 it is expected that the speed with which internal operations are performed will be on the order of 1 ns (nanosecond) for add time and 30 ns for storage cycle time. In a nanosecond (one billionth of a second) an electric pulse, moving at the speed of light, travels a distance of one foot. This will have an impact on the future designs of machines. Costs per bit of core storage will drop to less than $0.005. Systems will exist that permit both user-generated and user-alterable configurations of hardware and software. Thus the systems of the future will continue to approach the goal of maximum utilization of computers as a tool within specific problem environments.

EXERCISES

1. Diagram the development of computing aids from the abacus to UNIVAC I.

2. State the contributions to the field of computing machinery made by each of the following people: Jacquard, Pascal, Hollerith, Babbage, Aiken, von Neumann, and Mauchly and Eckert.

3. What was the significant development in computer technology of the design of the Bell Labs relay computer?

4. What characterizes each generation of computers?

5. Prepare a report on microprogramming.

6. Research and report on the current status of the fourth generation.

SELECTED REFERENCES

Aiken, Howard, "Proposed Automatic Calculating Machine," *IEEE Spectrum*, Vol. 1, No. 8 (August 1964), pp. 62-69.
Baer, Robert M., *The Digital Villain*, Reading, Mass.: Addison-Wesley, 1972.
Cashman, Thomas J. and William J. Keys, *Data Processing and Computer Programming*, San Francisco: Canfield Press, 1971.

Cole, R. Wade, *Introduction to Computing*, New York: McGraw-Hill, 1969.

Gruenberger, Fred (editor), *Fourth Generation Computers: User Requirements and Transition*, Englewood Cliffs, N.J.: Prentice-Hall, 1970.

Maisel, Herbert, *Introduction to Electronic Digital Computers*, New York: McGraw-Hill, 1969.

Rosen, S., "Electronic Computers: A Historical Survey," *Computing Surveys*, Vol. 1, (March 1969), pp. 7-36.

Weiss, Eric A. (editor), *Computer Usage: Fundamentals*, New York: McGraw-Hill, 1969.

Wilkes, Maurice V., "Computers Then and Now," *Journal of the ACM*, Vol. 15, No. 1 (January 1968), pp. 1-7.

Magnetic Storage Devices

Although punched cards and printer output provide a means of representing input to and output from computer programs, there is often a need to store programs and large amounts of data for a long period of time. Punched cards cause storage problems if the amount of information being retained is large and the main memory of the computer is not large enough to hold data on a semipermanent basis. Less expensive, slower, auxiliary magnetic storage devices have been developed to alleviate this problem. We shall discuss the characteristics of four such devices.

MAGNETIC TAPES

Magnetic tape is made from a flexible plastic material such as Mylar. The tape is one-half inch wide and is coated on one side with a thin film of a magnetic material such as iron oxide. The total thickness of the tape is approximately .002 inches and the oxide coating is about one-third the thickness of the Mylar backing. Tapes are commonly 2400 feet long and are wound on 10½-inch reels.

Data are recorded on the tape by first passing it by an erase head and then over a write head on a device called a *tape drive*. Figure A.1 pictures the read/write head used in IBM 2400 series tape drives. Writing occurs at the write gap of the read/write head and reading takes place at the read gap. Data are written by magnetizing small discrete spots on the oxide coating in either

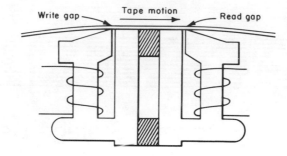

FIGURE A.1 Two Gap Read/Write Head

nine or seven parallel tracks along the length of the tape. Information is written on nine-track tapes in nine-bit groups (eight data bits and one parity bit) across the surface of the tape. Similarly, seven-track tapes record data seven bits at a time (six data bits and one parity bit) across the surface of the tape. In each case, the parity bit is set so that an even or odd number of one bits occurs in each nine-bit or seven-bit group depending on whether even or odd parity is used, respectively. Data are read by passing the tape over a read head which can detect the magnetized spots which have been written on the tape. When the tape is read, a check is made to see that each character still maintains the correct parity. If the parity is incorrect, an error has occurred in reading the character. The IBM 2400 series tape drives, with the two-gap read/write head shown in Figure A.1, read information back for parity checking purposes immediately after it is written. The bit patterns across a nine-track tape may represent EBCDIC or ASCII characters or eight bits of a computer word. The bit patterns across a seven-track tape may represent a BCD character or six bits of a computer word [see Fig. A.2]. The number of bits recorded longitudinally along the tape per inch is called the *bit density*. Commonly used densities are 556, 800, and 1600 bits per inch. On an IBM 2401 tape drive, the reel of tape (file reel) is mounted on a tape drive and the tape is threaded around capstans (rubber rollers on steel hubs) past the read/write heads around more capstans and onto a take-up reel (machine reel), as shown in Figure A.3. Approximately 10 feet of leader are needed before information is written on the tape. A piece of reflective foil on the edge of the tape nearest the operator marks the point on the tape where the recording of information begins (load point). A piece of reflective foil on the edge of the tape nearest the tape drive and approximately 15 feet from the physical end of the tape marks the end of usable tape [see Fig. A.4]. After the tape is mounted on

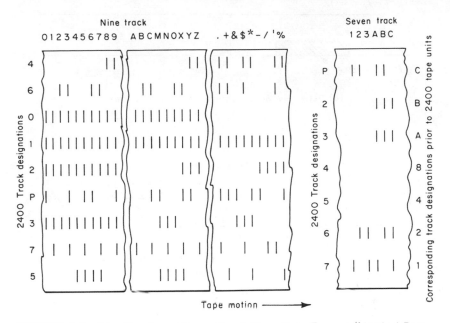

FIGURE A.2   Nine-Track and Seven-Track Tape Data Format (Vertical Bars Represent a One Bit)

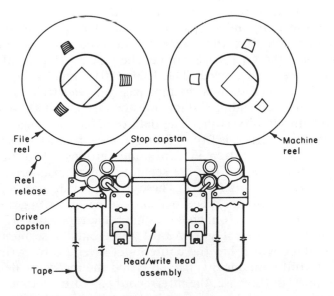

FIGURE A.3   IBM 2401 Tape Transport

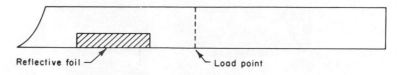

(a) Reflective foil at beginning of Magnetic Tape

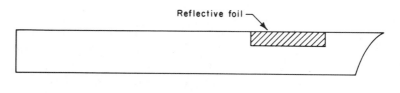

(b) Reflective foil at end of Magnetic Tape

FIGURE A.4

the drive it is wound onto the machine reel until the reflective spot passes the read/write head. The load button is pushed and the tape rewinds onto the file reel until the reflective foil is sensed photoelectrically by the tape drive. Two loops of tape are formed within two columns in the tape drive, one on each side of the read/write head, by pumping air from the bottom of each column. The resulting increased air pressure on the top edge of the tape maintains the loop and keeps the tape taut to prevent buckling. These loops minimize the stress on the tape when stopping or starting. Also, the tape drive can get the tape moving at full speed before the reels are moved. The IBM 2401 Model 2 tape drive, shown in Figure A.5, moves the tape past the read/write heads at a rate of 75 in./sec yielding a data transfer rate of 60000 bytes/sec at 800 bits/in. density (BPI). The data transfer rate range for IBM 2400 series tape drives is from 7500 bytes/sec to 90000 bytes/sec.

Information is written in continuous groups called blocks or records. Consecutive records are separated by unmagnetized areas called *interrecord gaps* (IRG). These gaps provide space for the tape to reach maximum speed before reading or writing a record. The interrecord gap is .6 inches on nine-track tapes and .75 inches on seven-track tapes. Figure A.6(a) represents a segment of a nine-track tape which has the contents of several cards written on it. Each record contains 80 characters and the recording density is 800 bits/inch. In this case, the interrecord gaps are six times longer than the data records, meaning that the tape drive will spend more time stopping and starting than reading. A remedy for this

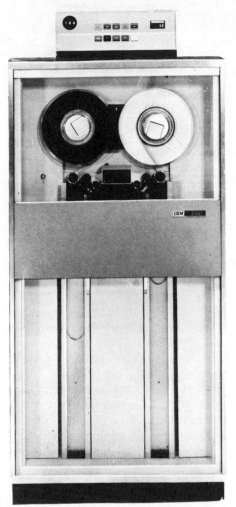

FIGURE A.5 IBM 2401 Magnetic Tape Unit (*IBM Corporation*)

situation is to write several records together as one large unit. This technique is called *blocking* the records. When the tape is being written, several records are stored sequentially in storage under program control. When a predetermined number of records has been grouped together, the entire group or *block* is written as a single tape record. To eliminate confusion, the term *record* is given to the amount of information which is considered as a logical unit within a program, and the term *block* is used to denote a physical record on the surface of the tape. If a tape is written with unblocked records, then record and block refer to the same physical entity. If cards are stored on tape using 50 cards per block, the length of a record is still 80 characters, but the blocksize is now 4000 characters. The resultant tape is as shown in

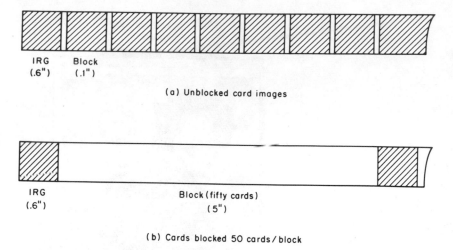

(a) Unblocked card images

(b) Cards blocked 50 cards/block

FIGURE A.6 Unblocked and Blocked Tape Records

Figure A.6(b). Each block on the tape is now 5 inches long, instead of .1 inch in the unblocked case. A single read now stores the equivalent of 50 reads of unblocked records. Since the program which is reading the tape still processes an 80-character record as a logical unit, special routines are necessary to deblock the records. Blocking of records decreases the total number of reads and writes on the tape and thus decreases the total amount of time a program has to wait for transfer of data. However, larger block sizes require more memory to hold the blocks and thus decrease the amount of memory available to the program using a tape, or tapes.

A group of logically related records is called a *file* or *data set*. The end of a file is denoted by a special character called a *tape mark*. Several files can be stored on a single reel of tape. Reels of tape, called *tape volumes*, are often initialized by writing a special file, called the *volume label*, as the first record on the tape. Depending on the computer system being used, this label can be checked by the operating system or by the tape user to verify that the correct tape has been mounted. Additionally, special records may be written as separate files preceding and following a particular file to identify its contents. These records are called *data set labels* or *file labels* and may be processed by the operating system or by the user. As further protection against inadvertant writing on a tape which contains needed information, the back of each tape reel contains a circular groove which allows a switch on the tape drive to remain off. As long as this switch is off, the tape can be read but not written, and it is said that the tape volume is

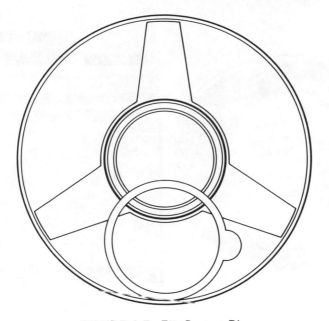

FIGURE A.7 File Protect Ring

file protected [see Fig. A.7]. By placing a plastic ring in this groove before mounting the tape, the switch is depressed and information can be written on the tape.

Magnetic tape thus provides the computer user with large amounts of demountable storage. The retrieval of information from magnetic tape, however, is strictly *sequential*. If record 10 of a file is needed, records 1 through 9 must be read first; if file 4 is needed, files 1 through 3 must be read first. Hence the speed at which data can be accessed is dependent on its position on the tape. Other magnetic storage devices permit *direct access* to data sets and records within data sets without reading intervening information. We shall now discuss three such storage devices.

MAGNETIC DISK

A magnetic disk is a thin circular sheet of metal 10 to 20 inches in diameter and coated with an easily magnetized material. Data are recorded serially, bit-after-bit, in concentric tracks on the surface of the disk. Several disks are grouped together by fastening them to a rigid bar which passes through their centers to form a *disk pack*. The disk pack is mounted on a *disk drive* which rotates the entire disk pack at a constant rate of speed [see Fig. A.8]. With

FIGURE A.8   IBM 1316 Disk Pack and 2311 Disk Storage Drive (*IBM Corporation*)

the exception of the top and bottom disks in the pack, data are recorded on both sides of the disks. Disk packs may be permanently mounted or they can be demountable, depending on disk drive design. There is a read/write head for each disk surface. The read/write heads may move independently, or may move as a unit. In the latter case, the positioning of a read/write head over a track automatically places the remaining read/write heads over the same track on the other disk surfaces.

The IBM 2311 disk drive [Fig. A.8] uses mountable disk packs which consist of 6 disks, each 14 inches in diameter. This provides ten recording surfaces of 203 tracks each. The usable tracks are numbered 000 to 199, from outside to inside, with the remaining three tracks used as spares. Each track has a capacity of 3625 eight-bit bytes, yielding a storage capacity of 7.25 million bytes per disk pack. The read/write heads move as a unit [see Fig. A.9]. One positioning of the read/write heads therefore provides access to 10 tracks on 10 different surfaces, or a total of 36250 bytes. This data (called a *cylinder of data*) consists of information from the same numbered track on all available surfaces. There are 200 cylinders of data on a 2311 disk pack. Data organized into cylinders can be more efficiently retrieved since 10 tracks can be read or written with a single movement of the read/write heads. The location of data on a magnetic disk is subject to two delays: *access-motion time* and *rotational delay*. The access-motion time is the time required to position the read/write head over the proper

FIGURE A.9   Read/Write Heads of IBM 2311 Disk Storage Drive (*IBM Corporation*)

track. This varies from 25 msec (milliseconds) to 135 msec on a 2311 disk drive, with an average access-motion time of 75 msec. The disks are rotated at a constant rate of 2400 revolutions per minute. The rotational delay is the amount of time required for the disk to rotate so that the required data are under the read/write head. A maximum of 25 msec is required to locate data on a track with 12.5 msec being the average time. The data transfer rate for the 2311 disk drive is 156,000 bytes/sec.

MAGNETIC DRUMS

Magnetic drums are hollow metallic cylinders coated with a material such as iron oxide that is capable of retaining a magnetic charge. Drums vary in diameter from 3 to 12 inches and may be up to 20 inches long. Data are stored in tracks around the surface of the drum. Each track is a fixed number of bits wide and there is a stationary read/write head for each track. Figure A.10 shows a schematic diagram of a magnetic drum. The IBM 2301 drum records data in four groups of four bits each on a track of the drum. Technically speaking, there are four read/write heads for each *addressable* track on the drum. This drum has 200 tracks

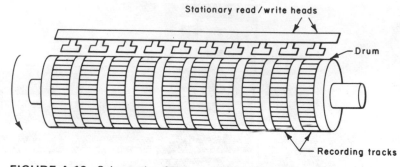

FIGURE A.10 Schematic of Magnetic Drum Storage

with a capacity of 20,483 eight-bit bytes per track, yielding a total storage capability of 4.09 million bytes. The drum rotates at a constant speed of approximately 3500 revolutions/minute. Data are located by specifying their position within a track. The maximum delay in locating data on a 2301 drum is 17.5 msec and the average delay is 8.6 msec. The delay is the time it takes for the data to rotate under the read head. Data are transferred from the drum at the rate of 1.2 million bytes/second [see Fig. A.11].

FIGURE A.11 IBM 2301 Drum Storage (*IBM Corporation*)

MAGNETIC CARDS

Magnetic cards are rectangular pieces of a flexible plastic material coated with a substance which is easily magnetized. Data are stored serially bit-after-bit in tracks on the surface of the card. The cards are stored in a cartridge and are withdrawn from the cartridge, wrapped around a drum which rotates past a series of read/write heads, one for each track or group of tracks on the card [Fig. A.12].

The IBM 2321 Data Cell is a representative magnetic card storage device. Each magnetic strip in the 2321 is 2¼ inches wide by 13 inches long. The surface of each strip is divided into 100 tracks with a storage capacity of 2000 eight-bit bytes/track, thus yielding a total storage capacity of 200,000 bytes/strip. There are 200 strips in a data cell and 10 data cells in the storage device with

FIGURE A.12 IBM 2321 Data Call Magnetic Card Storage Device (*IBM Corporation*)

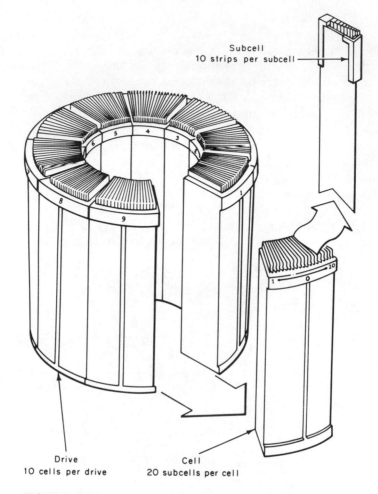

Subcell
10 strips per subcell

Drive
10 cells per drive

Cell
20 subcells per cell

FIGURE A.13

a total storage capacity of 400 million bytes. Each cell is further subdivided into 20 subcells containing 10 strips each [Fig. A.13]. Data are accessed by specifying the subcell number and the strip within a subcell where the data are stored. The data cells are rotated until the subcell containing the desired strip is positioned below a stationary drum. Each of the 10 strips in a subcell has two index tabs located in unique positions relative to the other strips within the subcell. Once the proper strip is located, a combination of separation fingers and a pickup head extracts it, and the movement of the drum causes the strip to be wrapped around it [see Fig. A.14]. There are twenty movable read/write heads above the drum and each head moves horizontally to access five

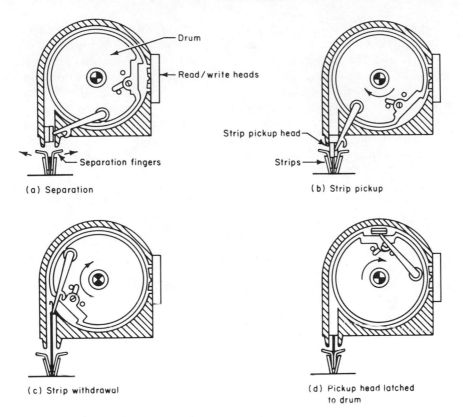

(a) Separation

(b) Strip pickup

(c) Strip withdrawal

(d) Pickup head latched to drum

FIGURE A.14 2321 Strip Pickup Cycle

contiguous tracks on the strip. The extracted strip remains on the drum until a request for another strip is made, or 800 msec have elapsed. The strip is replaced by reversing the direction of the drum and allowing the strip to slide back into its position directly below the drum. The minimum time required to access data on a strip is 25 msec and the maximum time is 600 msec, with the average access time being 350 msec. Once data are located they are transferred at the rate of 55,000 bytes/second.

The three direct-access devices just discussed have different physical characteristics, but they have in common the ability to directly access records within a data set. The use of these devices on the System/360 is greatly enhanced by the software support provided to the user. A standard data set appears on each volume (disk pack, drum, etc.) discussed which contains the name, location, and characteristics of each data set on the volume. This data set is called the *volume table of contents* (*VTOC*). Standard programs for interfacing with data sets on direct access storage devices allow them to be processed the same way regardless of the type of storage used. Data sets are located by name and volume name, and the actual transfer of a block of data is initialized by system I/O routines. The result is the storage of the block in memory regardless of the type of device from which the blocks were read. Records are often blocked on direct-access volumes to minimize the number of reads and writes required. It should also be noted that small data sets which access data sequentially are often maintained on direct-access volumes to take advantage of higher data transfer rates.

SELECTED REFERENCES

Cashman, Thomas J., and William J. Keys, *Data Processing and Computer Programming*, San Francisco: Canfield Press, 1971.

Dippel, Gene, and William C. House, *Information Systems, Data Processing and Evaluation*, Glenview, Ill: Scott, Foresman, 1969.

Farina, Mario V., *Computers, A Self-Teaching Introduction*, Englewood Cliffs, N.J.: Prentice-Hall, 1969.

Gear, C. William, *Computer Organization and Programming*, New York: McGraw-Hill, 1969.

Germain, Clarence B., *Programming the IBM 360*, Englewood Cliffs, N.J.: Prentice-Hall, 1967.

IBM System/360 Component Description, 2400-Series Magnetic Tape Units, Form GA22-6866, IBM Corporation, New York, 1970.

Introduction to IBM System/360 Direct Access Storage Devices and Organization Methods, Student Text, Form C20-1649-2, IBM Corporation, New York, 1966.

Schmidt, Richard N., and William E. Meyers, *Introduction to Computer Science and Data Processing*, (2nd ed.), New York: Holt, Rinehart and Winston, 1970.

INDEX